A History of the
Chinese Communist Party

Histories of Ruling Communist Parties

Richard F. Staar, editor

A History of the
Chinese Communist Party

Stephen Uhalley, Jr.

Hoover Institution Press

Stanford University   Stanford, California

The Hoover Institution on War, Revolution and Peace, founded at
Stanford University in 1919 by the late President Herbert Hoover,
is an interdisciplinary research center for advanced study on
domestic and international affairs in the twentieth century.
The views expressed in its publications are entirely those of
the authors and do not necessarily reflect the views of the
staff, officers, or Board of Overseers of the Hoover Institution.

Hoover Press Publication 361

First printing, 1988

Manufactured in the United States of America

94 93 92 91 90 89 88   9 8 7 6 5 4 3 2 1

Library of Congress Cataloging in Publication Data
Uhalley, Stephen.
  A history of the Chinese Communist Party.

  (Histories of ruling Communist parties)
  (Hoover Press publication ; 361)
  Bibliography: p.
  Includes index.
  1. Chung-kuo kung ch'an tang—History.   2. Communism—
China—History.   I. Title.   Series.
JQ519.A5U38   1988   324.251'075'09   88-765
ISBN 0-8179-8612-X

Design by P. Kelley Baker

**to Joan
with love and admiration**

Contents

Editor's Foreword

This is the twelfth book in a series on the histories of the sixteen ruling communist parties from their organization to the present time. The studies were initiated to fill an important gap in the modern English-language historiography of Albania, Bulgaria, Cambodia, China, Cuba, Czechoslovakia, (East) Germany, Hungary, (North) Korea, Laos, Mongolia, Poland, Romania, the Soviet Union, Vietnam, and Yugoslavia.

This new volume in the series covers the following:

- Historical background of twentieth-century China, including the early republic, warlordism, foreign involvement, the effect of World War I and its settlement, and the impact of the Bolshevik Revolution.

- The development of the communist party through years of factionalism and struggle into a unified, Sinocized, Marxist-Leninist organization with bases in the countryside, and the adroit use of Japan's invasion of China to consolidate and expand its ranks enormously.

- The unification of China and accession to political power in 1949 by means of military conquest.

- The establishment of the People's Republic, and reliance on the Soviet model.

- The search for a uniquely Chinese approach to socialism and economic development with a strong radical and ideological orientation, which exacerbated the evolving Sino-Soviet split, and led to the massive catastrophes of the Great Leap Forward and the Great Proletarian Cultural Revolution.

- After Mao Zedong's death in 1976, abandonment of radical ideology and, with the consolidation of power by Deng Xiaoping, promotion of the open-door policy to the world and sweeping domestic politico-economic changes.

As general editor of this series, I am pleased that such a distinguished scholar as Professor Stephen Uhalley, Jr., accepted our invitation to prepare this monograph.

Richard F. Staar
Coordinator of International Studies Program
Hoover Institution
Stanford University

Acknowledgments

I wish to thank Dr. Richard F. Staar, the editor of the Hoover Institution's series on the histories of the sixteen ruling communist parties, and the Hoover Publications Committee for extending to me the invitation to write a monograph for this fine series. The project was a welcome challenge, providing as it did an opportunity to relate afresh the story of the Chinese Communist Party at an opportune moment of history, albeit within the space limitations for such a volume in this series, and with a fairly tight deadline.

Time restrictions made it unfeasible to undertake intensive basic research in Chinese-language sources for the purpose of this project specifically, although such sources were used as far as practicable. There remained, of course, the inherent problems in treating a subject that is so shrouded in secrecy and distorted by polemic. However, the availability of excellent translated materials and the wealth of scholarship that has been produced over the years greatly facilitated my work. The Chinese-language *Guanyu jianguo yilai dangde rogan lishi wenti de jueyi: zhushiben, xiu ding* (Annotated Edition of the Resolution on Certain Issues in the History of the Party since the Founding of the People's Republic of China), compiled by the Central Committee's Party Literature Research Center, and which is said to reflect the newer "realizations" that have occurred since 1983, came to hand after my manuscript had been accepted and revised, and was consulted before going to press.

This book owes a great deal to earlier writers on the subject and to the many specialized monographs and academic articles and papers that have become available in recent years. Citations throughout the work acknowledge who these authorities are for the most part. I am grateful to each of them for his or her respective contribution to my understanding of Chinese communism. However, I am aware that there are other scholars and authorities whose works have had an influence on me, or who might otherwise legitimately have had an appropriate role or should have been recognized in a modestly comprehensive survey such as this, yet who may not be specifically noted in the endnotes or bibliography. I apologize for such omissions.

Professors of mine at the University of California at Berkeley helped lay the groundwork for my understanding, and deserve recognition even though so many years have gone by. Robert A. Scalapino, Franz Schurmann, and the late Joseph Levenson each provided important insights that still inform my thinking. Professor Scalapino has remained influential ever since. I have been moved also by the dedication and understanding of Father Louis Ladany, S.J., in Hong Kong, whose knowledge of Chinese communism is impressive. I am also grateful to a number of Chinese scholars and students who have thoughtfully and candidly shared useful observations and insights. No one, apart from myself, of course, is responsible for any misunderstandings and mistakes that may appear in this volume.

Introduction

Much attention is focused currently on the remarkable changes occurring in China—changes that have been instigated and promoted by the Chinese Communist Party. Most notable have been the economic reforms with their intriguing recourse to market economy ideas and practices, and the determination of party reformist leaders to bring about sweeping, if indeterminate, structural changes to accommodate them. Vast changes have already been brought about in rural China since 1978, as the collectivized ideal has been all but abandoned. There have been measurable improvements in agricultural production and in the livelihood of many peasants. However, it is uncertain what the long-term consequences may be from the decrease in attention to rural public needs and to the plight of truly distressed villages. Similar radical changes have been advocated, particularly since late 1984, for the rest of China's economy. Also, China has made tremendous strides in recent years in opening up to the world. It now has extensive political and cultural relationships abroad, and the volume and value of its international trade is steadily expanding. Most significantly, foreign loans, investments, and involvement in China's economy are again being earnestly sought, along with advanced technology from abroad.[1]

The party and government leaders have been highly eclectic in seeking to learn from a wide range of models and experiences abroad, from other reform-minded socialist nations, as well as from a variety of capitalist countries. Despite abundant evidence of resurgent nationalism in China, such learning from foreigners is done with greater humility than has often been the case in the past, which may be a consequence of the self-inflicted trauma of the Cultural Revolution. It also reflects a renewed awareness of the urgency for China to bridge the tremendous gap which had opened between itself and many other countries, including some of its close neighbors in East Asia. A readiness to consult with experts has become a distinctive characteristic of the government leadership.

Significant changes are also being pursued in government and in the Communist party itself. The objective clearly is to upgrade the leadership and its bureaucracy educationally and professionally, to streamline it, and to change its relationship to the economy and to the people in important ways. This has included a measure of decentralization of power and authority. The party had achieved some notable progress in these efforts by 1985, by which time impressive changes had been brought about in party and governmental personnel at all levels, reaching from the center down to the counties. A major rectification campaign was conducted from late 1983 to May 1987 that sought to support the reforms.

There has been some measurable progress with the reforms, but the conservative opposition has become emboldened as serious problems have developed and the difficulty of key reforms became clearer, resulting in a conscious slowdown of reforms during 1986 and early 1987. The mounting conservative resistance led to Hu Yaobang's enforced resignation of the party's general secretaryship in January 1987. Even so, Deng Xiaoping's reform program moved ahead cautiously, but determinedly. This determination was rewarded at the Thirteenth Party Congress in late 1987, when the reform program was reaffirmed and most of the octogenarian conservatives retired from the party's Central Committee.

The party countenances greater latitudes of style and behavior in society than had been the case before 1978. It tolerates more freedom of expression, even though cycles of cooling and thawing continue. The party seeks to erect a structure of laws, and a great many laws have been promulgated since 1979. This is designed to assure greater order in society, and more regularity and predictability for both political and economic purposes. The law is intended to make individuals feel more secure, even from the party itself. But the emphasis remains on "rule by law" rather than "rule of law."[2] The party even tolerates an unprecedented measure of religious expression among the people.

At the same time, however, the limits are made clear. Nothing will be tolerated that threatens the economic development program or the party. The purpose of such policies, the purpose of the entire reform program, is to facilitate and hasten the economic development and modernization of China. At the same time, it is expected that a renewed and more effective party, on the basis of popular and successful policies, will restore its credibility and legitimacy.

Thus, an imaginative, pragmatic current party leadership has moved adroitly and boldly to achieve these two all-important objectives. In doing so, it has been willing to make concessions in order to facilitate its efforts. Such concessions should not be misunderstood. They do not mean that the party is wavering in its commitment to socialism, although some individual party reformers may in fact have doubts about Marxism itself. Much less do the concessions suggest any intention to share real political power. The concessions were prompted by the recognition of two overriding imperatives. One is the need to modernize and develop the country seriously, both to improve the livelihood of the people and to make China a genuine world power. The other imperative is the need for political survival, for beginning in the late 1950s the party had fallen to a dangerous degree in popular esteem and confidence. By the late 1970s, it was apparent that only if the party became more responsive and effective was it likely to survive.

But the Chinese Communist Party is a proven survivor. The handful of able but impatient Chinese intellectuals who founded the party were, in fact, correct in their estimate that this particular form of political organization, judging from the Russian experience alone, would prove to be effective for seizing power and for undertaking sweeping changes. The review of the party's history that follows will demonstrate that the party subsequently survived many obstacles and many difficulties, and did go on to win power. It then sought to bring about a social revolution, in which it was partly successful, but at enormous cost to the Chinese people and to itself.

Some of the impediments the party confronted both before and after seizing power were imposed by outside forces. But many problems were occasioned by adherence to the ideology that came along with the party organization. With great difficulty and at great cost many problems were surmounted. However, such successes were partly due to an innate Chinese sense of pragmatism. Chinese pragmatism benefits, as Lucian Pye suggests, from "cultural dispositions which make totally acceptable behaviour that is guided by the logic of existing circumstances and which allows for unsentimental abandonment of past commitments and outdated rationalizations."[3] And, in this instance, recourse to pragmatic solutions was facilitated because the Chinese never, from the very beginning, really accepted Marxism at face value. This was the case even though, in the desperate straits in which China found itself when Marxism came to China, it did seem to provide needed explanations and guidelines. However, it was too facile, and the emphasis on social revolution divided the Chinese leaders on the priority of developing China economically.

It was really the Leninist party organization that the group of Chinese intellectuals had selected. Marxism was accepted because it was part of the package deal. The Chinese did not select Marxism, and *then* merely accept the party organization. It was the latter that was of primary interest, that met the urgent need. In such circumstances, Marxism was accepted largely on faith, to be understood when time permitted.

This order of priority partly explains the readiness of Chinese leaders to take liberties with Marxism, which they have long struggled to comprehend and to apply. There is, in fact, in China an unusual tradition of questioning Marxism and of interpreting it liberally. This has repeatedly offended the Soviets and many relatively orthodox Chinese Marxists. This tradition augurs well for the current reforms. Bending Marxism in China is not unprecedented by any means. And never has there been more questioning, more bending, than at present. Never, since 1949, has Marxism in China been weaker than at present.[4] This ideological weakness is amply compensated, however, by a pronounced sense of patriotism. This heightened nationalism in turn facilitates acceptance of the party's policies, to the extent that they are perceived to be in China's interests as a nation.

But this does not mean that Marxism will be allowed to wither and die. Whether it is actually much believed in or not, and however it is interpreted, Marxism-Leninism will remain the official ideology as long as the party exists. This is necessarily the case, for Marxism-Leninism, as amended by the thoughts of Mao Zedong and Deng Xiaoping and whoever is to follow, provides the rationale for the Chinese Communist Party. Furthermore, as the current state orthodoxy, Marxism automatically constitutes much of the contemporary "essence" of Chinese culture that satisfies the nationalistic need to distinguish China from other nations. Marxism can fulfill this psychological function, despite its foreign origin, because it has become so Sinocized.

The party itself remains a Leninist organization. It is changing its complexion. But being younger in average age, better educated, more professional, and partly decentralized simply makes it more efficient in the current environment and in addressing its main objectives. The Thirteenth Party Congress did underscore the need to separate the functions of party and government and the desirability of decentralizing power. But, in practice, how far and how well will the party succeed in withdrawing from government and economic work, and for how long?

The party is the vanguard, and the guardian. It is supposed to be dedicated to selfless service. There remain immense problems for China to resolve for its people to prosper and for it truly to become a major global power. Many in the party will continue to feel these great responsibilities, and some few will continue to call for bold changes to better meet them. Some will continue to call for greater democratization within and even without the party.

However, both as an organizational entity and as organized, notably ambitious individuals, the party is, at bottom, concerned with power—the gaining of power and the maintaining of power. It is only on the basis of power and authority that the party can exercise real leadership and, especially for those at the top, indulge in the resulting preferments for themselves and for their families. To what extent can the party voluntarily give up power, or even share it, meaningfully? Marxism, of course, conveniently justifies the retention of power, and this ultimately will explain its own preservation as the state's pliable orthodoxy. This logic reinforces the hand of the Chinese conservative Marxists in their current rearguard struggle, making it easier to dispute efforts to depart seriously from the current still basically Soviet-style structure. Nevertheless, that structure appears to be altering, albeit in a yet indeterminate direction. It has altered sufficiently and has created enough excitement among the socialist nations that it has had an affect upon the Soviet Union itself, and was undoubtedly one of the factors which led to the Gorbachev reform initiatives, with regard to both internal reforms and the enunciation of a new policy toward China and Asia.

A History of the
Chinese Communist Party

Without the leadership of such a party, without the flesh-and-blood ties it has formed with the masses through protracted struggles and without its painstaking and effective work among the people and the high prestige it consequently enjoys, our country—for a variety of reasons, both internal and external—would inexorably fall apart and the future of our nation and people would inexorably be forfeited.

From the *Resolution on Certain Issues in the History of the Party since the Founding of the People's Republic of China* (June 1981)

PART ONE

Onslaught of Revolution

· I ·

A Matrix for Revolution

China opened the twentieth century with the nadir of its declining fortunes fast approaching. Rock bottom came in the 1910s and early 1920s. In the midst of this malaise, as one specific response to it, was born the Chinese Communist Party, in mid-year 1921.

China's estimable, hardy civilization had reached its apotheosis long before, in the Song Dynasty (960–1279). And following the indignity of the Mongol occupation, it had glorious moments in both the Ming (1368–1644) and the Qing (1644–1911) dynasties. But the country's traditional order was not equal to the two unprecedented challenges of the nineteenth and early twentieth centuries.

One of these challenges was an internal one—a population explosion that reached nearly a half billion by the mid-nineteenth century, having expanded rapidly in the preceding hundred years from the centuries-old norm of less than 100 million. Even though the Chinese government had long done reasonably well in some respects and in some geographical areas in attempting to deal with the social consequences of this phenomenon, it was obvious by the end of the first third of the nineteenth century that it could no longer cope with this most unusual situation. An innate philosophical conservatism seemed to militate against technological innovation that might have helped to resolve the problem. Instead, China became dispirited as it succumbed to an ineluctable "equilibrium trap."[1]

Exacerbating matters considerably was evidence that the nineteenth century coincided with the late phase of another of China's recurrent dynastic cycles. Thus, the long-lived Qing Dynasty was displaying the characteristics of deteriorating performance that invited its overthrow, an act which in other circumstances might have established a new dynasty whose vigorous rule in its early years might have renewed the country as had happened so many times previously.

Unfortunately, the second major challenge precluded the possibility of any renewal along traditional lines. This challenge was the external threat posed by foreigners who arrived at this most unpropitious time for China. These foreigners, driven by the dynamics of the West's industrial revolution, clamored for trade profits and were well armed with superior weaponry. This new breed of visitor, persuaded of his own cultural superiority, was unimpressed by a civilization in decline and was therefore impervious to being culturally charmed, as had so many of his predecessors in centuries past. The consequences of this untimely encounter were traumatic for China, although it brought some benefits and ultimately stimulated responses that led to China's recovery as a nation and the reassertion of its independence. But the benefits and the eventual restoration of national dignity were scarcely apparent to prideful denizens of a country that was now compelled to endure several decades of humiliation and enormous losses of resources.

The encounter was accentuated because the two sides were so dissimilar—systemically and culturally. With so little common ground, misunderstandings abounded, and tempers flared by the 1830s as foreign demands mounted and were met by the stubborn resistance of Qing authorities. In 1836, even before the First Anglo-Chinese (Opium) War of 1839–1842, the importation of illicit opium from India had already caused the beginning of a net outflow of silver from China, reversing for the first time in history a pattern of external trade that had always favored China.[2]

The war of 1839–1842 resulted in the Treaty of Nanjing, the first of a long series of what were for China humiliating and unequal treaties.[3] Among the concessions, Hong Kong was ceded to Great Britain and five ports were opened to foreign trade. A subsequent agreement gave the British the "most-favored-nation" privilege, which was soon extended to other nations. In its treaty of 1843, the United States extracted the privilege of extraterritoriality, which placed its citizens in China under the jurisdiction of a U.S. official in both criminal and civil cases. Despite such sweeping concessions, however, trade frustrations remained. Chinese silk and tea exports continued apace, but the Chinese market for legal Western products remained disappointing. There were other grievances, too, but the trade balance continued adversely for China because of the increasing importance of the still-illicit opium. Additional hostilities led to the 1860 Peking Convention, which legalized the opium trade, opened additional ports including access to China's interior, and established foreign legations in Peking (later Beiping and, after 1949, Beijing). The British acquired the tip of Kowloon peninsula across from Hong Kong, while the Russians separately wrested away a huge tract of territory to the east of the Ussuri River.

Heavy foreign pressure and interference also severely affected domestic Chinese political developments. It exacerbated the conditions that hastened the deterioration of the already declining Qing dynasty. For example, the unprecedented trade deficit occasioned by the outflow of silver in payment of opium fueled inflationary pressures, ultimately lowering the living standards of the already distressed peasantry. Furthermore, opening new trading posts, especially Shanghai at the mouth of the Chang Jiang (Yangtze), had deleterious economic and social consequences for the established internal transport and service networks in the south. The defeat of the Manchus by other foreigners also seriously shook the dynasty's raison d'être, that is, justifying its political supremacy by providing security for the Chinese people.

The foreign presence also changed the character of domestic demands for change. Hence, the massive Taiping Uprising (1850–1864), which under other circumstances might have been merely the latest in the long tradition of peasant rebellions to displace a ruling house and to establish another, showed definite revolutionary ambitions instead.[4] Influenced by missionary tracts, the leader of the Taipings denounced Confucianism and espoused a new ideology based on Christianity. He sought to establish a new dispensation—not merely a new dynasty—that promised sweeping changes for China in every respect, from its structures for government, society, and economy to its cultural expressions. This revolutionary program contained not only wartime communistic impulses but also strong influences from Western institutional and cultural models. The Taiping challenge was a formidable one, affrighting the Manchus, many loyalist Chinese (concerned with preserving their concept of the traditional Chinese social and cultural order), and Western governments who feared a Taiping government that might not be as tractable as the weak Qing and that seemed to be unalterably opposed to opium.[5] The resulting coalition of interests finally turned the tide and the Taipings were ruthlessly suppressed. The scale of conflict and the loss of lives and property in this upheaval were unprecedented in human history.[6]

This first revolutionary challenge was throttled, but the Qing dynasty, and with it the traditional Chinese order, had been irretrievably skewed in the process. The very means of putting down the Taipings helped to undermine the ailing system and to accelerate its decline. The resort to Chinese provincial armies, which were also provincially financed (originally in order to suppress the Taipings), promoted a regionalism that sapped the authority and control of central political leadership for the duration of the dynasty.[7] A decentralized and hobbled polity was left to confront the powerfully intrusive foreigners and to resolve profound domestic problems.

In the meanwhile, foreign pressures on China mounted. The Chinese Communists refer to the period from 1842 to 1949 as one of "semi-feudalism and semi-colonialism." The latter term is not far off the mark, for even though foreign powers declined to take direct political control in China, they did severely compromise its sovereignty by exacting numerous further concessions through the turn of the century.

China's ability to modernize under such circumstances was severely inhibited. In a "self-strengthening" movement in the 1860s and early 1870s, a few able officials tried to learn about and reproduce Western military technology, for the purpose of protecting China's traditional culture and institutions.[8] Even this limited effort was opposed by reactionaries who clearly could see that such acceptance of modern technologies would inevitably affect basic values and ways of doing things.[9] The next rationalization undertaken by relatively progressive leaders in trying to accommodate to the world was modernization according to the *ti-yong* (substance-function) formula. By this means, China would also adopt or adapt Western-style institutions as well as technology (confirming the warnings of the reactionaries), but the traditions of the Chinese culture, or "spiritual essence," would remain the governing values of society.[10] Such agonizing, and the efforts it manifested, produced only modest results toward modernization. It also provided a pattern of response that seems to have informed subsequent reform programs, including the present effort of the 1980s.

The tragic experience of the 100 Days Reform in 1898 demonstrated just how forlorn progressive change was by the end of the century.[11] That famous effort was the culmination of a reaction to the humiliating defeat by Japan in 1895 and to the scramble for concessions that followed. The leading reformer, Kang Youwei, justified his reform proposals by claiming that Confucius himself had been a reformer in his day and by generally reinterpreting Confucianism. Kang and his colleague, Liang Qichao, won the ear of the young emperor and for a period of 100 exhilarating days one reform after another was proclaimed. But the entire program was suddenly crushed in a coup d'état by the empress dowager, who was supported by frightened reactionary interests and a calculating, sometimes progressive general, Yuan Shikai.

The subsequent mad Luddite-like Boxer paroxysm of 1900 accomplished nothing.[12] The Manchu government encouraged the Boxer movement in order to deflect the rage from itself. However, this venting of enraged feelings at foreigners saddled China with an additional staggering indemnity and subjected it to further humiliation. The crushing Boxer settlements did cause the government to consider seriously the need for change. The last decade of the Qing dynasty saw serious efforts undertaken, even if by leaders who were basically reactionary.[13] But such efforts came too late to save the dynasty and, ironically, rather than help shore it up, they served to hasten the undermining of the traditional, imperial political system. Thus, the extremely important abolition of the civil service examination based on the Confucian classics had major repercussions.[14] This induced students to take up Western-type learning and also removed the primary prop to the entire traditional ideology and polity. Likewise, beginning in 1905 the ambitious program of sending students to Japan (10,000 to 15,000 each year), and to a lesser degree elsewhere, for modern studies exposed these young people to radical ideas. Many returned to China convinced of the need to overturn the dynasty and to revolutionize the country.

By 1905 Chinese students and intellectuals in Japan founded the Tong Meng Hui, a revolutionary secret society, dedicated to the overthrow of the Manchus and the establishment of a republican form of government. Its leader was Sun Yat-sen, a young Cantonese who had been educated in Hawaii and Hong Kong.[15] After several failures over the years to begin the revolution in China, it finally did come about on October 10, 1911, in Wuhan when a planned uprising was discovered by the authorities and the revolutionaries were forced to act. Sun assumed the presidency of the new republic that quickly displaced the Qing dynasty.

The rapid success of the revolutionaries was due to more than their own appeal, program, and activities. Perhaps more important was the discontent on the part of local interests in central China over the building of a railroad linking Wuhan to Peking.[16] Provincial interests wished to be involved in the financing and ultimate control of the project. The central government, on the other hand, had desired to use the railroad as a means of reasserting central authority and had secured foreign capital in order to do so. Once again, the government ironically helped to unseat itself by doing what seemed necessary—although it also provided provincial critics with the argument that the country's interests were being sold to foreigners. The resultant sense of national outrage and resentment against the central government produced the coalition that made the relatively bloodless revolution possible.

But China at the time was hardly prepared to go much further than to remove the Manchus from power. People were generally not informed about what a republican form of government really was, and many old attitudes and practices remained little changed. Some areas, particularly the provinces of Hunan and Hubei, had seen the early and steady rise of progressive and revolutionary ideas and activity among a transforming elite, and there were growing numbers of people in a restive, changeful mood.[17] Nevertheless, for most of the country, the same endemic, basic problems of a deeply entrenched gentry landlord class on the one hand and continuing predatory foreign involvement on the other limited the prospects for the Chinese republic. Sun Yat-sen was compelled within three months' time to relinquish the presidency to Yuan Shikai, the military strongman who had earlier betrayed the reformers in 1898 and then the Manchus in 1911 by opportunistically throwing in with the revolutionaries.[18] He would soon betray the new republic as well.

There has been an ongoing debate on the effects of imperialism in China during this entire "neo-colonial" period, although it has lost steam in recent years.[19] Many observers even in the West agreed with the Communists that these effects were mainly deleterious. John Esherick, for example, maintained that imperialism actually transformed what was a stable, traditional, self-sufficient economy into an unstable and dependent one, in which millions of peasants became displaced and were subjected to deprivations caused by the vagaries of the international market. Foreign investment and trade also were said to have led to a geographical concentration that was not in the best interests of a balanced economic development. As a result of imperialism, the net capital flow was from China, and a great deal more in profits left China than was ever invested or reinvested. Albert Feuerwerker has shown that between 1895 and 1911 the costs of the Boxer and Japanese indemnities, including loans to help pay them, amounted to "more than twice the size of the total initial capitalization of all foreign, Sino-foreign, and Chinese-owned manufacturing enterprises established between 1895 and 1913."[20] Stephen C. Thomas's more recent analysis of the pivotal 1870–1911 period sees Chinese efforts toward industrialization as "rational, carefully planned reactions to almost overwhelming foreign assaults."[21]

There is, of course, much to be pondered in these arguments and, in any case, they have heavily influenced perceptions, especially among the Chinese. Actually, however, the total amount of money drained from China was not significant when considered against the massiveness of the Chinese economy. And foreign trade, in fact, led to no basic restructuring of the economy, which remained locally oriented. Also, the continuing backwardness of the Chinese economy was testimony to the weakness rather than to the strength of the effects of imperialism. And the backwardness of the economy—or to put it another way, the weakness of the treaty port sector of the economy—remained the result of inadequate transport, peasant impoverishment, the expensiveness of manufactured goods, and the continued use of traditional handicrafts and marketing channels.[22] Also, as Chi-ming Hou points out, "foreign capital was largely responsible for the development of whatever economic modernization took place in China before 1937."[23] It can be shown, too, that foreigners played a role in the modernization of institutions, for example, the Imperial Maritime Customs Service,[24] the salt administration,[25] and schools operated or advised by missionaries and others.[26] Ramon Myers has shown that there is, in fact, no evidence that pre-1937 peasant living standards declined as a result of the presence of modern industry in the treaty ports.[27] Regarding the Boxer indemnity, it is worth noting that the United States created with its share a fund that for almost 50 years enabled thousands of Chinese to study in the United States.

Nevertheless, the political ramifications of heavy foreign involvement were troublesome for China. This is suggested in the experience of the Yuan Shikai government. A Foreign Reorganization Loan was provided to Yuan in 1913, assuring the lenders that a strong man would provide the stability needed to continue a profitable trade.[28] Ironically, the very day that the loan was announced, a commission found that Yuan had been implicated in the assassination of Song Jiaoran, the outspoken parliamentary leader of the young republican government. The foreign loan helped Yuan avoid a closer relationship with Chinese reformers and encouraged his scheme to make himself the first emperor of a new Chinese dynasty. But the discarding of the republic and the declaration of dynastic restoration prompted a revolt. Fortunately, Yuan died in 1916, and the restoration aborted. The modern army that had been the basis of Yuan's power, and which had been loyal to him personally, came apart as his chief officers scrambled for military and political power. Modern warlordism, the real genesis of which might be traced back to the provincial armies that helped crush the Taipings, now came to dominate the country.

The malaise of warlordism would afflict China until after the victory of the Communists in 1949.[29] The years from 1916 to 1926 were the worst, for the country was plunged into anarchical chaos, and foreign exploitation peaked—except during the Japanese invasion of the 1930s and 1940s. The outstanding characteristic of warlordism was the fact of war itself. There was constant fighting and treachery and shifting of alliances, as the more ambitious warlords sought to enlarge their territory and perhaps gain control of Beijing and eventually the whole country. Beijing was the symbol and had the machinery of national government, the possession of which conferred legitimacy and eligibility for lucrative foreign loans.

Warlordism had nightmarish consequences for the Chinese people. There was very little constructive government anywhere. The effect on the economy was disastrous. Communications and transportation systems were dislocated. Warlords often enforced opium growing for revenue, displacing needed food crops, and their arms and munitions industries received inordinate investment. A brisk arms trade supplanted opium as imports of opium diminished because of increasing domestic production. Taxation was often confiscatory, with taxes at times assessed on every conceivable source. In emergencies such as floods and famines, which increased as a result of government neglect, unnecessary and inhumane obstacles were often placed in the way of relief.

The need of the Chinese people obviously was to awaken a sense of national consciousness and to organize themselves effectively in order to begin to cope with their overwhelming problems. A spirit of nationalism was requisite to the organization that would overcome the phenomenon of the Chinese being—to use Sun Yat-sen's despairing phrase—like a sheet of loose sand. Yet the emotions of nationalism were late developing in China. Despite the occasional isolated outbursts of antiforeign sentiment in earlier decades, nationalism seemed to run counter to the traditional sense of culturalism, in which the Chinese regarded their country the center of the world, whose boundaries ebbed and flowed with the rise of civilization itself. There was little sense of China as a political entity or a "national" one. China's cultural values were universal. Hence, the acceptance of nationalism was difficult, for it immediately relativized the universalistic cultural pretensions.[30] China as a nation-state meant that its values became those of China alone; and China, no longer the fountainhead of universal values, was merely a national unit, just as any ordinary nation. Such a concept was particularly difficult for the Chinese to adopt at the very time they seemed to need to strengthen traditional values in order to affirm their own identity in the face of the encroaching West. Since the traditional values were losing much of their essential appeal, at least as a coherent system, confusion abounded among Chinese intellectuals. This confusion and the ensuing desperation made many Chinese receptive to any new ideas or, better, any new thought system that would persuasively displace the increasingly untenable one. This would never mean, however, that the Chinese could abandon in its entirety their substantial traditional culture, no matter how many of them thought they were doing so in the years ahead.

In the midst of this domestic woe, the distant, essentially European conflict known as World War I took place. That event, along with its diplomatic settlement, came to have an enormous impact on China. The Chinese leadership had been adroit enough to join the Allied side during the war and China made substantial contributions to the war effort, primarily through the supply of large numbers of workers who helped to compensate for the dire labor shortage in France. Not unreasonably, therefore, China awaited the settlement following the armistice with high expectations. Thus, it was a jolting shock to learn that the Treaty of Versailles awarded the erstwhile German concessions in China to Japan rather than returning them to China. Chinese outrage manifested itself immediately in the demonstrations and strikes known as the May Fourth Incident (in 1919). This massive reaction, initiated by intellectuals and students, showed an unprecedented degree of cooperation and unity among the different social classes and among the various professional and occupational groups throughout the country. The Peking government was dissuaded from signing the treaty. Chinese nationalism had unmistakably asserted itself.

The name of this significant incident was given also to a more general and continuing movement that had begun in the 1910s and was then known as the New Culture Movement. It was to continue until the late 1920s as the exceedingly important May Fourth Movement, which brought a veritable explosion of intellectual, social, and political awakening to China.[31] Not only was the sense of nationalism cultivated and extended, but a new spirit of inquiry and criticism vigorously asserted itself. For the first time, in significant quantity and intensity, Chinese raised exciting questions regarding the state of their nation and culture, and they sought answers. Their questions were critical of the Western world, which had recently been tearing itself to pieces, but, perhaps more significantly they were self-critical too. Confucianism was scorned, while foreign "isms" such as Social Darwinism, pragmatism, and Marxism were studied appreciatively. Science, in particular, became popular. This led many to a particular fascination with Marxism, with its scientific pretensions, its ideological comprehensiveness and progressiveness, and its formula for revolutionary success—now validated by the successful Bolshevik Revolution in 1917.

The May Fourth Movement represented a structural breakthrough in the realms of both the spirit and the intellect. It was a necessary precondition for capitalizing on other opportunities that would enable

China to pull itself together and to modernize. The sense of national consciousness would continue to grow, and particularly so during the next period of national crisis in the 1920s with its great labor strikes and national unification effort, and in the 1930s and early 1940s during the Japanese invasion and occupation of large stretches of the country. Unfortunately, however, the buoyant spirit of inquiry and intellectual creativity would soon diminish as militarism and limiting ideologies gained ascendancy.

· 2 ·

. The Early CCP .

World War I did more for China than set off a national awakening. The preoccupation of the European powers gave China a respite that Chinese industry used to good advantage. As a result, both the small class of industrialists, managers, and merchants and the small working class or proletariat experienced pronounced growth. Although the size of these groups was very small proportionate to the peasantry and the gentry, this was another significant structural breakthrough. In the past, the all-powerful gentry class with its ties to officialdom had hampered the emergence of such new classes, with separate interests, that might have challenged its supremacy. Actually, for some time many of the gentry themselves had been looking for changes. But these new classes on the scene, emerging as they did in an atmosphere charged with new ideas and ways of looking at the world and the future, suggested the possibility of further meaningful change.

Still needed, however, was some means of fashioning these volatile new elements into a coherent, organized force with a sense of direction, continuity of program, and leadership. This was delayed somewhat by the very richness of the possibilities, at least in the realm of ideas. But the search was gradually given focus by circumstances and events. After the failure of constitutional democracy, many idealistic activitists were driven again to revolutionary activities, many living a clandestine, dangerous, and frustrating life as members of Sun Yat-sen's Chinese Revolutionary Party. These courageous patriots, along with numerous other intellectuals, became increasingly disenchanted with the Western democracies, partly because of the uncivilized spectacle of the European war, partly because of the failure of such nations to desist from taking advantage of China's distress, and partly because of their refusal to help the Chinese revolutionaries, despite Sun's repeated requests for help.

In sharp contrast was the heartening news of the Russian Bolshevik Revolution in 1917, confirming as it did that a small revolutionary party could succeed, and do so, furthermore, in a country that, like China, had only recently begun to industrialize. This positive impression was enhanced as the new Soviet government succeeded in surmounting its many obstacles. Impressive too was the new government's anti-imperialist posture and particularly the Karakhan Declaration of July 1919 renouncing all Russian rights and privileges in China. The Soviets would deny important parts of this declaration only weeks later, but since this crucial qualification was not widely known at the time the declaration reached China in early 1920, nothing detracted from the initial positive propaganda effect.[1] Of course, in the long run this example of Russian inconstancy undoubtedly damaged the Soviet image. Nevertheless, it is worth noting, as Don Price has pointed out, that Chinese revolutionaries had already, even before their own 1911 revolution, tended to view Russia as a "paradigm of revolutionary progress."[2] This predisposition facilitated Chinese acceptance of Soviet revolutionary leadership in the early years after the October Revolution. And many Chinese had already become sympathetic to socialism as an appropriate direction for China to travel.

But Marxism was new. Only after the Bolshevik Revolution did the Chinese begin to show interest in Marxism. The first major Chinese intellectual to declare his support for the Bolshevik Revolution was Li Dazhao, the Peking University librarian and professor of history who became the principal early interpreter of Marxism in China. He also began the tradition of adapting Marxism to Chinese perspectives, which combined, as Maurice Meisner phrases it, a voluntaristic interpretation of Marxism and a militant nationalism.[3]

It is important to note in this that Marxism arrived in China late and was accepted rather hurriedly by frustrated and impatient activists. Aside from being the ideology of the exciting Russian revolution, other elements of Marxism appealed to many Chinese. It seemed to be the latest and most fashionable body of ideas emanating from the West. Its scientific pretensions and comprehensiveness struck responsive cords among Chinese enamored of the promise of science in the modern world, disenchanted with their own traditional comprehensive thought system, and dubious about democratic ideals in China for the time being. This does not suggest, however, that many other Chinese intellectuals, equally anxious for change, did not either continue to search for what value and ideas could be legitimately salvaged from the past that might facilitate China's transition to modernity, or as in the case of Hu Shi, a leader in language reform, continue to study and espouse important Western ideas. Usually the search was for some congenial mix, as represented in Sun Yat-sen's own talks and writings. But for many activists, Marxism's apparent practicality, particularly its relevance to the building of a winning party organization, was the pièce de résistance. Even Li Dazhao's call for temporary abstinence from politics until Marxism was studied and understood was rejected in the general eagerness to actively participate in events.[4] As Li's protégé, Zhang Guotao, bluntly put it, "We fully recognized that it was due to the leadership of the Russian Communist Party that the revolution in Russia was able to register all of its achievements."[5]

The most impressive of the leaders of this period was the brilliant intellectual-activist Chen Duxiu. Chen was already a major personality before the 1911 revolution, by which time he had helped pioneer the vernacular revolution, introduce Western ideas, and engage in revolutionary activities in Anhui Province. Between 1915 and 1921, he founded and edited *New Youth*, the most influential magazine of the period, was dean at Peking University, and, as leader of the New Culture Movement, led the assault on Confucianism. But, as Lee Feigon asserts, Chen was not merely a Westernized intellectual. He was an "ardent nationalist, whose seeming cosmopolitanism was skin-deep at best."[6] More, he was a broad-gauged intellectual, deeply steeped in his country's cultural traditions. But he had already been long associated with an iconoclastic vein within those traditions. Thus, his espousal of Western ideas was a natural development for him, by means of which he could advance China's best interests and lose nothing of his personal integrity in the process. Chen's interest in Marxism was also late in developing. His earliest articles sympathetic to the Russian revolution did not appear until early 1919, but after he was forced to leave Peking late that year he declared Marxism to be the best prescription for China's ills. However, Chen did not accept Marxism without reservations, and often stressed the need to use Marxism as a guide, to be applied only as appropriate to the actual conditions in China.[7]

Nevertheless, it was Chen Duxiu who organized the Chinese Communist Party (CCP). The visit to Chen in August 1920 by Comintern representative Gregory Voitinsky and his overseas Chinese assistant, Yang Mingchai, the first of a succession of such Comintern advisers, facilitated this development. Voitinsky was an excellent point man for the Russians as they began to explore possibilities in China following a resumption of communications between the Chinese and the Soviets in

1920. The Chinese found Voitinsky to be cooperative, informative, humble, and enthusiastic. He also made the right connections from the start, establishing close ties with the Chinese Communists, but also meeting with Sun Yat-sen as well.[8] It bears noting that Voitinsky also met with and, along with other Soviets, came to have high hopes for the warlord Wu Peifu.[9]

By late August 1920, Chen established the first branch of the CCP, in Shanghai, comprising seven members. In September, a Shanghai unit of the Socialist Youth League (SYL) was begun, as was a foreign language school that sent its first eight students to Moscow's University of the Toilers of the Far East (later renamed Sun Yat-sen University) that winter.[10] Among these students was Liu Shaoqi, who would become a prominent leader. The Peking branch of the CCP began in September with nine members, expanding to fifteen by November, after allowing anarchists who had originally signed on to depart peaceably.[11]

In November 1920, Mao Zedong established a very active branch at Changsha, Hunan, and a large SYL unit at about the same time. Mao, a graduate of Changsha Normal School in 1918, formed an organization called the New People's Study Society and in mid-1919 had assumed the editorship of the *Xiang River Review*. He had already visited Peking and Shanghai. Mao was a brilliant young activist with a powerful personality. He had an early classical education, which, while not as deep and as sophisticated as Chen Duxiu's, nevertheless was to influence Mao throughout his life, despite the iconoclastic turbulence of which he was part and to which he contributed. Reared and situated in the politically sensitive crossroads province of Hunan, Mao responded to the vital ideas of his time, gaining a respect for science and technology, assimilating a heightened sense of nationalism and a growing conviction of the need for basic change for China. By 1919, Mao was briefly attracted to both political liberalism and a nonviolent anarchism, and for a time argued for a separate Hunan nation. Mao embraced Marxism in 1920, having been influenced by Li Dazhao and Chen Duxiu and greatly stimulated to do so by his friend Cai Hesen, who, while in France, corresponded informatively with Mao. But Robert A. Scalapino has made it clear that "Mao espoused Bolshevism at this point as a successful method of revolution, not as a philosophic truth."[12] Nevertheless, once he made his commitment to Marxism he did not waver, however many liberties he himself would take with its philosophy in the decades ahead.

Another CCP branch was organized in Wuhan in central China in November 1920. This group included Dong Biwu, who would survive to become a venerable party elder. Other branches appeared in Tianjing and in Jinan. Oddly, Guangzhou, which had long been the cradle of the modern revolution, was the last of the initial cities to have an organized branch. Anarchists, among revolutionaries, dominated this southern metropolis, which had been less influenced by the May Fourth Movement than cities in north and central China. However, things changed when Chen Duxiu accepted for a time the position of minister of education in "progressive" warlord Chen Qiungming's newly established government in Guangzhou in November 1920. Both a CCP branch and a unit of the SYL were soon established, although, in Chen's absence, developments in Shanghai slowed. Another important branch was organized in Paris, France, in February 1921.

These initial branches became very active in propaganda work, in publishing and distributing magazines and pamphlets, and in organizing and educating youth and workers. As the scope of the work of the branches widened, and perhaps because of the ideological confusion wrought by the influence of anarchists and others among the Marxists, whose own understanding of Marxism was deficient, sentiment for further developing the formal organizational structure of the party grew. Accordingly, plans were made in the spring of 1921 for the first national conference of delegates. This first national conference, the First Party Congress, was held in at least five sessions over a period of ten days during the month of July 1921 in at least three locations in or near Shanghai.[13] July 1 is celebrated as the party's birthday, but it is unlikely that the first session began until later in the month.[14] At least the first session was held in the Bo Wen Girls School in Shanghai's French Concession, while others were held in the apartment of one of the Shanghai delegates, Li Hanzhun. Because police suspicions were aroused, the final session was held aboard a boat on South Lake outside Shanghai.

Twelve delegates, representing 59 party members, participated in the First Congress. Two delegates had been invited from each of the six branches in China, and one came from Japan; one of the two Hunan delegates was returned home before the sessions began. The participants were Li Hanzhun and Li Da of Shanghai, Zhang Guotao and Liu Ranqing of Beijing, Chen Gongbo and Bao Huiseng of Guangzhou, Dong Biwu and Chen Tanqiu of Wuhan, Mao Zedong of Changsha, Wang Chinmei and Deng Enming of Jinan, and Zhou Fokai from Japan. Ironically, neither Chen Duxiu nor Li Dazhao attended. In addition, two Soviet Comintern representatives, Maring (Hendricus Sneevliet) and his assistant, named Nicolaevsky, attended.[15] Maring lacked Voitinsky's appealing personality and in the weeks prior to the convening of the congress managed to offend several of the Chinese leaders with his arrogance and aggressiveness. However, at the congress Maring did not intrude unduly. His talk to the session was interrupted by the fear of a police raid, and he was not invited to the more security-conscious meeting at South Lake.[16] Maring did not have a high opinion of the communist leaders. Also, he was not primarily concerned with the Chinese Communists at the time, but was focusing on Sun Yat-sen and his party, the Guomindong (Kuomintang; KMT).

The First Congress was therefore an exclusively Chinese affair, with but limited input from the Soviets. Maring did not even provide the delegates with the text of the resolutions of the Second Comintern Congress of July–August 1920 and he related only a vague idea of them to Zhang Guotao. Nor did the delegates have model constitutions of platforms of other communist parties to consult.[17] Without closer direction at this stage of development, it is not surprising that the delegates came to conclusions that were unacceptable to Moscow. In fact, aside from the election of absent Chen Duxiu as the first party chairman, the results must have been a shock to the Soviets. The adopted program was radical and independent, clearly astray from the line being promoted by Lenin and the Comintern.

The views of the moderate reformist Li Hanzhun, supported only by Chen Gongbo, who desired to support Sun Yat-sen, lost out to Liu Ranjing and Zhang Guotao, who argued for an exclusionist, independent party.[18] With regard to the party's relationship to the Comintern, although the delegates apparently intended to join the Third International (so named after the Third Comintern Congress in June 1921) they did not write this into their constitution nor did they formally join at this point. They did, however, undertake to make monthly reports to the Comintern. The fledgling Chinese Communist Party was probably unaware of the contradiction into which it had placed itself. Joining the Comintern would require submission to the latter's authority. Yet the new party had already opted for a policy of exclusivity that was in conflict with the Comintern.

One year earlier, the Second Comintern Congress had established Lenin's policy toward Asia, which semantically incorporated, or through sheer verbiage concealed, rather basic objectives. Even as Lenin concentrated on consolidating the revolution in the Soviet Russian Republic, he looked to Asia where the struggle could be extended. Lenin believed that with help backward Asian countries could overthrow imperialist control and actually dispense with the capitalist stage (between feudalism and socialism) of historical development. The rather imprecise and complicated way of achieving socialist revolution in Asia would have the peasants and proletariat join in "temporary alliances" with the national bourgeoisie, an enterprise that would be supported by the proletariat of the West. The alliance could be maintained until it was time to dispense with the national bourgeoisie.

This gradualist approach of Lenin's was objected to, however, by an Indian delegate, M. N. Roy, who believed that the focus of revolution should be in Asia and insisted that the growing proletariat-peasant movement should be kept separate from the bourgeoisie. Roy argued that the Comintern should support the former movement by forming communist parties. Collaboration with the unreliable bourgeoisie was to be avoided. Lenin compromised and allowed Roy's "Supplemental Thesis" to become a Comintern resolution, while in his own thesis the designation "bourgeoisie-democratic" was changed to read "national-revolutionary." Thus did the Comintern come to profess a policy line that was inherently contradictory and that would be interpreted to suit convenience. This was exacerbated by the unintentional printing and distribution of the earlier unrevised version of Roy's thesis, a mistake that went uncorrected until 1934![19]

Regardless of this ambiguity, however, Moscow's fundamental purpose was obvious enough. It sought to cultivate allies among promising national revolutionary movements that basically had bourgeoisie in leadership, while simultaneously helping communist movements to develop. Invariably, the priority would have to remain on supporting the former, at least as long as this served the interests of the Soviet revolution or state or until the time arrived to begin the next, socialist stage of revolution. Otherwise, the interests of the indigenous communist party were always secondary and, if need be, the party itself was expendable.

The Third Comintern Congress in June 1921 strengthened the notion of cooperation, for it coincided with the initiation of Lenin's New Economic Policy in the Soviet Union. The congress was at pains to have the European trade union movement concern itself with wages and working conditions and avoid political actions. Moderation characterized the Comintern's policy toward China as well, where the national revolution was to comprise a four-class alliance of the bourgeoisie, petty bourgeoisie, peasants, and workers.[20]

In the year between its First and Second Congresses, the youthful party became a beehive of activity. It further extended its work in propaganda and among youth, workers, and peasants, gaining invaluable experience in these areas. It expanded its own organizational network to embrace regional secretaries and branches in ten provinces; by mid-1922 some 120 members were spread throughout eighteen provinces.[21] At the same time, the party was becoming more disciplined, and it weeded out those who would not submit to the severe requirements of

Leninist democratic centralism. In September 1922, the magazine *Guide Weekly* replaced *New Youth* as the official party youth organ, the latter becoming a quarterly theoretical journal until it ceased publication in 1926.[22]

The SYL continued to grow faster than the party itself. After it had been dissolved in May 1921 in order to rid itself of non-Marxists, the SYL was reorganized that November. Its first congress was held in Guangzhou in May 1922, at the same time as the First National Labor Congress,[23] with 25 delegates representing 2,000 members. This membership figure expanded to 6,000 by the time of the SYL's second congress in August 1923.[24] It began to publish *Chinese Youth* in October 1923.[25]

Even more impressive were the party's early accomplishments in organizing workers. In mid-1921, the CCP founded a Labor Secretariat in Shanghai that published the *Labor Weekly* until it was suppressed in June 1922. Branches of the Labor Secretariat were established in Wuhan, Jinan, Guangzhou, Changsha, and Beijing. Despite the social barriers, and for reasons peculiar to the Chinese labor scene, the young intellectual activists were able to reach the workers. Their idealistic revolutionary enthusiasm enjoined them to go to the masses. But even so, organizing strikes might not have been possible had the activists not met a real need by opening and operating workers' schools. The first of these was founded by Zhang Guotao among railway workers in early 1921.[26]

Communist-led strikes began in Wuhan in October 1921. Meanwhile, Mao Zedong, Liu Shaoqi, and Li Lisan agitated at the Anyuan mines on the Hunan-Jiangxi border, and helped lead strikes on the Guangzhou-Hankou railway and elsewhere.[27] Communists were involved in the important strike of the 10,000-man Chinese Seamen's Union in Hong Kong, beginning on January 13, 1922. By February, this strike gained additional support in Hong Kong, in Guangzhou, and in Shanghai involving some 100,000 workers. The British finally conceded in March, allowing the union to continue and granting substantial pay raises. Afterwards, the Labor Secretariat called the first congress of what was to become the National General Labor Union. At this initial labor congress, convened on May 1, 1922, in Guangzhou, there were some 160 delegates, claiming to represent 100 unions and 200,000 to 300,000 workers.[28]

In the following year, Communists were reported to have led more than 100 strikes at such work sites as the coal mines at Anyuan and Kailan, the Shanghai textile mills, the Hanyang ironworks, and along the Beijing-Hankou railway in which 10,000 men participated. The climax of these strikes came with the bloody suppression of the Beijing-Hankou railway workers strike by the warlord Wu Peifu on February 7, 1923.[29] About 50 strikers were killed, hundreds wounded, and thousands were fired from their jobs. This event, known as the February 7 Massacre, was a notable setback for communist labor organizers. It also highlighted the problem of cooperating with potential enemies who were stronger than the party, and who had the power to erase quickly any gains made through cooperation. In this particular case, Li Dazhao, supported by Soviet diplomats, had clearly underestimated the wily warlord. An important lesson went unlearned in this, for "alliance" remained the Comintern watchword.

In the meanwhile, the earliest Communist organizing among the peasantry also was underway in the early 1920s, even though priority attention was not given this activity until after the urban debacles of 1927. Leading the work in the countryside was Peng Pai, the son of a rich landlord, who had studied in Japan for three years. Peng's activities were concentrated in two counties, Haifeng and Lufeng, known together as Hailufeng on the Guangdong coast northeast of Hong Kong. In January 1923, a 20,000-member peasant union was established in Haifeng.[30]

The First Congress of the Toilers of the Far East, held in Moscow in January–February 1922, was instrumental in making the Chinese Communist Party change its policy regarding cooperation with the Nationalists. The Moscow meeting, called to counter the Washington Conference that had excluded the Soviet Union, had as its theme the uniting of the proletariat with the oppressed peoples of the world. Thirty Chinese attended, representing both the KMT and the Chinese Communists. They listened to speeches stressing the priority of national revolution over social revolution and the need for Communists and non-Communists to cooperate. Three of the Chinese, including Zhang Guotao, privately met with Lenin, who discussed with them the possibility of KMT-CCP cooperation.[31] Zhang himself conceded that collaboration was possible, although certain difficulties had to be resolved.

Accordingly, the CCP soon came to change its own orientation to accord with that of the Third International. In June 1922, the party officially accepted the concept of the united front. Its first declaration on the situation in the country, on June 10, actually took the initiative in calling for a conference with KMT revolutionaries to discuss the creation of a united front to liberate the Chinese people from the dual yoke of foreigners and of powerful Chinese militarists.[32] The idea here was to undertake joint actions with the KMT, both collaborating as independent organizations.

This idea of a limited alliance was reiterated at the Second Party

Congress, which opened in Shanghai about July 10, 1922. The congress elected a new Central Committee that included Chen Duxiu, Li Dazhao, Cai Hesen, and Zhang Guotao. It also decided to join the Comintern, and in so doing formally submit the CCP to Comintern authority. Of course, such submission was qualified by distance and, as James Harrison has observed, Comintern representatives in China ultimately had to depend on the Chinese to carry out policy. But in the early years, the inexperienced Chinese tended, on the whole, to hew to the line with little reservation.[33]

Thus, Maring persuaded the CCP less than a month later at a special plenum of the party's Central Committee, at West Lake in Hangzhou, to accept another, more compromising plan for cooperation with the KMT. This was the technique of a "bloc within" whereby the Chinese Communists were to join the KMT as individual members. The idea had been introduced in meetings Maring held with Sun Yat-sen at Gweilin in late 1921.[34] In fact, Maring had used the same strategy in his work in the Indies and had promoted it at the Comintern's Second Congress before coming to China.[35] For his part, Sun must have seen this requirement as a means of keeping the Communists under observation, and thus insisted upon it as a condition of collaboration. Maring had then gone to Moscow where he received Comintern approval for it. Curiously, at the West Lake plenum, Maring misapplied the idea of the four-class alliance as articulated at the Third Comintern Congress the previous summer. Prior to this plenum, the KMT had been regarded as the party of the bourgeoisie, but now Maring on his own defined it as a "bloc of various classes," the four components that had been used to describe the entire advanced section of Chinese society.[36]

The Chinese Communists feared that by entering the KMT their own party would lose its independence and identity and that each Communist would become more vulnerable. However, despite such strong objections, they finally accepted the scheme in the end because they had no choice. The Communists *were* relieved of the need to be fingerprinted and to swear allegiance to Sun Yat-sen and, most important, they could maintain their membership in the CCP. Some of them did see, too, advantages for the party in working so intimately with the larger, more powerful organization. In fact, their intention, and that of the Comintern, was to use such opportunities to maximum advantage and, when the Communists were advantageously situated, to subvert and eliminate the KMT. However, this was a game played with equal cynicism and adroitness on both sides. Li Dazhao, who may have been Maring's only supporter at West Lake, was one of the first Communists to join the KMT. Chen Duxiu attended the Fourth Congress of the

Comintern from November 5 to December 5, 1922, at which the formation of such united fronts with Asian nationalists was promoted more strongly than ever.[37]

On January 26, 1923, a joint manifesto was issued in Shanghai by Sun Yat-sen and Soviet diplomat Adolph Joffe, which consummated the hard work of Maring during the previous year by formalizing the united-front policy of the KMT. The manifesto acknowledged that neither communism nor the Soviet system was suitable for China because of the absence of necessary conditions. This was an important point for Sun, but for the Communists it represented "just so much diplomatic verbiage which placed no restraints upon the CCP," according to Zhang Guotao.[38]

It is useful to keep in mind that, on the other side, Sun was allying himself with the Soviet Union, as Leng Shao-chuan makes clear, out of political expediency.[39] For Sun, 1922 had been another bad year. In June he was forced out of Guangzhou for the third time, and his pleas for Western help were unavailing. Hence his vulnerability to Soviet offers of substantial assistance. Maring worked unremittingly on Sun, so much so that he did not even bother to inform the CCP leaders about the Sun-Joffe talks, nor seek their concurrence, much to their chagrin.[40] Nevertheless, Chen Duxiu was given a place on the commission to reorganize the KMT, which was announced in January 1923. Sun was able to return triumphantly to Guangzhou in February where he began to build an independent army, sending Jiang Jieshi (Chiang K'ai-shek) to Moscow that summer and fall to study the Soviet military and to obtain arms.

The CCP's Third Congress was held in Guangzhou from June 10 to 20, 1923. Attending were 27 voting delegates claiming to represent 432 members. Maring was one of several nonvoting delegates present. A new nine-member Central Committee was elected, including for the first time Mao Zedong and journalist Qu Qiubai, along with the five carryovers from the Second Central Committee. Chen Duxiu was re-elected general secretary. Qu was made propaganda chief, and Mao replaced Zhang Guotao as director of the organization department. The united-front policy was the main topic at the congress. Maring was anxious to have confirmed the "bloc within" alliance concept that had been accepted at the West Lake plenum the previous August. He was further armed with a Comintern resolution of January 1923 and a May 1923 Comintern directive, both pushing the united front upon the CCP. There remained considerable opposition to the "bloc within" concept during and even after the congress, for many Communists refused to join the KMT for as long as a year later, and some simply left the party.

Contrary to what Maoist writers later claimed, the argument was not a simple left-right matter, with Zhang Guotao as the leftist opposition and Chen Duxiu leading the rightist deviation of capitulating to the KMT. Clearly, it was the Comintern, through Maring, that finally persuaded the recalcitrant Chinese. Ironically, it is Li Dazhao and other supporters of Maring who are extolled by party historiographers, while the maligned Chen Duxiu had long been an opponent of Sun Yat-sen.[41] As for Mao himself, on the important question of the labor movement, which Zhang Guotao and Li Lisan held should be exempt from KMT leadership, Mao shifted his vote to support joint Nationalist-Communist control. It should be noted, however, that the severe setback of the February 7 Massacre was on the minds of many Communists, underscoring as it did the weakness of the proletariat.

Zhang Guotao had himself journeyed to Moscow to report on that incident, only to experience indifference from a Comintern that was preoccupied by the challenge of the Trotsky-led opposition to Lenin's moderate policies.[42] Following Lenin's death in 1924, that opposition was then addressed to Joseph Stalin, who had assumed leadership of the Soviet party. Stalin defended Lenin's policies and, in confuting Trotsky's demand for world revolution, soon evolved the concept of defending "socialism in one country." Unfortunately for the CCP, Stalin's Chinese policy became the focus of fierce, unrelenting criticism by Trotsky. This compelled Stalin to defend himself and his policies regardless of the actual situation in China. Thus, Stalin, even more than Lenin, came to insist on Chinese cooperation with the KMT.

The manifesto of the Third Congress accepted the "bloc within" and did acknowledge that the KMT "should be the central force of the national revolution and should assume its leadership." But the CCP declared that it would attempt to move the KMT to the left and fuse the national and social revolutions by "deepening" the national revolution through the mass work that the Nationalists had neglected.[43]

Gregory Voitinsky returned to China in November 1923, replacing Maring as Comintern representative. Voitinsky's superior tact mollified the CCP and facilitated the implementation of the united front. Mikhail Borodin had arrived in China the previous month. This experienced Comintern adviser took on the reorganization of the KMT, which was soon operating along Soviet lines. The work of both men was assisted by the gunboat diplomacy indulged in by the Western powers at Guangzhou in December 1923. This was in response to Sun Yat-sen's not unreasonable demand for a portion of the maritime customs receipts that were administered by Western officials. This rebuke to Sun raised anti-imperialist sentiment. It also created a shift to the left by the KMT, which was to hold its First National Congress the following month, January 1924.

The Communists soon experienced the benefits of the awkward alliance. They were respectably represented in the congress and then were appointed to key positions. Three were elected to the 24-man Central Executive Committee, and one of these joined the eight-man standing committee. A Political Council, created in July 1924, prevented conservative Hu Hanmin's power bid and was controlled by the Nationalist Party's left wing. Two of eight KMT central bureaus were headed by Communists, including the important organization bureau, which they really dominated. As expected, Communists were prominent in the peasant and labor bureaus. Similarly, at the Whampoa Military Academy, established in the spring of 1924, Communists played significant roles. Zhou Enlai became a deputy head of political instruction, and several others who would later become famous leaders were instructors or students. They were denied, however, similar positions among the senior military leadership or a presence on the military council.

The CCP Central Committee held an enlarged plenary session in Shanghai from May 10 to 14, 1924, at which it decided to intensify mass and labor work. Also, in response to conservative Nationalist criticisms regarding CCP intentions to subvert the KMT, the party decided to give more attention to the preservation of its own independent organization. Finally, the plenum refined further the Comintern's advocated tactic of splitting the KMT into left and right factions by distinguishing a third faction, the center, which also could be won over in isolating the conservatives. Such initiatives were not appreciated in the Comintern.[44]

As the shock of the February 7, 1923, massacre subsided, and as the united front came to be realized, mass and labor activities began to revive. The Communists succeeded in penetrating the newly established labor bureaus of the KMT regional committees. Inflation, heavy taxes, and chaotic warlordism, along with a perceptibly increased foreign presence in China, were contributing elements in a new growing wave of discontent. A number of strikes occurred in 1924, some of them involving close Communist-Nationalist cooperation. The KMT left wing benefited from Sun Yat-sen's October 1924 defeat of the Canton Merchants Corps, which had opposed the radical orientation of his party. In the meanwhile, there was encouraging news that prospects had improved in north China where Soviet-aided warlord Feng Yuxiang had driven Wu Peifu from Peking with the help of Manchurian warlord Zhang Zuolin (Chang Tso-lin).

The Fourth Congress of the CCP was held in Shanghai from January 11 to 22, 1925. Some twenty delegates attended, claiming to represent over 900 members.[45] Chen Duxiu was re-elected general secretary for the fourth time. Mao Zedong, who may have been ill, but who in any case may have been under criticism for collaborating too enthusiastically with the KMT, did not attend. The Fourth Congress prophetically, as it turned out, initiated a recruitment drive to broaden the party from its narrow basis of intellectuals to a mass party of the workers. Accordingly, it lowered admissions requirements.

Thus was the CCP fortuitously poised to take advantage of the phenomenal May 30 Movement that summer, dramatically increasing its membership tenfold by the end of the year. This enabled the party in 1925 to surpass in size for the first time the Socialist Youth League, which changed its name to the Communist Youth League (CYL) at its third congress in February 1925.[46] The CCP Fourth Congress manifesto also emphasized the dangers of imperialism and insightfully predicted the imminence of the workers' and peasants' struggle against imperialism and capitalist oppression. However, the manifesto also stressed the "importance of the economic struggle of the working class."[47]

A promising new plateau for Chinese revolutionaries was reached in 1925. Sun Yat-sen died in March in Beijing, where he had gone to negotiate what the CCP could only regard as a dubious arrangement with the northern warlords. The negotiations had been unsuccessful, but the KMT had strengthened its Guangdong base and great results attended efforts in organizing labor. The second congress of the National Railroad Union was held in Zhengzhou in February, revealing strong continued Communist influence. Most of the leaders of the Chinese Seamen's Union now joined the CCP.[48]

The Second National Labor Congress met in Guangzhou in May, with 281 delegates in attendance, representing 166 unions with over 540,000 members. The congress established the National General Labor Union, replacing the Labor Secretariat that was formed in 1922. A Communist headed the union's 25-member executive committee, which also included Li Lisan and Liu Shaoqi among others. Again, timing for the Communist labor organizers turned out to be propitious, for soon after this congress adjourned, having put in place a national organization, the May 30 Movement erupted.

Protests in Japanese-owned textile mills had been going on since February, but on May 15, 1925, one of the factory guards shot and killed a striker in Shanghai. Ironically, Japanese factories were the most modern and provided the best working conditions in China, but they also exacted discipline and perhaps seemed the most "foreign" to Chinese workers, just because the working environment was so rationally efficient and impersonal.[49] Others were wounded and arrested as demonstrations spread to other cities.

On May 30, the CCP Central Committee, along with other groups in Shanghai, held a demonstration on Nanking Road to protest the arrest of student activists. Suddenly, police under a British officer opened fire, killing about ten demonstrators and wounding and arresting many more. This prompted further demonstrations and the Central Committee called a general strike for June 1. In a social upsurge reminiscent of the May Fourth Incident of 1919, merchants and student associations for a time added their support. The movement spread to other cities and brought about, climactically, the huge Hong Kong–Guangzhou strike. This strike began in Hong Kong on June 19, and on June 23 a large demonstration in Guangzhou was staged in support. Once again, trigger-happy armed men escalated matters beneficially for the radicals. In this case, British and French soldiers from the foreign concession on Shameen Island killed 52 of the demonstrators and wounded more than 100. The strike was quickly joined by others, until several hundred thousand workers, mostly under Communist leadership, were involved. The 16-month-long strike lasted until October 1926, making it the lengthiest in Chinese history. There was, in fact, an increasing proliferation of strikes throughout the country in 1925 and 1926, with 318 recorded for 1925 and as many as 535 in 1926. By April 1926, the figure for membership in the National General Labor Union had reached 1,240,000.[50]

The May 30 Movement was a watershed in modern Chinese history. The labor movement not only expanded enormously, but changed from a purely economic struggle to a political one. This was recognized in a resolution of the KMT's Second Congress in January 1926.[51] Nationalism became a more controlled and concerted force.[52] And in this assertion of it, the Chinese discerned that foreigners had blinked in the encounter, enabling the Chinese to take heart in the knowledge of the vulnerability of imperialism. In fact, both Great Britain and the United States eventually adopted new policies toward China.

Of course, the CCP benefited from this intensive labor activity and the surcharged atmosphere. However, as fast as the party was expanding, it was almost impossible, as Lyman Van Slyke noted, for it to keep up with the rapid developments.[53] Yet it valiantly tried. At the First Enlarged Plenum of its Fourth Central Committee in Peking in October 1925, the effects of the mass movement were discussed, and it was decided to formulate propaganda in ways that would be understood even by illiterate workers. However, at the Second Enlarged Plenum of the

Fourth Central Committee in Shanghai, July 12–18, 1926, it was rue-fully conceded that such popularization efforts had not been effective.[54] Renewed efforts were made, but the explanation of Marxism and CCP policies in terms comprehensible to the masses would take years of persistent experimentation. Simultaneously, the party also developed leftist schools where ideological training could be implemented on a more sophisticated basis. The most promising students from these schools were sent to Moscow for advanced training. Ironically, however, nearly half of these students would come to accept Trotsky's criticisms of Stalin's China policy,[55] and the youthful idealism of many others would be severely affected by Stalin's brutal handling of the opposition.

In the meanwhile, the restive peasantry was stirring, but the CCP was not yet equal to the task of leading their powerful movement. This formidable task was complicated by the priority given to the united front, which meant that peasants could only be organized to the extent that it did not threaten the interests of many Nationalists. Also the traditional bias of some leaders, such as Chen Duxiu, reinforced by Marxism, kept the CCP oriented to the urban proletariat, whose growth was already straining the party's leadership capacity. Thus, even though the Comintern had recognized the importance of Asian peasants for the revolution as early as 1920, and the CCP's Fourth Congress recognized the special importance of the peasants and the need to organize them, some very practical problems stood in the way.

Even so, the early efforts by the CCP in the countryside were im-pressive. Peng Pai's successes, noted above, were temporarily set back when his peasant association was bloodily suppressed in March 1924. For a while, Peng retreated to Guangzhou where he became a secretary of the new Communist-headed Nationalist peasant bureau. In the sum-mer of 1924, Peng also became director of the first class of the Peasant Training Institute. Each of the next five classes were directed by Com-munists, with Mao Zedong directing the final class of 318 in 1926. The graduates soon were instrumental in setting up peasant associations in Guangdong. In May 1925, the Guangdong Provincial Peasant Associa-tion was established, and by mid-1927 it represented about 700,000 peasants in 73 counties. Meanwhile, neighboring Hunan province soon overtook Guangdong in the organization of peasants. By mid-1927 there were more than 9 million association members in sixteen provinces.[56]

But in mid-1926, with only 600 communist activists working among all these restive peasants, the CCP had no real control. Mao, in early 1927, observed that the peasant movement had a dynamism of its own, independent of outside agitators.[57] Robert Marks has shown how, in fact, this was the case, pointing out that the upheaval in the 1920s in Haifeng, for example, was actually the result of changes in the socioeconomic structure that had been aggravated by imperialism and affected by the 1911 revolution, rather than the consequence of organizational activity by outside agitators.[58] Nevertheless, it should be acknowledged that Peng Pai had succeeded, as would many Communists after him, including Mao, because of a willingness to identify with the peasants, on their level, taking fully into account their concerns and interests.

As for the contradiction with Marxism and its urban proletariat, Peng simply regarded the peasants as the "new proletariat."[59] Despite its handicaps, and handicapped policy, the CCP gained from its limited involvement in this rural phenomenon. Eto Shinkichi noted that by March 1927 there were as many as 4,000 Communists in Peng Pai's Hailufeng.[60] The formation of active peasant associations also helped consolidate the Nationalist government's base in south China, enabling it to dispatch an expedition to reunify the country.

Much of the success the CCP did enjoy during this surge of labor and peasant unrest from 1924 to early 1926 was attributable to the united front with the KMT. On his deathbed, Sun Yat-sen left a final message, written in all likelihood by Wang Jingwei, his chief lieutenant, expressing the hope that his party would continue to cooperate with the Soviet Union. Wang, already chairman of the Political Affairs Council of the KMT, became the president of the Nationalist government on July 1, 1925, and chairman of the Military Council on July 6. However, Jiang Jieshi, his rival, was building his own support, particularly in the military. There was also an undercurrent of antagonism among many Nationalists against the Communists, fueled by distrust of their intentions, their dual-party allegiance, and their commitment to a foreign government.

On August 20, 1925, Liao Zhongkai, the leader of the Nationalist left and a friend of the Communists, was murdered. Hu Hanmin, the leader of the Nationalist extreme right was implicated, but no evidence of his guilt ever materialized.[61] Hu was sent to the Soviet Union for a time as a device to preserve the united front and to save his own life. In late 1925, two right-wing factions, one the Western Hills Group, later based in Shanghai, the other led by Tai Jitao in Guangzhou, called for the expulsion of the Communists.

This plea was rejected, however, at the Nationalists' Second Congress in January 1926 because the majority of the Nationalists still perceived the utility of the alliance. In fact, the congress elected seven Communists to the 36-member KMT Central Executive Committee, and among seven others who were elected deputy members was Mao Zedong. Communist Tan Pingshan continued as chairman of the organization bureau, while Lin Zuhan took charge of the peasant department and Mao, propaganda, although Wang Jingwei was its nominal chairman.

But three months later a violent incident took place that would shake the Communists' sense of security considerably. In the early hours of March 20, 1926, Jiang Jieshi arrested Communist cadres at the Whampoa Military Academy and elsewhere in Guangzhou. Pickets supporting the Guangzhou–Hong Kong strike were disarmed and the Soviet advisers were placed under house arrest. These actions were taken to prevent an alleged attempt by the Communist commander of the gunboat *Zhongshan* to kidnap Jiang. Thus, Jiang's coup was claimed to be a preemptive action. There is the possibility that certain Communists and Soviet advisers had provoked Jiang by arguing that the plans for a Northern Expedition were premature. Ironically, however, Borodin and a visiting high-level Soviet commission had recently met in Peking where they endorsed an early launching of the Northern Expedition. Borodin was still in the north when the March 20 coup occurred, but the members of the Soviet commission were visiting Guangzhou and were among those placed under house arrest.[62] Having made his point, and about to gain important concessions, Jiang released the Communists on the following day with an apology. The Soviet advisers, anxious to preserve the alliance with the KMT, smoothed over the incident. But it was to have serious consequences for the CCP, which was made to appear impetuously leftist and as such a threat to the alliance.

One consequence was that Wang Jingwei resigned the presidency of the Nationalist government, enabling Jiang to bolster his own position in the crucial months ahead. Also, on May 15, 1926, the KMT Central Executive Committee extracted tough concessions from the Communists. Henceforth all Comintern directives had to be channeled through a special committee composed of Nationalist, Communist, and Comintern representatives. The CCP could not criticize Sun's Three People's Principles. A list of all Communists in the Nationalist Party had to be given to its Central Executive Committee. Communists could constitute no more than one-third of the latter body and no Communist could be the head of a Nationalist government department. Thus, Mao Zedong, Tan Pingshan, and Lin Zuhan were forced to relinquish their new posts. Borodin counseled the CCP not to attach too much importance to the losses.[63] However, Zhang Guotao, for one, disagreed, believing that these events indicated "a course that weakened control of the KMT by the Soviet Union, doused the flames of the CCP, and strengthened the leadership of the bourgeoisie."[64] Suddenly, Borodin's immense influence on the Chinese revolution evaporated. For its part, the CCP, too, despite its increasing numbers and its frenetic work among the masses, was more handicapped than ever.

The military phase of the national revolution, the Northern Expedition, began in mid-July 1926, with a national revolutionary army consisting of about 100,000 men, an army that had been formed systematically since early 1924. Jiang Jieshi was commander in chief. Russian General Vasili Blucher (alias Galen), with other Soviet advisers, played important roles. The Communists had no military unit of their own, although a number of unit commanders, such as Yeh Ting, were Communists.

The expedition was a highly successful one. This was due to several factors: disunity among the warlord armies; adroit military diplomacy; and the tactics, the discipline, and the courage of the Nationalist army itself. Some of its success was attributable as well to the contributions of workers and peasants organized by the CCP, but such input has been overstated by the Communists, particularly by Trotskyite writers, as Donald Jordan has made clear.[65] There were too many instances when CCP-directed organized work threatened or distracted rather than supported the military campaign. In fact, it was the patriotic and favorable image projected by the army's behavior and by its political workers that elicited the cooperation of a responsive, unorganized population that was perhaps most important. By the end of 1926 the army had already taken key central provinces, and by the spring of 1927 it reached the rich lower Chang Jiang (Yangtze) Valley. Military operations then halted for about a year, during which time some fundamental political issues were settled.

The Nationalist movement had split geographically during the Northern Expedition. The Nationalist government, heavily influenced by the KMT's left-wing, based itself at Wuhan beginning in January 1927, while Jiang Jieshi conducted operations from Nanchang for a time. On the one hand, the Wuhan government condoned or pursued radical policies, giving the CCP considerable latitude for its mass organizing. Two prominent Communists, Tan Pingshan and Su Chaocheng, were appointed ministers of agriculture and labor respectively. Jiang, on the other hand, suppressed disorder and carefully avoided provoking foreigners. This was highlighted during the Nanjing Incident of March 24, 1927, in which he executed 30 or more soldiers implicated in the killing of about a dozen foreigners. Jiang was incensed when the Wuhan government that month stripped him of considerable political authority. Moreover, the government virtually annulled the restrictions that Jiang had placed on the CCP the previous year. On April 4, 1927, Wang Jingwei, just returned from abroad, signed a joint declaration with Chen Duxiu reaffirming KMT-CCP cooperation.[66] Wang and Jiang also held talks, but to no avail.

Only days later, in the early hours of April 12, 1927, Jiang Jieshi boldly disarmed the Communist-led unions in Shanghai and began a purge of the Communists themselves.[67] This has widely been regarded as a dastardly, if decisive, action, particularly since the workers had been instrumental in the taking of Shanghai for the Nationalist army. They had, in fact, tried to take the city three times from within in the previous several months, with sizable loss of life each time, including the third, successful attempt on March 21 and 22, 1927. But Jiang would not tolerate such a strengthened Communist presence in Shanghai, even if the CCP remained anxious to be cooperative. Jiang had reached an understanding with financial interests in the city and, with the help of even the powerful organized criminal element, the potential Communist threat was eliminated. This was a crushing blow to the CCP. As many as 300 were killed, while 5,000 were accounted missing in the suppression; many among these were promising young leaders. Zhou Enlai, the future premier, barely escaped with his life. The purge spread throughout much of the country. Meanwhile, in Peking, police had raided the Soviet Embassy on April 6, where they confiscated a number of compromising documents and arrested twenty Communists. One of these was CCP co-founder Li Dazhao, who was executed on April 28, 1927.

Given the debacle that had just occurred in Shanghai and elsewhere, the CCP's Fifth Congress, held in Hankou from April 27 to May 5, 1927, was a curious phenomenon. Here 80 delegates, representing the now completely misleading figure of 57,900 members, met with the newly arrived Comintern representative, M. N. Roy.[68] The key decision of the congress was to reaffirm the united front, and formally accept the Resolution on the China Problem passed by the Seventh Enlarged Conference of the Comintern Executive Committee, which had met in Moscow the preceding November and December. The resolution reflected Joseph Stalin's views that the Communists should remain within the KMT and sanctioned the holding of positions in the Nationalist government. Both of these had already been fulfilled at Wuhan, and the Shanghai disaster, which occurred later, had no effect on these policies. The congress merely acknowledged that the "big bourgeoisie" had opted out of the alliance, which had now become a "three bloc" affair, of proletariat, peasants, and petty bourgeoisie. In any case, the remaining options were not promising and there was concern that the KMT Left should be supported to prevent the Right from taking over the KMT.

Also discussed at the Fifth Congress was the agrarian question. The Comintern in December 1926 had indicated the need to seize real power in the countryside by means of the rapidly forming peasant associations. In appealing to the peasants, the Comintern advocated relatively moderate measures to be imposed on the Nationalists. This would enable the CCP to win control over the peasants. Such reasoning was not entirely inconsonant with the findings of an independent investigation that Mao Zedong made in Hunan from January 4 to February 5, 1927. Mao stated dramatically that soon "several hundred million peasants will rise like a mighty storm, like a hurricane, a force so swift and violent that no power, however great, will be able to hold it back." Mao charged: "There are three alternatives. To march at their head and lead them. To trail behind them, gesticulating and criticizing. Or to stand in their way and oppose them." For Mao the answer was obvious and he acknowledged and approved of excesses committed by the peasants in promoting revolution:

> A revolution is not a dinner party, or writing an essay, or painting a picture, or doing embroidery; it cannot be so refined, so leisurely and gentle, so temperate, kind, courteous, restrained and magnanimous. A revolution is an insurrection, an act of violence by which one class overthrows another.[69]

Mao's report was submitted to the Fifth Congress but was not placed on the agenda. He only attended the opening meetings of the congress and apparently argued against continuing the united front. But then, either from illness or in disagreement, he left the meetings. The congress, nevertheless, adopted a fairly strong stand in support of the peasant movement, although there would have to be a discrepancy between this stand and actual practice as long as priority was given to the united front. In any case, the peasant movement itself received a crushing blow only two weeks after the conclusion of the congress. On May 21, 1927, Xu Kexiang, the army commander at Changsha, commenced a severe repression of Communists, union leaders, and peasants who were threatening the city and confiscating land in the countryside. Hundreds perished in this brutal military reaction. A follow-up peasant march on Changsha on May 31, which the CCP now tried to restrain, was similarly defeated with much loss of life.[70]

The congress elected Chen Duxiu as general secretary for the last time and a Central Committee of 29 full members and eleven alternates.

Relations between the CCP and the KMT Left remained very delicate in the late spring and early summer of 1927, particularly over the peasant policy. Temporizing by the CCP leadership actually exacerbated the situation. The withholding of full and unqualified support for the peasants was deleterious to the development of the peasant movement, and irresolution only inflated the suspicions of increasing numbers of the KMT Left, whom the CCP leaders were hoping to mollify.

During this period, a number of inappropriate advisories or instructions were sent from Moscow to China, only confusing matters more. But none was as outrageous as a telegram from Stalin, received on June 1, 1927, which communicated as "instructions" the resolution of the eighth session of the Comintern's Central Executive Committee, which had concluded on May 30. Not unreasonably, the instructions confirmed the need to make agrarian concessions to Nationalist army officers and small landholders. But they also called for the "liquidation of untrustworthy Nationalist generals," the creation of an army of 20,000 Communists and 50,000 workers and peasants in Hunan and Hubei, and the placement of leaders with worker or peasant backgrounds in the KMT Central Executive Committee.[71]

The CCP could make little of such instructions at the moment. Accordingly, a reply was sent to Moscow acknowledging receipt of the instructions and indicating that they would be obeyed when it was possible to do so. But amazingly, M. N. Roy now showed the June 1 telegram to Wang Jingwei![72] Wang in turn shared it with the Nationalist generals, although he had initially wished to delay any separation from the CCP until Jiang Jieshi was dealt with militarily.[73] On June 3, the CCP sent an open letter to the Nationalists urging them to pursue agrarian reform, but was rebuked by Borodin for doing so, since the united front was in such precarious condition. An enlarged conference of party leaders met about June 20 and decided on measures to preserve the alliance. Tan Pingshan and Su Chaocheng resigned from the Wuhan government, perhaps to reduce friction.[74] On July 13, the CCP issued a manifesto preparing for the worst in the face of an expected coup d'état by the Nationalists. Even so, the party continued to make concessions so that the KMT would continue to cooperate.[75]

On July 15, KMT leaders called on the Communists in their party to renounce their Communist affiliation. This forced the CCP underground. Chen Duxiu resigned as general secretary that day. Many Communists fled. Many were soon killed. Meanwhile, on July 27, with fanfare provided by the leaders of the KMT Left, Borodin departed for Moscow— without, it bears noting, bidding farewell to the distressed CCP leadership.[76]

On August 1, 1927, there occurred a very significant event, the Nanchang Uprising, even though at the time it was but another stinging defeat for the Communists. Despite the new traumatic setback for the CCP and for Soviet influence in China, this time at the hands of the

KMT Left, Stalin continued to insist that the alliance endure! Stalin was compelled to do so since any break at this juncture would confirm the correctness of Trotsky's consistent charge that the alliance was a terrible mistake. Stalin also adopted a contrary estimate of China's revolutionary prospects, seeing a revolutionary wave now ascending to its crest there, and holding that Trotsky had been wrong in having seen the wave ascending two months earlier. Thus, Stalin, in need of victories in China, did indeed try to force the trend of events just as his antagonist claimed.[77] The CCP complied with a large-scale military assault on the city of Nanchang, drawing upon Communist-led units that had defected from the Nationalist army. The enterprise was nevertheless carried out under the Nationalist flag, indicating continued adherence to the united-front policy. A revolutionary committee was installed in the city preparatory to the establishment of a government. But the action failed to ignite an uprising among the workers and peasants as expected in a rising revolutionary tide. Instead, the Communists were soon badly defeated. Nevertheless, the event marks the shift of the Chinese Communist movement to a military phase that would last for more than two decades and leave a much longer-lasting military imprint on the CCP. The date of the Nanchang Uprising, August 1, has ever since been commemorated as the birthdate of the Red Army.

On August 7, 1927, the CCP Central Committee held an emergency conference at the behest either of the new Comintern representative, Besso Lominadze, or of Qu Qiubai, a 28-year-old writer trained in the Soviet Union, who was now named the party's general secretary.[78] The conference criticized and removed Chen Duxiu and his supporters as "opportunists" and "rightist capitulationists," thereby preserving for the party itself an image of infallibility. The conference endorsed the Comintern's new line, which still advocated working within the KMT, although the latter was now held to be merely a front to be manipulated by an independent CCP in the process of advancing to the establishment of workers', peasants', and soldiers' soviets.[79] Emphasized now was the agrarian revolution as the crux of the bourgeois democratic revolution, although this did not mean that the urban proletariat was to be abandoned.

The CCP, compelled to go underground, adopted organizational measures to this end. A seven-man Emergency Political Bureau was formed within the Central Committee, with its own secret communications system.[80] Branch organizations were similarly reorganized. Of necessity, secrecy was the order of the day, for Communists and their sympathizers were relentlessly hunted down by both the Wuhan and Nanjing governments. During this period, Communist control and influence in labor unions was ended. Even so, since the line discerned a rising revolutionary tide, it was necessary for the CCP to call boldly for armed uprisings by workers and peasants alike.

This led to the Autumn Harvest Uprising in September, which was another dismal failure. Mao Zedong conducted the main operations in areas that he himself had estimated to be ripe for revolution. But the military effort begun in early September 1927 did not prompt the peasantry to rise in support, nor did it spark a rural conflagration. It was, in fact, a disastrous defeat.[81] With much difficulty, Mao finally led his small military force into the fastnesses of the Jinggangshan mountains athwart the borders of Hunan and Jianxi provinces. The only success at this time, and this was merely temporary, was the occupation in October of Lufeng and Haifeng in eastern Guangdong by Ho Lung and Yeh Ting. Here Peng Pai established the first Chinese soviet government in November. The authority to do so had been granted by the Comintern in late September when the alliance with the KMT was finally laid to rest. But the Hailufeng soviet only lasted until February 1928, when it was crushed by an overwhelming application of armed force.[82]

The CCP Central Committee held an enlarged session on November 9 at which it surprisingly reiterated the view that the wave of revolution was still rising. The recent failures at Nanchang and in the Autumn Harvest Uprising were blamed on Tan Pingshan and Mao Zedong respectively, rather than on party policy. It was acknowledged, however, that inadequate attention had been given to the cities and to the divisiveness within the ranks of the KMT. The sagging fortunes of the party could be recouped, it was determined, by taking the city of Guangzhou. This objective was enthusiastically urged by Stalin, who wanted his China policy dramatically vindicated in time for the Fifteenth Congress of the CPSU.

Even though the prospects were frankly unpromising, the CCP fortuitously was able to take control of Guangzhou for a total of three days, from December 11 to 13, 1927. This was possible because the troops of General Li Jishen had recently been driven out by General Zhang Faguei, whose troops were still deployed heavily in defenses outside the city. This created the opportunity seized by Ye Jianying, who was sympathetic to the Communists and who was the leader of the training regiment that remained behind in Guangzhou. During the brief occupation, a soviet government was established, which announced radical intentions that clearly went beyond the purview of a bourgeois democratic regime and were actually suggestive of the dictatorship of the proletariat that Trotsky advocated.[83] In any case, there was again no general rising of the workers and peasants and the "Canton Commune" was brutally crushed. This defeat was so overwhelming that it became fatuous to speak any further of a rising revolutionary wave in China. In fact, the CCP had now been deprived of its urban support; the urban proletariat was no longer a revolutionary force. However, the Canton Commune did perhaps play a significant ideological role by setting "appropriate proletarian political parameters," as S. Bernard Thomas maintains, for the rural soviet period that was to ensue. Moreover, it figuratively placed the CCP revolution more clearly within the internationalist orbit of the Comintern-led world revolution, and gave a clue as to the shape of the Chinese revolution in the future.[84]

·3·

The Chinese Soviet Republic

The Chinese Communist defeat in 1927 had been so stunning that Joseph Stalin had no choice but to adjust his China policy. This was done at the Ninth Plenum of the Comintern's Central Executive Committee in February 1928. The plenum acknowledged the errors of its own representatives in China (*not* its own line) and outlined the initiation of a new line that, lo and behold, anticipated the upsurge of yet a new revolutionary wave in China. But the new line somewhat more realistically advocated the building of a political and military force in the hinterland that would eventually challenge the KMT. Hence, it advocated the establishment of soviet bases at safe distances into the countryside, their consolidation by means of agrarian revolution, and the gradual development of an army. Guerrilla warfare was espoused and, while the emphasis was on activity in rural areas, attention was also to be given in this strategy to the inciting of unrest in the cities as a diversionary ploy.[1]

This new line, which would be elaborated upon over the next two and a half years, informed the deliberations of the Sixth Congress of the CCP, which was held in Moscow from June 18 to July 11, 1928. The Moscow venue provided security for the distressed Chinese Communist leaders and assured Stalin, who was now consolidating his victory over Trotsky, of maximum influence over them. The CCP meeting also conveniently preceded the Comintern's Sixth Congress, which was held from July 17 to September 1, 1928, so that there was ample opportunity for Chinese and Soviet comrades to compare notes. There were more than 30 delegates to the Sixth CCP Congress, including Qu Qiubai,

Zhang Guotao, Zhou Enlai, Li Lisan, Xiang Zhongfa, and Deng Zhong-xia.[2] No one from the rural bases, including Mao Zedong, was present. Some Chinese delegates, perhaps under suspicion by Stalin, were prevented from attending. Nikolai Bukharin and Pavel Mif participated. The Sixth Congress approved new statutes for the party. Xiang Zhongfa, a rare genuine proletarian worker among the Chinese Communist leaders, replaced Qu Qiubai as general secretary, although the post had become a nominal one. The real new power was Li Lisan. Li had studied in France and was an important labor leader in the May 30 Movement. Li headed the new political bureau. Mao Zedong, was elected to the Central Committee, after having been removed from party posts in November 1927 because of alleged errors during the Autumn Harvest Uprising.

From the resolutions of the Sixth Congress it is evident that the Chinese Communists duly assimilated Stalin's new line. Thus, despite the disasters of recent experience, the CCP seemed as dependent on the Kremlin as ever. Yet, in actual fact, the party had changed considerably over the course of its first eight years. Martin C. Wilbur has astutely observed that the CCP had "developed a vigorous leadership with many talents, wide contacts with various strata of society, and much useful experience in revolutionary work." Wilbur also noted that the party had become toughened by violence and thus became committed to warfare, which was quite a transformation for largely young people who had started out as intellectual idealists, albeit with an activist orientation. Finally, Wilbur noted the more intangible psychological transformation that was underway, that is, the "shift from dependency upon ideology to empiricism." Especially in the practical realm of strategy, theory was adjusting to China's social realities.[3]

Ironically then, even as Stalin's China policy was becoming fine-tuned, and even though the CCP appeared to be as dependent, the Chinese had learned a great deal. Moreover, circumstances in China would preclude the line being implemented according to Stalin's expectations or desires. This is not to suggest that the CCP did not continue to maintain a subordinate relationship to the Soviet Union, proffering, as necessary, at least lip service to the Comintern line in order to maintain Communist legitimacy.

Mao Zedong was joined at Jinggangshan by Zhu De and his Fourth Army in April 1928, increasing the new Red Army three- or fourfold. Zhu De was made commander in chief of the now-designated Fourth Red Army, while Mao became party representative. This brief interlude at Jinggangshan was busy and eventful. The army undertook training and grew to as many as 10,000 in this barren, sparsely populated wilderness. The Communists also attempted to implement educational programs and a radical agrarian reform program. But there was little time for such civilian activities because the shooting war continued. The area was under repeated attack with respite afforded for a time only by the resumption of the KMT's Northern Expedition. Additionally, the Red Army was itself requested to launch in July an ill-fated assault on Bingxian in south Hunan. One heartening development at about the same time, however, was the defection from the Nationalist army of Peng Dehuai, who would become a very prominent Communist army marshal and ultimately a celebrated opponent of Mao.[4] Peng's unit was designated the Fifth Army. When Mao and Zhu were ordered to relocate to the east in the Fujian-Jiangxi border region, which they did beginning in December 1928, Peng's Fifth Army was left to defend Jinggangshan. Peng could do so only for a couple of months, until he was forced to withdraw, but he then regained control of the area in the summer of 1929.[5]

On the eve of his departure from this initial mountain refuge, Mao reasoned out some of the elements of an independent regime of "workers and peasants." He wrote that what was necessary was "(1) a sound mass base, (2) a sound Party organization, (3) a fairly strong Red Army, (4) terrain favorable to military operations, and (5) economic resources sufficient for sustenance."[6] This was in addition to a split opposition, for when the opposition applied undivided attention to the Communist stronghold, the Red Army would still be put to flight, as basically happened at Jinggangshan and would eventually recur elsewhere.

The new main base was established on the boundaries of Jiangxi, Fujian, and a portion of Guangzhou, in mountainous terrain only marginally more hospitable than Jinggangshan. But it was a much larger territory with several market towns and a population of 5 or 6 million mostly poor people. It proved to be temporarily a most suitable base in which to experiment with policies and to develop a strong army. Other smaller base areas were established in similar terrain spread over ten provinces in central China. By the summer of 1930, there were as many as fifteen such bases, while the regular military forces had grown to sixty or seventy thousand men organized into thirteen armies.[7]

Much attention was given to the organization, training, and behavior of this growing military force. This effort proceeded under trying circumstances, given the disparate locations of units and difficulties of communication, as well as the inclusion of numerous undesirable elements in the ranks. In December 1929, at Gutian, Jiangxi, Mao wrote a resolution for the Fourth Red Army's ninth party congress entitled "On Correcting Mistaken Ideas in the Party."[8] This memorable resolution summarized the mistakes recently made by the Red Army. It emphasized the military's subordination to politics and deplored becoming conceited in victory, dispirited in defeat, having limited vision, or surrendering to revolutionary impetuosity. Mao also addressed such errors as "ultra-democracy," poor discipline, absolute egalitarianism, subjectivism, individualism, the ideology of "roving rebel bands," and putschism. In order to correct such mistakes, Mao recommended intensified educational programs, recruitment of experienced workers and peasants, encouragement of criticism, discussion of military work, and establishment of clear rules and regulations.

A year earlier, Mao had already articulated what would become the famous Three Rules of Discipline and Eight Points of Attention, designed to make the army responsive and well behaved among the population from which it sought support.[9] These "rules and points," as they came to be pridefully practiced in the years ahead, did indeed make the Red Army a popular one.

Mao's efforts to concentrate on the building of the base area and the army were disrupted by continued differences of views with the central party leadership, now dominated by the strong-willed Li Lisan after his return from the Sixth CCP Congress in Moscow. Mao and Li had known each other since school days in Changsha, but had never taken to each other. The irony of the struggle between the two men was that Mao's efforts in the hinterland did, in fact, coincide closely to the Comintern's new line in many, if not all, respects. This was particularly so inasmuch as Mao did not deny a role for the urban proletariat to the extent that one was feasible. But Li, as Richard Thornton has insightfully concluded, found himself "caught between Comintern pressure to build up the soviet movement and the recognition that the growing power of the field commanders would eventually lead to his eclipse as party leader."[10] Li initially sought to disperse the Red Army, presumably to deter a concentration of power in Mao's hands. This did lead to a reorganization of military designations in 1929, but Li reversed himself on this score later in the year.

Li Lisan consolidated his power in the CCP by the time of the Second Plenum of the Sixth Central Committee in June or July 1929, which Li himself called, but which was attended by only about half of the members of the Central Committee. The plenum's resolution of July 9, 1929, suggested Li's future course as it descried the further awakening of the proletariat.[11] But other events quickened the pace of developments both outside and inside China. The autumn of 1929 saw a worldwide economic crisis that seemed to bear out Communist predictions of the demise of capitalism. In November, a Soviet Russian force invaded Manchuria and restored control over the Chinese Eastern Railway, which had fallen into Nationalist hands that summer. The CCP was compelled to endorse the Soviet action under the slogan "defend the Soviet Union," despite the obvious adverse domestic political consequences. It was on this issue that, on November 15, Chen Duxiu finally came to be expelled from the party of which he had been the principal founder. Chen subsequently became the leader of the faction-ridden Trotskyite opposition in China. He died a distraught figure in 1942, having seen little materialization of the idealism he had espoused.[12]

For his part, Li Lisan felt the need to exceed Comintern instructions in response to the crisis of 1929. On December 7, a CCP circular spoke of the need to attack and occupy important cities. By February 1930 the central party leadership called for a national congress of soviet area delegates to convene in May in order to make plans. A February 26 directive rebuked Mao and Zhu De for continued "hide-and-disperse" tactics[13] and placed priority on creating urban unrest. In fact, as James Harrison makes clear, Mao in early 1930 did not disagree with Li's objective of taking cities, but he would increasingly come to disagree with Li's timing.[14]

The National Congress of Soviet Area Delegates was held from May 31 to June 4, 1930, near Shanghai with 47 such delegates, not including Mao. Most important among the decisions of the congress was approval of Li Lisan's policy to use the Red Army to attack key cities, after which a central soviet government would be established, hopefully, at Wuhan. A manifesto called for the first national congress of the Chinese Soviet Republic to be convened on November 7, 1930. As things were to turn out, however, this congress was postponed for a year and was not held in Wuhan or any other key city. On June 11, 1930, the Politburo (the top leadership organ elected by the Central Committee) issued a resolution entitled "The New Revolutionary Rising Tide and Preliminary Successes in One or More Provinces," which proclaimed China to be the weakest link in the chain of world imperialism yet "it is there that the volcano of world revolution is most likely to erupt."[15] The June 11 resolution laid out the details of the "Li Lisan line" of eschewing guerrilla warfare in favor of resolute attacks on the cities. Accordingly, the four main Red Armies were reorganized into four army corps. The Zhu-Mao forces were now designated the First Red Army Corps; He Long's units were the Second; Peng Dehuai's the Third; and Xu Xiangqian's the Fourth. All local guerrilla units were to meld into these regular units, but this was rejected by Mao and Zhu for fear of rendering the base areas defenseless.[16] The Comintern also disagreed with the June 11 resolution and unsuccessfully sought to dissuade Li Lisan from implementing his plans. A Comintern letter of July 23 contradicted virtually all of Li's policies over the previous several months.[17] In response, Li simply suppressed the July 23d letter, as he had done with previous Comintern telegrams, and pressed on with his scheme.[18]

On about July 27, 1930, Peng Dehuai captured Changsha and held it until August 6.[19] After this initial success, however, Li's plans quickly deteriorated. Mao and Zhu failed in their attempt to take Nanchang. Worker uprisings in Wuhan and elsewhere did not materialize. Nor did peasant restiveness inflame rural areas. Nor did expected KMT military defections occur. Furthermore, the Comintern became more insistent that Li desist, and dissent within the CCP became outspoken. Nevertheless, the stubborn Li ordered a new attack on Changsha to be followed by the taking of Wuhan. Mao opposed this unpromising venture but was overruled by other commanders who obeyed Li. However, the assault on Changsha in early September failed and the attack on Wuhan was thus averted. The Red Army, whose losses were considerable but might have been even worse, retreated to its bases. The Li Lisan policy had collapsed.

The Comintern eventually brought the CCP back into line, but it took several months and increasing pressure to do so. The Third Plenum of the CCP's Sixth Central Committee was held at Lushan from September 24 to 28, 1930, apparently in secret, with only fourteen Central Committee members present, although there were a larger number of organizational representatives also in attendance. The configuration of power within the Central Committee was such that Li Lisan was not removed from the leadership at this time, although he did share power for several months with Qu Qiubai, who with Zhou Enlai had recently returned from Moscow. The Third Plenum was a cover-up, since it claimed that Li's policies had been basically in agreement with the Comintern and that only minor tactical mistakes had been made.[20]

The Comintern communicated its disagreement with the Third Plenum in a letter of November 16, 1930, contradicting the plenum's conclusion and calling upon the CCP to oppose Li Lisan.[21] Moscow also sent to China its top CCP specialist, Pavel Mif, who had been rector of Sun Yat-sen University. Thus, on January 16, 1931, the Fourth Plenum of the CCP's Sixth Central Committee was held. At this plenum, with Mif as chairman, the Comintern's intentions were ramrodded through. Li Lisan was attacked and his line, according to official party reckoning, the "second left line," was repudiated. The errors of the Third Plenum were dissected. Most important was a major change in leadership, clearly wrought by heavy-handed Soviet intervention, for even though Li Lisan's tenure was clearly over (he had already departed for Moscow in December and did not return to China until 1945), other Chinese Communists would have come to the fore.[22] Li's lieutenant, He Mengxiung, was the most likely candidate at the time. Lo Zhanglong, a seamen's union leader, was a prominent ally of He.

The plenum elected a new Politburo of sixteen full and alternate members. Xiang Zhongfa and Zhou Enlai remained in their positions, respectively, as general secretary and member of the Politburo's Standing Committee—a reward for siding with Mif during the power struggle. Zhou had deftly managed to be forgiven for his own key role in the Third Plenum. All other positions were monopolized by the 28 Bolsheviks, the returned student protégés of Mif. The most important of these was Chen Shaoyu, better known as Wang Ming, who was on the Politburo Standing Committee and head of the Jiangsu party organization. He Mengxiung and Lo Zhanglong, among other disaffected party stalwarts, set up an "Emergency Committee" to consider a course of retaliatory action, which, however, led to their expulsion from the CCP. Any further threat from this faction was largely eliminated with the arrest and execution of He by the KMT. It was suspected that He had been betrayed by his erstwhile comrades.[23]

Mao did not attend the Fourth Plenum. He remained in the remote countryside where he busily surveyed the actual conditions of the region, devising what he believed to be the appropriate policies for building base areas while ruthlessly eliminating enemies, undesirable lumpen-proletariat elements, and, on notable occasions, rivals and their supporters. Mao's "Investigation of Xingguo" is an example of the detailed care with which he analyzed the situation of agricultural laborers, affording himself insight into rural conditions.[24] Such intensive, factual studies led Mao to favor agrarian reforms that were, on the whole, moderate, although implementation tended to be violent. His opponents, particularly the 28 Bolsheviks, were to advocate more radical measures.

The investigation into the activities of the disruptive Anti-Bolshevik (AB) Corps, which was reportedly organized and funded by the KMT to operate as spies among the Communists, afforded Mao's General Front Committee the opportunity to purge both AB Corps suspects and rivals, namely, Li Lisan's Jiangxi Provincial Action Committee. This was the essence of the Futian Incident, which began with arrests in November 1930 of some 4,000 officers and men of the Twentieth Army in Huangpo district, Jiangxi. These were genuine AB Corps suspects, but at the same time the entire Provincial Action Committee, save for two of the members at Futian, were arrested on the same charge.[25] In early December a battalion of the Twentieth Army revolted, releasing some twenty members of the Action Committee at Futian. The revolt was serious not only because of the profound differences among the Communists that it brought to the surface, but because it happened just as the KMT was launching the first of its encirclement campaigns against the soviet areas.

The rebels sought to establish their own soviet base in Yongyang across the Gan River, from which they attacked Mao's moderate agrarian policies and his arbitrary behavior.[26] Unfortunately for the rebels, Li's fall from power and the KMT offensive beginning in December weakened their position. Also, in January 1931, the Central Committee in Shanghai abolished both the General Front Committee and the Provincial Action Committee. In their stead, it created a Central Bureau for the Soviet Areas, in which Mao and his supporters were given enhanced authority. Between May and July 1931, Mao's forces finally were able to foreclose on the rebels, whose leaders were taken by deception.[27] Up to 4,000 "counter-revolutionary elements" were arrested by July. Public mass trials followed. Five principal rebel leaders, who received death sentences, were sent on a tour of Soviet areas and were forced to undergo repeated public exposures as the Mao version of the affair was thus dramatically propagandized. Three of the five were then executed.[28]

Mao was in a strong position in early 1931, dominating the Central Bureau for the Soviet Areas. But his considerable strength was continually eroded by the maneuvering of his new political opponents, the 28 Bolsheviks, who had taken control of the Politburo at the Fourth Plenum in Shanghai in January 1931. This was sanctioned by the Comintern in June 1931.[29] Mao gradually relinquished control of the party apparatus as members of the Central Committee moved into the soviet hinterland. This large area was now divided into six administrative districts, the principal one being the Central Soviet District in southwest Jiangxi and the Xiang-o-gan areas of Hunan, Hubei, and Jiangxi. Mao was also director of the General Political Department of the Revolutionary Military Council. It is apparent that Mao and Zhu De maneuvered to gain control of the electoral machinery for the National Soviet Congress. They had reason to be apprehensive of the new Politburo leadership. On September 1, 1931, the latter sent to the rural soviets a directive attacking Mao's rural policy and the concept of guerrilla warfare, and once again urging the Red Army to occupy large cities.[30]

The First National Soviet Congress was convened in Ruichin, Jiangxi, on November 7, 1931, the anniversary of the Bolshevik Revolution, with 610 delegates present. The congress formally established the Chinese Soviet Republic and elected its government. It also approved a political program, a constitutional outline, land and labor laws, resolutions on the Red Army and economic policy, and other laws and decrees.

None of these matters originated at the congress, but had been decided earlier.[31]

The constitutional outline held that the Chinese Soviet Republic was a workers' and peasants' democratic dictatorship, transitional to a proletarian dictatorship. Since both workers and peasants were represented by the CCP, the republic was, in fact, a Communist party dictatorship. Between congresses the dictatorship was to be governed by a Central Executive Committee (CEC), which would appoint a Council of People's Commissars (CPC), the highest state administrative organ. Sixty-three members were elected to the CEC, which then held its First Plenum on November 27, 1931. Mao Zedong was elected chairman, making him, in effect, chairman of the Chinese Soviet Republic, a post he held until the end of the Soviet Republic itself in October 1934. Xiang Ying and Zhang Guotao were vice chairmen. The CEC appointed the CPC on the same day, and the same three top leaders occupied the equivalent positions in that body as well.[32]

The establishment of the Chinese Soviet Republic was a significant development in the CCP's evolution. It constituted a concrete symbol of an "alternative way" for the Chinese people to that offered by the KMT. It also institutionalized the shift of the party's focus from the cities to the countryside, where it would remain until 1948–1949. It afforded the CCP the opportunity to refine governance techniques and policies. The lessons learned from the agrarian policies of this period would be useful later. The labor law, designed primarily for the urban proletariat, while necessary for ideological purposes, could only have been meant practically for later implementation.[33]

Mao's domination of the Soviet Republic continued to erode, especially because the 28 Bolsheviks were supported by Moscow. Mao's struggle with the 28 Bolsheviks can also be seen as an effort to assert greater independence from the Soviets. This rivalry intensified when the Central Committee moved from Shanghai to Juichin, the exact date of which remains unclear. Incidentally, Maoist historiography subsequently designated the work of the 28 Bolsheviks in Shanghai as being a cause for abandoning that metropolis. Such criticism served to bolster the legitimacy of Mao's subsequent accession to supreme power. But Lawrence R. Sullivan, in his study of the Jiangsu Provincial Committee in 1931–1934, has shown that the 28 Bolsheviks did, in fact, devote attention to strengthening urban party organization, educating cadres, and mobilizing mass support.[34] In the Soviet Republic itself, as Ilpyong Kim points out, Mao and the 28 Bolsheviks did not always struggle against each other, but sometimes cooperated.[35] Since there existed what can be regarded as a third element comprised of leaders such as Zhou

Enlai, there was also the phenomenon of shifting alignments and compromises among the three groupings. In any case, Mao gradually lost
control of the party apparatus in the course of such maneuvering.

Mao was next shorn of his military posts. The Red Army had managed to stave off the first three of the KMT encirclement campaigns by
the summer of 1932 and had conducted several offenses of its own. Still
there were reverses in 1932, associated with the fourth encirclement,
that led the Central Committee to convene a conference at Ningdu in
August 1932. Mao's tactics of mobile guerrilla warfare had just recently
been criticized in an article by another military leader, Liu Bocheng,
and such criticisms highlighted the conference. In the end, Zhou Enlai's
concept of positional warfare and capturing cities prevailed. Mao was
removed from the Central Committee's Revolutionary Military Council, and he was subsequently replaced by Zhou as political commissar
of the Red Army.[36] Zhu De's authority was also reduced on the Revolutionary Military Council. The new tactics were successfully employed
in the course of the fourth encirclement campaign, even further eroding
Mao's position at the time, although Mao later claimed that this victory
had come about because of his continuing influence in the Red Army.[37]

The 28 Bolsheviks continued to expand their influence and control
through the year 1933, and by mid-year the party was actively preparing
its Second National Soviet Congress. This congress was to have convened on December 11, 1933, the anniversary of the Canton Commune
in Guangzhou. But it was actually held from January 22 to February 1,
1934, following on the heels of the Fifth Plenum of the Sixth Central
Committee, at which the major decisions to be taken up at the congress
were made. The congress was attended by 693 full delegates, 83 alternates, and 1,500 observers, although the new auditorium in which it
was held only seated 1,000.[38] Mao played a prominent role at the congress
and was elected chairman of the newly established Presidium of the
Central Executive Committee, but was not re-elected to the Council of
People's Commissars' chairmanship, nor was he any longer on that more
active body. Lo Fu, or Zhang Wentian, one of the 28 Bolsheviks, became
chairman of the CPC. Mao had already progressively lost control of the
government before the Second National Soviet Congress and this was
merely formalized at the congress. He continued to play a role in the
government although a less influential one, presumably by agreeing to
go along with the new policies, many of which he would later criticize.

The 28 Bolsheviks now began treating landlords and rich peasants
more harshly than Mao had done. Following the first phase of the Land
Investigation Movement in October 1933, Mao had tried to mitigate the
class struggle so insistently advocated by the 28 Bolsheviks. He did so

by clarifying the criteria for determining class and by broadening the definition of the middle and rich peasant. Mao's efforts were now repudiated and by March 1934 the agrarian policy became radicalized. Almost all rich peasants were drafted into labor brigades and their property was expropriated. The judicial policies of the Soviet Republic were similarly radicalized, according to Trygve Lotveit, changing a system that had been relatively lenient and standardized into a "Red Terror."[39]

Whatever success may have been achieved by jettisoning counterproductive lumpenproletariat from the Red Army and in earlier constructive mass work with the poor peasants and with women in the base areas was undone by the unrealistic role ascribed by classroom Marxists to the tiny number of agricultural workers.[40]

The Second National Soviet Congress had met while the fifth encirclement campaign, which had begun in October 1933, was still in its early stages. This campaign, unlike the previous four, was much more deliberate, employing the tactic of an ever-tightening ring of concentric blockhouses as counseled by a German military adviser, Von Seeckt. It was also a much larger operation, using 800,000 men. The Red Army now came under the command of Otto Braun, a young German Communist adventurer, better known as Li De at the time, who dictatorially pushed the positional warfare response that had already been decided on.[41]

At the time of the congress, there was also another development of apparent major significance for the Communists. In November 1933, several of Jiang Jieshi's generals, dissatisfied with Jiang's preoccupation with the Communists rather than with Japanese inroads into China, established an embryo revolutionary government in what was called the Fujian Revolt. The Communist leadership was generally responsive to the former Nationalist Nineteenth Army's plight, but there was disagreement on the means of cooperation. The 28 Bolsheviks wished to send troops to assist the revolt. Mao, however, counseled prudence, suggesting that the dissidents join the Red Army in Jiangxi instead. By February 1934, however, before anything could be done, the revolt was crushed. Mao was blamed for thwarting the Central Committee's intentions and therefore contributing to the rebels' defeat.[42]

The turning point of the fifth encirclement came with the hard battle of Guangchang, from April 10 to 12, 1934, which the Communists lost. Mao claimed that before Guangchang there still existed the possibility of mobile warfare, of luring the enemy to penetrate deeply into the base area and then wiping them out. After Guangchang this was no longer possible. In May, however, Mao unexpectedly and without authority went to the southern front where he issued orders to sympathetic comrades to conduct a guerrilla-like operation. Those who participated were subsequently punished and kept under surveillance until Mao came to power on the Long March. This audacious conduct was the likely reason for Mao himself being placed under house arrest in August 1934, rather than for his lack of cooperation on the Fujian Revolt matter—if, in fact, he was so incarcerated, about which there remains some question.[43]

Jiang's fifth campaign ground on relentlessly. By mid-October 1934, a general withdrawal from Jiangxi, organized by Li De, commenced in secret. Mao was ill, and many of his own supporters were left behind as part of the 6,000-man rearguard defending some 20,000 wounded. The crossing of the Xiang River by some 90,000 men of the First Front Army must have been a costly one and dissatisfaction quickly mounted over the current leadership. Then the marchers were frustrated in the effort to reach their objective in northwest Hunan because of a large Nationalist blocking force. Mao is said to have stepped in at this critical juncture with a plan that won support. The army now wheeled westward into Gueizhou, aiming for a new destination—Zhang Guotao's soviet base in northern Sichuan. On this new line of march, the army paused at the town of Liping in western Hunan. Here, on December 18, the Politburo met, and probably restored Mao's membership on that body and approved his military proposal. An interesting recent account holds that Zhou Enlai shifted his support to Mao at this time,[44] but this is doubtful.[45] In any case, the most important meeting of the Long March would take place three weeks later.

The Red Army rested at Zunyi (Tsunyi) in Gueizhou from January 6 to 18, 1935, during which time an enlarged meeting of the Politburo was held. This meeting is now officially regarded as *the* turning point in the history of the party, marking its passage from childhood to maturity. Consequently, it is considered to have been the party's first "independent" conference.[46] The conferees passed resolutions[47] that sharply criticized the policies of Bo Gu and Li De. Many of the criticisms were probably justifiable, but a dubious one is the charge that the Bo Gu leadership mishandled the Fujian Revolt—since Mao's own role in that affair remains less than clear. In any event, the mistakes were labeled as "right opportunism." This is to be kept distinct, of course, from the more general appellation of the "third left line," which subsequently would be applied to the now largely superseded policies of the 28 Bolsheviks!

The Zunyi Conference was a personal triumph for Mao, who in recent years had been treated with ever-diminishing deference by the party leadership. Mao had consummately exploited the military crisis to political advantage. In all likelihood, even though Wang Ming was in Moscow, Mao's opponents had a majority in the Politburo at Zunyi. But because the military situation was *the* life-and-death issue, this was an "enlarged" meeting, complemented by the presence of ranking military leaders, who for the most part supported Mao.[48] Lin Biao's support in recent months may have been especially important. Thus did Mao emerge in the key decision-making role in the CCP. He was not to be designated chairman until later and his power was not total, nor was it completely unchallengeable. In fact, in terms of formal position, Mao had only been advanced to the Politburo's Standing Committee, and technically was Zhou Enlai's assistant in military matters.[49] But from this new policy-making vantage point, Mao began to assert increasing control, and he would never again relinquish his dominant position in the Chinese Communist movement. Zhou Enlai, obviously perceiving Mao's rising star and deferring to his strong personality, soon came to accept the role of faithful lieutenant.

The story of the rest of the fabled Long March is well known.[50] Instead of attempting to breach strong Nationalist defenses in southern Sichuan, the Communists made successive feints toward Gueilin and Kunming while the main body of the Red Army unexpectedly crossed the Chang Jiang in its upper reaches, where it is called the Jinsha or Golden Sands River. Even Lin Biao's force, which had made the feint at Kunming, was able to doubleback in an amazing forced march to cross the Jinsha River. The Red Army now made its way through hostile Lolo territory and then forded the frightening Datu River, which had proved impossible to fighting heroes of Three Kingdoms and Taiping Revolution vintage. Then there were seven towering mountain ranges that took a terrible toll in victims exposed to the elements with unsuitable clothing and equipment.

Finally, on July 20, 1935, the weatherbeaten and exhausted Communists linked up with Zhang Guotao's Fourth Front Army in the more agreeable Mou Gun area of Sichuan. The First Front Army had been reduced from 90,000 to only 10,000 men, while the Fourth Front Army had 45,000 men, who were in much better physical shape.[51] The Communist leaders held two notable meetings during this rendezvous of the two armies. The initial one, at Fupian, became the scene of a sharp disagreement between Mao and Zhang over the destination of the march once it resumed. Zhang preferred establishing a new soviet in the Sichuan-Gansu-Xigang border region. Mao claimed that if the Red Army were to become blockaded in such a location, "we would become turtles in an urn."[52] Instead, Mao wished to proceed northward toward Inner Mongolia.

The second meeting was held further north near Maoergai. This was a secretive, inconclusive meeting, generally regarded as the site of the policy decision to forge a new united front to fight the Japanese. In fact, no one even suggested such a policy at this meeting, although there was talk about resisting Japan.[53] Coincidentally, in Moscow, the Seventh Congress of the Comintern was held in the summer of 1935. The chairman of the congress, Dmitrov, stressed that an anti-imperialist national united front was to be set up in colonial countries, especially in China where an anti-Japanese united front should be established. This policy was designed to safeguard Soviet Russian national interests. Accordingly, it was Wang Ming in Moscow, the CCP's representative at the Comintern, who issued the August First Declaration on behalf of the CCP, proposing an all-China united national defense government and allied armies to resist Japan.[54]

In the meanwhile, in a curious arrangement, Zhu De remained with Zhang Guotao, and Mao, departing secretively in the middle of the night, willfully continued the march of the First Front Army northward. Yet additional arduous trials had to be endured as the marchers traversed treacherous swamps and grasslands. Finally, in October 1935, the Red Army, now numbering only 7,000, arrived in Baoan, Shaanxi. Here the survivors were met by troops led by Liu Jidan and Gao Gang. Baoan served as the capital for a few months, but in 1936 the move was made to Yan'an, a more advantageous location in northern Shaanxi. In late 1936, the Second and Fourth Front Armies also arrived in Yan'an. The Second Front Army under He Long had completed its long march from northern Hunan, after having joined with the Fourth Front Army following the departure of the First Front Army. Zhang Guotao had finally to concede that Shaanxi afforded better prospects after all.[55]

As magnificent an achievement as the Long March was, it was also an enormous defeat for the Chinese Communists. They had been driven out of their southern bastion with overwhelming loss of life, and were now in a barren, impoverished corner of China where they surely would have been exterminated had it not been for the Japanese threat to China. But the fact that the CCP had endured so much, and had survived, caught the imagination of the nation and the world. This was especially so in the patriotic atmosphere of the times, and most particularly since the Communists claimed brassily that they had merely repositioned themselves the better to lead the nation's fight against Japan. Hence was defeat transmuted into victory.

PART TWO

Seizing Political Power

· 4 ·

The Yan'an Transformation

Over the next several years, the CCP underwent a fundamental transformation and experienced spectacular growth. This was largely due to
the war against Japan, but the CCP creatively used the opportunities
presented by the conflict. Mao, for a time, continued to be beset by
Comintern directives and their advocacy by the 28 Bolsheviks, but
eventually he consolidated his power and placed his own unmistakable
stamp on the party. The CCP had by this time learned to place the
loosest construction on its Marxist ideology, even as Mao and his comrades became more knowledgeable in it. The party had learned the value
of timely alliances, and their limitations. It had similarly come to know
intimately the desirability of external aid, and its costs, and this had
created greater appreciation for the principle of self-reliance. The party
had certainly learned the need for its own military capability; Mao's
dictum that "political power grows out of the mouth of a gun" brooked
no compromise.[1] The Yan'an period also afforded the Communists further opportunities to experiment with various policies and programs.
Some of these were sufficiently successful in the élan of the time that
they would become for Mao a tempting but elusive model for the attempted solution of problems decades later. But at Yan'an it was the
patriotic war that was the key ingredient.

The CCP proved to be more responsive to growing national sentiment to resist Japan than was the Nationalist government. Japanese
inroads into China began in September 1931 with the occupation of
Manchuria. The Chinese Soviet government in 1932 had actually declared war on Japan from its sequestered lair in Jiangxi. But the Nation-

alists had merely made concessions to the Japanese in subsequent months and years, while ruthlessly suppressing Chinese protests. However, after four years of such enforced quietude, students took to the streets in Beiping on December 9 and 16, 1935, with as many as 7,700 participating on the second date. Many of these demonstrators would join the CCP in the following year or two. Subsequently they came to comprise a distinctive later leadership group within the party.[2]

The CCP Politburo met at Wayaobao, Shaanxi, in late December 1935 and called for the "broadest national united front" to fight Japan.[3] Earlier in the month, the CCP land policy had been moderated to ensure that rich peasants would also have the right to own land. The moderation was reinforced by the experience of a massive Communist thrust into neighboring Shanxi province on February 20, 1936. This military adventure succeeded initially in winning recruits and securing supplies, but, by May, Shanxi had to be abandoned in the face of determined enemy assaults. Thus, the CCP came to see the need for a consistent and workable united front policy. By March, the CCP had already begun to suggest that the Chinese suspend their civil struggle and fight Japan instead.[4] Such appeals were ignored until the Xian Incident of December 1936.

Jiang Jieshi, frustrated by the inaction of his armies in carrying the fight to the Communists' base in Shaanxi, made the mistake of visiting his commanders in Xian on December 4, 1936, even though an earlier visit in October had already failed to persuade them to act. One of these generals, Zhang Xueliang, the son of the late Manchurian warlord, Zhang Zuolin, was particularly disenchanted by Jiang's policy of, in effect, enjoining Chinese to fight Chinese while the Japanese were occupying his Manchurian homeland. Hence, Jiang was placed under arrest by his own officers and had to suffer the indignity of having his release negotiated by a Communist, Zhou Enlai. Jiang was thus compelled to agree to a new united front with the CCP.[5] The party maintains that the decision to save Jiang was the result of its own correct analysis of the situation with an eye to the national interest,[6] although it is suspected that the party actually responded to pressure from Moscow to spare the generalissimo.

The CCP made four concessions in order to bring about the second united front: it abandoned armed insurrection; the Soviet Republic would be made part of a special region of the Republic of China and the Red Army would be redesignated as a unit of the national army; a universal suffrage-determined democratic system would be set up in the special region; and the confiscation of land from landlords would end. For its part, the KMT had to agree to five points: end the civil war;

bestow democratic freedoms and release political prisoners; convene a conference with broad representation to discuss national salvation; accelerate preparations to resist Japan; and improve the livelihood of the people. The formal agreement to these points was signed on September 22, 1937.[7]

But the Japanese, sensing impending Chinese unity, moved up their timetable of conquest. They had already launched their general invasion following the Marco Polo Bridge Incident of July 7. Despite the urgency of the situation, Mao had held out in negotiations with the KMT for the essentials of Communist autonomy.

Wang Ming arrived in Yan'an from Moscow in October 1937 and soon renewed an assault on Mao's preeminence and policies. In general, Wang promoted a line that sought to accommodate both the Nanjing government and the propertied classes much more than did Mao, but this was an approach Wang attributed directly to Stalin's instructions. The Wang line relied heavily on the united front and returned the focus of activity to the cities—Wuhan in particular—once more. The new line was adopted at the December 1937 meeting of the Politburo and Wang improved his own political position.[8] Accordingly, much attention was devoted to the defense of Wuhan throughout most of 1938, since the city was the last important urban center in Chinese hands and the keystone of Wang Ming's policies. Unfortunately for Wang, Wuhan fell to the Japanese in October.[9]

Thus, at the important Sixth Plenum of the CCP's Central Committee from October 12 to November 6, 1938, the party switched lines again, this time embarrassing Mao's alternative program of rural revolution and resistance. This program had already been implemented since the summer of 1938 in bases created behind Japanese lines, particularly in Jin-Cha-Ji (Shanxi-Jahar-Hebei). Carl Dorris has contended that the programs worked out in these base areas constitute the real origins of what later came to be known as the Yan'an model of communism. This is especially the case inasmuch as Yan'an politics between 1937 and 1941 were characterized by a bureaucratic work style, as Mark Selden has observed.[10] The exigencies of survival at the bases led the party leaders to modify the reliance on narrow class interests and class struggle that had been the hallmarks of the Jiangxi Soviet in mobilizing the masses and in building revolutionary bases. In the early months and years of such experimentation in the War of Resistance, the CCP developed a strategy of "struggle within unity" and shaped a new movement for national resistance that cut across class lines.[11] Campaigns to promote rent and interest reduction were generally productive, and campaigns for progressive taxation or democratic government challenged the elite in the many villages where tenancy was nonexistent.[12] Mao also began to argue more pointedly at the Sixth Plenum for the Sinofication of Marxism, "making certain that in all of its manifestations it is imbued with peculiarities" and "using it according to these peculiarities."[13]

For a time, Wang Ming's fulsome commitment to the united front remained in effect under the authority of Xiang Ying and his New Fourth Army, which operated in central China. This provided Wang Ming with a chance to demonstrate the viability of the policy in a rural situation, and enabled him to remain active in party affairs. However, in January 1941, Xiang Ying, who had delayed too long in responding to orders to move behind Japanese lines, was killed by the Nationalists in the New Fourth Army Incident.[14] Mao now moved quickly to consolidate his power. The Politburo met in secret session in the fall of 1941 and considered the report of Peng Zhen on the promising policies of the border region. It also heard strong criticism of Wang Ming's line.[15] Mao soon followed this favorable turn of events with a massive and intensive rectification campaign throughout the party.

This *zheng feng* campaign from early 1942 to 1944 was multipurposed. Not only did it remove from power Mao's principal political opponents, Wang Ming and the remainder of the 28 Bolsheviks, but it addressed other concerns as well. There was an urgent need to ensure the commitment and the adequate indoctrination of a party membership that had increased twentyfold, from 40,000 to 800,000 between 1937 and 1940. Yan'an had attracted a flood of well-intentioned and patriotic intellectuals and others during these years, but many exhibited urban-elitist and other undesirable attitudes and values, and few were schooled in Marxism, particularly in Mao's Sinocized version of Marxism. New institutions such as the Central Party School and the united front Kangda University helped, but could not resolve all the needs quickly.[16] There was concern, too, about the responsiveness of the bureaucracy that had mushroomed in Shen-Gan-Ning, where by 1941 some 7,900 full-time salaried officials worked, especially now that the KMT had reimposed its blockade and the pressure from the Japanese remained. There was concern about the effective communication of the new ideology and policies among the disparate bases and under such trying circumstances.

The *zheng feng* campaign was launched on February 1, 1942, with Mao addressing over 1,000 party cadres in Yan'an on the evils of subjectivism and sectarianism. Mao pointed out that Marxism-Leninism was not studied "because it is pleasing to the eye, or because it has some mystical value . . . Marxism-Leninism has no beauty . . . It is only extremely useful."[17] As for dogmatists who regard Marxism-Leninism as a ready-made panacea, they must be told, Mao said, "Your dogma is less useful than excrement" for the latter can be used as fertilizer while dogma cannot. However, Mao also criticized those guilty of empiricism, for failing to be guided by theory. He used the simile of the arrow and the target, noting that it was necessary to use the arrow of Marxism-Leninism to hit the target of the Chinese Revolution.[18]

The campaign was conducted, it was claimed, on the basis of two principles. The first was expressed by the slogan "Don't repeat past mistakes." The second, in another slogan, "Save men by curing their ills." Thus, past errors were to be exposed regardless of "personal feelings and face." But the purpose of such exposure "is to save people, not cure them to death."[19]

Mao gave a second lecture one week later, on February 8, this time on "formalism" in the party. To rid the "patient" of this malady, Mao suggested an unusual technique of "reasoning" by first providing a powerful stimulus to the patient. That is, "yell at him, 'You're sick!' so the patient will have a fright and break out in an over-all sweat; then he can be started on the road to recovery."[20]

The *zheng feng* campaign was conducted systematically, beginning within the Central Committee itself, and then in three stages throughout the party.[21] The first stage was a two- to three-month period of study and discussion of selected readings, followed by an examination. The readings consisted of 22 documents, including several written by Mao, two by Kang Sheng, one by Liu Shaoqi, and one by Chen Yun. There was nothing from the 28 Bolsheviks; however, one essay by Stalin was included, as was the "Conclusion" from the *History of the Communist Party of the Soviet Union.*

This was a most important exercise in the Sinofication of Marxism-Leninism. The period of study, discussion, and examination was followed by one of investigation of party work. This was done by the organ or school itself on a decentralized basis, rather than being conducted by a central agency. The third stage was given to the drawing of conclusions, each person reporting on the work of another, with reports sent to higher authorities. Thus, the campaign was basically an educational one, conducted in small groups, using the method of criticism and self-criticism to enhance comprehension. The war situation was a constraint that also helped to keep the campaign a moderate one. A yet third principle, of "unity-criticism-unity," was utilized to enjoin a positive outcome. While some individuals were expelled from the party and some were demoted, the entire experience was a refreshing contrast to the spectacle of Stalin's dreaded purges of 1933–1935, which terrorized, tortured, imprisoned, and executed so many members of the CPSU. Wang Ming, Mao's principal nemesis in this period, was given an unimportant post, but retained his membership on the Central Committee.

During the first stage of the *zheng feng* campaign, Mao had also set down the party's line with regard to literature and art. This was done at two successive talks (the Yan'an Talks), on May 2 and 23, 1942, to audiences of intellectuals with indeterminate commitment to Marxism-Leninism. Mao made it clear that writers and artists produced their work for the people and it had to be done on the basis of a proletarian standpoint. He held that such proletarian consciousness did not depend on economic class origin alone. It could be achieved by an act of will and through appropriate education. This unorthodox Marxist view applied by extension to society as a whole, hence a revolutionary movement's consciousness did not necessarily rely on the economic substructure. Mao insisted that art and literature served political objectives. He agreed that Marxism destroys creative moods, but these were "feudal, bourgeois, petty bourgeois, liberalistic, individualist, nihilist, art-for-art's sake, aristocratic, decadent or pessimistic, and every other creative mood that is alien to the masses of the people and to the proletariat."[22]

Mao was supported in these views on literature and art by his attractive young wife, Lan Ping, who had been an actress in Shanghai. This marriage was a controversial one. Lan Ping was a relative newcomer, whose romance with Mao after her arrival in Yan'an in 1937 caused Mao to divorce his second wife, a veteran of the Long March. Mao's marriage to Lan Ping, whom he renamed Jiang Qing, never was fully accepted by many of the Yan'an comrades. This, along with her strong opinions, especially in the cultural field, would cause a great deal of trouble within the party and without in future years.

Other campaigns were also conducted that collectively represent the synthesis that took place in the CCP during these war years. Intellectual workers were encouraged to integrate with the masses. A "crack troops and simple administration" campaign throughout 1942 reduced personnel and organs in the bureaucracy, strengthened lower-level leadership, and increased popular government participation.[23] A year earlier, in July 1941, the heralded *xia-fang* (*hsia-fang*) or "to the village" campaign had been initiated.[24] This was first intended to resolve the labor shortage problem, but the practice grew into a much broader concept wherein the urbanites shared experiences with the masses, supposedly learning from the latter, and thereby helping to bridge the gulf between the cities and the countryside.

A campaign to reduce rent and interest, applied with determination after Mao's major statement on land policy on January 28, 1942, was important in identifying activist peasant leadership.[25] The mutual aid, cooperative campaign, started on January 25, 1943, was a significant experiment for the CCP, since it was an effort to create a new institution in the village beyond the family unit.[26] It was only partly successful. However, according to Elizabeth Perry, even in the Huai-bei border region, with its well-established societal patterns, the small but significant successes of the party in its slow and painstaking implementation of mutual aid seemed to establish the feasibility of cooperative, productive effort.[27] Also in 1943, a production movement was launched to counter the effects of economic blockade.[28] One notable experiment in this campaign was the technique of "organizational production" wherein self-sufficiency was promoted by again having party, government, and military cadres participate in physical productive labor. This was intended to reduce the distinction between mental and manual labor, a strong influence from the traditional past.

The strategy used in Shen-Gan-Ning was employed in the other border regions in the base areas behind Japanese lines as well, where, according to Peter Schran, the effects were implicitly similar, even though adaptations were made according to circumstances.[29]

The campaigns of the later Yan'an period were permeated by the "mass line," a distinctive characteristic of Mao's mobilizational politics. The expression "mass line" best epitomizes the ability of the party to be sympathetically involved with and responsive to the rural masses at critical times in the pre-1949 period. It also best suggests why the Communists were so successful in securing the support of the peasantry. The contrast of this policy with that of the KMT could hardly have been more dramatic inasmuch as the latter appeared to be basically oblivious of the peasants and their needs. Nanjing did attempt to expand control over the villages in the 1930s by enlarging the size of the local bureaucracy, but without improving services to the rural communities. Consequently, such rural reforms only added to the burdens of the peasants. The famous scholar Hu Shi (Hu Shih), for one, pleaded that these rural efforts be stopped and that the number of local officials and soldiers be reduced.[30]

It should be acknowledged in passing that the Nanjing government in the 1930s had brought about some reforms overall. These reforms were, under the circumstances in which Nanjing was compelled to operate, impressive in some respects. The unification of the national currency, the standardization of weights and measures, improvement in education, a respectable growth in industry, and the extension of the railway system are among its achievements. It has been pointed out, however, that progress in industry, education, transportation, modern banking, improved sanitation, and electrification had already been made even under the earlier warlord administrations.[31]

Furthermore, the Nanjing government might have done more to encourage and support industrialization than it did. Unfortunately, because it was compelled to deny itself revenue from adequate agricultural taxation, it was forced to tax regressively the modern industrial-commercial sector.[32] The powerful Chinese cotton industry managed, however, to defend its interests.[33] Of course, once the government retreated to Zhongjing it did little but stagnate. Finally, the employment of fascist-like tactics, justified by Japanese and Communist threats to national security, created serious disenchantment among intellectuals, reducing support for the government and resulting, as we have noted, in sympathy and recruits for Yan'an.

The most distinguishing characteristic of the Nationalist regime was its militarism, which it was so reluctant to deploy against the Japanese. Nevertheless, once the war began, Nationalist armies acquitted themselves bravely and sustained enormous casualties in the early months of the conflict. This heroism, incidentally, was publicly acknowledged by the Chinese Communists themselves, but only many years later (as part of a propaganda campaign to foster Taiwan's unification with the People's Republic of China).[34] However, the decision to breach the dykes of the Yellow River near Zhengzhou, Henan, in 1938 to slow the Japanese advance was a highly questionable one since it inflicted such great suffering on so many Chinese peasants. In any case, despite these costly early measures, the Nationalists soon settled on a strategy of waiting out the war, which would eventually be won by other nations, a prospect that was assured with the Japanese bombing of Pearl Harbor on December 7, 1941.

The Communists themselves fought bravely at the outset of the war, and Lin Biao achieved a notable early victory over a Japanese column at Pingshanguan.[35] They subsequently succeeded in becoming identified as the leading force in the fight against the Japanese, and this made them the chief beneficiaries of the patriotism that was so strongly aroused.[36] This national consciousness was the natural response to the indignity of Japan's military and political ambitions on China's soil, but it was greatly exacerbated by senseless Japanese atrocities. This has scarred so deeply into the Chinese consciousness that in 1985, forty years after the end of the war, at a time when Sino-Japanese relations were otherwise hailed as being the best in a century, the Chinese media also gave much publicity to the infamous Rape of Nanking of December 1937–January 1938, wherein the Japanese executed 340,000 people in that one city alone.[37] Nevertheless, the Communists adopted a posture essentially similar to that of the Nationalists as far as real fighting was concerned, except for establishing bases in areas much closer to the Japanese, and also except for the forthright yet curious One Hundred Regiments Campaign of August–December 1940, which elicited a punishing Japanese response and was not repeated.[38] Instead of fighting, the CCP concentrated on expanding its roster and territory, and on the campaigns and social experiments that enhanced its unity and viability.

Negotiations between the Nationalists and the Communists had been suspended for about two years following the New Fourth Army Incident in 1941. Efforts to resume these in 1943 made little progress, but by 1944 world events began to suggest a new pattern of relationships and opportunities ahead that disposed both parties to consider talks more seriously. The tide of World War II was clearly turning. The unequal treaties had been laid to rest and China was declared to be one of the five great powers. The Comintern was dissolved. Even so, the negotiations, which resumed in May 1944 at Xian, then at Zhongjing, made little headway.

Both the United States and the USSR favored CCP-KMT cooperation. During most of the war the Soviets had been too preoccupied on the European front to have had much influence on the Chinese. But the United States took a more active role in providing aid to the Nationalists and by mid-1944 in seeking to mediate between the Chinese rivals. Following the visit of Vice President Henry Wallace in June 1944, an American military observer mission was established at Yan'an, from which some Americans filed reports indicating that the Chinese Communists were an emergent force worthy of serious consideration and inviting invidious comparisons with the Nationalists.[39] General Joseph Stilwell sought unsuccessfully to encourage greater attention by Jiang Jieshi to the war against Japan, and came away with a jaundiced view of Jiang and his government.[40] His successor, General Albert Wedemeyer, was more congenial to Jiang and commensurately less tolerant of the Communists. President Franklin Roosevelt's envoy Patrick Hurley misleadingly gave the Communists an initial impression of willingness to cooperate with them, but he soon became firmly oriented toward the Nationalists. This experience gave pause to the leaders in Yan'an. For the time being, by early 1945, they did not feel they could depend much on real help from either major power. In any case, it was time for the party to take stock generally of where it was and where it was going.

This stocktaking began at various regional party meetings in early 1945, followed by the Seventh Plenum of the Sixth Central Committee on April 20. The Seventh Plenum approved the important Resolution on Some Questions in the History of Our Party, which set the historical record straight from the perspective of a triumphant Mao, analyzing the correctness or incorrectness of previous policy lines. Wang Ming's defeated policies were now designated as having been successively a leftist line (in fact, the "third left line") in the Jiangxi period (even though Mao had castigated them as rightist ten years earlier at Zunyi) and then as a rightist line in Yan'an. Explicitly praised was Mao's integration of the "universal truth of Marxism-Leninism with the actual practice of the Chinese Revolution."[41]

The plenum also set the agenda for the historic Seventh Congress of the CCP that followed, meeting from April 23 to June 11, 1945, in Yan'an, the first CCP congress since the sixth in Moscow in 1928. Of the 1.2 million party members at this time, no more than a thousand remained from those who had joined before 1927, and no more than 20,000 from those who had joined between 1927 and 1937.[42]

The CCP celebrated the Seventh Congress as one of "solidarity and victory." Some 544 delegates and 208 alternates attended 22 plenary sessions and many small meetings, listening to many speeches. The most important items were Zhu De's report on military matters, Liu Shaoqi's report on the revision of the party constitution, and Mao's speech "On Coalition Government." The congress approved a new constitution. It also elected a new Central Committee.

As indicated by the title, Mao's speech on April 24 was a proposal for a "democratic coalition government" with the Nationalists, although the latter would have had to become reorganized to make it possible.[43] For their part, Mao said the Communists would long adhere to their minimum New Democracy program in the protracted present stage of the two-staged evolution to socialism. But the Communists would lead the coalition, "an alliance based on the overwhelming majority of the people, under the leadership of the working class." The envisioned state even allowed for the growth of private capital and the protection of private property—during the present New Democratic stage. "It is not domestic capitalism," Mao averred, "but foreign imperialism and domestic feudalism which are superfluous in China today; indeed, we have too little of capitalism."[44] Mao did make it clear, however, that

> We Communists do not conceal our political views. Definitely and beyond all doubt, our future or maximum programme is to carry China forward to socialism and communism. Both the name of our Party and our Marxist world outlook unequivocally point to this supreme ideal of the future, a future of incomparable brightness and splendour.[45]

Elsewhere in this important speech Mao referred to foreign culture, saying "it would be a wrong policy to shut it out, rather we should as far as possible draw on what is progressive in it for use in the development of China's new culture; it would also be wrong to copy it blindly, rather we should draw on it critically to meet the actual needs of the Chinese people." Mao, incidentally, applied the same reasoning to China's traditional culture, enjoining selective continuities from the past.[46]

Mao also gave the concluding address of the congress on June 11, 1945. Here he recalled an old Chinese fable entitled "The Foolish Old Man Who Removed the Mountains" to illustrate his resolution to remove the two big mountains of imperialism and feudalism that "lie like a dead weight on the Chinese people."[47] Mao could speak confidently and boldly, for the Seventh Congress had been a huge personal success for himself and for his policies. His personality cult reached an early peak at this time. Many of his ideas had been incorporated into the new party constitution, referred to in the text as the "Thought of Mao Zedong." The party was basically unified under him, with allegiance pledged by members in the base areas and in the "white" (a term signifying the need for underground party organization and activities) areas of the cities under Nationalist or Japanese control; and those of the ilk of the 28 Bolsheviks were fully subdued.

Mao's victory translated into power. The Seventh Central Committee had 44 members and 33 alternates. At its First Plenum, the Central Committee elected its Politburo, including Mao, Zhu De, Liu Shaoqi, Zhou Enlai, Ran Bishi, Chen Yun, Liu Bochu, Kang Sheng, and either then or later added Dong Biwu, Peng Zhen, Gao Gang, and Peng Dehuai. The Politburo chose a Secretariat comprising Mao, Zhu De, Liu Shaoqi, Ran Bishi, and Zhou Enlai; alternate Chen Yun replaced Ran upon the latter's death in October 1950. Mao was chairman of the Central Committee, the Politburo, and the Secretariat.[48] He was never to relinquish the first two essential chairmanships until his death 31 years later. With such prestige, power, and strength of personality, Mao Zedong was destined to make an enormous impact upon the party and the country over these three momentous decades.

· 5 ·

Military Victory

As the war against Japan wound down, the Chinese Communists became increasingly optimistic about their prospects. They had compiled for themselves a respectable record during the national struggle, and they had taken advantage of the opportunities the war afforded. From a state of near extinction just before the war, they now emerged with a spirited party membership of well over a million.

Despite the optimism and high morale, however, the Communist leaders remained sober in their estimate of the difficulties ahead. It was generally conceded that the impending civil war would take at least a decade to win. The Soviet leaders thought even less of the chances of their Chinese comrades and in consideration of their own national interests continued relations with the Nationalist government, sealing this orientation with a Sino-Soviet Friendship Treaty on August 14, 1945.[1] Stalin even tried to discourage the Chinese Communists from making a military effort to capture power.[2] In the event, however, Soviet assistance in Manchuria was helpful to the Chinese Communists. A CPSU Central Committee writer, O. Borisov (actually Borisov-Rakhmanin), claims that the Soviet Union's contribution to the latter "played a determinative role at the concluding phase of the Chinese people's liberation struggle." And this was manifested "most forcefully in the direct political, economic and military assistance which was made available to the revolutionary forces in Manchuria."[3] Nevertheless, there remains the question as to how much assistance was rendered. For their part, the Chinese sought to avoid the kind of relationship that would even appear to subordinate themselves to the Soviets, as had happened to local communists in Eastern Europe. Nor, for that matter, did the CCP presence in Manchuria deter the Soviets from systematically stripping machinery from Manchurian industries as they departed. Still, Soviet assistance was from the outset a factor in striking a balance, since the Japanese had ruthlessly exterminated Communist guerrillas in Manchuria during the war.[4] On the other hand, Steven Levine points out that the Japanese occupation similarly had had a "shattering effect on the hierarchy of power in Manchuria," thereby "preparing the ground for the postwar revolutionary movement."[5]

The caution of the CCP certainly seemed justified. The Nationalists did appear to have an overwhelming advantage in terms of conventional war capability. They had an almost three-to-one superiority in fighting men, and this was at least five-to-one in terms of men in arms more generally. The Nationalists also enjoyed an impressive monopoly in air and naval units. They had tremendous superiority in firepower, and this could be brought to bear with artillery, aircraft, and mechanized forces. The Nationalists also had the advantage of being recognized as the legitimate government of China, whose leader was considered the head of one of the five world powers, thanks to American insistence. Finally, Jiang Jieshi enjoyed his highest degree of national popularity in the relieved atmosphere attending Japan's defeat, and he had the important support of the powerful United States.

American support was critical. Not only did it mean huge supplies of war equipment, financial assistance, and military advice, it was also important in tactical deployment. At the end of the war, the Chinese Communists had the important advantage of being situated in northern China, the result of the penetration and work during the war and following their offensive during the summer of 1945. However, this advantage was neutralized by American intervention. General Douglas MacArthur, the supreme commander of the Allied Powers in Japan, warned the Japanese of the importance of surrendering only to the Nationalists.[6] Also, the Americans transported as many as 500,000 Nationalist soldiers to the northern and eastern parts of the country, where they were able to disarm more than 1.25 million Japanese troops. The Soviets obstructed and delayed some of this operation.[7] But the Communists disarmed only 30,000 Japanese in China proper, although they may have had somewhat greater success in Manchuria.

The CCP leaders appear to have been divided at war's end in terms of how to deal with the Nationalists. Mao complained that some comrades were too willing to put faith in political tactics, instead of being determined to fight. Liu Shaoqi much later admitted that he had "illusions of peace" during this period.[8] Of course, Mao himself had set the tone for this disposition to talk rather than fight in his famous speech "On Coalition Government" at the Seventh Party Congress. The Communists also debated the respective roles of the United States and the Soviet Union in China. The former nation appeared particularly threatening to many now that it possessed and had already used an atomic bomb. However, Mao argued that the new weapon could not decide wars.[9]

Nevertheless, even though the Communists were determined to achieve ultimate victory and to continue to build and train their military strength to that end,[10] they did not overlook the opportunities that negotiations, encouraged by both the Americans and the Soviets, might bring about. Thus, on August 24, 1945, the Communists accepted the Nationalist leader's third invitation to reopen the negotiations that had gone on intermittently during the war. Mao and Zhou Enlai flew to Chongqing on August 28, along with U.S. Ambassador Hurley. At the welcoming banquet in Chongqing, Mao astonished observers with his toast to Jiang's long life.[11]

The negotiations took a month and a half. The main issues discussed were political representation, the "nationalization" of armies, the method of selecting local officials, and the disposition of Communist base areas. The Communists made concessions. They agreed, for example, to withdraw from certain base areas, although in fact this signified a prudent redeployment and an actual further expansion and consolidation of their strengths. Thus, by the end of 1945, the Communists had basically withdrawn from south China, with the exception of some guerrilla units that were left behind. Their forces were now concentrated well to the north of the Chang Jiang. As a result of this basic reshaping of their territory, they could now claim control of 149 million people in about a quarter of the most populous area of China. The negotiations concluded in an agreement on October 10, 1945. This agreement proposed the convening of a Political Consultative Conference (PCC) that would represent all groups to discuss the democratic reorganization of government and to approve a new constitution. It created a committee of three, composed of a Nationalist, a Communist, and an American, to supervise the military reorganization. Mao returned to Yan'an. Zhou remained behind to deal with the details.

These details, however, proved impossible to settle. The Communists, for their part, would not give up real control of the appointment of officials in their own base areas. This problem, along with continued hostilities, soon voided the October 10 agreement. On November 26, 1945, Ambassador Hurley resigned his post, blaming several American foreign service officers, including the perceptive John Stewart Service, for undermining his policy.[12] On the following day, President Harry S.

Truman appointed war hero General George C. Marshall as his special representative to China.[13] J. Leighton Stuart took up the post of ambassador in July 1946.

The Chinese Communists demonstrated new interest in negotiations very quickly. Moscow had concluded an agreement with the Nationalists on November 27 that removed the Communists from the cities of Manchuria.[14] Thus, the Communists agreed to participate in the PCC, scheduled to meet in January 1946. They welcomed General Marshall's arrival in China, and took President Truman's assertion on December 15, 1945, calling for a "strong, united, democratic China," as an indication of support for a coalition government. Zhou Enlai proposed a cease-fire during the PCC meetings, and with General Marshall's help this was agreed to. With the exception of those areas south of the Chang Jiang and in Manchuria, all troop movements were to stop after January 13. During the January 1946 meetings of the PCC, it was agreed that a National Assembly would be convened in May and that local officials, including provincial governors, would be popularly elected. In February, an agreement was reached by the "committee of three" to reorganize the military, in a way that would still ensure the Nationalists a five-to-one ratio of superiority. However, these agreements soon proved to be as illusory as had been those of the previous October.

Following considerable military moves and countermoves in Manchuria, the situation superficially appeared to become more satisfactory to the Nationalists by May, when their forces occupied the city of Changchun. At this point, Jiang Jieshi yielded to U.S. pressure and agreed to a two-week cease-fire on May 24, 1946, which was subsequently extended to the end of June. However, the positions of the two sides had hardened. Neither was willing to concede what the other insisted on. By the end of June, it became clearer that the final test of arms was about to begin. Jiang was anxious, finally, to press his apparent military advantage. For their part, the Communists had succeeded in buying some time to regroup and expand, and in making it appear that the Nationalists were primarily responsible for the resort to a military solution. In any event, the Communists had not banked too heavily on the success of the negotiations, and while they were not oblivious of the desirability of U.S. or Soviet assistance, they had learned by now the importance of self-reliance.[15]

General Marshall did not leave China until January 8, 1947. By that time it was abundantly clear that his perhaps impossible mission had failed. The Third Revolutionary Civil War, as the Communists call it, had already begun in earnest during the preceding summer of 1946. By late June, the Nationalist armies began an offensive in the Central Plains.

In July there was a great deal of fighting in Shandong and in northern Jiangsu.

The civil war was fought in three well-defined stages. As seen by the Communists themselves, the period from July 1946 to June 1947 was the defensive stage. During this initial period, the Communists accepted the brunt of the Nationalist offensive, allowing it to extend deeply into north China and Manchuria. The Communists used a policy of strategic withdrawal and mobile warfare, abandoning the cities and towns for the countryside. Lin Biao's troops moved to the north of the Sungari River, leaving the rest of Manchuria to the Nationalists. Li Xiannian moved out of central China into Shanxi. The Communists consolidated within their areas of strength and otherwise fought a war of attrition. The Nationalist offensive reached its peak symbolically with the capture of the city of Yan'an in March 1947, which was conceded without contest. Jiang must have been cheered by the news, initially, of his troops' pursuit of Mao himself in the back country of Shanxi.

Stage two of the war began in the summer of 1947. This was the stage of limited counteroffensive. The Communists continued to concentrate on mobile warfare. They eroded the strength of the Nationalist forces while simultaneously extending the range of engagements. The Communists shared the U.S. assessment that Jiang had overextended himself by deploying most of his best troops in important, but remote, Manchuria. Thus, the principal objective of the Communists was to direct the counteroffensive against the "soft underbelly" of central China and at the major north-south railways that moved through north China. In July and August 1947, the Communists crossed the Huang River in three separate areas and established new base areas in central China. By the end of the year, the People's Liberation Army (PLA), which is how the Communists now designated their military organization, threatened the railways that ran from north China into Manchuria. They would soon cut the lines both north and south of Mukden (soon to be called Shenyang). In November 1947, they took Shijiazhuang in Hebei, and this linked together two base areas that lay directly athwart the important Beijing-Hankou railway.

Mao Zedong gave a well-publicized explanation of the Communist war strategy on December 25, 1947.[16] This frank and public disclosure of military plans must have been intimidating to Nationalist generals, who were only too aware of their many points of vulnerability, even though their strategy had appeared to be so successful to date. Mao listed ten principles of operations for the coming counteroffensive. The main Communist objective was to eliminate the effective strength of the Nationalists rather than to acquire land or towns. The PLA would operate against enemy units that were dispersed and isolated, and this would continue until the balance of forces began to swing to the Communist side. The PLA would defer attacks on enemy concentrations and large towns. Battles of attrition that might result even in equal losses were similarly to be avoided. The old Maoist maxim of attacking only when numerically superior forces could be brought to bear was enjoined. The main source of supply of both arms and personnel was to come from the enemy. The success of this measure led Mao later to refer to Jiang Jieshi as his quartermaster. U.S. Ambassador Stuart noted: "It is perhaps a mark of Communist contempt for Nationalist military thinking and intelligence that the Communists have so little hesitation in explaining their strategy, which, it must be admitted, has to date not been without success."[17]

Communist success did not depend exclusively upon the fighting. We have already noted the weaknesses of the Nationalist government. But now its poor government practices, rampant corruption, and predilection toward repressiveness began to take a bitter toll. As the population generally began to lose confidence in the Nationalist regime, the situation was only exacerbated. The press-ganging of conscripts who were told to risk their lives in a seemingly endless and hopeless war became ever more distasteful and resented. A ruinous inflationary spiral, which the government lacked the sense and courage (ironically for fear of taking unpopular measures, or perhaps of offending vested interests) or the ability to deal with satisfactorily, contributed mightily to the erosion of confidence. The resultant extreme economic instability was followed by the "total collapse of political and social morals."[18] The Nationalists could only respond by implementing increasingly repressive police measures.

In contrast to the disastrously negative Nationalist record, not only did the Communists have a very appealing record, but, refusing to rest on laurels already won, they promoted programs designed to gain even greater popular support. Their winning tactic was to emphasize positive and effective programs, which they then implemented in order to demonstrate they meant what they said. The implementation of programs often resulted in mistakes, but the Communists appeared to demonstrate yet another virtue in being able to continue to learn from such mistakes and to adjust their programs and tactics accordingly.

The principal program that the Communists were able to use effectively to serve their own immediate political and military interests was land reform. This program appealed immediately and profoundly to millions of the country's destitute peasants. The promise of a just share of land was sufficient to mobilize most of the volunteer soldiers necessary to conclude the civil war, but coercive methods of recruitment were also used.

There is the very real question, of course, as to just how "feudal" the land tenure system in China was by the 1940s. The Communists employed statistics that probably distorted the actual situation in land-ownership. They claimed that in the newly liberated areas the landlords and rich peasants composed only 8 percent of the population but owned 75 percent of the land.[19] This would suggest that there was a great deal of interest in and pressure for land redistribution because tenancy was widespread. Thus, the majority of peasants would naturally support the party that promised to give them land. But, in fact, the land tenure system was much more equitable. Given the size and the heterogeneity of China's physical endowments, there were many variations in the system. Undoubtedly there were even locales here and there where relatively well-off peasants actually constituted a majority of the local population. In north China the majority of peasants actually did own their own land.[20]

Nevertheless, the absolute majority of peasants were not well off. Whether they owned their own land or were tenants was almost beside the point. Thus, the Communist program was not aimed at tenants alone, but at the much larger number of impoverished peasants and farm workers, whether or not they were tenants. The Communist program would in fact eliminate tenancy, but this was only one of several issues. As Suzanne Pepper has noted, the CCP attacked broadly "the more basic fact of socio-economic life in the countryside, namely the inequality of wealth."[21] There can be little doubt but that the Communists had seized on an issue of vital concern to a great many among China's vast rural population. It is remarkable, by comparison, that the Nationalists had ignored such a fundamental issue.

The Communists conducted a tentative experimental phase of land reform between May 4, 1946, and October 10, 1947, that departed radically from the moderate policy pursued during the war against Japan. The lessons learned during this phase were discussed at a National Land Conference held in September 1947 in Xibaipo village in Hebei, which was attended by about 1,000 delegates. The conference passed an Outline Land Law, which was published on October 10 and which became the basic text for similar meetings throughout the liberated areas.[22] The document regarded China's present land conditions as the root of its "being the victim of aggression, poverty, backwardness and the basic obstacle to our country's democratization, industrialization, independence, unity, strength and prosperity." Thus did the Communists focus on the gentry class. The new law was radical and systematic. It aimed at the elimination of the landlord class, as a class, and the equalization of landownership. It sought to implement Sun Yat-sen's old slogan of "land to the tiller." The program was administered by the village peasant associations, poor peasant leagues, peasant congresses, and subsidiary organs. Land was distributed equally regardless of sex or age, and it was given on the same basis to Nationalist soldiers and to landlords, as long as they were not traitors, collaborators, or civil war criminals. Land disputes would be decided by people's courts. The peasant associations were responsible for maintaining order.

There were numerous complications and contradictions in the implementation of the program. Some were the result of the exigencies of the war, some were caused by insoluble contradictions in the objectives themselves. Hence, the Communists sought on the one hand to make the reforms sufficiently radical to satisfy the yearnings and whetted appetites of the aroused impoverished masses, but, on the other hand, tried to keep them moderate enough to retain the support of noncommunists during the early New Democratic stage, especially while the civil war raged on. Thus, the poor and landless rural population came to expect a meaningful share of the spoils of land distribution, and the Communists did seek to make available to all something tangible from the program. But the Communists also wished to placate and protect the better-off middle peasants. They were solicitous of the middle peasant, whom they saw as an important and productive asset in the countryside and whose standard of achievement and pleasanter livelihood should remain the goal of all peasants. It was hoped that the middle peasants might be won over to the revolution, rather than alienated from it.

Unfortunately, in all probability the Communists themselves did not initially recognize that the fundamental problem was that the countryside was too poor overall to make the equalization of wealth possible—without taking from the numerous middle peasants.[23] In other words, as wealthy as some landlords and rich peasants may have been, their redistributed properties were insufficient to make the sizable destitute rural population into middle peasants. Thus, particularly as the Communists sought to gain the support of the poor and landless peasants early in the civil war, there was a strong tendency to commit leftist errors, and this invariably meant encroaching on the middle peasants. Eventually this leftist excess was addressed and corrected. It undoubtedly helped the cadres who implemented the program when, in January 1948, Mao defined the distinction between middle and rich peasant. A middle peasant, it turned out, was one who derived only 25 percent or less of his income from the exploitation of the labor of others, while a rich peasant exceeded this percentage.[24]

This became an important matter during 1948, for while calculated violence was useful, excesses could not be permitted to impede the developing military situation. Mao also insisted that the different types of areas be discriminated among properly and appropriate policies be used in each area.[25] "Old liberated areas," that is, those areas that had been under control from mid-1945, required only minor adjustments of land conditions. The "semi-old areas," occupied between 1945 and mid-1947, had seen a rapidly changing military situation. While the land problem here had been dealt with in a preliminary fashion, it was not solved. The middle peasants retained a wait-and-see attitude, while the poor peasants were in a demanding mood. Poor peasant leagues were to be organized to deal with the situation. The "new liberated areas," taken since mid-1947, were to experience land reform only in stages. The one remaining area, the "guerrilla zone," adjoined enemy territory and the new liberated areas. Here work had to be confined to propaganda, covert organizational work, and the distribution of certain movable property. To avert the possibility of people being subjected to persecution, mass organizations could not be organized openly, nor reforms implemented in these marginal areas.

The CCP took advantage of the improving war situation in the winter of 1947–1948 to conduct a new *zheng feng* or rectification campaign. Not only was such a campaign necessary in order to deal with errors in the massive, complicated land reform program, it was needed for other reasons as well. The most urgent was that the CCP had expanded from the 1,210,000 members of April 1945 to 2,700,000 by mid-1947. This figure acknowledgedly enabled many "landlords, rich peasants, and riffraff . . . to sneak into" the CCP.[26] Mao believed that these elements did "control a number of Party, government, and people's organizations, tyrannically abuse their power, ride roughshod over the people, distort the Party's policies, and thus alienate these organizations from the masses." The *zheng feng* campaign, one of the truly distinctive innovations of the Chinese Communist movement, sought to educate those who could be redeemed and to reject those who could not. The 1947 *zheng feng* differed from the 1942–1944 campaign in that it invited criticism for the first time from nonparty individuals. Interestingly, the Nationalist government demonstrated no similar effort to seriously regenerate itself from time to time. Through the technique of persuasion, rather than naked coercion, the CCP continued to grow in numbers as it purified itself, in stark contrast to the drastic reductions of Soviet party membership during the purges. Early in 1948 a similar renewal program was conducted in the PLA, where the objectives were greater political unity, improved living conditions, and the learning of better military techniques.

Thus, the Communists productively used the respite represented by the second stage of the civil war. Their land reform program reached monumental proportions with essential lessons being learned in the process, and at least some of the excesses were corrected. The program was suspended in 1948 as attention turned to the final military showdown. As much as one-third of the land had been redistributed by this point. The CCP continued to expand, but at the same time it tried to reform and streamline itself. Simultaneously, the party promoted mass organizational work throughout the population, particularly among women, youth, and workers. The PLA continued to grow, yet still took time to become more intensively indoctrinated. The military also began to practice the new tactics to be employed in the next stage of the war, that is, the use of massed armies in more conventional positional battles. Greater attention was given to industry and commerce in the communist areas, and production increased.

The late summer of 1948 saw the beginning of the third and final stage of the civil war.[27] The PLA now numbered over 2 million men, and for the first time had parity with the Nationalist army. The latter army was now clearly on the defensive. Three hundred thousand of its best troops were isolated in Manchuria, while another 100,000 were tied down at Jinan in Shandong. In the meanwhile, in the cities behind Nationalist lines, inflation sapped morale, and political unrest flared in Nanjing. The Communists took full advantage of this situation. They launched an all-out strategic offensive. While most observers by this point figured that the Nationalists would undoubtedly lose the war, few were prepared for the spectacular successes the Communists now achieved.

Within five months in the fall and winter of 1948–1949, in four major campaigns, the Communists broke the back of the Nationalist army.

The first campaign saw Communist general Chen Yi capture Jinan on September 24, 1948, which Jiang Jieshi insisted upon defending despite advice to the contrary by General David Barr, director of the Joint U.S. Military Advisory Group to China.[28] The Nationalists lost 100,000 men and 50,000 rifles at Jinan, primarily, it was said, because of psychological rather than military reasons.[29]

The second campaign saw Lin Biao's Northeast China Field Army, which by now had grown to twice the size of the Nationalist army in Manchuria, move onto the offensive. Jinzhou, an important rail junction and supply base, was captured in mid-October. This had the effect of disorienting the Nationalist army in Manchuria by destroying their communication system.[30] The city of Changchun fell on October 19, as did Shenyang (Mukden) on November 2, after brilliant maneuvering by Lin Biao.[31] Nationalist troops were already defecting in droves, and the few remaining positions quickly gave in.

The third campaign, the Huai-Hai, was a classic set-piece battle that lasted from November 6, 1948, to January 10, 1949. It came to be regarded as Jiang Jieshi's "Waterloo." Some 600,000 men of the East China and Central Plains Field Armies surrounded about the same number of Nationalist soldiers in a wide area north of the Huai River around the city of Xuzhou. The choice of the battle site was in itself surprising; the more defensible line would have been along the Huai River itself.[32] Despite generous air support, the Nationalist army finally succumbed to the tightening siege of the Communists. The way was now cleared to the Chang Jiang (Yangtze).

The fourth and last of these crushing campaigns was in the Beiping-Tianjin area. Tianjin surrendered on January 15, 1949. One week later, Nationalist general Fu Zuoyi, who had been secretly negotiating with the Communists, turned over to Lin Biao the city of Beiping.[33] Another half million men were lost by the Nationalists in this campaign, and a pattern was established for other Nationalist generals to follow in turning over cities to the Communists. Beiping would become the capital of the Communist government, and by March the new administration moved in.

The Second Plenum of the Seventh Central Committee was held in Xibaipo, Hebei, from March 5 to 13, 1949, attended by 34 full and 19 alternate members. Mao's report of March 5 looked to the period of rule ahead, and to the establishment of a firm united front policy that would include nonparty democrats. Accordingly, the plenum approved the establishment of a new Chinese People's Political Consultative Conference (CPPCC) and the establishment of a democratic coalition government. It also approved Mao's conditions for talks with the Nationalists, which he had enumerated on January 14. The plenum also dismissed Liu Zujiu from full membership in the Central Committee for having "betrayed the revolution" in the Henan "white" areas.[34]

Mao used the occasion to caution his jubilant comrades as they prepared to move into Beiping. "To win countrywide victory," he declared, "is only the first step in a long march of ten thousand li." Among the many considerations prompting such sobriety in victory was the shift of the center of gravity now taking place in the work of the party. For years the party had based itself in the villages, from whence it surrounded the cities and gathered strength. Thus, Mao announced: "The period of 'from the city to the village' and of the city leading the village has now begun."[35] The plenum accordingly decided to restrict further recruitment of peasants and to increase the percentage of workers in the party. As a matter of fact, the CCP had already been acquiring some experience in this new area since 1945. In the course of this experience it had already made mistakes, but was learning how to correct them.

By mid-1948, the Communists already held 586 cities, which included municipal units down to the size of county towns.[36] Most of the larger cities were in Manchuria, and of these, Harbin was the largest. It was occupied by the Communists as the Soviets withdrew from Manchuria in 1946 and thus afforded them considerable urban experience throughout the civil war period. Their earliest opportunity to administer a city, however, had been during their occupation of Zhangjiakou (Kalgan), located to the northwest of Beiping, from late August 1945 to early October 1946. The experience generally followed the same pattern of behavior as was manifested in the land reform program, with initial radicalism or overenthusiastic idealism necessarily giving way to more moderate measures.

In the cities, a continuing problem was the lack of even rudimentary urban experience on the part of many cadres, and their reluctance to change rural habits and a guerrilla mentality. It was also very difficult for many cadres to comprehend the reason for the difference in rural and urban policy regarding exploiters. In the countryside, even though land reform had moderated in order to protect the middle peasant, the erstwhile gentry elite had effectively been dispossessed and removed from real power in much of north China. In the cities, however, except for monopoly capitalists and those who had been traitors, an accommodation was made with private capital. Capitalists had to be protected from more radically oriented workers, and this the CCP became determined to do. This was a necessary proviso during New Democracy and while the need was so great to marshal all resources for national economic reconstruction and development. Thus, as urban policy developed from 1947 to 1949, the CCP became more conservative. Leftist excesses were corrected. This trend was also influenced by the increased attention to learning from the experience of the Soviet Union.

Temporary peace negotiations slowed the Communist advance in early 1949. Jiang resigned as head of the Nationalist government and his successor, Acting President Li Zongren, sent a delegation to Beiping. These talks broke down on April 20, 1949, when the Nationalists rejected the Communist ultimatum. By April 21, the Second and Third

Field Armies of the PLA began moving across the Chang Jiang. Demoralized Nationalist armies offered little resistance. The Communist armies swept the Chang Jiang Valley: Nanjing fell on April 23, Hangzhou on May 3, Wuhan on May 17, and Shanghai on May 27. Peng Dehuai, in the meanwhile, led his First Field Army into the northwest. Lanzhou, in Gansu, was captured on August 26. The other northwestern provinces soon surrendered. August saw the beginning of a new offensive in south China. The entire southeastern littoral was taken by fall. The western provinces of Guizhou, Sichuan, Yunnan, and Xikang fell by December 1949. In April 1950, Hainan Island was captured. Tibet fell in late 1950. Only Taiwan eluded capture. The island province became the refuge for what was left of a viable Nationalist government and its military.

It would be a tragic irony of history that as the Nationalists retreated it was the Soviet ambassador, rather than the American, who followed the fleeing government as far as Guangzhou in the south. The Soviets thus seemed to demonstrate their determined orientation toward the Nationalist government and their serious underestimation of the Chinese Communist movement. In fact, they were probably underscoring, at this point, the "correctness" of their policy so as to avoid triggering a U.S. reaction in one area of the globe where the U.S. and the USSR tacitly avoided another cold war confrontation.[37] For its part, the United States was not ready to abandon the Nationalists either, even though Ambassador Stuart remained in Nanjing. The Communist leaders, who had permitted the abuse of American consular officials in Shenyang (Mukden) by subordinates, did invite Stuart on May 13, 1949, to visit Mao and Zhou in Beiping (less than a month after Nanjing's occupation) to discuss U.S.-China relations. However, Stuart's qualified authorization from Washington, which was not acted upon, did not arrive until July 2. By then Mao had already announced that China would "lean to one side," that is, toward the Soviet Union. This policy represented a strong predisposition on the part of Chinese Marxist-Leninists, despite any qualms they might have had about Soviet attitudes in the past, despite anything that Ambassador Stuart might realistically have been able to negotiate, and despite any desire to have an economic relationship with, or even assistance from, the United States in the future.[38]

· 6 ·

. Establishing the People's Republic .

With victory the CCP now had the responsibility of governing the huge land and population mass of China. As patriotic Chinese, the Communists desired to bring sound rule to their people and to develop the country economically, to make China modern, strong, and secure. But as social revolutionaries they were also committed to transform society and culture. In general, the economic, nationalistic goal would have priority, which was in any case compatible with Marxist reasoning regarding sequential stages of development. This would be particularly evident when economic development and united front policies were center stage. But the CCP, as a Marxist-Leninist organization, would also maintain its commitment to social revolution. Under Mao's leadership this radical, idealistic purpose would be dramatically articulated occasionally, and sometimes given priority attention, even if this deleteriously affected the economic, nationalistic goal.

In June 1949, following the decision of the Second Plenum, some 134 delegates representing 23 "democratic" organizations held a preparatory committee meeting in Beiping, prior to the convening of the Chinese People's Political Consultative Conference (CPPCC).[1] Mao was elected head of the standing committee of this temporary body, which would make basic decisions before the September meeting of the full CPPCC. The latter body—which, differently constituted, had been used by the Nationalist government in January 1946—would set up the new government of China. Before it did so, the CCP had to make clear its own fundamental orientation.

This was done by Mao on June 30, 1949, in his major article "On the People's Democratic Dictatorship," written to commemorate the 28th anniversary of the CCP.[2] He noted that three main weapons were used to defeat the enemy: "A well-disciplined Party armed with the theory of Marxism-Leninism, using the method of self-criticism and linked with the masses of the people; an army under the leadership of such a Party; a united front of all revolutionary classes and all revolutionary groups under the leadership of such a Party." Mao declared:

> To sum up our experience and concentrate it into one point, it is: the people's democratic dictatorship under the leadership of the working class (through the Communist Party) and based upon the alliance of workers and peasants. This dictatorship must unite as one with the international revolutionary forces. This is our formula, our principal experience, our main programme.

Mao rhetorically repeated an accusation often addressed to the party: "You are dictatorial." His reply: "My dear sirs, you are right, that is just what we are. All the experience the Chinese people have accumulated through several decades teaches us to enforce the people's democratic dictatorship, that is, to deprive the reactionaries of the right to speak and let the people alone have that right." Mao defined who "the people" were.

> At the present stage in China, they are the working class, the peasantry, the urban petty bourgeoisie and the national bourgeoisie. These classes, led by the working class and the Communist Party, united to form their own state and elect their own government; they enforce their dictatorship over the running dogs of imperialism—the landlord class and bureaucrat-bourgeoisie, as well as the representatives of those classes . . . suppress them, allow them only to behave themselves and not to be unruly in word or deed. If they speak or act in an unruly way, they will be promptly stopped and punished.

The power of the state would be used to protect the people, Mao said, and enable them to educate and remold themselves by democratic methods, with everyone taking part, to eliminate unwanted influences and "advance towards a socialist and communist society." Persuasion, not compulsion, was the method to be used, Mao emphasized. Even well-behaved reactionaries would be given land and work "in order to allow them to live and remould themselves through labour into new people." However, if they were not willing to work, "the people's state will compel them to work."

The national bourgeoisie would be subjected to suitable educational work at present and this would be carried forward a step when it would be time to "realize socialism, that is, to nationalize private enterprise." However, in the meanwhile, this class was of great importance, to be united with in common struggle. The current policy "is to regulate capitalism, not to destroy it."

Mao conceded that the education of the peasantry was a serious problem, because the peasant economy was scattered and the socialization of agriculture, judging by the Soviet Union's experience, would require a long time and painstaking work. Nevertheless, Mao maintained that "without socialization of agriculture, there can be no complete, consolidated socialism."

With regard to China's international orientation, Mao repeated the accusation: "You are leaning to one side." "Exactly," he replied. "The forty years' experience of Sun Yat-sen and the twenty-eight years' experience of the Communist Party have taught us to lean to one side, and we are firmly convinced that in order to win victory and consolidate it we must lean to one side." Thus, China would "unite in a common struggle with those nations of the world which treat us as equals and unite with peoples of all countries. That is, ally with the Soviet Union, with the People's Democracies and with the proletariat and the broad masses of the people in all other countries, and form an international united front."

Mao again counseled humility in facing the awesome new tasks ahead. "We must learn to do economic work from all who know how, no matter who they are. We must esteem them as teachers, learning from them respectfully and conscientiously. We must not pretend to know when we do not know. We must not put on bureaucratic airs." In this, he singled out the Soviet Union, holding that its party "is our best teacher and we must learn from it."

This was a forceful statement of the basic CCP position, and it informed subsequent discussions shaping the new government. But, having been reminded of the Communists' outlook at the time, it is useful to reflect on the country's situation as well.

Aside from the very important fact that the Communists had won the war, 1949 was a very difficult year for them and for China. Military operations on a large scale continued throughout the year, by the end of which the PLA had secured the entire mainland with the exception of Tibet. Hainan Island and Taiwan remained to be taken (as late as June 1950 there were still 400,000 Nationalist soldiers on the mainland, disbanded, but many of them in touch with the new seat of operations of the Nationalist government in Taiwan). Naval and air units of the former regime continued to blockade at least partially the main coastal ports, and occasionally to bombard them. This was, of course, a serious problem for the new Communist government, for the coastal cities and their huge populations were heavily dependent on shipping to provide essential food and other necessities. This dependency reflected the normal trade orientation of the seaports, but it was made all the more urgent because of the inadequacy of Chinese agricultural production and the disruption of already limited transportation facilities in the interior. The problem was intensified by the loss of almost all commercial ships, which had fled to Taiwan. It was necessary to deal with vast numbers of surrendered and captured military personnel, who had fallen into the hands of the PLA much more quickly than had been anticipated, and to assist millions of refugees to return to homes in their native provinces. On top of all this, in 1949, of all years, bad weather and floods plagued the countryside, so that food production was 20 to 25 percent below the pre-1949 peak level.[3] Reportedly, the floods were the worst since 1931.[4]

Also, the CCP lacked sufficient numbers of trained personnel for the enormous tasks now confronting them. In 1949 there were 4.5 million party members, mostly peasants—and they lacked adequate appropriate experience. As we have noted, the CCP was initially at a disadvantage in running large cities with their many unfamiliar and complex institutions and unique problems. Many Communists were simply illiterate. They made great use of the many idealistic young people—regardless of their political persuasions at the outset—in the takeover of certain institutions. They also made use of officials who had carried over from the previous regime. It was said that as many as 95 percent of the former Nationalist officials remained at their posts after the Communists arrived in Shanghai.[5] This was, of course, a boon to the new administration. However, CCP cadres were now thrust into an environment of cooperation that would eventually create problems of adverse influence, backsliding, and corruption.

Underlying the current confusion and difficulties were the more fundamental and endemic problems the new regime now inherited. There were the problems of extensive war destruction, of prolonged and acute inflation, of the great population pressure on scarce resources, and of the yet relatively limited and superficial degree of modernization. The late Alexander Eckstein noted that the economy "by practically all available measures was near the bottom of the world development scale."[6] China, by the mid-twentieth century, had a GNP per capita that was only one-half to one-third of the level achieved in England in the late seventeenth century. Agriculture produced about half of the Chinese GNP, while all of the modern sectors combined contributed only about 20 percent.[7] Agriculture still operated mostly within a framework of traditional technology and institutions, resulting in very low labor productivity. Furthermore, since the 1930s at least, agricultural production had virtually stagnated.

The CCP responded to the challenge, pragmatically reasoning that success would require continued united front tactics under the rubric of New Democracy. But first, Mao declared, "We should get ourselves better organized." Thus, everyone was to be placed in appropriate organizations, in order "to put an end to the disorganized state characterizing the old China, so that the great collective strength of the masses may be tapped."[8]

The CPPCC was held in Beiping from September 21 to 30, 1949. It had 662 participants, of whom 510 were full members and 77 alternates.[9] The Communists did not provide majority representation for themselves in the CPPCC. This was not necessary since they controlled all the instruments of power already. But the gesture did support the pretense of a coalition government and democracy. This was a practice the CCP had followed during the War of Resistance that tended to give institutional and legal support to the continuing united front policy. Thus, among the full members of the CPPCC, 142 of them represented both the CCP and other small political parties that had agreed to cooperate with the CCP, 102 were regional representatives, 60 represented the PLA, 75 were "guests," and 206 represented various professions, cultural associations, overseas Chinese, and minority nationalities. The CPPCC would continue to serve as a national congress until 1954 when a new constitution established a new form of government. However, the CPPCC, as an institution in its own right, still exists. It is the foremost symbol of the united front, maintained with varying use and emphasis over the years.

The most important tasks of the CPPCC were accomplished during its first plenary session. It enacted rules governing itself, but most important it enacted the Organic Law of the People's Central Government of the People's Republic of China (PRC) and a Common Program, which served as an interim constitution for the new regime. The CPPCC also made Beiping, now called Beijing, the capital of the PRC, adopted a flag with five stars on a field of red as the national flag, and made the song "March of the Volunteers" the national anthem. The Christian calendar was adopted as the country's chronological system, displacing the system of the former regime, which had computed years beginning with the establishment of the first republic in 1912. Finally, the CPPCC elected its own First National Committee, with Mao as chairman, and officers of the new People's Central Government Council.

Mao drafted the declaration that recorded these decisions on September 30, 1949, saying: "Fellow-countrymen, the founding of the People's Republic of China is proclaimed, and the Chinese people now have their own Central Government."[10] This assertion was repeated in a simple public ceremony on Tiananmen Square the following day. October 1 has ever since been celebrated as National Day.

The new central political structure was an effective stopgap means for enabling the Communists to get on with the governance of the country, making use of the nonparty human resources available in order to greatly complement their own limited ranks. In the meantime, the CCP would continue to develop means for making further changes. Despite the New Democratic facade, the regime was clearly Communist and authoritarian from the beginning. The CCP exercised ultimate authority and provided essential leadership in all other organizations.

At the apex of the Central Government was the People's Central Government Council, which promulgated laws and managed domestic affairs, foreign policy, and the budget. Mao was chairman. The council also had a vice chairman and 56 members. Directly responsible to it were the very important People's Revolutionary Military Council chaired by Mao personally, and the Supreme People's Court and an affiliated organ, the Supreme People's Procuratorate. At the next echelon was the State Administrative Council, chaired by Premier Zhou Enlai, which put into effect the decisions of the higher council. The State Administrative Council was subdivided into four functional organs. There were about 30 ministries and agencies under the general direction of the premier. Some posts were given to non-CCP members, but such assignments had limited authority, and party members held all strategic positions.

Moving down the hierarchical structure of the new government administration there were relatively fewer trained or administratively capable Communists to fill government positions, particularly as the CCP fanned out through the huge country. Yet, at the regional, provincial, and local levels, there was a host of complex problems requiring urgent attention. Additionally, the Communists, from the very beginning, were anxious to penetrate politically more deeply and more effectively into society than had any previous Chinese government.

Innovation was demonstrated at the regional level. The government divided China into six large administrative regions, each one corresponding to the zones of responsibility of the major military units of the PLA, particularly the four field armies. In each region was a party bureau representing the Central Committee.[11]

Dorothy Solinger has studied the Southwest Great Administrative Region for the period 1949 to 1954 in an effort to understand the role played by the regional government in bringing about greater national political integration and control. She found that the system, as paradoxical as it seemed to be, that is, by using decentralization in order to develop centralization or, in other words, by using regional organization in order to abolish regionalism, actually did promote greater political control from Beijing. The regime simply countered local diversity in all its forms—political, economic, and cultural—by parceling out the country in intermediate-size packages. Thus, the regional administrations were able to apply national policy to areas that were somewhat similar, while being aware of local peculiarities.[12]

On the one hand, it is possible that Mao and other central party leaders eventually became concerned that Gao Gang, chairman of the Northeast Region, and (less convincingly) Rao Shushi, who succeeded Chen Yi as chairman of East China, were attempting to turn their respective regions into independent "kingdoms," thus contradicting the intention of regional government. On the other hand, however, the use of this administrative device did help to lay a basis for the greater level of centralization that the country's economic development program would require. At the same time, the disposition to experiment with techniques of decentralization when necessary was also promoted. The regional administrations were abolished in 1954, but would be revived in the period 1961–1966, and once again in 1977.

The next level of governance was that of the provinces or *sheng*. These remained pretty much the same as they had been in the past. With some few alterations, the number of provinces finally came to be 23. Enjoying roughly the same rank as provinces were five autonomous regions—for principal minority nationalities—and two special municipalities, Beijing and Shanghai.[13]

Below the province the next level of administration was the county or *xian*, although special districts, *zhuan chu*, were created at a level between the province and county to act as conduits and coordinating mechanisms; with about ten *xian* to each *zhuan chu*. The *xian* has been an important administrative entity for 2,000 years in China. In traditional and republican times, it represented the deepest penetration of formal government at the local level. The *xian* magistrate was an exceedingly busy man, but rarely became well acquainted with the common folk under his jurisdiction. Because of the determination of the CCP to penetrate more deeply into the local political arena, and partly to displace the erstwhile gentry who had assisted the old magistrate in local governance, the *xian*, while retained under the new regime, lost some of its distinction.

Thus, in rural areas the next major lower level of administration became very important. This was the *xiang*, which comprised several villages and is often referred to as an administrative village. Interposed between the *xian* and the *xiang* was a coordinating mechanism known as the district or *chu*.

In the cities, even though at the outset former Nationalist bureaucrats were retained in their positions, important changes were made in the government. According to Franz Schurmann, the one place where continuity of structure was maintained was in the police system, and this was probably to ensure the maintaining of order.[14] The most important change was that government was now conducted by committees. This was true from the people's committee at the central municipal level down to the urban district level.

One way in which the new regime began to penetrate more deeply into society was by expanding the functions of the police. Local police stations expanded their personnel and took on civil administration responsibilities in addition to regular police duties. One police staff member came to be particularly important—the policeman who registered households and who consequently became acquainted with all the people of a neighborhood. This use of the police for civil administration purposes represented the deepest penetration of government authority "from the top down."[15]

But the process of organizing urban society came from the "bottom up" as well, through "organizations of mass character." Initially these were groups of residents who were led by local CCP members or activists, in either case known as *ganbu*, for the purpose of explaining and implementing government policies. However, because of the ad hoc character of these initial groups and their eventual profusion, there came to be considerable confusion in their operations and jurisdictions.

The solution was to establish uniformly structured residents committees. These were first introduced experimentally in 1951 and 1952 in Tianjin and Shanghai, the two cities in which the *bao jia* system under the Japanese had been most successful. The *bao jia*, also used by the Nationalists, was purely a control and surveillance system. The Communists had abolished the *bao jia*, but the new residents committees did bear a resemblance to it, particularly since the latter came to be closely associated with the local police. However, the residents committees had more constructive functions than just public security. They also made citizens aware of government policies; had a hand in fire prevention, culture and recreation, public works and sanitation, relief, and arbitration matters; and they were supposed to collect and reflect the opinions of residents to higher authorities. This would be done through police or through the street mayoralties, later to be called street committees, that were established at a level just above the residents committees.[16]

Women played a very important role in the residents committees from the beginning. This is because these committees and the street committees were established in residential areas exclusively and seemed to serve the purpose of organizing those citizens who were not already organized at their places of work or study. However, these committees do not seem to have been popular with the residents themselves. People resented the interferences and feared the police connections. The committees do not seem to have spread throughout the country very extensively before the 1954 reorganization of government.

Mass organizations became exceedingly important mechanisms for involving all members of society in the new politics and social life of the country.[17] Many mass organizations came into being, but the most important were the following: The New Democratic Youth League (later to be called the Communist Youth League) was the equivalent of the Soviet Komsomol, and comprised young people between the ages of 14 and 25 who aspired to become regular members of the CCP. By May 1954 its membership had reached more than 12 million.[18] An affiliated junior youth organization, the Young Pioneers, for youngsters from 9 to 14, had eight million members by May 1953.[19] During the 1950s the Sino-Soviet Friendship Society was very important. By February 1954 it boasted a membership of 58 million, and was extremely active. The All-China Democratic Women's Federation, at the time of its Second National Congress in April 1953, had 76 million members.[20] This organization has been vitally important in the very difficult struggle in China to promote women's rights. The All-China Federation of Trade Unions in May 1954 had 11 million members, and played a highly important role in the organization and discipline of China's small—but soon to grow greatly—industrial proletariat.[21]

Mass organizations were developed for every sphere of social and professional activity: academic groups, artists, actors, writers, and religious groups. In the countryside, peasants joined state-run monopolies called 'cooperatives' and peasant associations. In September 1953 each category of these rural organizations had a membership of 141 million or more.[22]

The structural aspects of the new regime's administration revealed both continuities from the past and innovations; the innovations being primarily in those features that required involvement and participation in the political process. This objective was promoted through other means, too, particularly through techniques of mass mobilization politics. Hence, from the beginning, people were encouraged to participate in mass demonstrations and meetings (of all sizes), and to march in or observe festive parades. These events were designed to make the participant feel a part of the collective might of the new China, and to instill in him or her a welcome sense of purposefulness as the regime set about achieving its various goals. Such participation would hopefully encourage continued consciousness of and involvement in politics.[23]

One particularly distinctive feature of such mobilization politics in China, as compared with other such authoritarian states, is the innovative and intensive use of nationwide mass campaigns. Again, this is a form of political expression that has roots in modern Chinese history, but it came to be highly developed by the Communists.[24] Each of these campaigns generally had a distinct target or objective of its own, ranging from the promotion of a particular government policy to the promotion of literacy or certain sanitation procedures. They were often instigated indirectly, with a number of individuals or organizations "spontaneously" asking in letters to the press that attention be given to some issue or problem. Once sufficient "demand" was noted, the party would respond by formally announcing and organizing a campaign, which was distinguished by appropriate slogans that were publicized repeatedly for the life of the campaign, and sometimes long afterwards. In the period of New Democracy, through 1953 (and later), there were many such campaigns, and they played a significant role in stimulating political consciousness.

A very important and distinctive characteristic of political life introduced by the CCP was the requirement that every individual belong to a *xiao-zu*, or small group, in one of the organizations with which he or she was affiliated. The small group is composed of between eight and fifteen members. Within this unique institution the individual is, or is supposed to be, involved in perpetual political study and mutual criticism. The small groups have remained a perennial and pervasive feature of life in China, with the exception of the period of the Cultural Revolution in the late 1960s, when the regular political structure and processes were temporarily suspended, and they have been in low profile or dormant in the post-Mao period. Martin King Whyte found that even in organizations that were not working as they were supposed to, the small groups and their "political rituals" still contributed to organizational effectiveness. The small group was also successful in informing the individual of official goals and policies, in inhibiting him from expressing or finding support for opposition, and in making him work harder or volunteer for new and difficult tasks. However, Whyte questioned whether the small group was as successful "in transforming and unifying the varied hopes, fears, needs, aspirations, and loyalties" of the participants as the regime had intended it to be.[25]

The mass organizations, the mobilization campaigns, and the small groups constituted techniques of communication between the party and society that the party generally used adroitly. Of course, the CCP also soon came to establish control over the conventional mass media, from newspapers to radio (and later television), making full use of this extremely important realm for its purposes.[26]

The apex of political power in China continued to be the Central Committee of the CCP, composed during the early 1950s of party members elected at the Seventh Party Congress in 1945. The Seventh Central Committee continued to entrust the formulation of policy, of course, to its Politburo and chairman. Politburo members held commanding positions in the government. The CCP was, in fact, the alter ego of the state government and of all other organizations as well, including the PLA and the mass organizations.

Key decisions and policies were and still are made by the Politburo, and then communicated to the government and other organizations. Strategically placed party members were placed in either the top or deputy leadership positions, so there would be assurance that the policies would be carried out. The structure of the CCP also vertically paralleled that of the government, so that at each level from central, to regional, to provincial, to county, to village, or to street committee there was at the same horizontal level a committee or branch of the CCP. The same held true for other organizations as well; wherever there was an organized unit, there was a unit of the CCP too. The latter was then able to give direction to and monitor the government administration both vertically and horizontally.

The relationship and the distinction between the CCP and the state (whether in its New Democracy or subsequent socialist expressions) is, as Franz Schurmann explains, theoretically the same as the distinction in any organization between the executive function on the one hand, and the staff and line functions on the other. The executive propounds policy, which is translated by the staff and line into concrete commands.[27] Thus, the CCP tries to avoid—with, as we shall see, varying success—becoming too involved with the implementation of its own decisions, which would tend to bog it down in routine technicalities. Like the imperial mandarins of the past, the CCP cadre or *ganbu* is a political generalist who tries to see the whole picture through his party's ideological lenses. This is in keeping with the self-image of the CCP as possessing the competence to represent the will of the proletariat, while the state is the bureaucratic instrument through which this will is realized.[28]

PART THREE

Shaping the New China

· 7 ·

From New Democracy to Socialism

The Common Program adopted by the CPPCC on September 29, 1949, gave legal nationwide expression to the ideas of New Democracy and united front politics that the CCP had discussed for some time. The Common Program was deliberately reassuring to most elements in the population because of the new government's need to elicit massive cooperation in order to make effective headway quickly toward the immediate objectives of consolidation, recovery, and reorganization. During this transitional period, the national bourgeoisie and the petty bourgeoisie, even though marked for eventual elimination as distinctive classes, were to have a constructive role to play, along with the workers and peasants.

As we have seen, from the very beginning the party imposed organizational mechanisms that would limit any genuinely democratic and liberal features of New Democracy and that would facilitate the transition to socialism when the signal was given. Nevertheless, the Communists themselves probably expected New Democracy to last longer than it actually did. The time of the transition to the next stage could not readily be foretold at the outset; this was to depend on circumstances. But beyond such a logical assumption, there are at least two reasons why New Democracy might have had a longer life.

First, the CCP perceived its triumph as the victory of the new democratic revolution in modern Chinese history. The CCP recognized China's economic backwardness and the essentially agrarian character of the country. Marxist theory provided the expectation that the country would now have to industrialize, and this is what New Democracy was to facilitate. Once China was industrialized and had a substantial working class, the time for socialism would have arrived. Second, given the arrangement of China's economy, with the external orientation of the major coastal cities, it made sound economic sense to retain the services of those Chinese who were most familiar with this pattern of economic relationships and who could keep it intact and productive. This was the natural role of the national bourgeoisie, for it was this class of industrialists and commercial entrepreneurs who had the needed expertise and invaluable contacts both within China and without.

The Third Enlarged Plenum of the Seventh Central Committee met from June 6 to 9, 1950, in Beijing, attended by 35 full and 27 alternate members, and by 43 party committee secretaries of provinces and municipalities. Mao cautioned the party to "try earnestly and painstakingly to make a success of its united front work."[1] He was anxious lest his comrades unnecessarily antagonize the national bourgeoisie, who were to be struggled against on the one hand and united with on the other, so that effort could be concentrated on the immediate targets. These were: "first, the imperialists; second, the reactionaries in Taiwan and Tibet; third, the remnant Kuomintang forces, the secret agents and the bandits; fourth, the landlord class; and fifth, the reactionary forces in the missionary schools established in China by the imperialists and in religious circles and those in the cultural and educational institutions taken over from the Kuomintang. These are our enemies."[2] The plenum also discussed the land reform program that would begin again soon. Later that month, on June 23, 1950, Mao spoke to the Second Session of the CPPCC's First National Committee and reaffirmed that the time for nationalizing private industry and socializing agriculture was "still quite far off." And he said that in the future the country "will enter the new era of socialism unhurriedly and with proper arrangements . . . and when the transition has been fully considered and endorsed by the whole nation."[3]

Two days later, on June 25, 1950, the Korean War began. This event, which burst like a sudden unexpected thunderclap, would have profound consequences for the new PRC and for the party's program of New Democracy. It is useful to remain aware of this important conflict that raged in the neighboring country of Korea and into which China was inexorably drawn. No longer were China's domestic programs simply the efforts of a new revolutionary regime trying to reconstruct and govern a huge population in moderate ways preparatory to further socioeconomic transformations over the long haul. Now it became a regime and a people fearful of being attacked once more by foreign enemies. The problems suddenly increased; the psychology and the mood changed, and so did the pace of developments.

The new regime set the target date of 1952 to restore agricultural and industrial production to pre-1949 peak levels. It succeeded for the most part in doing this; the achievement being impressive but not spectacular. A fundamental reason for the success, after all, was the restoration of peace, national unity, and political order for the first time in over two decades. Additionally, the Communists made tactical concessions to the capitalists and industrialists, encouraging them to stay in China and cooperate; overtures were made to many who had fled to return. New Democracy, it was made clear in the official pronouncements, was a period in which capitalism was to be regulated, not destroyed.[4] Liu Shaoqi spoke to businessmen and industrialists in Tianjin, asking them to keep their capital in that city and to invest it in plant expansion.[5] Nor were workers to make excessive demands, regardless of their theoretical privileged status in the new order. A new trade union law saw that labor was organized in such a way that it was under close CCP supervision and discipline.

The recovery in all fields was also facilitated by favorable agricultural harvests three years running—1950, 1951, and 1952—compensating for the dreary situation in 1949. It may be that the 1952 harvest reached or even exceeded pre-1949 record levels, even though land reform was then in progress.[6]

Substantial progress was made in the production of steel, cotton, cloth, paper, flour, and cigarettes. The rise in steel production seemed impressive, particularly in light of the fact that the Soviets had removed over one-half of the capital stock of Manchurian industry in 1945.[7] However, economist W. W. Rostow points out that even at its peak the Japanese iron and steel industry in Manchuria had produced at only about 60 percent of capacity, so that full restoration was not required in order to reach the 1952 record.[8] However, in pig iron, coal, electric power, sugar, soybeans, and wheat, production still lagged behind prewar levels.[9]

One dimension of the economic program was this rapid recovery, particularly in heavy industry. Another dimension was the bringing under government control of an increasing share of output. Thus, the sizable state enterprise sector inherited from the Nationalists was consistently enlarged, although in the period of recovery this was only partly at the expense of private enterprise; between 1949 and 1952 the state-controlled share of industrial production went from 44 percent to 67 percent. By October 1952, all railways, 80 percent of heavy and 60 percent of light industry were state operated, as was 60 percent of domestic shipping. Also, the government controlled 90 percent of all loans and deposits through the People's Bank; state trading companies handled 90 percent of foreign trade, half of the wholesale trade, and about 30 percent of the retail trade. Of course, the area of effective government control was more extensive than these figures indicate.[10]

W. W. Rostow and his associates assert that these developments, along with the land reform program, constituted the outstanding economic achievements of the early regime, in that it was now able to mobilize and to allocate higher proportions of China's national income to investment and other purposes than ever before.[11]

One such area to which the regime could apply this new power effectively was the military, and this was particularly helpful during the costly Korean War. Another such important and urgent investment area was the improvement of domestic transportation. In 1950 and 1951 a high proportion of investment was made in railway construction. This produced results. Whereas in October 1949 less than half of the country's railways were in operation, by mid-1951 all lines were restored and used with greater intensity, and new construction was underway. This was a promising beginning, but decades later transportation remains a serious bottleneck in China's development program.

The new regime's concerted effort to deal with the severe fiscal and financial crisis was remarkably successful. By March 1950 the vicious inflationary spiral was broken and, after some fluctuations, price stability was gradually instituted by 1952.[12]

During these first months, the emphasis was on economic recovery. Revolutionary transformation was deliberately eschewed. Nevertheless, two important laws were enacted that in themselves brought about a genuine social revolution. These were the Marriage Law of May 1, 1950, and the Agrarian Reform Law of June 30, 1950.

Aside from the laws that established the new government in 1949, the Marriage Law was the first new law of the land. Mao's phrase "women hold up half the sky" expressed a genuine commitment on the part of many in the party leadership. For the first time in history, women in China were legally liberated. The new law struck a body blow at the very heart of the traditional male- and elder-dominated family system and its values, where women and children had had no rights of their own. An old Chinese saying "A wife married is like a pony bought; I'll ride her and whip her as I like," conveys an image of the lot of women.[13] The new law also was claimed to counter bourgeois ideas about women as well.[14] In fact, some urban families had been greatly influenced in recent years by modern liberal ideas regarding the role of women, but there had been no legal safeguard to protect either women or the young.

The vast majority of the population in the countryside still adhered rigidly to the traditional practices.

Implementation of the Marriage Law was not easy. A campaign was launched to publicize the new law, but it met with only very limited success, owing to considerable resistance, even on the part of many cadres. Almost three years later, Deng Yingchao, the wife of Premier Zhou, acknowledged that arranged marriages still took place.[15] A new nationwide campaign was launched in March 1953, and this time special effort was given to teaching the cadres themselves about the "great meaning" of the campaign. Even this campaign produced disappointing results, but it made evident to the idealists of the Communist leadership just how great a problem this would be. Accordingly, the CCP decided to make the implementation of the Marriage Law a task that would require continuous effort over the long haul rather than seeking to enforce it overnight. Provisions were made throughout the judicial and administrative system and in the mass organizations to see that this would be carried out.[16] Years later it would be seen that results have been mixed, for as Kay Johnson has shown, the policies of the CCP, despite its intentions, have often reinforced traditional roles for women.[17]

With the promulgation of the Agrarian Reform Law in late June 1950, the land reform program that had been suspended in 1948 was finally resumed. About one-third of the country's rural population had already undergone land reform during 1947–1948. The Agrarian Reform Law was a relatively moderate instrument. Except for bad elements among the landlords, even the latter were to retain sufficient land to work themselves. Rich peasants were not a target of the campaign. They had not been targeted by the 1947 law either, but many were in fact victimized during the terror of leftist excesses. The CCP was serious about protecting the rich peasants because they were obviously very productive, and because any threat to them would negatively affect the morale of the much larger group of middle peasants, who were also highly productive. Actually, even the hiring of labor and the renting of some land by certain privileged groups were allowed.[18]

Significantly, the program did not aim to distribute land equally as was attempted under the 1947 law. Again, the CCP had learned its lesson, and now sought only to bring about an "equitable and rational" distribution. But the provisions implementing this objective actually reinforced some of the inequalities of the old system. John Wong has pointed out that the "only part of the old pattern of ownership now missing was the concentration of land in the hands of the landlords."[19]

The land reform program was conducted on the basis of a decentralized administration. Land Reform Committees were established at each level of government, from the regional to the *xian*, to oversee the program; no coordinating mechanism existed at the central level in Beijing.

People's tribunals were established at the *xian* level, governed by regulations sent down from Beijing. The tribunals presided over the *gongshen*, or mass trials, which were organized conjointly by land reform and judiciary cadres. The *gongshen* were staged in the villages before huge gatherings of local people. The accused would stand before the tribunal as an object of *douzheng*, or struggle, while cadres and those who would cooperate fanned the emotions of the crowd. Obviously, the *gongshen* was not intended to be a fair trial; for anyone subject to it was already considered guilty. Its purpose was to achieve one of the basic objectives of the land reform program, that is, to mobilize and to educate the peasants in class struggle. It also implicated the peasants in the elimination of the old power structure.[20]

Land reform below the *xian* level was run by the peasant associations, membership in which was open to agricultural laborers, poor peasants, middle peasants, rural handicraftsmen, and impoverished rural intellectuals. Landlords and rich peasants were excluded. Additionally, the *minbing*, or people's militia, were formed at this time. These became the rural law enforcement officers, and a spearhead for social revolution as well. During land reform the *minbing* acted as a special land reform police organization. The PLA itself refrained from participating in land reform.

Ganbu, comprising land reform teams, played a key role in making the movement work, for they had to promote and agitate as well as organize and supervise the movement in their jurisdictions. On top of this, they had to try to give credence to the official position that land reform was a spontaneous peasant movement. Unfortunately, well-trained and highly motivated *ganbu* were in short supply. There were three kinds of *ganbu* basically: the full-time professional organization leaders; the intellectuals who came out from the cities temporarily; and, most important, the peasant activists. The latter eventually became party members, and most remained in the villages as the new power elite.

Land reform began with the arrival in a *xiang* of a work team, which acquainted itself with the local situation. The team then converted a few chosen poor peasants, who were deliberately made to feel discontented and resentful against the old tenure system and those who had enjoyed the fruits of it. Once this handful of poor peasants became committed to change, they were considered to have undergone *fanshen* (literally to have been turned over),[21] and they began to convert their friends.

The second stage was exceedingly important, for it brought about the differentiation of rural classes. The entire process of confiscation and reallocation rested on the classification of the rural inhabitants. However, this proved to be an extremely complicated matter, fraught with many subjective considerations, so that many inequities and injustices resulted. To be wrongly classified a landlord rather than a rich peasant was sometimes the difference between life and death, or it could result in qualitatively different treatment for one's family for decades. Only in 1979 were the "rich peasant" and "landlord" designations, which had been assigned to children as their class origin, abolished.[22]

The land reform program resumed in mid-1950 was conducted more painstakingly than it had been in the north and northwest during the civil war. Even so, the entire program, for most parts of the country, took only two years to complete rather than the three that had been projected. This quick success was due to the organizational skill of the Communists and to external circumstances.

The Korean War provided great stimulation to accelerate and to complete the program; there being a fear that the landlords would cooperate in a Nationalist attack on the mainland. As China became involved in the Korean War, the land reform program assumed a harsher tone.[23]

A major regional exception to this general success was the Central-South Region, particularly Guangdong and Guangxi provinces, which did not complete land reform until the spring of 1953. The southernmost part of this region lacked the necessary preconditions for launching the campaign in the first place. Also there was an insufficient number of *ganbu* to deal with a population that was especially reluctant to cooperate fully, and this was made more difficult because of conflict between local *ganbu* and those sent in from the north.[24] The present general secretary, Zhao Ziyang, directed the program in Guangdong. This experience made it clear, as John Wong says, that "contrary to the official claim, land reform in Guangdong, and likely in other provinces as well, was not a self-actuated and self-generating peasant movement but was kept going only by strong political pressure and organizational effort by the authorities."[25]

In any case, the CCP achieved its purpose in the land reform program. It succeeded in parceling out the land, essentially taking from the landlords and giving to the poor peasants. This was no long-term solution for agriculture because individual family farms were on the average considered too small to be farmed efficiently with modern mechanization. Furthermore, the party believed there was danger that the relative equilibrium brought about would disintegrate, as the rich became richer and the poor, poorer once again. Ironically, thirty some years later, after years of collectivization experimentation, the party would find itself confronted with a strikingly similar situation, albeit the land would no longer be privately owned.

But the real achievement in 1952 and 1953 as far as the CCP was concerned was in the destruction of the power of the former local power elite. The landlord class and its monopoly of power was broken. In its stead a new local power structure comprised of poor and lower-middle peasants—who owed what they had gained to the CCP and its new regime—became established.

The Korean War, which spanned these critical years of 1950 to 1953, made a severe impact on domestic developments in China. At a time when the new regime was concentrating on economic recovery, the war was a costly distraction that upset plans for a smooth military demobilization and siphoned off precious human and material resources that were urgently needed in the civilian sector. While some demobilization did in fact continue during the war itself, it was still necessary to enlist new personnel. A recruitment drive in December 1950 took 250,000 of the country's best students and skilled workers into the PLA. A similar drive in June 1951 recruited another 270,000 students. This disrupted both the conduct and the completion of education, a situation that was then given attention and corrected during the following academic year. Similarly, as many as 7 to 8 percent of the doctors in China—where the ratio of doctors to the population was only one to every 10,000 people— served in Korea by the middle of 1951; and by the end of the war in 1953 twice that number had done so. Transportation was an endemic problem; yet by the end of the war more than 4,000 railwaymen from Shanghai alone had served in Korea.[26] Worst of all, China suffered between 700,000 to 900,000 casualties (out of which perhaps as many as 300,000 died).

But the war also provided an opportunity for the CCP that it was quick to seize: the foreign war was so close to China's border and the growing threat from Taiwan and along the coast was so obvious that it was enabled to capitalize on the inflamed sense of patriotism to mobilize people more quickly and effectively and to step up the timetable for social and economic change. However, the anxiety over security resulted in serious counterproductive manifestations as well. Excesses were committed and an atmosphere of apprehension and terror was induced among many whom the New Democratic policies had been designed to assure.

All of the mass movements of the New Democracy period, except land reform, were launched after China's intervention in Korea. As we have seen, the implementation of land reform was itself affected; its pace was accelerated and it lost some of its moderate luster. Over the next year or so, six nationwide campaigns burst upon the scene. Their objective was to win the commitment of everyone to the regime's policies. These policies were continued economic recovery, political consolidation, continued ground-laying for future (now near future) basic social and economic changes, and fighting the Korean War and all elements that might threaten the regime's security because of the war.

The first three of these massive campaigns were grouped together, the first two beginning in November 1950, and the third in February 1951; all were concerned at least in part with the war and its domestic ramifications. These were the Volunteer campaign, the Resist-America and Aid-Korea campaign—which led to the ancillary Patriotic Pact campaign and the Donation for the Purchase of Planes and Heavy Artillery campaign—and finally the fearful Suppression of Counterrevolutionaries campaign.[27] The other three major campaigns began later in 1951: the *san-fan* (Three-Antis) campaign, which started in September 1951 and ended in late April 1952; the Increase Production and Practice Economy campaign; and the *wu-fan* (Five-Antis) campaign. These last two began in October 1951 and ended in June 1952.

The Volunteer campaign called for volunteers to fight in Korea as members of the Chinese People's Volunteers. Pressures of different kinds were applied so that quotas were filled. The campaign was related to land reform insofar as the Agrarian Reform Law of 1950 provided special privileges for soldiers and their families. They could even be exempted from the hated "landlord" classification, and unless they owned an excessive amount of land, it was not confiscated.

The Suppression of Counterrevolutionaries campaign was brutal. Begun in February 1951, the campaign was basically completed by midyear. It took more than 100,000 lives. But its psychological ramifications were untold. The public was encouraged to participate in the witch hunt. Youngsters who denounced their own parents were praised. Party members who tried to protect targeted family members were themselves punished. While undoubtedly some genuine spies or bad elements were arrested, the word quickly spread that many people were being taken arbitrarily and then subjected to frightening mass trials before being executed. Many others were sentenced to forced labor or imprisonment.

The *san-fan* and *wu-fan* campaigns were far less bloody but still fearfully sobering to many Chinese. The former was addressed to *ganbu* and government employees. The object was a legitimate one—to combat corruption, waste, and bureaucratism. The party leaders were aware that many new recruits to government service needed to be made aware of such dangers that would threaten to alienate the party from the people; moreover, many officials held over from the former regime were in need of such consciousness-raising and warning, as were older party members who had begun enjoying the spoils of victory. This campaign did make *ganbu* more careful, for a time.[28]

The *wu-fan* campaign was aimed against bribes, fraud, tax evasion, theft of state property, and leakage of state economic secrets in the business community. The campaign consciously employed terror to intimidate industrialists and businessmen, large numbers of whom were secretly denounced, compelled to endure public accusation meetings and then condemned, heavily fined, or saw properties confiscated. Hundreds were driven to suicide. The campaign helped finance the Korean War and fatten state coffers. It prepared the bourgeoisie for further trials they would undergo.

Intellectuals constituted a scarce national resource, but, being petty bourgeoisie, they had to be brought under control and eventually either transformed or eliminated from influential positions. A National Writers and Artists Federation had already been founded in July 1949 with Guo Moro as chairman and Mao Dun and Zhou Yang as vice chairmen. But by late 1951 intellectuals, too, came in for greater attention, especially writers, academic humanists, and social scientists. The party publicized certain cultural or literary affairs in order to communicate its concerns. Prominent among these were the Wu Xun, Liang Shuming, and Hu Shi campaigns.

A film about a Qing dynasty beggar named Wu Xun who became an exemplar because he later contributed to schools for poor boys appeared in late 1950, to the acclaim of party critics. However, by mid-1951 these critics were severely rebuked by Mao for not having an adequate grasp of Marxism. Mao's identity in this affair was not revealed until 1972, when Mao's wife, Jiang Qing, told American scholar Roxane Witke that she had played the lead role in instigating this campaign in order to sharpen Marxist thinking.[29] Guo Moro made a public self-criticism over this affair.

Liang Shuming, a well-known traditional scholar and rural reconstruction leader, was instructed to write a self-criticism for failing to use Marxism in his most recent book and was publicly criticized by Mao himself. Liang was again heavily criticized in 1955 and his reputation within China did suffer as a result. Mao was finally satisfied with a public confession that Liang made in February 1956.[30] Liang was considered the "feudal counterpart" of another famous scholar, Hu Shi, the student of John Dewey and leader of the vernacular language movement decades earlier, who was subjected to similar campaigns *in absentia.* Hu had to suffer the indignity of having his own son denounce him.[31]

These campaigns were overshadowed by the Thought Reform campaign, which was aimed initially at professors in late 1951 and subsequently at other teachers in the educational system. The purpose of this campaign was to begin the remolding of education and intellectual discourse along acceptable Marxist-Leninist lines.[32]

These campaigns appeared to be successful in the short run. They traumatized many individuals and generally sensitized China's urban elite to the party's outlook. They began the process, along with the Marriage Law and land reform, of transforming the way people thought and expressed themselves in public. But in the longer run, such ideological forced feeding created resentment and resistance. Many intellectuals, along with other citizens, became polished practitioners in the art of dissembling. But this behavior only exacerbated the differences between many intellectuals and the party, especially its leader who had long been distrustful of China's intellectual elite.

The CCP and China came to be profoundly influenced by the CPSU and the Soviet Union during these crucial formative years of the early 1950s. This course was already set by the new Chinese leaders' Marxist-Leninist orientation. It was strengthened by the CCP's "Lean to One Side" policy, initially articulated by Mao in mid-1949 and reaffirmed by Mao's visit to Moscow for more than nine weeks beginning on December 16, 1949. Although Mao was not pleased by the difficulty of negotiations with Stalin, nor with the concessions that he had to make, the resulting Sino-Soviet Treaty of Friendship, Alliance and Mutual Assistance on February 14, 1950, facilitated cooperation between the two parties and nations. The treaty, which Mao called "eternal and indestructible,"[33] provided China assurance of Soviet support should Japan or any state cooperating with Japan attack China. The Soviets also agreed to extend credits to China, amounting to $300 million over five years. But the Chinese had to agree to a continuation of Soviet presence in Dalian (Dairen) and Port Arthur. The Chinese also signed a 30-year agreement establishing two Sino-Soviet joint stock companies to exploit oil and mineral resources in Xinjiang. Nevertheless, the alliance with the Soviet Union was popular in China. The Soviets provided air force divisions that spring, which soon ended Nationalist air raids on Shanghai and other places.[34] And whatever reservations the Chinese still had were removed by the Korean War. Some Chinese believed that the alliance deterred a U.S. assault on China.[35] No one at the time expected that China would subsequently have to repay with interest the assistance provided by the Soviets in the fighting of that war.

The United States's nonrecognition of the PRC and the relative isolation of the latter from the Western world, which the United States promoted, made the Chinese all the more vulnerable and receptive to their Soviet mentors, despite the enormous differences that divided the Chinese and Russian peoples. Some ten to twenty thousand Soviet advisers and another 1,500 East European experts labored in China during the 1950s.[36] In the meanwhile, more than 80,000 Chinese studied in various programs in the Soviet Union in the same decade. In addition, some 700 Soviet professors and other lecturers taught in China, while some 7,500 Chinese pursued higher studies in the Soviet Union.[37] These individuals collectively brought about what was regarded at that time as "the most comprehensive technology transfer in modern industrial history,"[38] even though the amount of aid was much less generous than what the United States was providing to various countries.[39] Their efforts sovietized all Chinese institutions, most particularly imparting a distinctive centralization of authority throughout government and society, just as Chinese architecture pervasively and indelibly took on Stalinist features. Soviet influence left its stamp on the Chinese military establishment. It would do so on the economic development program, beginning with the First Five-Year Plan, which began without fanfare in 1953, and on the 1954 state constitution and the consequent restructuring of the Chinese government.

As Soviet influence mounted, a serious but limited internal party power struggle, not entirely unrelated to the Soviets, came to a head. Gao Gang, a Politburo member and chairman of the State Planning Commission with a strong power base in Manchuria, and Rao Shushi, head of the party's Organization Department and influential in East China, may have cooperated with each other, even though they were quite dissimilar personalities. That they formed a conspiracy was staunchly denied by Rao to the end. They did oppose Mao's intention to accelerate the collectivization of agriculture and disputed regional investment allocation decisions. In addition, they allegedly aspired to higher positions already occupied either by Mao himself or by Mao's supporters. Liu Shaoqi felt particularly threatened. Furthermore, Gao and his northeast base afforded extraordinary influences from and connections with Soviet officialdom. Party historian Liao Gailong says that Stalin regarded Gao as the "Chang Cuolin of contemporary China, a local warlord." "These are not empty words," Liao continues, for Gao "had indeed made secret reports on the situation of China to the Soviet Communist Party."[40]

The party split first became evident at the National Conference on Financial and Economic Work convened by the Central Committee and held from June 13 to August 11, 1953.[41] But moves against Gao and Rao did not begin until after they were transferred to new posts in Beijing and thus removed from their respective constituencies in Manchuria and Shanghai.[42] Liu Shaoqi led the attack on the pair at the Fourth Enlarged Plenum of the Seventh Central Committee, February 6 to 10, 1954, which Mao, who was said to be "on vacation," did not attend. The Fourth Plenum decided on a party national delegates conference to discuss the First Five-Year Plan, which was not held until March 1955. When it was held, Deng Xiaoping gave a report on the "Gao Gang–Rao Shushi Anti-Party Alliance." Gao was accused of setting up an independent kingdom; Rao, of moderatism and personal ambition. Both were expelled from the party. Rao was imprisoned. Gao committed suicide "as an extreme expression," it was said, "of his betrayal of the party."[43] The March 1955 conference also passed a resolution establishing party control committees at the local, county, and provincial levels to pursue the purge and to forestall future factional activities.

This internal threat, readily dealt with, was not a major distraction. The affair's Soviet dimension was tactically ignored. The party, in the meanwhile, continued to foster major decisions in government and the economy. The First National People's Congress (NPC) met from September 15 to 28, 1954. It adopted the first state constitution on September 20. This document consisted of a preamble and 106 articles, and held China to be a people's democratic dictatorship in transition to socialism. Mao estimated that it would take about fifteen years just to lay the foundations for socialism, and "50 years for China to actually become a great socialist country."[44] The NPC, elected for four years, became the supreme vehicle of formal state power, represented by a standing committee between its sessions. Mao, as state chairman (in addition to being party chairman), now presided over a more centralized machinery of government, including a National Defense Council. He also commanded the military, appointed and dismissed the premier of the new State Council (the central government organization), and represented the country in important foreign affairs. He also now convened and chaired the Supreme State Conference, a consultative body with ex-officio members and others appointed by Mao himself. Mao employed this useful body about twenty times over the years ahead.

The Soviet influence in this constitution with the strong emphasis on centralized control, while not the only influence, is evident. The regional governments were abolished, as were, for a number of years, the regional party bureaus. These administrative units either had fulfilled their purposes or were casualties of the Gao-Rao purge.

Publicity was finally given the First Five-Year Plan at the Second Session of the First NPC in July 1955, after having been reviewed by the National Party Conference in March. In a speech, Li Fuzhun, the chairman of the State Planning Commission, spelled out the economic development program, which stressed mining and heavy industry. Soviet aid was sufficiently forthcoming to make this possible. Within only two years, rather impressive results were to be registered by this consciously lopsided Stalinist development strategy. Unfortunately for Chinese workers and consumers, there would be few perceptible benefits for them inasmuch as light industry and agriculture were given little attention. On the contrary, peasants were expected to work even harder to supply industry with raw materials, repay Soviet loans, and feed a population increasing by more than 10 million a year. Under these circumstances, Soviet-style planners sought to avoid any undue agitation among peasants that might jeopardize agricultural production. Hence, Li Fuzhun informed the NPC that farm cooperativization would have to proceed slowly. In fact, Deng Zuhui had already proposed at a Central Committee rural work conference in May 1955 that 200,000 early agricultural cooperatives be retrenched and dissolved. That there was a major disagreement within the party's leadership on this issue became known only days later.

On July 31, 1955, Mao spoke to a conference of secretaries of provincial, municipal, and district party committees, strongly demanding faster, not slower collectivization, and angrily castigating those who were "tottering along like a woman with bound feet."[45] Mao believed the risk to the economic development plan was worth taking because he perceived an adverse momentum building. "The spontaneous forces of capitalism have been steadily growing in the countryside in recent years," he noted, with new rich peasants increasing in numbers while many poor peasants still lived in poverty.[46] Mao sent the cadres back to their local posts with his instructions to accelerate rather than retard collectivization.

The timetable was abruptly changed. Mutual aid teams had been under experimentation for four years already and had spread across the country. Also already in place were a modest number of lower agricultural producers cooperatives (APCs). Each of these comprised from twenty to forty households, in which the income of members derived from payment for both labor and the use of property that had been "contributed" to the cooperative. The APC constituted a particularly significant step in the collectivization process because it fundamentally altered the organization of farming, with farming decisions now taken from the family household and placed in the hands of a newly created level above the household. And now, following Mao's instructions in July 1955, there was a sudden mushrooming of lower APCs throughout China.

The next step also came quickly. The higher APCs, comprising one to three hundred households, were formed by combining numbers of lower APCs. At this stage, payment for contributed property ceased, although use of contributed animals was still compensated. Title of land passed from the family to the collective. The ostensible advantages of these larger units of organization were that they would use labor and resources more efficiently, increase savings and investment potential, and improve the delivery of social services. Among the initial disadvantages was the inexperience of local *ganbu* in administering such a new complex organization, particularly since so many were still illiterate. There was also the very real possibility that the incentive to work would diminish.

In early 1955, only about 14 percent of the rural population was organized into lower APCs. By the end of the year this figure had reached 60 percent, and by early 1956 virtually all peasants had joined a lower APC. Furthermore, by the end of 1956 almost 90 percent of the lower APCs had amalgamated into higher APCs, so that the amazing "high tide of cooperativization" was almost entirely completed by mid-1957. It was remarkable that such a fundamental change in local decision-making and social organization took place so swiftly throughout such a large country and rural population without having caused more disruption than it did. Not only was there little disruption but agricultural production continued to increase. That the Chinese eschewed the harsh tactics that had been employed during Stalin's collectivization program in the early 1930s undoubtedly made a great deal of difference in the Chinese experience. It also helped that collectivization in China generally conformed to the contours of the natural village.[47] But this early apparent success misled the Chinese into making the serious mistake only a year later of once again forcing the pace of change in the countryside, and the real difficulties regarding productivity under collectivization would not be fully appreciated for some time to come.

The Sixth Enlarged Plenum of the Seventh Central Committee met October 4 to 11, 1955, in Beijing, with 38 full and 25 alternate members of the Central Committee in attendance, along with 325 other nonvoting *ganbu* from throughout the geographical and hierarchical reach of the party organization. Agricultural cooperativization was, of course, the main agenda topic, and the plenum agreed to its acceleration. Liu Shaoqi purportedly criticized himself for going slowly with APCs, while Deng Zuhui and the party's Rural Work Department were criticized for "rightist empiricism."[48] Deng Xiaoping explained the Politburo's decision to convene the Eighth Party Congress in the following year.

The apparent success of the "socialist upsurge" underway in the countryside by the end of 1955 led the party to move up the timetable of socialization in the cities as well. As Mao put it in December 1955, "we must try to accomplish the transformation of China's handicrafts and capitalist industry and commerce ahead of schedule in order to meet the needs of an expanding agriculture."[49] In fact, Chinese industrialists and businessmen had long expected this day. The CCP had inherited a substantial state sector in industry and commerce from the Nationalist government. Socialization under the party began with the outset of the First Five-Year Plan in 1953 as government extended control over all critical resources, prices, and distribution channels. Joint stock ownership of private firms began on a volunteer basis in 1954. Capitalists, who had already felt threatened in the *wu-fan* campaign of 1952, were subjected to both an intensive press campaign against them and another campaign against counterrevolutionaries in 1955. Thus, when the party held meetings with leading capitalists and others from October to December 1955, the audience submissively listened to plans for the accelerated socialist transformation of their enterprises. In December 1955, Mao projected a target date of 1957 for completion of the conversion to joint-stock format.

Suddenly, however, Peng Zhen in Beijing took the extraordinary step of converting all industry and commerce in this major municipality within the first ten days of January 1956, with handicrafts following suit by January 12. Mao was not pleased at this precipitate action, which appeared to be an insubordinate retaliatory gesture in response to his own hasty maneuver in agriculture. But Mao had little choice but to accept the fait accompli. Shanghai took up Beijing's challenge and by January 20 had similarly completed the transition. The fervor spread so quickly that by the end of January all the main industrial cities could report the task completed.[50] This rambunctious move precluded a more orderly changeover and as a result there were many problems, including dislocations in supply, production, and marketing. However, the transition was accomplished and did not appear to affect the booming First Five-Year Plan, which was at its zenith. The party did appear to treat cooperating capitalists with some humanity for a time, allowing them to draw interest on their shares of the joint-stock companies and sometimes using their services.[51]

With China assuming a socialist form, Mao himself became anxious to move ahead on all fronts in order to liberate the productive forces that he believed to be the aim of socialist revolution. He criticized rightist conservatism among his comrades and called for "more exertion." Along with lower-level *ganbu* and without much input from economists, Mao drafted a very ambitious and unrealistic Twelve-Year Plan for Agriculture, comprising 40 points, which was adopted by the Politburo on January 23, 1956, and then by the Supreme State Conference two days later.[52] Liberal policies were favored toward rich peasants and landlords, even admitting them to membership in APCs. Similarly, an appeal was made to intellectuals, signaled by a major speech by Zhou Enlai in January 1956, seeking to enlist their talent and efforts in economic development.

But such aspirations to push ahead, particularly with the help of bourgeois intellectuals and without the concurrence of the party's Soviet-influenced economic planners, provided ample opportunity for Mao's detractors, who were increasingly concerned about his arbitrary style of leadership, to close ranks in opposition. They were greatly assisted in this by the astounding news that came from the Twentieth Congress of the CPSU, where on February 25, 1956, Premier Nikita Khrushchev had delivered his secret speech denigrating the late Joseph Stalin. This led to pointed discussions among ranking party leaders in China on the desirability of promoting collective leadership and avoiding a Chinese "cult of personality." However, the official Chinese response to the Khrushchev secret speech was an article in the *People's Daily* entitled "On the Historical Dictatorship of the Proletariat" on April 5, 1956, which noted that Stalin had made positive contributions as well.

Mao continued to promote his unfolding vision, with adjustments, in the face of a growing and determined opposition within the party. His speech of April 25, 1956, at an enlarged meeting of the Politburo on the "Ten Great Relationships" was a particularly important comprehensive analysis that boiled down the reports of 34 departments and many subsequent discussions on finance and economics held by the Politburo in the preceding several weeks.[53] The official unexpurgated version of this speech was not published by the party until as late as January 1977, more than twenty years later, when it was finally revealed that Mao had made a number of critical remarks about the Soviet Union at that early date.[54]

This was the beginning of a concern on the part of the CCP to avoid some of the Soviet Union's more obvious problems. The speech was also notable for the decision to restrain development of conventional military capabilities in favor of a limited nuclear capability. Mao also called for a new policy of "long-term coexistence and mutual supervision" between the CCP and the token noncommunist parties. Mao suggested a two-thirds cut in the size of the government and party bureaucracies, which, along with "supervision" by anyone outside the party, certainly created anxieties and helped consolidate opposition within the party. Undaunted, Mao urged "greater, faster, better and more economic results." But he already had had to make realistic concessions in agriculture.

Mao made it evident to everyone in the spring and summer of 1956 that if in 1954 he had been in poor health, as had been rumored, he was certainly robust now for he swam across the Chang Jiang three times. The message was that this was a party chairman who was physically able to stand behind his policies. On May 2, 1956, Mao delivered a secret speech to the Supreme State Conference calling for a policy toward intellectuals under the slogan "Let one hundred flowers bloom, let one hundred schools of thought contend."[55] This policy appeared to be advocated by propaganda chief Lu Dingi at a meeting of intellectuals on May 26. But, in fact, there remained considerable reluctance within the party to promote this policy. Also, opposition to Mao's economic policy manifested itself at a party meeting in Beidaihe in early June, an opposition that probably influenced Li Xiannian's budget report to the Third Session of the First NPC on June 15.[56]

The Eighth Congress of the CCP was held from September 15 to 27, 1956, with 1,026 delegates and 107 alternates. These participants represented a party that had grown ninefold, to 10,730,000 members, since the previous congress in 1945; with more than half of this increase having taken place in the entirely changed circumstances following the victory of 1949. Nevertheless, the social composition of the party remained roughly constant, with almost 70 percent of the members of peasant stock, only 14 percent workers, and 11.7 percent intellectuals.[57]

Obviously, there was a pressing need to align the party membership more closely to the main tasks that the party itself was addressing, principally the industrialization of the country. This was recognized implicitly in the policy of Mao and Zhou regarding intellectuals, and others such as Deng Xiaoping recognized the need for technological expertise. Thus, one might have expected a greater effort to have been made to take the steps necessary to see that the party transformed itself appropriately so that younger better-educated individuals would join the party and rise to leadership positions. Instead, priority was given to seniority, even by Deng Xiaoping, while Mao and Liu Shaoqi stressed Marxist training. This reconfirmed a process, already well underway, by means of which the party's leadership, like that of the CPSU, inexorably became older rather than transformed. Moreover, even though an impressive number of members (38 percent) had been recruited since 1954, the heaviest influx still came from the peasantry, despite the decision in 1950 to increase the percentage of workers.[58] The newly elected Central Committee was enlarged from 77 to 170 members and alternates, but not even one representative of the next younger generation was included. The new Politburo, elected at the First Plenum of the Eighth Central Committee on September 28, consisted of seventeen members and six alternates, and did constitute a rough balance among party, state, and military representatives. But in 1921 the average age of a Politburo member had been 29. In 1945 the figure was 49, and in 1956 it reached 60.[59]

The atmosphere at the congress was understandably jubilant. There were about 140 foreign delegates and observers from 56 foreign communist parties. The participants heard a total of 133 speeches, including 43 from the visitors. The party was conscious of the fact that it was presiding over a continuing series of nation-building and economic development successes, and it could declare at this time that the socialist system had been basically established in China. The party announced that the principal contradiction in China was no longer between the working class and the bourgeoisie but between the advanced socialist system and the backward productive forces of society.[60] Such was the sentiment of the majority of the party's leadership. But it was not universally shared.

The party chairman himself did not agree. This disagreement was not apparent to outsiders at the time. In the wake of the Gao-Rao purge, the theme of unity was being emphasized, and rhetoric regarding party democracy and the desirability of avoiding a personality cult was prominent. Hence, the fact that some of Mao's own policy preferences were getting short shrift was not immediately apparent. In fact, Mao himself was being overruled or ignored. The congress was dominated by Liu Shaoqi and party-apparatus cadres, including Deng Xiaoping, who now won the important reactivated post of general secretary, curtailing Mao's own effective control of the party Secretariat. This is not to imply that Mao's opposition was united. The situation was more complex. Leaders realigned depending upon the issue at hand. Liu, for example, tended to agree with Mao regarding aspects of economic policy, while Deng Xiaoping did not, but Deng did tend to agree with Mao on the question of mutual supervision among the parties, but Liu did not. An honorary chairmanship of the Central Committee was established, but Mao failed to accommodate any expectation that he would actually relinquish real power in order to take it up. The congress approved a new party constitution, which, in sharp contrast to the former statute with its effusive references to the "Thought of Mao Zedong," neglected to include even a single such reference.

Reforming the party, already on Mao's mind, was given even greater urgency by the crises in Poland and Hungary in the fall of 1956. The Second Plenum of the Eighth Central Committee met from November 10 to 15, 1956. It heard from Liu Shaoqi, who had just returned from Moscow, on these developments. The plenum's communiqué supported the Soviet suppression of the Hungarian Uprising. But Mao was becoming increasingly skeptical and critical of Soviet behavior. He called for a rectification campaign in his closing speech, although this was not reiterated in the plenum's communiqué.

The Chinese were concerned primarily about preventing Soviet mistakes from producing more serious results, rather than with criticizing the perpetrators. On December 29, 1956, the *People's Daily* article "More on the historical experience of the proletarian dictatorship," ostensibly attacking Yugoslav President Joseph Tito, developed the idea that contradictions could exist within a communist state and these could be exacerbated by a leader if not properly handled. Through neglect, in other words, they now could change from being nonantagonistic to antagonistic contradictions. The problem was not a systemic one, but of certain links within the system. The article also introduced, but did not emphasize, the notion of revisionism, that is, the fostering of a trend against Marxism-Leninism.[61] The emphasis was still on dogmatism, which remained Mao's primary concern at home.

In mid-January 1957 the magazine *Chinese Youth* revealed that the Central Committee had recently decided that a rectification campaign would be held beginning in 1958, so the decision may in fact have been made by the Politburo following the Second Plenum.[62]

On February 27, 1957, Mao delivered another of his most memorable speeches, again to the Supreme State Conference, entitled "On the Correct Handling of Contradictions Among the People."[63] Mao distinguished between two kinds of contradiction that continued to exist even under socialism. For the most part these were "nonantagonistic" differences among the people, as opposed to "antagonistic" ones between the people and the enemy. Prior to liberation, the latter had dominated. Mao went on to make the candid concession, once again, that contradictions can still exist between the government and the people, between the leaders and the led. As a remedy for such contradictions, Mao again proposed the Hundred Flowers policy. The purpose was to enable China to avoid the unfortunate upheavals that had beset Poland and Hungary. Mao believed that ideological struggle was necessary, but that it had to be conducted correctly and argued that "Marxism as a scientific truth . . . fears no criticism." Mao reiterated these arguments in another secret speech on March 12, 1957, to more than 500 leading cadres and others at a national conference on party propaganda work.[64]

These talks were very heartening to many Chinese intellectuals. Strongly supportive of such liberalization was Zhou Enlai, who had recently visited Eastern Europe, the Soviet Union, and Asian countries. Deng Xiaoping was also supportive. But Peng Zhen, who also had just returned from a visit to Eastern Europe and the Soviet Union, had an entirely different view of the problem and joined the majority of party leaders who remained opposed. Peng feared that solicited criticisms would be exploited by the imperialists.[65]

The directive for the rectification campaign was dated April 27, 1957, while the reluctant Liu Shaoqi and Peng Zhen were both out of town, but was not issued until their return on the 30th, by which time it was probably another fait accompli for Mao.[66] The numerous cadres who had resisted the idea of the campaign became further disgruntled by the way it had actually been brought about. In any case, Mao's directives and recent speeches became the ideological guidelines for the campaign, and bureaucratism, Mao's concern, rather than Liu's subjectivism, the principal target. The campaign utilized small meetings, rather than large struggle sessions, and was to be conducted as a "gentle breeze and mild rain." An important element of the campaign was its enjoining of cadres to participate once again in physical labor. And, in accord with Mao's insistence, nonparty criticism was invited.

What followed for the next five weeks, from May 1 to June 7, 1957, was a stunning surprise to the party, which had been congratulating itself, and perhaps especially for Mao, who clearly had not anticipated the virulence with which the criticism would be voiced. Among the issues addressed were injustices that had been suffered during the counterrevolutionary campaigns; the role of the party in educational institutions, including its attitude toward nonparty teachers and students and courses; and the role of the party generally in society and whether it was actually raising living standards. Some of the latter criticism eventually became threatening in tone and actually got out of hand, especially as viewed by less tolerant party members.

Ironically, the criticism came to be universally shared and perhaps made even more telling because much of it was publicized by the party-controlled press. Mao's party critics, of course, could point to the rising tide of criticism and to its increasingly immoderate tone. For his part, Mao was in a dilemma. In this difficult situation, he began to consider that the danger of revisionism within the party was becoming a more serious one. But he was constrained from attacking revisionism straight-away because he still had hopes of winning over intellectuals who would otherwise also be attacked again. However, in the end, Mao basically was compelled to give up on the bourgeois intellectuals. On June 19, his secret contradictions speech of February 27 was finally published, but with revisions, including a list of six criteria that would henceforth guide criticism. The text made important concessions as well, and received favorable publicity abroad. But in China, Mao's position had worsened. He suffered, in effect, from a double credibility gap by having to appear to concede that party critics had been right, and by having drawn out the nonparty critics, only to see them retaliated against in an anti-rightist campaign. It would be a campaign that would cause great hardship among many thousands of China's intellectuals and their families for many years to come.

Mao's party critics provoked him by rubbing in their triumph of the summer of 1957. The party leader even had to endure innuendoes that his own policies were rightist as intellectuals came to be condemned for advocating positions he himself held. For the first time, as Roderick MacFarquhar has shown, a *People's Daily* editorial of July 28, 1957, reflected Mao's growing conviction that rightists also existed among party members themselves.[67] This seriously threatening split within the party was set aside for the time being by a compromise reached at the Third Plenum of the Eighth Central Committee, which met from September 20 to October 9, 1957. Deng Xiaoping delivered the report on the rectification campaign. Apparently, Liu and Peng accepted that party cadres had erred, while Mao finally abandoned the intellectuals as the essential element in the national economic development program.

It was a crisis in agriculture that compelled the party to make this compromise and to close ranks. Food grain production was increasing by only 1.3 percent in 1957, which was only just over half the rate of the population increase. The effect of this was more clearly seen in the cities, where in the period between 1952 and 1957 the population had grown by almost 30 percent, while the rural population grew by 9 percent.[68] Party leaders were not clear about what was going wrong, but in the fall of 1957 they could feel the effects.

· 8 ·

. Radical Redirection .

It is difficult to comprehend the magnitude of the disaster into which the party now steered itself and, with it, the Chinese people. There is a tendency almost three decades later to lose sight of the enormous suffering caused by the Great Leap Forward of the late 1950s, partly because of the calamity of the Cultural Revolution of the 1960s, the unfortunate consequences of which are still quite evident and are still consciously being recalled in order to justify some of the reforms of recent years. The Great Leap Forward was, in fact, much harsher for the common people, particularly the peasantry, with as many as 16 to 30 million people perishing in what was one of the worst famines in history.[1] This compares with perhaps a million victims in the subsequent tumultuous Cultural Revolution, which, without taking from its destructive impact on China, was essentially an urban phenomenon affecting primarily the party itself, although its victims and destruction extended well beyond party ranks.[2]

How did such a tragedy come to pass? To begin with, the economic situation was already very bad by 1957. This was the result of policies that had appeared successful for a time, but were actually producing widespread dissatisfaction, apathy, and deteriorating living conditions among the populace, and intensifying political divisiveness within the party leadership.[3] The party's response to the economic dilemma and distress in 1957 was not necessarily an irrational one conceptually.[4] It attempted to expand agricultural output by relying on mostly traditional methods—mobilizing the peasantry, emphasizing water conservancy projects, and introducing small-scale rural industries that made use of dual technology as available. In the meanwhile, it hoped to maintain the momentum in heavy industry as well. This did not begin as a comprehensive integrated strategy in late 1957. There was only a growing awareness that something had to be done to achieve an economic breakthrough to bring about self-sustained growth. There is little in the prior record to suggest that the leadership would become so adventuristic or so foolish once unanticipated setbacks occurred, and especially when the facts became apparent. Mao himself had perhaps been inconsistent on economic policies and had impatiently pushed for faster results in the past, but one would not have expected him, on this basis, to become as doggedly single-minded as he did.

The CCP sought to avoid some of the mistakes the Soviets had so prominently made over the years as it fashioned the new uncertain strategy. It is ironical, therefore, that in all probability Mao got the notion for a "great leap" from the attempted reforms of Premier Khrushchev, which Mao learned about during his visit to Moscow in November 1957, on the occasion of the 40th anniversary of the Bolshevik Revolution.[5] Mao was obviously impressed by Khrushchev's economic boldness and by the celebration itself, held, as it was, in the wake of the launchings of the first Soviet ICBM in August and the first two sputniks in October and early November. Mao was moved to tell international party comrades that China would overtake Britain economically in only fifteen years. And he exclaimed to Chinese students at Moscow State University that the east wind now prevailed over the west wind, a neatly turned phrase but hardly realistic. Mao was in a militant mood toward the West, partly in response to his perception of heightened U.S. military pressure (an agreement had been reached in May to place Matador missiles, capable of striking deep into China, on Taiwan). Mao was sobered somewhat by Khrushchev's insistence on the desirability of peaceful coexistence, and he must have become aware that the Soviet need to divert more funds to Eastern Europe would mean less for China. But Mao was certainly mollified by the secret agreement that had just been concluded on October 15, whereby the Soviets undertook to assist China's nuclear program, an agreement that was not publicly revealed until six years later. Mao returned home with mixed thoughts, but nonetheless excitedly and with a renewed determination that China meet the enormous challenges at hand boldly and self-reliantly.

At the beginning of 1958, Mao made an extended tour of the country, visiting basic-level units and getting ideas for the forthcoming all-out effort. The party also held a series of conferences in different cities in which the specifics of a new approach evolved. In January, at Hangzhou (from about the 2d to about the 5th) and at Nanning (the 8th to about the 22d) work conferences discussed what was to emerge as a document known as the Sixty Work Methods, constituting a very broad range of issues. At Hangzhou, Mao vigorously promoted a campaign against the four pests (rats, sparrows, flies, and mosquitoes). At Nanning, he berated upper-level bureaucrat specialists, especially conservative officials at the Ministry of Finance, for producing documents that were too technical for the Politburo.[6] Mao spoke at a Supreme State Conference, held January 28–30, and called for a continuation for six months of the party's rectification campaign, which was also to be continued less severely among the democratic parties. He also asked that the *xia-fang* program, in which cadres from the central organs were sent periodically for productive labor, be regularized. Completion of the Twelve-Year Plan for Agriculture was to be hastened.

A work conference at Chengdu, from February 28 to about March 22, heard three speeches from Mao, and took time out for rural inspection tours. The notion of simultaneous development of both industry and agriculture was promoted at Chengdu. So was the acceleration of the pace of administrative decentralization, a move that would considerably strengthen the provinces, especially the provincial-level party committees, at the expense of bloated central government ministries. The State Council soon afterwards placed agricultural machinery under the administration of the agricultural producers cooperatives, decentralizing even further this responsibility—as well as assigning the task of financing such mechanization to the local level.

These work conferences were a major source for the reports subsequently approved by the Fourth Plenum of the Eighth Central Committee, which met on May 3 in preparation for the Second Session of the Eighth Party Congress, which immediately followed.

This important Second Session, held from May 5 to 23, 1958, heard the comments of 117 participants, most of whom undoubtedly reflected the growing sentiment to act boldly. As a consequence, the congress reversed itself from the orientation of its 1956 session, and now formally approved the strategy of a Great Leap Forward. Liu Shaoqi sounded much more the way he did in 1945 rather than in his 1956 public support for Mao's ideas. There did remain, however, important differences between Mao and Liu. For example, while Liu outspokenly supported the notion of a mass mobilization economic effort at this juncture, he believed that the party's role was essential in organizing and directing such mass energy. Mao would not have disagreed, had he been queried, on the primacy of party leadership. But, as Roderick MacFarquhar has suggested, Mao probably "envisaged the great leap as a voluntarist explosion of energy more than a supreme example of mass mobilization."[7] In any case, Mao did not mention the party's leadership in any of the five speeches he made to the congress.

The congress also approved the continuing rectification campaign and approved in principle the Twelve-Year Agricultural Plan. Finally, it endorsed the results of the Moscow conference of the previous November. Mao's congress speech of May 17 noted the international situation wherein a united socialist camp faced the divided imperialists, a condition he believed should be exploited. As for the danger of a nuclear confrontation, Mao optimistically held that even if only a third of the world's population survived "it is not a bad thing," inasmuch as plans could be developed under such circumstances for the total elimination of capitalism.[8]

The Fifth Plenum of the Eighth Central Committee was held on May 25, immediately following the congress. The plenum elected Lin Biao, who had apparently recovered only recently from a lengthy illness, as an additional party vice chairman and, as such, a member of the Politburo's Standing Committee. Lin's elevation was a calculated tactical move by Mao to regain greater influence over the PLA. Also elected to the Politburo were Ke Qingshi, Li Qingchuan, and Tan Zhenlin, indicative of the greater strength of the provincial-level party committees as represented by Ke and Li, and of more overlap with the Secretariat, of which Tan had been a member.

Overall, the party had gained considerable power vis-à-vis the government as a result of decisions made in May 1958. It became much more intrusive into the affairs of government than had heretofore been the case, although the party's assumption of a central role in policy implementation really dates from the period of agricultural collectivization.[9] The journal Hongqi (Red Flag), under the editorship initially of Chen Boda, was also founded at the Fifth Plenum, and it soon became very influential. On the same day these decisions were made, Mao led a group of senior party officials to work on the Ming Tombs Reservoir, signifying the determination of cadres to resume a Yan'an-style acceptance of hardship and physical labor in the all-out mobilization of China that was about to begin.

Mao did not encounter serious opposition in these meetings. The prevailing climate of opinion seemed to follow Mao's belief that something extraordinary had to be done. It is also likely that both the severe anti-rightist campaign of 1957 and the extended, continuing rectification campaign silenced many who might otherwise have spoken up. This reticence was reinforced in the months ahead by an intensifying militarized atmosphere.

A lengthy, enlarged meeting of the Military Affairs Committee was held between May 27 and July 22, 1958, with over 1,000 senior officers in attendance. The meeting discussed how the PLA might modernize and still maintain its Yan'an traditions. Defense Minister Peng Dehuai, an avid modernizer and promoter of closer cooperation with the Soviet Union, had sought to reduce the role of the political commissar and the importance of the party committee, in the interest of military efficiency. But the meeting saw strong resistance to this trend and a reassertion of the need to study Mao's military writings, which some had come to consider obsolete.[10] Mao and his supporters similarly wished to renew the tradition of close officer-enlisted relationships marked by appropriate egalitarian practices. Only two months after the meeting, officers were once again ordered to spend a month each year in the ranks, and by February 1959 some 150,000 performed this or a similar such requirement.[11] The meeting also promoted renewed development of the militia under the slogan of "everyone a soldier."[12]

A surprising phenomenon during the summer of 1958 was the emergence of the people's commune, an organizational entity that had not even been mentioned as recently as the Second Session of the Eighth Party Congress in May. This third and final major stage in the evolution of agrarian collectivization was in part a response to the desire for large labor battalions as had been used in the widespread water conservancy projects during the preceding winter.[13] Thus, higher APCs began amalgamating, a trend that was endorsed at the Chengdu meeting, and although this development was not yet regarded as particularly significant, the endorsement encouraged more mergers. The designation *renmin gong she*, or people's communes, began to appear in June and by August came into general usage. The new unit of organization was now conceived to be a multipurposed one, encompassing not only agriculture, but industry, commerce, education, and military affairs as well.

The enlarged Politburo conference at Beidaihe from August 17 to 30, 1958, was a major turning point in the Great Leap Forward. Actually, up to this point China may have been making some significant progress economically. The leadership had the opportunity at Beidaihe to make appropriate adjustments to assure success. Unfortunately, what happened was the converse. The conference produced a series of ambitious policies covering the communes, agriculture, industry, education, commerce, the militia, and participation in physical labor by cadres.

Communes were to be developed throughout China, with roughly one per *xiang* to include about two thousand households or about ten thousand people. Party and administrative units of the *xiang* were to be the same as those of the commune, hence the latter now became the basic unit of state power in rural China. The communes were to have a collectivist life-style, fostered by means of common mess halls, child-care facilities, schools, tailors, barbers, public baths, and homes for the aged. The resulting reorganization of labor was expected to produce immediate results. Hence, grain output was predicted to reach as high as 350 million tons for the year. The 1958 steel target was raised to 10.7 million tons, twice the output of 1957.[14]

As this enthusiasm for new forms and new targets escalated, a foreign affairs crisis reached dangerous proportions. In the wake of heightened tensions, initially quickened by developments in the Middle East during the summer of 1958, Mao decided to put the Soviet Union to a real test. Premier Khrushchev made a secret visit to Beijing with Defense Minister Marshal Malinovsky on July 31, and discussed the Middle East crisis with Mao. More important, however, Khrushchev proposed joint military cooperation efforts that Mao regarded as an infringement of Chinese sovereignty. Hence, the Chinese refused to allow Soviet communications facilities in China or the advantage of submarine refueling and recreation ashore along the China coast. This insensitive Soviet overture may, in fact, have been *the* turning point in Sino-Soviet relations.

Khrushchev's disregard for Chinese sensibilities was rewarded by Mao's decision to begin heavy bombardment of Quemoy Island (Jinmen) about three weeks later without informing the Soviet premier ahead of time. The Soviets dutifully made public propaganda statements in support of China, but the Chinese determined by means of this exercise that they could not depend on the Soviet Union's backing if such a crisis threatened to evoke a confrontation with the United States. The Chinese themselves took the further initiative in easing the crisis. Zhou Enlai, in his speech to the Supreme State Conference on September 6, proposed a renewal of ambassadorial talks with the United States at Warsaw. But Mao's remarks during a Politburo meeting at this time, to the effect, once again, that China would survive a U.S.-Soviet nuclear conflict, may have alarmed Soviet Foreign Minister Gromyko, who was present.[15]

The Quemoy crisis contributed to the deterioration of Sino-Soviet relations, but within China, while the event was not widely publicized, it helped nonetheless in the implementation of the radical new policies. It facilitated the rapid formation and expansion of the people's militia. By January 1959, 220 million adults had been recruited into this huge organization.[16]

The commune movement was affected. The term "commune" itself connotes a militant communist tradition. Subunits within the commune came to be designated as production teams and production brigades, replacing respectively the erstwhile lower and higher APCs. The pace of commune formation accelerated incredibly, so that in the single month of September 1958 the number of communes mushroomed from 8,730 to 26,425, representing an increase from about 30 percent of the rural population at the end of August to 98 percent of that population by the end of September. Clearly, much of this reorganization can have been on paper only. Nevertheless, the pace of developments continued unabated and confusion abounded.

Curiously, despite this major effort to reorganize agricultural labor along more "rational" lines, insufficient attention was given to gathering the harvests of 1958. This was due primarily to the great diversion of manpower into other pursuits, especially into the steel production drive. At Beidaihe in August the party had endorsed the doubling of the steel production target for 1958, from the 1957 production figure of 5.35 million tons to 10.7 million tons. This later was claimed to be the crucial error that unbalanced the entire economy during this frenetic period. But Mao actually predicted even more extravagant goals for steel in the years ahead, suggesting that by 1959 output would reach 30 million tons, by 1960, 60 million tons, and by 1962, as high as 120 million tons![17] This obsessive concern for steel manifested itself in the famous backyard steel furnaces that now dotted the rural landscape, and that soon consumed many usable pots and pans and other metal implements. Yet steel was only one of the many distractions besetting the peasants, for many of them were drawn off into other projects of local industry and construction. But the basic tragedy was that the all-important harvests were neglected. The use of shock teams working all hours, once the error was discovered, did not entirely resolve the problem. It did contribute to the exhaustion of the peasants, who were also being called on for militia training, and who were experiencing difficulties in adjusting to communal living.

Of course, it did not take long for the party to realize that things were going awry. Accordingly, adjustments were made at three major meetings in November and December 1958, following nationwide inspection trips by leading cadres, but a realization of the full extent of the impending disaster would take longer still. At the Zhengzhou conference, from November 2 to 10, Mao spoke about Stalin's book *Economic Problems of Socialism*, cautioned against making changes in rural areas, and affirmed the need to go slowly in making the transition to communism.[18] At the Wuchang meeting of November 21 to 27, production targets were notably reduced, but, as events would prove, insufficiently. At the Sixth Enlarged Plenum in Wuchang (often referred to as the Wuhan Plenum) from November 28 to December 10, the leadership was somewhat more realistic but remained optimistic. The communes were to be consolidated and rectified over the next five months and exaggeration was discouraged. But targets, though scaled down, were still much too high. Steel output, for example, was now expected to reach 18 million tons in 1959, rather than 30 million tons. And grain production was to increase from the estimated 375 million tons in 1958 to 525 million tons in 1959.

A surprising development was the plenum's approval of Mao's decision not to stand for election again as chairman of the PRC, a decision explained to cadres by way of a telephone conference among the provinces during the meeting.[19] Mao voluntarily relinquished the state chairmanship with its ceremonial obligations, but retained the more important party chairmanship.

In the following months, the party came to realize that the planned consolidation phase, rather than providing a base for further advance, would have to be retreated from even further. One of the serious problems, labeled "departmentalism," initially publicized by Tao Zhu in Guangdong, saw brigades and teams hide their harvest from authorities, rather than submit to a more equitable distribution of income among less affluent units. Such concealment also contributed to the impending food shortages. A similar phenomenon was occurring at a higher level, too, as larger units concentrated exclusively on their own plans and needs. This led some higher-ranking cadres to propose some measures of recentralization, using the simile of the country as a chessboard that had to be considered as a whole in making and implementing economic decisions. Within the communes, too, accounting and distribution problems abounded, along with many other very unsatisfactory experiences.

Thus, at the so-called Second Zhengzhou Meeting, an enlarged session of the Politburo held from about February 27 to March 10, 1959, further modifications were made. However, here Mao ironically argued against those who criticized departmentalism, seeing such behavior as an understandable defensive reaction by peasants, even though this defense was admittedly rightist. Mao even threatened to give up his party membership, if necessary, in order to carry out his "right opportunism" on behalf of the beleaguered peasantry.[20] Mao also recommended that the team, rather than the brigade or commune, be the basic level for accounting and for the allocation of work and wages, even though this ideologically represented a considerable retreat from the prospects of an early realization of communism.[21] Even so, Mao remained, on the whole, optimistic about the faltering Great Leap.

An enlarged meeting of the Politburo took place in Shanghai from March 25 to April 1, 1959, at which rectification of the communes continued. The steel output target for 1959 was trimmed back again, to

16.5 million tons, despite arguments, reportedly by Bo I-bo, that they be raised instead. Such an argument was said to have been, ostensibly, a covert attempt to sabotage the Great Leap Forward.[22] The Seventh Enlarged Plenum was held immediately afterward, from April 2 to 5, also in Shanghai.

The Seventh Plenum approved a number of policy proposals that had been made at recent party meetings, but changed a recommendation that Mao himself had made, although on a point on which Mao may have been ambivalent, that is, that the production team be the basic level accounting unit. Instead, the brigade was assigned this responsibility, a more radical decision.[23] The plenum also saw a skirmish between Mao and Peng Dehuai, the latter taking umbrage at the chairman's "assuming command in person."[24] The plenum was followed by meetings of the Supreme State Conference on April 15, at which Mao discussed, among other matters, the Tibet crisis and the desirability of less criticism of rightists and more respect for teachers; and then by the First Session of the Second NPC, from April 17 to 28, at which Liu Shaoqi was elected chairman of the PRC.[25] At this point, Liu was a reliable supporter of Mao and had, in return, received the latter's support for this position.

An exceedingly important enlarged Politburo conference was held during the entire month of July at Lushan in Jiangxi, during which the long-festering feud, partly professional and partly personal, between Mao and Peng Dehuai came to a head. The way in which this clash was handled was to have the severest repercussions for the CCP. The Lushan conference was structured to elicit criticism of current policies, and thus began with small discussion groups. This encouraged cadres to speak more boldly than might have been the case normally. But added to this was a sense of crisis, and this may have been sufficient for Peng Dehuai, who was not a reticent personality, to speak his mind. Peng was primarily concerned about the compromises being demanded of the military, which he had striven to professionalize over the past several years. But his concern extended beyond the PLA to the nation as a whole, particularly since food shortages and distress in the countryside necessarily had a deleterious effect on the morale of his soldiers.

Peng made his criticisms in a long "Letter of Opinion," which was presented to Mao and others on July 14.[26] It was a systematic and trenchant critique of the Great Leap Forward and of the communes. Peng may have had the sympathetic ear of a number of other participants, but his support evidently was primarily among military colleagues. Zhang Wentian, an alternate Politburo member and one of the 28 Bolsheviks of earlier days, also forthrightly aired his criticisms at the conference.[27] Since both Peng and Zhang shared similar views, had traveled to Eastern Europe together that spring, and otherwise met with some frequency, the two probably tried to coordinate their efforts.[28] But this was not a major conspiracy, even though Zhang may well have provoked Peng into making his criticisms.[29] As a result, Zhang, along with several military leaders, came to be castigated as part of the Peng "right opportunist, anti-party clique," although it is not likely that these men really conspired to topple Mao.

Mao gave an eloquent response on July 23.[30] He was annoyed at the charge of "petty-bourgeois fanaticism" that was leveled against some of the radical policies, even though he had been distancing himself from some of these recently. He believed that the mistake of the "wind of Communism" had been corrected. Mao did not evade self-criticism: "I have committed two crimes, one of which is calling for 10,700,000 tons of steel and the mass smelting of steel. If you agreed with this, you should share some of the blame. But since I was the inventor of the burial puppets, I cannot pass on the blame: the main responsibility is mine. As for the people's communes, the whole world opposed them; the Soviet Union opposed them."[31] Mao owned up to not having understood economic planning and for taking too much into his own hands. Mao admitted: "The chaos was on a grand scale and I take responsibility." But Mao would not accept exclusive responsibility.[32] At one point, he provocatively exclaimed that under certain circumstances he would return to the countryside to lead the peasants to overthrow the government. "If those of you in the Liberation Army won't follow me, then I will go and find a Red Army, and organize another Liberation Army. But I think the Liberation Army would follow me."[33] Subsequently, the two old antagonists engaged in a heated exchange of barbed comments. Mao won this contest, for few of the leaders would have exchanged his leadership for Peng's in such an implied direct challenge. Yet many must have wondered why the redoubtable party chairman had been so intolerant of criticism he had himself solicited, especially from an old comrade who was bluntly speaking what was self-evident to so many.

Immediately following the conference, Mao convened the Eighth Enlarged Plenum of the Central Committee which met, also at Lushan, from August 2 to 16, 1959. Mao employed the occasion to remove Peng from further contention. He fortuitously was able to use to advantage the Soviet decision of June 20 to renege on their 1957 agreement to help develop China's nuclear technology, announced soon after Peng's return from Moscow. Furthermore, Mao exploited Khrushchev's criticism of the communes expressed on July 18 during the latter's visit to Poland, promoting the suspicion that there had been collusion between the

Soviet leader and Peng. The implication of foreign involvement, however improbable, isolated Peng, rendering support for him all the more imprudent at this point.[34] Peng and his clique, most of whom were referred to as the "Military Club," were said to have had connections with Gao Gang. The plenum dismissed Peng as defense minister.

It was perhaps inevitable that Peng had to be displaced, given Mao's views on the role of the military. But Mao overstepped himself at Lushan, providing the first real demonstration of his abuse of personal power. In the meanwhile, party stalwarts such as Liu Shaoqi and Zhou Enlai stood firmly with Mao, doing little or nothing to temper his vengefulness toward Peng. As a consequence, the "Yan'an Round Table" was cracked, as Roderick MacFarquhar has perceptively put it, to be shattered by the Cultural Revolution, yet to come.[35] After Mao's death years later, the party would officially judge that this plenum's resolution regarding the "so-called" anti-party group of Peng and the others "was entirely wrong" and that politically this struggle "gravely undermined inner-Party democracy from the central level down to the grass roots."[36]

Peng wrote a letter to Mao on September 9, asking permission to study or to undertake physical labor.[37] The latter option was disallowed owing to the age of the old soldier, so that he was able to study with but annual visits to work sites over the next several years. Mao must have been grateful to Peng in retrospect, because Peng promised not to commit suicide following his disgrace at the Eighth Plenum.[38] Such a suicide might have damaged Mao's image. Even so, Mao carried the castigation of Peng even further, perhaps in order to justify the latter's dismissal. This took place at a protracted enlarged meeting of the Central Committee's Military Affairs Committee, which was held sometime between late August and October 1959. Here, Peng was accused of never having been a true Marxist, but an opportunist who had infiltrated the party without changing his world outlook. Peng railed once again, despite having made a confession, but to no avail. The public was notified of Peng's dismissal, and Lin Biao was installed as minister of defense on September 17.[39]

Another beneficiary of the Peng Dehuai purge was a little known official in Hunan who would rise to high positions at the end of Mao's life. This was Hua Guofeng, who might have played some role in the making of a case against Peng, or perhaps more likely against Zhou Xiaozhou, the party first secretary of Hunan who was implicated with Peng.[40] Incidentally, Deng Xiaoping, who had played a prominent role in the Gao Gang affair, was little involved in the Peng case. He is said to have broken his leg playing ping pong (!) at Lushan and left the meeting early.[41]

Unfortunately for China, the Peng affair prompted the party leadership to arrest its recent retrenchment of Great Leap policies and to reaffirm them once again, in an overreaction to Peng's rightist criticism. The Eighth Plenum did acknowledge the serious problem of exaggerated claims and accordingly reduced both the output figures for 1958 and output target figures for 1959. The 1958 grain output figure was now reduced from 375 million tons to 250 million tons, and steel output was reduced from 11.08 million tons to 8 million tons. Grain for 1959 was now targeted at 275 million tons rather than 525 million tons, and steel was reduced from 18 to 12 million tons.[42] Some adjustments were made. Backyard steel efforts would no longer be counted in the state plan, and were to be pursued more in keeping with local needs and resources. Otherwise, however, the Great Leap rhetoric reappeared, and warnings were publicized against rightist opportunist backsliding. Collectivist features of the communes were reasserted. The inexhaustible energies of the people were to resolve all problems. Tao Zhu, for one, enjoined the people to stand firm, like rocks on the coast, unwavering under the assaults of storm and tide.[43]

In the meanwhile, relations with Moscow continued to deteriorate, with consequences that would only exacerbate the difficulties that were engulfing China. Premier Khrushchev visited Beijing again on September 30, en route back to Moscow from his summit meeting with President Dwight Eisenhower at Camp David. The Soviet premier was not pleased at the news of Peng's fate and of those who advocated a cooperative stance strategically with the Soviet Union, and he continued to advocate peaceful coexistence with the United States. Also at this time, the Sino-Indian border dispute flared following Indian detection of a Chinese road being built in the Aksai Chin, a territory along China's far west and India's northwest that was claimed by both countries. Much to the chagrin of the Chinese, the Soviets chose to take a neutral position, rather than demonstrate fraternal socialist solidarity.

The Chinese seriously reappraised their position vis-à-vis the Soviet Union over the next several months in a series of high-level foreign policy conferences. The upshot was a major polemical attack on the Soviets on April 22, 1960, the 90th anniversary of Lenin's birth. This was the long-delayed rebuttal of the ideas presented by Khrushchev at the Twentieth CPSU congress in 1956. The Chinese moved the debate onto the ideological plane and, in contrast to the Soviets, argued that the imperialists were implacably hostile to the socialist nations. More specifically, they held that most U.S. leaders disagreed with the concept of peaceful coexistence, again contrary to Khrushchev's contention.[44]

Concurrently, the Chinese began to lobby their position within international communist front organizations; presented their views at a meeting of the Warsaw Pact powers in Moscow on February 4, 1960; and seized the initiative at a plenary session of the communist-dominated World Federation of Trade Unions in Beijing in early June 1960, where they forcefully expressed their position.[45] Peng Chen, who attended the congress of the Romanian communist party in late June 1960, infuriated the Soviets by circulating a private communication from the CPSU to the CCP, the harshness of which detracted from another document criticizing the Chinese that the Soviets themselves had earlier distributed and that was more reasonably argued. Khrushchev responded with vitriolic personal criticisms of the Chinese on the floor of the congress.[46]

The exasperated Soviets now took a fateful step, and one which they must often consider to have been imprudent despite the aggravation which prompted it. On July 16, 1960, they informed the Chinese of their decision to withdraw all Soviet advisers. The reasons for this were primarily because the Chinese neglected to heed Soviet technical advice and often scorned it, and they imposed intolerable conditions on the advisers, including spying on them, searching their possessions, opening their mail, and sometimes molesting and attacking them. The Chinese denied all of these charges. Nevertheless, by the end of August, all 1,390 Soviet advisers in China at the time had left the country. The Soviets also scrapped 257 scientific and technical cooperation projects.[47] The relationship had been an imperfect one at best. Yet, in the perspective of Sino-Russian relations over a longer period of history, the 1950s had seen unprecedentedly good relations between the two countries, which now had similar political systems and professed similar values. Certainly, Soviet patience had been tried in recent months. But the Soviets might have taken a more optimistic view of the future. They had, after all, invested heavily in transferring expertise to China. Some ten thousand advisers had served in China in the 1950s and many more thousand Chinese had studied in the Soviet Union. There had been established a complex network of human relationships at many levels between the two countries. There was a reservoir of goodwill that had continued to compensate for the disagreements between the top leaders. Now, all of these achievements became forfeit, and the willfulness of the leaders was allowed to poison sentiment throughout both countries. Relations would, in fact, continue to deteriorate even further in the years ahead, but the vindictive withdrawal of advisers and the abrogation of the aid program at this critical moment would leave a deep scar the Chinese would not forget.

The Chinese, for their part, took care to treat the departing Soviet advisers with courtesy to the very end. Yet, more than twenty years later, when a much more balanced view of the Great Leap finally became possible, the Chinese would still officially regard the "perfidious" behavior of the Soviet government as one of the reasons for the disaster that befell them.[48] But, in fact, other factors played as great or greater a role. Three successive years of adverse weather conditions contributed mightily to the poor performance in agricultural production. Still, it is difficult to avoid the conclusion that errant leadership decisions and irresponsible behavior were the most decisive factors.

Both Mao and Liu began to take economics more seriously. Each man separately studied a Soviet textbook on political economy. Liu became convinced that economic development would have to be emphasized in the 1960s, with industrialists and businessmen given an important role. Mao read more critically, noting the unsatisfactory experience of the Soviet model. He dwelt upon important distinctions between China and the Soviet Union.

In response to doubts that were raised at Lushan regarding Mao's policies, the fourth volume of his *Selected Works* was published in September 1960. This volume covered the period 1945 to 1949, and was apparently intended to remind readers of how Mao's farsightedness had finally proven correct in that critical period as well.[49]

The party initially responded to the rural crisis by instituting a *xia-fang* campaign to correct errors of implementation on the part of local cadres. However, by June a new policy of "agriculture as the foundation and industry as the leading factor," reaffirming the priority on grain production, was implemented. In order to strengthen the party's central control, the six regional party bureaus were restored. And in November 1960, the Central Committee issued an urgent directive on rural work, usually referred to as the Twelve Articles. This document provided guidelines for the communes, underscoring the importance of the production team and making it a unit of partial ownership. It also restored private plots, family sideline pursuits, and free markets.[50]

But the Chinese leaders became heavily preoccupied with the dispute with Khrushchev. Two important subalterns, Deng Xiaoping and Peng Zhen, spent most of the second half of 1960 at meetings abroad. Six Central Committee conferences that year focused on foreign affairs, which meant primarily on policy relating to the Soviets. As many as one-fourth of the active Politburo attended the lengthy 81-party Moscow conference in November.[51]

The party thus entered the 1960s with the country in radical turmoil, and with a party leader whose enthusiasm for idealistic change had largely brought this about. Moreover, the leader's increasing intolerance of criticism was eroding the party's camaraderie. At the same time, both the party and the country were becoming increasingly isolated, from the socialist camp as well as from the West.

If one can look beyond the disasters of this period of the Three Red Banners (that is, the Great Leap Forward, Communization, and the General Line for Socialist Construction), there were, in fact, some accomplishments, and a forceful statement was made regarding an optional, radical approach to development and the future that for sometime impressed many observers. The accomplishments included the beginnings of a determined effort to spread industry into the countryside using intermediate technology and local labor. There was the effort, too, to awaken the consciousness of the peasant masses as to possibilities for their progeny, even if these were achievable only by dint of self-reliant resourcefulness and hard labor. This mass line approach encouraged local initiative and experimentation. In the cities, a number of construction projects still commemorate the enthusiasm of the peak of the period, and none more symbolically than the monumental Great Hall of the People on Tiananmen Square, which was built in well under two years' time.

·9·

Retrenchment and Class Struggle

The next several years saw a deepening of the cleavage within the party that was already becoming apparent in the period before the Great Leap Forward. On the one hand, many party leaders were anxious to return to a more regularized, centralized regimen that would emphasize economic development under party leadership, with concessions as needed to encourage productivity. Cadres of this persuasion were quick to seize upon the severe depression occasioned by the Great Leap to implement their cautious, incremental policies. On the other hand, while Mao himself was sobered by the experience of the Great Leap, he saw in it memories of the successful Yan'an past and flashes of a distinctive Chinese future that he would continue to cherish. Implementation of this vision required continued mobilization efforts, relying upon the masses as much as the full cooperation of the party. Mao would become increasingly anxious to follow this line as he came to have an increasingly negative view of developments in the Soviet Union, fearing that China would follow suit unless a conscious effort was made to avoid doing so. The divergence within the party was exacerbated as leaders differed over the lessons to be learned from the Great Leap. And as William Joseph aptly puts it, "This divergence showed that there was an ultimately irreconcilable disagreement over the fundamentals of the Chinese revolution."[1]

The party organization itself chose to emphasize the more cautious option as it sought to deal with the disorder besetting the country. In January 1961, an enlarged Politburo meeting was convened, followed by the Central Committee's Ninth Plenum. At this meeting the party ended the rapid progress emphasized in the General Line, one of the Three Red Banners, replacing it with the slogan "readjusting, consolidating, filling out, and raising standards." Reaffirmed again was the foundational role of agriculture and the priority of grain. Mao himself keynoted this veritable New Economic Policy, emphasizing realism by referring to the party's tradition of "seeking the truth from reality," that is, by investigating local conditions before making decisions.[2] With Mao withdrawn, however, from the first line of state decisionmaking, a collective leadership under Liu Shaoqi now asserted itself.

In the next year and a half, the party carried out sweeping reviews and articulated the results in a series of broad directives. The reviews covered agriculture and forestry, industry and communications, finance and trade, culture and education, and politics and law. Central work conferences were frequently used in promoting and consolidating these studies.

The first of the major readjustment documents to emerge from this process was the Sixty Articles, consisting of the draft regulations on the rural communes. This study was conducted by Deng Xiaoping and Peng Zhen, who in doing so neglected to consult with Mao. Consequently, during the March 1961 central work conference at which this draft was discussed, a resentful Mao asked, "Which emperor decided this?" He also uttered the famous phrase "Without investigation no one has the right to speak."[3] Nevertheless, the document did summarize the experience of the past three years, taking into account the party's own piecemeal decisions during this period, including the recently issued Twelve Articles. It also provided essential guidelines to the communes and facilitated the new change of direction. This change, even though it promised relief to the rural population, was understandably confusing to local cadres and peasants alike because it was so contradictory to the strong previous signals. Implementation of the directive took two forms, one in which local party committees did the work, and the other in which central and provincial special task forces did so, often "squatting" in a given locale in order to carry out a thorough investigation. In some places, experimentation went beyond the Sixty Articles, taking the form of *san-zu i-bao*, that is, permitting the expansion of private plots, free markets, and sideline enterprises, and the fixing of quotas by individual households. Such latitude provoked Mao.

Similarly, in September 1961, a document known as the Seventy Articles, dealing with industry and mining, was sent out by the Secretariat. Again, Deng Xiaoping was prominently involved. This document contradicted the radical 1960 charter of the Anshan Iron and Steel Company that had been enthusiastically endorsed by Mao. The 1960

Anshan charter had in its turn been drafted as an alternative to the so-called Magnitagorsk charter, from the period of the Soviet model. The Anshan charter stressed politics over profits and mass participation over domination by experts in the running of industry. The Seventy Articles turned China back in the direction of the Soviet model once again.

In the easier atmosphere of 1961, the party's propaganda department issued regulations that were intended to encourage artists and intellectuals. A document entitled "Sixty Articles on Universities" became a party directive in November 1961. This directive restored the ideas that the main function of universities was teaching and research, that research and specialized training are necessary, and that faculty should be relatively independent of party control.

As a consequence, the period of 1961–1962 saw the emergence of a modified Hundred Flowers campaign. This time, however, the writers who ventured articles and plays were mindful of the six restrictive criteria imposed by Mao in the summer of 1957. Furthermore, encouraged by elements in the party, some indulged in satire charged with double-meaning expressions and themes. The most famous of these critics was Wu Han, the Peking University historian who specialized on the Ming dynasty and who served as deputy mayor of Beijing. Wu Han cleverly followed Mao's own suggestion in writing about a famous Ming magistrate.[4] His play, *Hai Rui Dismissed from Office*, published in January 1961, was actually a defense of Peng Dehuai, although this meaning was understood by relatively few informed Chinese at the time. Deng To, editor of *Frontline*, started a column in that newspaper in early 1961 entitled "Night Talks at Yenshan," and subsequently joined with Wu Han and Liao Mo-sha in writing, under a combined pseudonym a new column called "Notes from the Three Family Village."[5] However, the very existence of such double entendre literature at the time was unknown to most Chinese and to virtually all foreigners until four or five years later when a counterattack was launched by Maoists.[6] Mao accepted this criticism without comment, but it was not to be forgotten.

In January 1962, an enlarged central work conference was convened with some seven thousand cadres from five levels of the party hierarchy in attendance. At this meeting, the party sought to further the recentralization of authority that had been eroded during the Great Leap. The policy reviews undertaken during the previous months were endorsed, even by Mao himself. A preliminary summing up was undertaken of the positive and the negative experience of the Great Leap Forward, including further criticism and self-criticism of mistakes. This was the culmination of a process that Mao had encouraged and was initiated by his own self-criticism in June 1961, which was now revealed at the

January 1962 conference. Mao again had acknowledged that he had to be the first to bear responsibility for the mistakes of the Central Committee because of his position.[7] Nevertheless, it remained clear enough that others were expected to make similar self-criticisms, and this was done.

However, in summarizing the effects of the Great Leap, an appointed committee, under the direction of Deng To (the responsibility for this having been delegated to him by Peng Zhen), had come to conclusions the previous month, December 1961, that only confirmed the criticisms Peng Dehuai had made in 1959![8]

Thus, major differences remained evident at the January conference. Basically, Liu Shaoqi, reflecting the committee analysis, contended that the Great Leap had been a failure and the economy was in poor shape. Hence, he stressed the need to concentrate on its restoration. Mao, on the other hand, held that the difficult period had now passed. But Mao's style of leadership also came under criticism, particularly his bypassing of regular party processes. While Mao agreed on the desirability of collective leadership and the need for democratic centralism (the specific topic of his speech), he continued to maintain that the minority had the right to its views and that these sometimes were right.[9] The party chairman, who was on the defensive, received timely support from both Zhou Enlai and Lin Biao at this important meeting.[10]

An enlarged meeting of the Politburo in February underscored the seriousness of the crisis in the economy. Chen Yun even suggested that land be redistributed to rural households, agreeing with Deng Xiaoping that this was tantamount to a restoration of private farming.[11] Many cadres who had been targeted during previous anti-rightist campaigns were now rehabilitated. These included Zhang Wentian and Peng Dehuai. Zhang went on to collaborate on a book on economics with Sun Yefeng. Peng undertook an investigation in the countryside that produced a lengthy report vindicating his previously expressed views.[12]

Liu Shaoqi encouraged doing what was necessary to restore the economy and to provide a sound material base upon which socialist development might proceed. It was in agreement with this position that Deng Xiaoping in July 1962 made his famous comment: "Whether cats are white or black, so long as they can catch mice, they are all good cats."[13] This strong tide of concentrating on the improvement of the economy, regardless of the means, reached its peak under Liu's leadership in August 1962 with the publication of a new edition of his book *How to Be a Good Communist*.

Mao had not been exclusively on the defensive while developments so contrary to his wishes continued to unfold. Ever since Lin Biao had been appointed Minister of Defense in 1959 the PLA had been undergoing a major overhaul. In 1960 the PLA's general political department initiated an intensive ideological revitalization program both in the military and among its dependents. The Four Firsts principle, said to be the key to political work, now permeated the PLA, with its emphasis on man over weapons, political work over other kinds of work, ideology over administration, and practical ideology over bookish ideology. Lin Biao's injunction to "read Chairman Mao's works, listen to his words, do as he instructs, and become a good soldier of Chairman Mao" was incorporated into a 1960 resolution of the Military Affairs Committee. The PLA reaffirmed prominent themes and slogans of the Great Leap Forward. Intensive campaigns were conducted within the PLA to make such ideas and their significance well understood. By February 1961, 85 percent of the PLA's party branches had been rebuilt, clearly in line with Mao's ideas rather than with those of his party critics.

Two distinctively different lines had emerged within the party, and by the summer of 1962 these were on collision course. The first overt clash came at a month-long work conference at Beidaihe in August. This conference was given to discussions on agriculture, commerce, industry, and party unity, as well as the expansion of the Central Control Commission and the transfer of cadres. Mao specifically criticized the spread of *san-zu i-bao* concessions in the countryside. He did not proffer an alternative program. Instead, he warned his comrades not to forget class struggle. He also suggested that the current debates within the party constituted a struggle between two roads. Socialist education, he said, was needed.

In September 1962, the Tenth Plenum of the Eighth Central Committee was held in Beijing. This famous meeting is perhaps best known for Mao's warning, already issued earlier at Beidaihe, to "never forget class struggle."[14] Almost twenty years later, after Mao's death, the official party view would be that Mao had "widened and absolutized the class struggle" at this meeting. Furthermore, this revised historical judgment would hold that Mao even "went a step further" by asserting that "throughout the historical period of socialism, the bourgeoisie would continue to exist and would attempt a comeback and become the source of revisionism inside the Party."[15] At the plenum, Mao warned against Soviet-style revisionism. He wished to be assured that real revolutionary successors would emerge from among China's youth. He said prophetically that such successors "come forward in mass struggles and are tempered in the great storms of revolution."[16]

Thus, Mao persuaded the plenum to approve of a new rectification campaign, which was to include a socialist education campaign, a crackdown on intellectuals, and a new *wu-fan* (five-antis) campaign within the party. The plenum also strengthened the party's Central Control Commission.[17] Ironically, however, while the plenum duly reflected Mao's ideological line, and accepted his veto on further concessions in agricultural policy, it also basically legitimized the adjustment program, which he disliked.[18] The readjusted communes would remain relatively stabilized for the next two decades.[19]

There was a misleading air of unity at the plenum because the deepening differences were kept from coming to the surface, where they might be resolved. The leadership seemed to be uniting behind Mao, but only on the assumption that they would not carry out his directives, as Ellis Joffe has observed.[20] The gap between the chairman's wishes and the cadres' deeds would thus widen and party unity would disintegrate. It was under such circumstances that the Tenth Plenum proved to be the last large formal party meeting to be held for the next four years.

Mao and the PLA gained prestige from the latter's breathtaking performance in the swift Sino-Indian border war in the fall of 1962. This dispute had reached a flashpoint following refusal by the Indians to agree to negotiate a general border settlement, and after the adoption of a so-called forward policy, which in the end either provoked or provided the pretext for the Chinese military response. After having eliminated all forward Indian positions in several days in November, the Chinese returned to their side of the disputed border as they had said they would do.[21] The Chinese were greatly offended when the Soviet Union set aside its neutrality, and sided with India, even providing military assistance to the Indians. For the Chinese, this scandalous behavior was of a piece with the Soviet's adventurism in precipitating the concurrent Cuban missile crisis and then abjectly retreating from it.

Years later, after Mao had left the scene, the party would concede that the socialist education campaign that unfolded fitfully between 1963 and 1965 "did help to some extent to improve the cadres' style of work and economic management."[22] In fact, the socialist education movement was a classic confrontation between the two lines.[23] The campaign was carried out in stages. The first stage, from late 1962 to mid-1964, concentrated on errors committed by basic-level cadres. The problems were to be corrected patiently, by means of education and indoctrination. By the middle of 1963, however, there clearly had developed disagreement within the party with regard to implementation. Three Central Committee work conferences were held in 1963 to discuss the campaign.

At the second of these work conferences, held in May, Mao's own ideas still prevailed. This conference produced a draft resolution called the First Ten Points.[24] Cadres were to participate in productive labor, and poor and middle peasant associations were formed (rather liberally constituted so as to include those who had formerly collaborated with landlords but had reformed) to monitor local cadres. Thus, Mao once again sought to temper the party by exposing it to external review. Mao conceded that, while 95 percent of lower-level cadres performed acceptably, there were, nonetheless, 5 percent who did not and must be removed. He presumably believed that external involvement would facilitate this and perhaps improve relations between the party and the people.

By September 1963, however, those who disagreed with this approach were able to assert themselves. This occurred at the third work conference, which was held following a period of "spot-testing" in certain areas.[25] Here a revised program was drafted under Deng Xiaoping's supervision, known as the Second Ten Points.[26] The peasant associations were relieved of their supervisory function, something that many of them had been reluctant to carry out anyway, and were instead transformed into auxiliaries to assist the basic-level cadres. Material incentives were reintroduced as a means of garnering support and improving productivity. The Second Ten Points did extend the rectification campaign to include middle-level cadres, although this was to be conducted mildly.

The implementation guidelines were changed again in September 1964, becoming now the Revised Second Ten Points.[27] This revision incorporated the experience and pessimistic findings of high-ranking leaders, including Liu Shaoqi and his wife, Wang Guangmei, each of whom had spent lengthy periods of time with work teams in the countryside. Their experiences led them to distrust many of the local cadres and the peasants and to see the need for strengthened work teams. They called for secretive means to investigate cadre corruption, a phenomenon which was more widespread than initially believed. By this stage, the masses had themselves become the object of the campaign rather than the vehicle for its implementation. And the local party members and cadres became subjected to the most intensive purge to date, with between 1.25 and 2.5 million basic-level cadres dismissed from their positions.[28]

Mao objected to the change of character of the campaign. He was distressed by the concentration of attention on corruption to the neglect of the greater need to rectify revisionist tendencies among cadres and peasants. Mao also objected to the large number of cadres accused of corruption and the harshness of their punishment. But, most of all, he criticized the size and behavior of the work teams, with their preference for secret investigations and avoidance of mass mobilization techniques. Consequently, in January 1965, a yet new version of the guidelines was circulated, called the Twenty-three Articles, which embodied Mao's own prescription for pursuing the socialist education campaign.[29] While smaller work teams would continue to conduct the campaign, they were to eschew secretive work and rely on the masses once more in order to rectify basic-level cadres. More ominously, Mao now made it clear that there were people in positions of authority who were taking the capitalist road.

In fact, the party chairman's intentions were no more heeded at this point than they had been earlier in the campaign. Although local cadres were relieved of some of the pressure they had been under, only in a few places were the masses seriously mobilized. A rectification campaign was finally begun as late as October 1965 at the higher, county level, but this never targeted revisionism specifically. Instead, the aim was merely to increase the efficiency of county party committees, but the effort does not seem to have been very successful.[30]

In the meanwhile, efforts had been underway to combat corruption, inefficiency, and revisionism at higher levels of the party and state bureaucracies, in accordance with decisions of the Tenth Plenum. These campaigns did not initially receive as much attention in the countryside as did the socialist education campaign. Thus, a five-antis campaign was carried out, middle-level cadres were *xia-fanged* again beginning in 1964, and procedures were set up for regularizing productive physical labor by cadres at lower levels in their own organizations.

Additionally, the PLA came to have greater influence on the party and state bureaucracies. The PLA had been successfully overhauled under Lin Biao along Maoist lines. Moreover, it had enhanced its professional image and heightened national pride by its dramatic triumph over India in the fall of 1962. Its stock was further heightened by the successful detonation of a nuclear device in 1964. Thus, in that same year, political departments modeled after those that had already been established successfully throughout the PLA were set up in the state's economic agencies. The PLA provided a model soldier, Lei Feng, and a model unit, the Good Eighth Company of Nanking Road, to be publicized throughout the country. In fact, by early 1964 the country as a whole was enjoined to "learn from the PLA."

On January 4, 1964, ten poems written by Mao over a period of fourteen years were published with great fanfare. Here, Mao employed the technique of indirect criticism that his own critics had been using. But the most likely intended targets of his poems were protected by propaganda department officials who interpreted the poems as implicit attacks on Soviet revisionism, rather than on China's own cultural officials and others. The most prominent example of these poems was one entitled "Reply to Comrade Guo Moruo," composed in January 1963, which speaks menacingly of the need "to wipe out all harmful insects . . ."[31]

Up to this time, fascinating debates among intellectuals continued to appear in the media, mirroring aspects of the intraparty split.[32] Historian Liu Jie, for example, was scolded for contending that the Confucian concept of *ran* (*jen*), that is, benevolence, transcended class affiliations. Another historian, Lo Ergang, was vilified for his interpretation regarding the Taiping hero Li Xiucheng's behavior after his capture by Zeng Guofan. Lo held that Li heroically sought to deceive his captor by means of a false confession. But this view was unacceptable to Mao, who wished to use the centennial of Li's death to make an urgent contemporary political point. Thus, whatever the merits of the case, ipso facto, the Taiping hero had to be seen as a traitor. He was held up during the centennial as a negative example in emphasizing the slogan of "continuing the revolution to the very end."[33]

The senior party theoretician, Yang Xianzhen, who may have been sacrificed by higher authorities, again to deflect attention from themselves, was criticized for his slogan "two into one," which signified that opposites were permanently united despite appearances.[34] The implication was that problems could be studied in order to identify the relevant opposing contradictions, following which a solution could be determined based upon the common ground that was revealed. This deemphasized class struggle and recommended compromise and conciliation instead. And it provided theoretical rationalization for Mao's opponents who questioned his mobilization-style development concept. But Mao countered with his own slogan "one into two," connotating a concept that eschewed harmonization and relied on class struggle rather than study. This was more in keeping with his dedication to "uninterrupted revolution," a prescription for preventing in China the backsliding into revisionism that now characterized Soviet behavior.

The Soviet Union continued to be a disappointment to Mao, in both its domestic and its foreign policies. A final parting of the ways came in July 1963 when the Soviets signed the Nuclear Test-Ban Treaty, which Beijing denounced as indicative of Soviet "collusion" with the United States.[35] Sino-Soviet bilateral talks were now postponed indefinitely, and polemics became completely unrestrained on both sides. In July 1964, Mao delivered his trenchant polemic "On Khrushchev's Phoney Communism and Its Historical Lesson for the World." However, this piece, which traced the deterioration of Soviet communism since Stalin's death, was primarily a warning to the CCP to arrest a similar slide toward revisionism.[36] The dispute quieted down for a time following Khrushchev's resignation in October 1964, but the Chinese regarded the Moscow meeting of March 1965 a failure, and the mutual polemics were resumed.[37] The Chinese, undoubtedly off balance because of their preoccupation with the Soviet Union, behaved in such a way over the eventually postponed Second Afro-Asian Conference scheduled for Algiers in June 1965 that they were widely criticized.[38]

The Chinese were now increasingly concerned about the intensifying war on their southern flank as well. In 1965, the United States greatly expanded its involvement in the Vietnam War. If the Soviet Union and the United States were truly colluding, this could be a very serious matter. In any case, the war only complicated differences with the Soviet Union, rather than serving as a convenient pretext for resolving them.

The Vietnam War promoted further divisiveness within China too. Suddenly, the PLA's return to its old defensive people's war image seemed less congenial to its chief of staff, Lo Ruiqing, an erstwhile supporter of Mao's concept. The situation required adequate preparedness; hence, Lo began to argue for retaining some measure of military professionalism. With such a ready army, China could afford a more aggressive posture toward the United States and consider active entry into the war. Nevertheless, Mao's and Lin Biao's program continued unabated. By May 1965, the PLA had once again rid itself of rank insignia and officer-enlisted distinctions. Furthermore, it was clearly maintaining its basically defensive character. In September 1965, Lin Biao delivered his address "Long Live the Victory of the People's War," which ostensibly commemorated the victory over Japan but actually signaled China's warning to Vietnam that it would not enter the war.[39] Instead, the Vietnamese were enjoined to emulate the essential element in China's own revolutionary war: self-reliance. Lo disagreed. In December 1965, he was removed from office. There were, of course, others who would have preferred involvement in the Vietnam War at this juncture. But not party chairman Mao Zedong. He had another kind of conflict in mind for China. It would be a cataclysmic one, but confined basically to China itself.

PART FOUR

Protracted Trial

· IO ·

The Great Proletarian Cultural Revolution

Despite the increasing tensions within the party and the mounting concern over external pressures, the Chinese economy was reviving as the mid-1960s loomed. China had by 1965 repaid with interest all the debts it owed to the Soviet Union, which had accrued mostly through arms purchases during the Korean War. China even had a modest aid program for other developing countries and revolutionary movements. The Third NPC met from December 21, 1964, to January 4, 1965, and was able to announce that the national economic readjustment had in the main been achieved, and that soon the economy as a whole would enter a new stage of development. But this was a very misleading estimate of the situation. It did not take into account the seriousness of the party chairman's concern with revisionism.

Mao had not been amused with the difficulties encountered in the implementation of the socialist education campaign. He was concerned that the political departments that had been established in the economic agencies of the bureaucracy in 1964 and 1965 were not producing results.[1] He was annoyed at the resistance to his ideas from party comrades and the veiled criticisms directed at him from party intellectuals and others. Specifically, he was disturbed that rectification had become moribund, and that his call for a veritable cultural revolution at the beginning of 1965 had been ignored. This unresponsiveness was particularly alarming to Mao inasmuch as he had been making clear to his comrades his apprehensions that the CCP might be in danger of emulating the CPSU's wayward development. Therefore, at an enlarged meeting of the

Politburo's Standing Committee in September 1965, Mao noted the possibility of revisionism in the Central Committee and the need to counter bourgeois ideology.[2] More important, he now began to think anew what had to be done to deal with such revisionism. He directed Peng Zhen to implement the criticism of Wu Han's 1961 play *Hai Rui's Dismissal from Office.* But at the Politburo meeting that followed, his recommendations were parried.

Mao also wanted basic changes in the institutions that transmitted and implanted the values of socialism. He believed, for example, that work-study programs should be substituted for the prevailing regular college curriculum. In November, a national conference on urban part-work, part-study schools was held, where the concept received support. However, Deng Xiaoping, who saw the pressing need for regularly trained professionals, suggested that such a work-study program not be hastily carried out.[3]

An ideological study campaign had been approved in September to be conducted at all echelons. By early 1966 this campaign seriously began promoting the preeminence of politics and the need to control private economic growth. By early February, even Deng Xiaoping's famous phrase regarding the unimportance of a cat's color as long as it caught mice was criticized in a newspaper editorial. But this campaign too, while discussed earnestly enough, came to be basically disregarded and derailed by the party leaders it was directed against.

Mao's insistence in September 1965 on a public critique of Wu Han's play had also been ignored for some time. Mao would later explain that the "watertight kingdom" established by his opponents in Beijing "could not be penetrated even by a needle."[4] The frustrated but irrepressible Mao left Beijing for six months to be "alone with the masses" and to initiate a flanking maneuver against his entrenched foes.

Thus, on November 10, 1965, the attack began with the publication of a critique of Wu Han's play in the Shanghai *Wen Hui Bao.* The critique, signed by Yao Wenyuan, was a scathing one. The play had praised Hai Rui for returning land to the peasants. This was disputed as a historical fact. But, more important, Yao asked if Wu Han was implying that land be returned at present, to whom was it to be returned since it now belonged to the people's commune? It took almost three more weeks before the critique was republished by the reluctant authorities in Beijing. But a nationwide campaign was now underway and one that elicited considerable interest, and a surprising amount of support for Wu Han. However, the campaign extracted two confessions from him as well. It bears stating that, for most foreign observers, this was the first inkling that such double-meaning literature had been published several years earlier.[5]

Mao shrewdly entrusted this campaign to a Group of Five headed by Beijing mayor Peng Zhen and party propaganda chief Lu Dingi. The group resolved its dilemma by producing an outline report between February 3 and 7, 1966, that tried to deflect the strengthening campaign away from political issues and leaders by stressing the academic side of the disputation.

In contrast, Mao's wife, Jiang Qing, presided over a forum on literature and art in the PLA also in February that came to dramatically different conclusions. Subsequently, a *Hongqi* editorial would call Peng's report "a black banner," while the PLA's forum summary was "a red banner representing the general counterattack launched by the proletariat on the handful of Party persons in authority taking the capitalist road."[6]

In the meanwhile, Mao's supporters attacked other writers such as Deng To, who was to be "grabbed, have his words rooted out and impaled," and Liao Mosha.[7] In May and June the earlier articles of Deng and of his clique were intensively and publicly scrutinized in the media.

On May 16, 1966, the Central Committee issued a circular denouncing Peng Zhen's outline report.[8] Years later this circular would be regarded critically as the "programmatic document" of the impending Cultural Revolution.[9] On June 4, Peng Zhen and Lu Dingi, the latter now called the "king of hell," were both fired from their jobs. The Group of Five was supplanted by a new Cultural Revolution Group, chaired by Mao's personal secretary, Chen Boda, and included Lin Biao, Zhou Enlai, Jiang Qing, and Kang Sheng. The presence in the capital of Lin Biao's PLA in some force added visible teeth to the party leader's moves. Mao now wanted another thoroughgoing anti-rightist campaign to be conducted within the party on a scale exceeding the campaigns of 1957 and 1959.

Ironically, the conduct of this campaign was left to Liu Shaoqi, while Mao remained away from Beijing for six weeks. From June through mid-July, Liu obligingly pursued his impossible assignment. He sought to demonstrate his compliance in ferreting out revisionism, but not to the point that he and his own supporters would be undermined. Liu sent more than 400 work teams consisting of more than 10,000 members into institutions of higher learning, secondary schools, and some agencies of the bureaucracy, where administrators were placed under investigation.[10] The style of operation of these teams was similar to that of teams during the socialist education campaign's Revised Second Ten

Points phase. This style focused on the errors of lower-level administrators rather than those of their superiors. There was also anxiety to keep the operation from being taken over by Mao's supporters, and hence on an orderly basis. This intense but well-controlled campaign lasted for a period known as the Fifty Days.

But this approach conflicted with Mao's. Already on May 25, Mao-encouraged faculty and students at Peking University (Beida) had erected a large poster criticizing university officials. This resulted in much turmoil on campus, with individuals taking sides in the dispute. The work team sent to Beida included Liu's wife, Wang Guangmei, but it was soon perceived to be protecting the original targets. On July 28, the Beijing Municipal Party Committee disbanded the work teams. In their stead, Cultural Revolution committees were to be elected in every school and university.[11] These would be extended beyond educational institutions by the impending Eleventh Plenum, broadening considerably the scope of the movement. However, these particular committees would come to be supplanted by other mass organizational forms in the months immediately ahead.

Because of Mao's protracted absences from Beijing in late 1965, early 1966, and again in June and July 1966, rumors abounded regarding his health. These were set aside on July 16, 1966, when he made a reportedly spectacular swim in the Chang Jiang, swimming a distance of ten miles (with the current) in only one hour. Disregarding the accuracy of the reportage of this event, it produced the desired propaganda effect. The message was clear once again that Mao was in good health and ready to deal with the opposition to his policies. This swim became yet one more exploit to fuel the intensifying cult that was making Mao into a superhuman personality. There was much that was nonsensical in the manipulation of this cult, the product alike of both clever detractor and naive devotee. But the cult was the design of Mao himself, who came to wield it as yet another weapon in the political struggle, along with the PLA and the mobilized masses. He told visiting Edgar Snow on one occasion that Khrushchev may have fallen because he lacked such a cult.[12]

Mao triumphed over Liu Shaoqi by hurriedly calling together a plenum of the Central Committee, the first such meeting in four years. The Eleventh Plenum of the Eighth Central Committee was held in Beijing from August 1 to 12, 1966, attended by only 80 of its 120 members, but augmented by many "revolutionary teachers and students."[13] During the plenum, on August 5, Mao wrote his own famous wall poster "Bombard the Headquarters," implicitly inviting criticism of the party's highest levels. Liu was dismissed from the Politburo's Standing Committee, ostensibly for not making the work teams responsive to the masses, but was spared public vilification by name for some months to come. Lin Biao became the only vice chairman of the party and was designated Mao's heir-apparent.

On August 8, the Eleventh Plenum issued the Sixteen Articles, apparently a compromise document that just managed to pass with a majority vote. The Sixteen Articles provided the first guidelines for what was now called the Great Proletarian Cultural Revolution, which was finally to get underway. This was to be a movement, it was exclaimed, to "sweep away all monsters" and "touch men to their very souls." It was also to "put daring above all else and boldly arouse the masses."[14]

The daring organizational instrument created initially for this purpose was the Red Guard movement, comprising mobilized youth across the nation.[15] The youngsters first enthusiastically assaulted the Four Olds, that is, old ideas, culture, customs, and habits. Such direct experience, which involved struggle and self-questioning, was to provide the personal "steeling" that would ostensibly transform them into the revolutionary heirs for whom Mao longed. But neither the Sixteen Articles nor the August 12 communiqué at the end of the Eighth Plenum gave specifics. They merely provided exhortations, apparently to give the masses a free hand, for the latter were to be trusted, relied on, and respected for their initiative. Fear, particularly of "disturbances," was to be thrust aside.[16] This rhetoric, however, failed to impress municipal and provincial party leaders who from the beginning actively resisted the Red Guards or tried to subvert them.[17] For her part, Jiang Qing used this initial campaign in October to have the homes of writers and artists in Shanghai who were in her disfavor, for reasons that went back to her experience as an actress in the 1930s, searched and ransacked. Items that were found to relate to her contact with them were burned in January 1967.[18]

Between August 18 and November 16, 1966, about 10 million Red Guards traveled to Beijing, where they took part in eight successive monster rallies. During this period, the youngsters were encouraged to travel extensively in order to exchange "revolutionary experiences," and transportation was provided free of charge in order to make this possible. In this way, the Cultural Revolution Group disrupted the control of local party officials over the Red Guards and made it clear that Beijing and the PLA were supportive of the new organization. At each of the large Beijing demonstrations, they were greeted by Mao, along with Lin Biao and Zhou Enlai. However, this "revolutionary tourism" was suspended on November 16 because of the strain placed on the country's inadequate and overburdened transportation system, an order that some were re-

luctant to obey. Subsequent exchanges of revolutionary experience undertaken afoot were known, therefore, as "long marches."[19]

The party committees responded to this massive support for the
Red Guards from the Center Cultural Revolutionary leadership in Beijing (which I will refer to as the Center for the time being) by forming
alternative Red Guard organizations that would be supportive of them.
By the end of October it was apparent that a stalemate had been reached.
Nevertheless, the Center now raised the ante and made the situation
even more complicated. It lifted the restrictions on membership in the
Red Guards for those with a "five red" background. This attracted into
the movement many youth who had become disenfranchised as a result
of earlier party policies, as Hong Yung Lee has described so well. Thus,
even sons and daughters of disgraced intellectuals might hope for opportunities in a real shake-up of the system, particularly if class was
defined as a mental attitude or consciousness rather than a matter of
birth or economics.[20] Also, the Center now permitted student activists
to enter factories and communes in order to complement mobilization
efforts among workers and peasants. Finally, the Center attempted to
make it clear that targets were not limited to local party committees
but should focus on high-ranking leaders who opposed the movement.
To underscore this, in December 1966, several such leaders were paraded
in the streets of Beijing. For some time already, Red Guard tabloids and
wall posters had been criticizing by name Liu Shaoqi, Deng Xiaoping,
and Tao Zhu. The latter had replaced Lu Dingyi as propaganda chief and
by his outspokenly radical rhetoric for a time appeared to be a Maoist.
The fact that he was now termed a "double-dealer" suggests a talent for
having been able to use radical arguments to arrive at conservative
conclusions.[21]

But none of these efforts seemed to produce the desired effect of
eliciting self-criticisms from party leaders throughout the country. Instead, many leaders sought ways of ingratiating themselves with workers. This was said to have resulted in the error of "economism," whereby
wages were raised and bonuses bestowed for this purpose.[22] However,
Andrew Walder has shown that, in fact, it was a decision of December
26, 1966, by the Cultural Revolution Group in Beijing, making concessions to temporary and contract workers, that more than any other single
event triggered "economism" in Shanghai.[23]

By mid-January 1967, the Center abandoned its efforts to win compliance from the party establishment. On January 23, a Central Committee directive announced plans to form a "great alliance to seize power
from those in authority who are taking the capitalist road," to which
the PLA was to give its active support. As Harry Harding has noted, the

role of the masses had now changed. They were no longer merely critics and monitors of cadre performance, but were now enjoined to become part of an alliance and rise in rebellion to depose those who had usurped power.[24]

But, of course, the masses were hardly a unified constituency or force with which to work, for they included many different interests. They could be manipulated by party committees that exploited such differences. As a result, there was great confusion for a time and very few of the initial power seizures proved to be acceptable to the Cultural Revolution Group in Beijing.

On February 1, 1967, a new model for seizing power was provided, the "three-in-one combination." In its final format, this would include representatives of revolutionary mass organizations, the PLA or militia, and revolutionary party cadres. The latter representative was crucially important for the CCP itself, since the party was assured a meaningful role in the shifts of power that would be taking place everywhere. There was for some time some difficulty in translating the participatory concept into an appropriate ongoing institution that could effectively use the power that would be seized. Initially, the concept of the Paris Commune was influential, and many of the newly established power seizures referred to themselves as a form of people's commune.[25] On February 5, Shanghai declared itself to be a people's commune. However, Shanghai officials were quickly summoned to Beijing to meet with Mao, who disabused them of the appropriateness of this hasty action. The problems with the concept at this juncture included the uncertainty of the results of elections that would be necessary, the incompatibility with the notion of the three-in-one combination format, and the indeterminate role of the party in such an organization of power. Hence, on February 19, 1967, the Central Committee forbade the use of the people's commune designation by municipalities and provinces.[26]

Within a month the Center began advocating that revolutionary committees, based on the organization of power in Heilongjiang province, be established at every level of administration throughout the country. These committees were subsequently formed as a result of hard bargaining among conflicting groups and with the ultimate approval of the Center in the case of the provinces and important municipalities. In Shanghai, Zhang Chunqiao merely changed the designation from commune to Shanghai Municipal Revolutionary Committee.[27] But elsewhere this proved to be a very long and painstaking process. It would take about eighteen months before all of the provincial revolutionary committees were worked out and approved.

This sudden moderation of the Cultural Revolution became known as the February Adverse Current. Mao himself had become persuaded that the masses could not carry out power seizures by themselves and furthermore insisted on a policy of leniency toward erring cadres. This respite enabled Premier Zhou to restore some order in a government that had become nearly defunct.[28]

The PLA, in the meantime, inexorably became more and more drawn into the maelstrom. Of course, under Lin Biao, it had for years been preparing for a major role in such a situation. It had initially provided logistical support for the new Red Guard organization in the late summer and fall of 1966. But by early 1967 it was successively ordered to support the left (specifically so on January 23); to participate in revolutionary committees; to resume on March 7 a military training program for the Red Guards that originally began in December 1966; and also, on March 28, to "support industry and agriculture." The latter assignment amounted to ensuring that production not be interfered with, as the radicals began to counterattack the moderate reorientation of February.[29] Needless to say, these were difficult orders to obey uniformly. Moreover, the PLA, while better organized and disciplined than other institutions, had its own divisions regarding the Cultural Revolution. In any case, even if it was in the main ideologically sympathetic to Mao and the radicals, it was basically a conservative institution, strongly oriented toward maintaining order rather than promoting disorder in its own social setting. Its conservatism was particularly aroused when radicals actually attacked the PLA itself, abusing soldiers and acquiring weapons. Thus, the PLA often exercised its authority to disband counterrevolutionary organizations by suppressing radicals instead. Time and again, subtly and otherwise, it opted to support conservative mass organizations. The PLA, despite Lin Biao's leadership, frequently found itself at odds with the Cultural Revolution Group in Beijing.

In March 1967, the Center did counterattack the February Adverse Current. This resulted in further compromises. The revolutionary committees and their three-in-one combination composition was reaffirmed, and a greater role given to revolutionary mass organizations, although conservative mass organizations were also recognized. Liu Shaoqi was now attacked personally in the official media for the first time. His wife, Wang Guangmei, was forced to undergo a humiliating interrogation at Qinghua University on April 6.[30] The conservative mass organizations continued, however, to receive increasing PLA support. The struggle between the two kinds of mass organizations reached epic proportions, with numerous casualties, during the spring and early summer, at which time a stalemate had clearly been reached.

This inconclusive conflict gave rise to a secret conspiratorial organization that prompted the mass movement to attack officially prohibited targets.[31] This extremist faction, called the May 16 Group, aimed its barbs at Zhou Enlai and at the PLA. The PLA, in turn, sought to defend itself by instigating conservative mass organizations to attack the radicals. This contributed to the rising tide of violence that reached a particularly dramatic climax in Wuhan.

As in most other places, the military authorities in Wuhan had been siding with their local conservative mass organizations, the most important of which in Wuhan was called the One Million Heroic Troops, rather than with the radicals' lead unit, the Workers' General Headquarters. In fact, in March the PLA had arrested 500 leaders of the latter organization. This had been appealed to Beijing and discussions between the Wuhan military authorities and the Center ensued without much satisfaction to the local radicals. In June and July, as elsewhere, the fighting in Wuhan became intense, with more than 1,000 persons killed and a sharp reduction in factory production in that metropolis alone.[32]

In July, two Center leaders, Xie Fuzhi and Wang Li, were sent to Wuhan to investigate the situation. Following their review, the Beijing emissaries basically decided against the conservative mass organization and the PLA's actions in Wuhan. Thereupon, the One Million Heroic Troops kidnapped Wang Li from his hotel and beat him badly. Zhou Enlai, who flew to Wuhan to mediate this grave situation, narrowly averted being kidnapped himself. Beijing responded decisively by dispatching an airborne division and naval forces. Wang Li was retrieved and, with Xie Fuzhi, returned to Beijing. The PLA's commander in Wuhan, Chen Zaidao, was compelled to return to Beijing as well, but in the end received only a light punishment. The affair can be read as an example of disagreement with and hostility to the Cultural Revolution Group by powerful elements in the PLA.[33]

The Cultural Revolution Group and leftists throughout the country now became even more radicalized for a time, perhaps as an expression of their own dissatisfaction with the trend of developments. On July 22, Jiang Qing advised the radicals to seize weapons with which to defend themselves. During this wave of radical extremism, leftists drastically disrupted China's foreign affairs work when they forcibly occupied the Ministry of Foreign Affairs for five days or more in August 1967.[34] Elsewhere they did their best to provoke foreign incidents. Among the worst instances were the sacking of the Soviet Consulate on August 17 and, more seriously, setting afire the British Embassy on August 22. China's foreign policy was in a painful, self-imposed crisis. All ambassadors were withdrawn from abroad for study, with the exception of

Huang Hua in Cairo. In this phase, the radicals simultaneously attacked sensitive areas of the establishment military and bureaucracy elite, as well as the conservative mass organizations below. This imprudent strategy threatened important government functions and arrayed against the radicals a united front of formidable proportions.[35]

On August 11, 1967, the Center changed the movement to a more moderate direction again. Jiang Qing and Chen Boda exposed the May 16 Group. An enlarged meeting of the Beijing Revolutionary Committee was held on September 1 at which the radicals were further restrained. Jiang Qing was soon compelled to reverse herself regarding the use of weapons, and had to ask her followers to lay them down. She also praised the PLA, and criticized ultraleftism. Prominent leftists Wang Li, Guan Feng, and Lin Jie were given no opportunity to backtrack and were purged from the Cultural Revolution Group. They were charged with promoting a counterrevolutionary line, regarded as " 'left' in form but right in essence."[36]

The Center announced that the party would be rebuilt and a campaign to rectify class ranks would get underway. This campaign was to put the radicals on the defensive since so many of them hailed from families with less-than-satisfactory revolutionary backgrounds. Military training was begun anew on campuses, and the study of Mao's thought was to be undertaken throughout the bureaucracy. Educational reform was to be emphasized, as was the public criticism of Liu Shaoqi and Tao Zhu. Also, official propaganda shifted its attention from students to workers, who were now regarded as the main force of the movement. Mao agreed with these deradicalization measures at this time, and he made it clear that the PLA's integrity was to be preserved. The Cultural Revolution was again to emphasize the theme advocated by the PLA for the past year, i.e., that the movement constituted a "Great School of Mao Tse-tung Thought."[37]

The PLA clearly gained ascendancy over the leftists of the Cultural Revolution Group in this shift. Renewed approval of the PLA and the implicit support of the conservative mass organizations from Beijing only fueled the disillusionment that many earnest, idealistic Red Guards had begun to experience when the PLA first cracked down in March 1967. Some decided to leave China altogether.[38] Some protested all the more vigorously, as did a group called the *Sheng-wu-lian* in Hunan. Following its formation in mid-October 1967, this group published three documents that provided a blistering critique of the revolutionary committees and called for an armed uprising to overthrow them and establish communes in their stead.[39] A major point made in this critique was that participation by experienced cadres in political institutions was not necessary, that people could prosper without such bureaucrats. The *Sheng-wu-lian* was greatly disappointed with Mao for having abandoned the urban commune.

But the tide against the leftists continued. Another prominent leftist in the Cultural Revolution Group, Qi Benyu, disappeared from sight by the end of 1967. The *Sheng-wu-lian* was suppressed in January 1968. As the revolutionary committees continued to be formed, radicals saw their share of participation and influence decline. But they were outraged to see the wholesale reinstatement of cadres who were attacked at the beginning of the movement, and the revival of the old work methods as well.[40]

This renewed moderate trend appeared to be arrested briefly in March 1968. Following several high-level meetings that month in Beijing, Yang Chengwu, the PLA's acting chief of staff, was purged. Among other charges, Yang was said to have improperly influenced personnel appointments, especially to the revolutionary committees.[41] This may have appeared to be a gesture of encouragement to the Cultural Revolution Group and the radicals, but in fact, Yang, a close associate of Lin Biao, had been forced out at the insistence of several of the regional commanders.[42] Yang was replaced by General Huang Yungsheng from the Guangzhou Military Command. With Yang's purge, the Cultural Revolution entered its final phase. This phase, initiated by Jiang Qing, was basically a campaign against "rightist trends." A classified radical pamphlet, for example, reprinted in Guangzhou in March, warned that the handful of "capitalist roaders" already dragged out were not "dead tigers," but were only waiting to counterattack.[43]

The revival of the leftists' hopes only exacerbated tensions once again, with the result that armed struggle resumed, and reached serious proportions by June and July of 1968. Weapons were again seized, including the hijacking of trains carrying arms bound for the Vietnam War. Numerous incidents were reported involving great property damage and considerable loss of life. This time even the PLA felt its organizational integrity and morale threatened, because now some of its units were more actively supportive of the left. In many places throughout the country, the PLA came down hard on the radicals. Most students had by now become disenchanted with the movement, but there were diehards who continued to carry on a bitter fight, even disregarding direct orders from authorities, including Mao. On July 3, a small war erupted on the Qinghua University campus in which fifteen students were killed.[44] The Red Guards held a secret nationwide conference in Beijing in late July.

At this point, Mao stepped in. He scolded five student leaders at his residence in the middle of the night. Mao also decided that the Red Guards had served their purpose. He turned to more mature individuals with whom to work in seeking to achieve his objectives. These were none other than the proletarians themselves, who had already been getting the lion's share of media attention since the previous fall, and who had already shown themselves to be more restrained.

Thus, on July 30, 1968, thousands of soldiers, workers, and peasants descended on Qinghua University, and a Worker-Peasant Mao Zedong Thought Team began to administer the school. This pattern was repeated throughout China's cities. In the countryside, poor and middle peasant associations performed the same function. These teams, numbering in the hundreds on occasions, were supported by the PLA. This shift in organizational and personnel format was symbolically stated when, on August 5, Mao sent the team at Qinghua a well-publicized gift of mangoes.[45] The shift did not mean that Mao had given up his own radical aspirations. He told a delegation of visiting Albanians at the end of August that China was paying a very high price in the current Cultural Revolution. He added that such a "struggle between the two classes and the two lines cannot be settled in one, two, three, or four cultural revolutions." He thought it would take fifteen years to consolidate the present movement, while two or three such revolutions should be carried out every hundred years.[46]

Plans for the Ninth Party Congress were initiated by Mao in the fall of 1967, and entrusted by him to the Shanghai radicals, Zhang Chunqiao and Yao Wenyuan. This gave the radicals the opportunity to see that the party's reconstruction would serve their own interests. Thus, the decisions were reached that the delegates would be selected and not elected, that a national party congress would be held first and then followed by lower echelon congresses, and that the congress would be held sooner rather than later in light of the growing conservative trend in late 1967. These measures were thought to favor the radicals.

On December 2, 1967, the Center also decided to begin the reconstruction of the party structure itself and issued guidelines to that effect. Discussions of the guidelines revealed the usual differences that beset the Chinese political leadership. The Shanghai Revolutionary Committee, being Maoist, predictably favored the inclusion of nonparty Cultural Revolution rebels who had been performing party-like functions. Only after argumentation did the Guangdong Revolutionary Committee concede that leaders of mass organizations might attend, without voting privileges, the "nuclear party meeting."[47] On this and similar issues, the radicals tended to favor an opening up and reforming of the party, while conservatives desired a normalization of the party along previous lines. The work of party reconstruction proceeded apace as the provincial revolutionary committees themselves came to be formed. The last five of these, located in border areas, were organized in August and September, perhaps with special haste dictated by Chinese concern over the Soviet invasion of Czechoslovakia on August 21, 1968.

The Twelfth Plenum of the Eighth Party Congress was held from October 13 to 21, 1968. The plenum concentrated its fire on Liu Shaoqi, removing him from all offices and expelling him from the party as a "renegade traitor and scab." His removal from the state chairmanship was illegal, since this could be done only by the NPC. Liu would be mistreated over the next few years and die a miserable death. For his part, Deng Xiaoping was not named in the plenum communiqué, even as "that other top Party person in authority taking the capitalist road."[48] A new draft party constitution was adopted. The plenum also approved two so-called mass line programs that were shortly implemented. One of these was a massive shift of urbanites, mostly young people, among whom were many of the most radical Red Guard leaders, to rural villages. This comprised a movement of as many as 30 million people by the spring of 1969. The other program revived certain Great Leap Forward economic policies. This saw the abolition of private plots and work points at some communes.

In the month just before the Ninth Congress, there occurred two heavy military clashes with the Soviets on an unimportant island on the Ussuri River, called Zhenbao by the Chinese and Damansky by the Russians.[49] The first clash took place on March 2; the second on March 15. From appearances the Chinese may well have won the engagements.[50] They had the geographical advantage since the island was closer to their bank of the river. As to who started the affair, both sides claimed that the other was to blame. In all likelihood it was the Chinese who provoked the crisis, perhaps to deflect attention at the impending party congress from domestic factionalism and problems.[51] Less convincingly, it was claimed that the Soviets chose this means of warning Chinese comrades preparatory to the congress.

The Ninth Party Congress, of "unity and of victory," met secretly in Beijing from April 1 to 24, 1969. Mao gave two short speeches to the 1,512 delegates, almost three-quarters of whom were from the PLA. Lin Biao delivered the principal report, in the course of which he made as many as 148 references to Mao.[52] Lin affirmed that the Cultural Revolution had been "absolutely necessary and most timely for consolidating the dictatorship of the proletariat, preventing capitalist restoration and building socialism." He described in fulsome detail the "crimes" of the fallen Liu Shaoqi. Although a great victory had been won, Lin cautioned his comrades, using Mao's words, that "the defeated class will still struggle . . . We must not lose our vigilance."

With regard to the international scene, Lin spoke truculently about both superpowers. He quoted Mao: "Working hand in glove, Soviet revisionism and U.S. imperialism have done so many foul and evil things that the revolutionary people the world over will not let them go unpunished."

The congress adopted a new party constitution, the briefest yet in the history of the party.[53] Mao and many of his precepts were again extolled. Mao Zedong Thought was now seen as the "Marxism-Leninism of the era in which imperialism is heading for total collapse and socialism is advancing to world-wide victory." The constitution also recognized that socialist society covers a considerably long period of history, during which "there are classes, class contradictions and class struggle, there is the struggle between the socialist road and the capitalist road, there is the danger of capitalist restoration and there is the threat of subversion and aggression by imperialism and modern revisionism." These contradictions can be resolved only by depending on the Marxist theory of continued revolution . . . Such is China's Great Proletarian Cultural Revolution."

Most important, and unusual, was the inclusion in the new party constitution of the provision that Lin Biao was the successor to Mao. Thus, despite all the rhetorical adulation of Mao and his thought, the congress was perhaps a greater victory for Lin than it was for Mao. The party chairman had, after all, made many painful compromises during his Cultural Revolution. Many of his most ardent ideological supporters had been ground under during the convoluted twists and turns of the movement.

It did appear that some of Mao's ideas had born fruit. The countryside was now sharing in more of the benefits of the revolution. At least rudimentary health care and education were now extended to most of the production brigades, or villages, although the expense for these had to be borne locally. The bureaucracy had been reduced in size, at least in the number of its ministries and agencies. More urbanites and cadres than ever before were regularly sharing some of the physical labor of workers and peasants, so that it could be said that the life of the latter was better understood than ever before. The Dazhai model brigade provided a well-publicized example of the virtues of self-reliance and hard work that might inspire the entire nation. The Dajing Oil Field similarly underscored China's determination to pull itself up by the bootstraps. May 7th Cadre Schools were instituted to improve the ideological understanding and coincidentally the physical well-being of cadres throughout the party and state bureaucracy.

Such institutions and such practices, in Mao's reckoning, represented China's forthright and timely response to the danger of revisionism and capitalist restoration. They were the means whereby the ideal Maoist man would begin to come into being. This beginning would be nourished by the distinctive value-laden artistic productions and propaganda of the radical-controlled media and cultural forums. Ultimate success was to be assured by means of an overhauled, simplified, and more relevant educational system, even if this meant keeping universities and colleges closed for several years. Such efforts comprised the heart of the much-touted alternative Chinese way in socialism. It was an effort that found sympathizers throughout much of the world, who often saw what they hoped to see, especially as uncritically presented by the Chinese media.

Of course, little of this Maoist vision had been shared or supported by the party itself. Most of the elite party leadership found much in the vision that was anathema to them. The fiction of party support would not long outlive the visionary party leader. Nor would many of the new institutions and some of the practices that hailed back to Yan'an and to the Great Leap.

The reality in 1969 could be perceived somewhat better in the composition of the Ninth Central Committee, which was elected at the congress.[54] Of the 170 members and 109 alternates of the new Central Committee, about 45 percent were from the PLA, about 28 percent were revolutionary cadres, and 27 percent from the revolutionary masses. This breakdown reflected the popular three-way alliance of the ubiquitous revolutionary committees. Only about one-third of the new Central Committee had survived from the Eighth Central Committee.

The Ninth Central Committee elected a new Politburo, consisting of 21 members and four alternates.[55] Mao was chairman and Lin Biao vice chairman. Only nine of those elected had been on the Politburo prior to the Cultural Revolution. About half were from the PLA. The military had become exceedingly prominent in Chinese politics. This was hardly an original aim of the Cultural Revolution. Instead, the Politburo's composition graphically illustrated one of the disquieting consequences of that chaotic adventure for the party.

· I I ·

Aborted Military Domination

The party survived the Cultural Revolution only because Mao, the party's larger-than-life leader, chose to enable it to do so. In fact, he had from the beginning no other intention. Mao merely wanted to shake the party to its foundations to rid it of revisionism. He did not wish to destroy such a useful organizational instrument. The shaking, however, was cataclysmic. The party was nearly destroyed and for a time actually ceased to perform its leadership function. This it had perforce surrendered to successive experimental organizational devices and to coalitions representing varying interests. In the end, however, it was the PLA that quieted the political storm and tamed the chaos. Thus, the reviving party had to deal with a formidable military whose appetite for rule had been whetted, and whose ambitious leader, now Mao's constitutionally designated successor, intended to radically refashion Chinese society. Ideally, from this perspective, a more compliant party would no longer constitute the intractable obstacle to such plans that it did before the Cultural Revolution. As Jurgen Domes has pointed out, at the height of Lin Biao's power, the party "was about to become a mass organization of the PLA, particularly at basic unit, county and provincial levels."[1]

The major challenge of the party at this important watershed in its history, therefore, was to rebuild without being dominated by the military, precisely avoiding the compliant status that Lin Biao wished it to have. The military was not the only source of concern, although it was the most overwhelming for the moment. The Cultural Revolution radicals, although their power and influence continued to decline, superficially (as it turned out) did seem to have an initial advantage in the rebuilding of the party. Mao, even as he stood somewhat apart by this time, had tried to provide them this edge at the outset of the rebuilding process. Exhortations to "absorb proletarian fresh blood," that is, those rebel fighters who have "a high level of consciousness of the struggle between the two lines, a keen sense of class struggle, boldness in stepping to the forefront of the struggle in defense of Chairman Mao's revolutionary line and, especially, firmness in opposing revisionism," supported the radicals' effort.[2] A campaign of "struggle-criticism-transformation," in which nonparty masses participated, served the same purpose. Initially, beginning in May 1969, after the creation of the new Central Committee and its Politburo, the rebuilding took place at the basic level, in the commune brigades and in enterprises.

The second stage of party rebuilding began in late 1969 and lasted until the Second Plenum of the Ninth Central Committee in August 1970.[3] During this stage the focus shifted to the county level, even though basic-level rebuilding would continue for some time. Mass participation continued, but the rebuilding was now more carefully directed by higher-level party authorities. This stage saw further erosion of the influence of the Cultural Revolution Left, as millions of Red Guard and revolutionary rebel leaders were sent to the countryside, and as the military demanded the acceptance of discipline as the most important criterion for membership in the party. Progress was slow during this stage. Not only was there the rearguard struggle from the disorganized and declining radicals, but disagreement mounted among other leaders as to which cadres purged during the Cultural Revolution should be rehabilitated.

This disputation took place primarily between two factions. One of these factions favored the consolidation of military dominance, while the other sought an independent party organization. Hence, the latter faction sought the rehabilitation of organizationally competent cadres who would restore the party's leadership, while the former emphasized a "correct" political orientation. The May 7th Cadre Schools were used to facilitate the systematic rehabilitation of cadres who had not erred seriously. By mid-1970 as many as 100,000 cadres from the national capital and some one million at the provincial level had been sent to these rurally located schools. The PLA, which ran these schools, took advantage of this opportunity to prevent the rehabilitation of many veteran party cadres as a means of maintaining its own power. But this angered Mao, who considered this abuse of authority an "ultra-Leftist" deviation.[4]

The next stage of party rebuilding began after the Second Plenum in August 1970. Now the focus was shifted to the provincial level, even though a great deal yet needed to be done at the lower echelons. Significantly, the PLA regional commanders supervised the reestablishment of the provincial party committees. By the time the last of the provincial party committees was established in August 1971, they were utterly dominated by the military commands. There was actually a larger proportion (62 percent) of military in the secretariats of the new provincial committees than there had been in the revolutionary committees, and nearly all regional military commanders assumed leading party positions in the provincial committees. Only 5.1 percent of the secretariat personnel could be said to represent the Cultural Revolution mass organizations.[5] Interestingly, however, a large proportion of the new secretaries and deputy secretaries of the provincial committees were recruited from areas outside their new posting.[6] Shanghai alone remained a bastion of radical civilian strength. Efforts were made concurrently to reestablish both central control over the party and the party's control over the military. But this would prove to be a long, painstaking process, if only because the military's presence was so pervasive and actually fulfilled the obvious need for providing order. The efforts took the form of directives from Mao and the Central Committee instructing the PLA to defer to the party committees, and to respect the party constitution's stipulation regarding party control of the military. A study campaign was launched in the fall of 1970 specifically focusing on this theme, using the 1929 Gutian Resolution and a Military Affairs Committee directive of 1960 as study materials. An enlarged Politburo meeting in December 1970 and a central work conference in April 1971 saw Mao call for self-criticism on the part of Lin's collaborators for their "arrogance and complacency."[7] Criticisms of the work style of army representatives on party and revolutionary committees increased, both publicly and privately.[8] Finally, Mao told his military commanders in the late summer of 1971 that they should pay attention to military affairs. "You should not only be civil officials but also military officials."[9]

Also importantly, the state bureaucracy was slowly reviving and its leadership, under Zhou Enlai, became more assertive, even though for a time military leaders were assigned important posts in the ministries as well. Initially, these agencies were much smaller than previously and some of their functions had been transferred downward. Moreover, many of their cadres were still undergoing reform. Many second-level cadres began to be rehabilitated and reassigned to government positions in the spring of 1970, and by the fall of 1971 purged high-level cadres began to reappear. On this basis, the State Council began regular meetings in March 1970, the first since 1967.[10] Reflecting the priority issue of the period, one of the first of the ministries to be reestablished with adequate staffing was the Ministry of Foreign Affairs.

Similarly, mass organizations of the pre-Cultural Revolution period began to re-emerge. These were important mechanisms through which the party traditionally extended its authority. The Communist Youth League, which before the Cultural Revolution had been the principal feeder organization for party recruits, was reconstructed nationwide by the fall of 1970. The All-China Federation of Trade Unions was mentioned in the press in February 1971.

The impressive position of Lin Biao and the military in Chinese politics was neutralized in the end, however, by a combination of more immediate and serious factors. First, Mao soon after the Ninth Party Congress apparently began to lose confidence in Lin as a suitable successor after all. Second, even as the military consolidated its power, it experienced a widening split within its own ranks. Finally, an effective coalition of forces arrayed themselves against Lin. This combination of factors in the end drove Lin to take or become party to drastic measures that led to his own destruction.

Mao's displeasure became apparent in March 1970 when he approved the removal of the post of state chairman from the new draft PRC constitution. This decision confirmed Premier Zhou Enlai as the de facto head of government, and suggested to Lin that Mao was now considering a collective leadership rather than a single successor when Mao should leave the scene.[11] In the meanwhile, criticisms of "arrogance and complacency" in the PLA continued.

The increasing pressure on Lin Biao and on the Left, which despite its own declining fortunes remained for a time partly allied with Lin, led to a showdown at the Second Plenum of the Ninth Central Committee. This important meeting was held at Lushan from August 23 to September 6, 1970, and was attended by 155 members and 100 alternate members.[12] Lin Biao and several of his generals used the occasion to launch a "surprise attack." They were joined by Chen Boda, a member of the Politburo's Standing Committee, who had apparently begun to feel very insecure as a leading ultraleftist at a time when the atmosphere was shifting to the right. This surprise attack actually constituted a challenge to Mao's authority, but was aimed at Zhou Enlai. The premier had opposed the restoration of the post of state chairman as well as another provision in the draft state constitution, which extolled the "genius" of Mao. The implication of the attack was that it was actually Zhou who opposed Mao by deleting these two provisions from the document.

However, an apparently stunned Mao reacted sharply. He quickly defended Zhou and reminded Lin that he, Mao, had already told Lin on six earlier occasions that a state chairman was not needed. Nor did Mao think much of the imputation to himself of the "genius" characterization, perceiving that it was really designed to serve Chen Boda's own purposes. Realizing the real nature of the challenge at this juncture, Mao would later refer to this encounter as the tenth major struggle between opposing lines and headquarters in the history of the CCP.[13]

Mao now began using indirect tactics to undermine Lin's PLA power base. The first such tactic was, to use Mao's depiction, "throwing stones," which meant criticizing Chen Boda's views as expressed at Lushan, with the implication that blame attached to Lin as well, inasmuch as he and Chen had conspired together. Chen disappeared from public view and was now attacked as an ultraleftist and a "political swindler." Lin's top military supporters were weakened by being made to recant and by sharing their self-criticisms at the April 1971 Central Committee work conference. Mao then "added sand to mud" by reorganizing the party's Military Affairs Committee. Finally, in January 1971, he employed the third tactic of "undermining the cornerstone" by reorganizing the Beijing Military Region.[14] These tactics weakened Lin's support in the Central Committee and in the central military organs. Mao employed a more general campaign to criticize revisionism and to rectify work style, which was directed towards senior cadres, most of whom were military leaders, as a means of undermining support for Lin generally. This campaign would last for many months, even beyond the demise of Lin Biao himself.

In the meanwhile, Lin pursued other policies in line with his own concept of a Maoist state, provoking opposition and facilitating a coalition among opponents. The most important of these were in the areas of agricultural social policy and foreign policy respectively.

Jurgen Domes has shown that Lin was determined to make a new effort to revive the essential elements of Mao's agricultural social policy, which had failed to survive either the Great Leap Forward or the Cultural Revolution. This time Lin was prepared to use the military and its disciplinary ethos to achieve results, rather than depend on either youthful enthusiasm or the spontaneous efforts of the masses as in the past. Hence, the central military organs implemented mobilization programs, three of which were of particular importance between the summer of 1969 and the spring of 1971.[15]

The first of these was the Four Good, Five Good Movement, which basically extended the features of a successful campaign of 1960 that had been conducted within the PLA to the rest of Chinese society in

1969. Once again, political thought was given priority over professionalism, and clearly understood hierarchical relationships and discipline were extolled as the means to achieve the leadership's idealistic vision for society.

The second program was the convening of congresses of activists in the living study and application of the Thought of Mao Zedong. These congresses, heavily influenced by the PLA, sought to identify dependable activists who would zealously uphold Mao's ideas, and military virtues as well. This program seemed to compete with the rebuilding of the party itself by creating a separate corps of *ganbu*.

The third program was the "down to the countryside," or *xia-fang* movement, in which as many as 15 million young people throughout the country were deported from the cities to rural areas.[16] Red Guard leaders were sent to military camps and PLA farms, where they were subjected to strict supervision. Active Red Guard members who had not actually been leaders were sent to marginal lands to engage in irrigation and forestry work. Some activists were resettled for life in villages in other provinces. But some who had been less active were sent to villages closer to home. This rustification program caused enormous hardships and incurred great resentment on the part of millions of young people and their families, and on the part of villagers, who felt imposed upon and threatened. Some small measure of this reaction was registered graphically in the statistics and testimonials of youthful escapees to Hong Kong during this period. But official propaganda made the program appear idealistic and largely voluntary.

The controversial *xia-fang* campaign may also have been meant to contribute to the radicalization of the countryside once again, as had occurred during the similar campaign in 1957–1958 that ostensibly facilitated the implementation of the Great Leap Forward. With the breakdown of civil administration during the Cultural Revolution, a massive restoration of individual farming and free trading of farm production had taken place. Specifically, the system of production advocated by Liu Shaoqi and Deng Xiaoping in 1962 had become fairly well established on a widespread basis. With his new power and authority after the Ninth Party Congress, Lin sought a return to the Maoist model of 1958, with its emphasis on the primacy of the commune, on nonmaterial incentives, and on egalitarianism. Thus, a new campaign to "learn from Dazhai" began by the spring of 1970, with an unprecedented emphasis on the principle of "politics in command" and political reliability. But this effort to return to regimented collectivization, along with the requirement to make increased grain deliveries to state procurement agencies, resulted in widespread peasant resistance.[17]

This rural resistance was noted and supported by most of the regional military commanders, who basically opposed Lin Biao's objective of making renewed heavy demands on the peasantry. On the contrary, these regional commanders were more sympathetic to a rural program that was popular with the peasants and that was more likely to assure social stability and higher productivity. Hence, the breach within the military became more apparent. Lin Biao's strength was confined to the central military apparatus and to the air force and the navy, both of which relied on the center logistically.[18] The concurrent campaign against the radical Left, which particularly concentrated on the "pseudo-Marxist swindler like Liu Shaoqi," the designation accorded Chen Boda after his fall, facilitated the efforts of those who resisted the radical rural policies that were so closely identified with Chen in the past.

Lin Biao also encountered what would prove to be overwhelming opposition in the area of foreign policy. Following the Zhenbao firefights in March 1969, China found itself under considerable duress from an aroused Soviet Union. In the course of that year, troop strength on both sides of the border escalated dramatically. Nor were all the new Soviet deployments in merely defensive positions. The stress reached maximum proportions when, after a number of border incidents in the preceding several months, the Soviets, on August 13, assaulted a contested position in the region of the Dzungarian Gates in western Xingiang province. Here the Soviets had a clear advantage and they struck in strength, killing 30 Chinese soldiers.[19] Chinese apprehensions heightened considerably during these months, particularly as the Soviets actively considered a preemptive "surgical strike" inside China as the crisis peaked in September 1969. Chinese fears led to an extensive program of digging underground shelters and would continue for many months.

This crisis eventually motivated the Chinese to seek a rapprochement with the United States. But first, either because of the immediate need to mollify the Soviets before they were provoked to do something more drastic or because of a desire to seek a genuine rapprochement with the Soviet Union, a tilt toward the latter was brought about.[20] This initial tilt toward the Soviets may have been agreed to by both Lin Biao and Zhou Enlai, but was probably advocated by Lin as the first step of a process designed to drive the United States out of Asia.[21] Thus, Chinese rhetoric toward the Soviet Union became much more cordial during this interlude. Sino-Soviet border negotiations formally began in October 1969, and during 1970 formal diplomatic relations were restored, with the respective ambassadors at their posts late in the year. In the meanwhile, Chinese rhetoric against the United States actually intensified during this period, reaching its height with Mao's exhortation of May 20, 1970, that the "People of the world unite and defeat the U.S. aggressors and all their running dogs." Despite all of this, Sino-Soviet border negotiations did not accomplish much at this juncture, and overall relations did not improve further. The CCP and the CPSU remained estranged. But this brief pro-Soviet tilt may have had the effect of making it easier for Moscow to accept the impending U.S.-PRC rapprochement, as well as making American policymakers more anxious and therefore more ready to make concessions.

It is generally conceded that the most important factors in the establishment of the U.S.-PRC rapprochement were strategic ones.[22] For once, the assessment of the situation on the part of leaders in power in both Beijing and Washington coincided. Mao and Zhou Enlai perceived that China's best interests would be served by developing relations with the United States, a change in policy that would help keep the Soviets at bay and also enhance China's economic development prospects. They saw that the United States was actually desirous of becoming disentangled from Vietnam, and no longer constituted a threat to China from the south. For its part, in withdrawing from Vietnam the United States was interested in a new understanding with China, and one that the Soviet Union would henceforth have to take into account. The desirability of this new relationship finally prevailed in Beijing. Zhou had won another policy victory over Lin Biao, a victory signaled by Edgar Snow's presence next to Mao at the October 1 celebrations in 1970 and made evident among Chinese leaders by Henry Kissinger's secret visit to Beijing in July 1971.

But by the time this major foreign policy decision had been made, Lin had long realized that his prospects were darkening, commensurate with Mao's increasing opposition. Thus, by late February 1971, Lin had already set in motion, or agreed to the setting in motion of, plans for an armed coup. His son, Lin Liguo, as deputy director of operations in the Air Force, was entrusted with the responsibility of directing the clandestine planning and organizing. Huang Yongsheng, PLA chief of staff; Wu Faxian, air force commander in chief; Li Zuopeng, navy first political commissar; and Qiu Huizuo, director of the General Logistics Department, were complicit in these plans. Between March 22 and 24, Lin's son and several conspirators worked out plans called the "Outline of 'Project 571'" (the number 571 in Chinese is a homonym for "armed uprising") in Shanghai.[23]

This clandestine document provided an assessment of the situation, a justification for action, the strategy and tactics, and even the slogans to be used. Noting that their "fleet" (the code name for Lin Biao's forces) had a number of advantages, they acknowledged that "B-52" (the code name for Mao) was wary of them. But, the conspirators reasoned, it would be better to "burn our bridges" rather than to sit still awaiting capture. "This is a life-or-death struggle—either we devour them, or they devour us." The enemies, except, ostensibly, for Chen Boda, included the radical Left, who were regarded as a "Trotskyist clique wielding the pen." Particularly targeted was Zhang Chunqiao, who was seen as a rising favorite of Mao.[24] As for B-52 himself, they held that he now behaved like the despotic Qin Shihuang (the Qin Dynasty emperor) and abused the people's trust. Noted was Mao's tactics of dividing and conquering and of turning against his supporters. The writers acknowledged that the Red Guards had been "cheated and used," "served as cannon fodder," and eventually "suppressed and made into scapegoats." The sending of young intellectuals to rural areas was "really a disguised form of labor reform." Sympathy even seemed to be evinced for administrative cadres who were sent to May 7th Cadre Schools, "which amounted to losing their jobs."

However, acknowledging Mao's continued popular status, the conspirators decided that B-52's forces were to be attacked "while waving B-52's flag." Various means were to be employed, including poison gas, biological weapons, bombs, auto accidents, assassination, kidnapping, and small urban guerrilla bands. The document also claimed that "our action will have the support of the Soviet Union."[25] A controversial secondary source holds that Lin Biao indirectly sought to present a proposal to the Soviet Union, but that this was not responded to by the Soviets.[26]

Mao learned of this plot and made an "inspection tour" of the provinces between mid-August and September 12, 1971, during which he explained his differences with Lin Biao and consolidated his support. Lin's co-conspirators allegedly tried to assassinate Mao en route from Shanghai to Beijing on September 12. When this attempt failed, according to the official report, Lin, along with his wife and son, tried to escape to the Soviet Union, but their plane crashed in Mongolia in the early hours of September 13. Lin's daughter it was said, had revealed the plot to Zhou Enlai.[27] Of course, many questions remain regarding this incident. These range from how is it that the clever Lin Biao could have been so easily foiled had he really committed himself to such an enterprise, to whether he was actually in the plane that crashed in Mongolia although recent evidence suggests that he was.[28]

This fascinating political development was kept secret from the outside world for months. Observers could only speculate that something important was occurring at the time of Lin's flight because

Chinese authorities ordered a cessation of all air traffic for two days and the air force remained grounded for three weeks. Speculation was further fueled by the cancellation of October 1 National Day celebrations in Beijing. *Hongqi's* September issue had on its cover for the third time in 1971 a color photograph of Mao and Lin together. But as Lin failed to appear in public after several weeks, then months, it became abundantly clear that something had happened to him. Lin's whereabouts was presumably too awkward a topic to raise during the visit of President Richard Nixon in February 1972. The first official explanation to outsiders began to surface in the summer of 1972. A full official explanation awaited the convening of the Tenth Party Congress in August 1973.

With Lin Biao's fall, the party was relieved of the imminent danger of becoming dominated by the military for the indefinite future. The military's presence in politics would remain noticeable for years to come, but the worst threat had now passed. However, one troublesome legacy of the Lin Biao incident was the additional incalculable strain it placed on the credibility of China's political leadership. The unresolved Cultural Revolution had already shaken confidence considerably. Then the surprising purge of Chen Boda, who had been Mao's secretary and confidant since 1937, certainly added to the image of leadership confusion. Moreover, Chen had been closely identified with the most notable features of Mao's radical programs from the Three Red Banners of 1958 through the Cultural Revolution. For him suddenly to be exposed as a swindler and brusquely abandoned by Mao raised serious questions, and had serious implications for the Left's continuing programs.

But this question-provoking situation was magnified by the revelation of Lin Biao's alleged deed and of his inglorious death. Like Chen Boda, Lin had long been known as a strong and dependable supporter of Mao and of his idealistic vision for the future, at least in the popular mind. That Lin had had serious shortcomings, as subsequent criticisms would reveal, and that he had actually tried to kill Mao was hard for many to accept. And if the charges against Lin were true, it only raised questions about Mao's judgment in his choice of successors, especially considering the towering crimes still being attributed to Liu Shaoqi. Mao's credibility and infallibility were seriously jeopardized, as, by extension, were the party's. This had to remain the case even though official accounts would emphasize that Lin's plot had been "ingeniously thwarted" by Mao and Zhou.[29]

· I 2 ·

Chairman Mao's Last Years

The party had averted domination by the military in 1971, but its own recovery was not to be an easy one. The next five years saw continued intensive political struggle. Indeed, the official party view would hold that this period comprised the remaining half of the ongoing Cultural Revolution, which was later seen as having passed through three stages. The second of these stages, which had been underway since the Ninth Party Congress in April 1969, would continue until the Tenth Party Congress in August 1973. The final stage would then last until October 1976, when, following Chairman Mao's death in September, the radicals were removed from power.[1] The continuing factional struggle during this period did little to arrest the diminishing credibility of the party.

The first need, however, was to purge all who had followed Lin Biao. This led to the dismissal of 60 leading military officers. Most of these were in the central military administration, the air force, and in Lin's Fourth Field Army loyalty group. Except for the Beijing Military Command, few of those who were cashiered were to be found in the regional military commands, for the majority of the latter had been part of the coalition that had toppled Lin. Thus, only two of the eleven regional military commanders were dismissed.[2]

The party was quick to take advantage of this purge of military leaders in order to improve its own position. It intensified the process of rehabilitating party and government cadres who had been attacked during the early Cultural Revolution. The primary justification for this was the obvious need for experienced administrators, although there was resistance. Such resistance came primarily from those who had originally criticized those being rehabilitated or who had benefited from their absence. The rehabilitated cadres were usually transferred to a locality different from where they had been when they had come under attack, but normally they stayed within their own area of functional competence. Yet, even as these veteran officials were being quickly reinstated, the party continued to cultivate new, younger cadres.[3] Hence, by the end of the ten-year Cultural Revolution, it would be reckoned that nearly half of the party's membership had joined during the Cultural Revolution.[4]

The reconstruction of the state administration, which had proceeded very slowly while Lin Biao was in power, now began to accelerate, although it remained evident for some time that the military was still visibly present even in this area. Of the eleven leading officials in the State Council who were appointed over a number of months after Lin's fall, five were PLA generals.[5] Nevertheless, as the bureaucracy reconstituted itself, it became increasingly clear that more and more veteran cadres were being rehabilitated and restored to office. In the meanwhile, the military remained entrenched in the provinces while radical representatives on the provincial revolutionary committees continued to be displaced.[6]

The very efficient Zhou Enlai, with Mao's support, had taken over the day-to-day work of the party. This led to a number of rapid improvements. It was also leading, as Ahn Byung-joon has put it, to "another institutionalizing regime under the party," similar to what had occurred in the early 1960s.[7]

Along with the restoration of previously criticized veteran cadres and reinstitutionalization, there also was a concerted effort between September 1971 and the fall of 1973 to promote policies that were highly reminiscent of the post–Great Leap Forward readjustment and basically contrary to Mao's development policies. This was the post–Lin Biao "New Course." The autonomy that had devolved to the regional leaderships in economic planning and administration during the chaos of the Cultural Revolution, which was contrary to Mao's emphasis on centralized control over key industries, was now largely confirmed. Technicians regained importance in enterprises, and management gained at the expense of workers' committees. A clearly differentiated salary structure allowing for sizable salary differences was re-established, as well as the use of material incentives, negating the Maoist preference for egalitarian remuneration and nonmaterial incentives.[8]

These New Course policies were particularly apparent in rural China, which saw a return to a distribution of labor and property at three levels, with the most important responsibilities assigned to the production teams. Small plot usage was once again guaranteed and sideline activities were encouraged. Remuneration was again related to productivity. The use of political criteria with regard to remuneration and distribution was rejected. Thus, even though the "Learn from Dazhai" slogan continued to be promoted, its intent and purpose were changed from the enjoining of a collectivist ideological orientation to that of encouraging technical innovation and productivity.[9] Self-reliance was still encouraged, but with less emphasis.

Perhaps most dramatic of all was the radical change in foreign policy. Under the aegis of Mao's so-called Revolutionary Line in Diplomacy, China gained success after success in opening to the world. China was admitted to the United Nations in the fall of 1971. President Nixon's visit in February 1972 was fraught with symbolic significance. To help explain to rank-and-file party members and the Chinese public this stunning turnaround toward the foremost capitalist nation, two of Mao's 1945 essays, "On Peace Negotiations with the Kuomintang" and "On the Chungking Negotiations," were widely circulated.[10] These had earlier promoted the concepts of flexible tactics and of a broad united front for dealing with a principal antagonist, and by implication were seen as relevant in the present situation.

But the Shanghai joint communiqué of February 28, 1972, set the framework for the continued improvement of relations with the United States in the years ahead. Similarly, Prime Minister Kakuei Tanaka visited China in September 1972, initiating an even quicker normalization process between China and Japan.[11] Over the next several years, a floodtide of nations formally recognized the PRC. China was now viewed more charitably and with greater tolerance by Americans and other nonbloc peoples than at any time since before 1949. The CCP and its PRC, with deft diplomacy, managed to achieve unprecedented international acceptability in the midst of the continuing bitter internecine political struggle.

The New Course policies were readily implemented in those areas dominated by veteran cadres directly under Zhou Enlai and where most of the regional military commanders held sway. This success emboldened these moderates to test even the remaining bailiwick of the radical leftists. Thus, even in the fields of education and culture, developments began to take place that were not generally consonant with the main thrust of Maoist ideological aspirations. For example, recently reopened institutions of higher education were gradually given some say in the admission of new students, although these were now heavily recruited from the ranks of peasants, workers, and soldiers. Even entrance examinations were reviving at some schools. Discipline was re-introduced into classrooms at all levels. By early 1972, some academic publications began to reappear. Even in the sphere of performing arts and the media, which were the main strongholds of the Left, there were indications of some change toward more variety and less political control. Beginning in early 1972, there were increasingly severe attacks throughout China on egalitarianism and ultraleft deviations. Much of this was under the guise of the campaign against "swindlers like Liu Shaoqi," which now included the yet unnamed Lin Biao, but which merely cloaked actual criticism of the Left in general, and certain features and excesses of the Cultural Revolution in particular.[12] Even the previously sacrosanct little red book of Mao's quotations, vulnerable because of its association with Lin Biao (Lin had written the introduction to the ubiquitous book and vigorously promoted it), came under attack as encouraging too superficial an understanding of Marxism.

The radical Left had not been oblivious of this rightist trend. For a time they had been powerless to respond effectively. Their fortunes had been on the decline since well before the Ninth Party Congress. They had participated in the coalition that eliminated Lin Biao, but this may have been merely a means of assuring their own survival for the time being. Nevertheless, the rightist trend from 1971 into 1973 finally galvanized the Left into action. They succeeded in enlisting more support from Mao. They strengthened ties with the secret police and built support from the ranks of the regular mass organizations that during 1973 began to revive in place of the abandoned mass Cultural Revolution organizations. They also had support from Li Desheng, who directed the PLA's General Political Department. And they still maintained tight control of most of the media and propaganda mechanisms.

During early 1973, the radical Left succeeded in changing the theme of the characterization of Lin Biao's crimes from ultraleftist to ultra-rightist, which shifted the onus from themselves, and from the Cultural Revolution, back in the direction of the moderates. The radicals argued that Lin had been guilty of empiricism and pragmatism, not of idealism or apriorism.[13] The media also began again to use more heavily the rhetoric of the Cultural Revolution. By mid-1973, the radicals began a fuller counterattack on the policies of the New Course. Symbolizing this gambit in the field of education was the case of Zhang Tiesheng, an examination candidate in Liaoning who protested being examined on academic subjects because he had been at work harvesting. His protest was defended by the radicals, who took the occasion to criticize the revisionist policies being reintroduced into education. In August

1973, the radicals began extending their counteroffensive with a new campaign criticizing the traditional sage Confucius. This was actually a renewed attack on Zhou Enlai.[14]

Also in August, from the 24th to the 28th, the Tenth Party Congress was held in the strictist secrecy and with unprecedented brevity. It had not been preceded by an announcement or even by a Central Committee plenum.[15] Even foreign newsmen, who for many months had been closely observing the Great Hall of the People in Beijing for signs of such a long-expected meeting, were taken by surprise when the official congress communiqué was publicized on August 29, the day after the congress had concluded! The 1,249 elected delegates to the congress represented a total membership of 28 million. This was the first official membership figure since the 17 million announced twelve years earlier in 1961. The congress seemed intended to settle matters following the Lin Biao purge and not to undertake new initiatives.[16] Hence, the rhetoric of the Tenth Congress emphasized continuity with the line of the previous Ninth Congress. The diction of the Cultural Revolution dominated the proceedings. The congress itself was said to represent a new three-in-one combination, bringing together representatives of three age groups: senior, middle-aged, and younger leaders.

Zhou Enlai delivered the intriguing political report, with its long-awaited official explanation of the Lin Biao Incident. In agreement with the growing tide in 1973, the incident was labeled an ultrarightist phenomenon. Surprisingly, Zhou alleged that Lin's "crimes" were designed to produce revisionism. To elaborate this point, Zhou disclosed more information regarding Lin's political report to the Ninth Party Congress. Before that congress, Lin was said to have drafted the report with Chen Boda. The two were supposedly against continuing the revolution under the dictatorship of the proletariat, arguing that the main task now was to develop production. However, this was seen to be merely a new version of the "revisionist trash" that Liu Shaoqi and Chen Boda (again!) had "smuggled" into the resolution of the Eighth Party Congress, and which was consequently rejected by the Central Committee. Lin also secretly supported Chen's "open opposition" to the final report drawn up under Mao's guidance. He only grudgingly accepted the Central Committee's political line and then read the report to the congress. Certainly an interesting revelation, but not terribly convincing. Zhou called Lin a "bourgeois careerist, conspirator and double-dealer," and his followers were described as a clique "who never showed up without a copy of *Quotations* in hand and never opened their mouths without shouting 'Long Live' and who spoke nice things to your face but stabbed you in the back." Inside China, "they wanted to reinstate the landlord and bourgeois classes," and internationally "they wanted to capitulate to Soviet revisionist social-imperialism and ally themselves with imperialism, revisionism and reaction to oppose China, communism and revolution."[17] This remarkable array of charges had probably been necessary to facilitate a compromise for the purpose of the congress, deflecting further criticism of the Left, the Cultural Revolution, and the military, while the rehabilitated cadres gained ground.

Zhou noted Mao's prescription for distinguishing the correct line from the erroneous line: "Practice Marxism, and not revisionism; unite, and don't split; be open and aboveboard, and don't intrigue and conspire." Zhou emphasized the need to strengthen the centralized leadership of the party, again quoting Mao that "it is the Party that exercises overall leadership."[18]

Interestingly, in the light of Zhou's own pragmatic handling of China's new diplomacy, the premier felt constrained to say that the international situation was "characterized by great disorder on earth" and that "such great disorder is a good thing for the people, not a bad thing."[19] Thus, Zhou counseled the party to uphold "proletarian internationalism" and to form the broadest united front against imperialism and "in particular, against the hegemonism of the two superpowers."[20] Suggesting a greater feeling of security as a result of the new diplomacy, Zhou declared that the USSR was merely making "a feint to the East" while preparing to attack in Europe.

The main reason for revising the party constitution, of course, was to delete the embarrassing reference to Lin Biao as Mao's successor.[21] But it was highly significant that 32-year-old Wang Hongwen was selected to explain the revised constitution, the second most important speech at the congress. Wang had risen quickly during the Cultural Revolution, and it was his factory in Shanghai that was said to have formed the first of the restored party committees after the Ninth Party Congress.[22] His sudden prominence was the most surprising development at the congress. This meteoric rise was confirmed at the Central Committee plenum that followed the congress, at which Wang was ranked number three in the party, ahead of even his radical seniors, Jiang Qing and Zhang Chunqiao. Wang's youthfulness symbolized a new image for the party, even though this was misleading since the average age of the overall political leadership continued to advance.

Both Zhou's and Wang's speeches spoke of the need for many more cultural revolutions in the future. Wang agreed with Zhou on the need to strengthen the party's centralized leadership and to promote its traditional style of work. He warned that privilege was to be resolutely opposed, as were such unhealthy tendencies as "going in by the back door." There was the need to train millions of revolutionary successors and to "give full play to the role of the revolutionary committees, the other sectors and organizations at all levels." He also gave attention "with special emphasis" to the favorite Maoist feature of accepting criticism and supervision from the masses. Wang added that "it is absolutely impermissible to suppress criticism and to retaliate," an injunction that was incorporated into the constitution. The party was to "have faith in the masses, rely on them, constantly use the weapons of arousing the masses to air their views freely, write big-character posters and hold great debates."

The congress elected a new Central Committee of 319 members and alternates (195 and 124 respectively), 204 of whom were continued from the Ninth Central Committee.[23] The overall total had increased by 40 over the size of the original Ninth Central Committee. Overall military representation declined, particularly among central military figures. The number of central party and government officials increased somewhat. Foreign affairs officials were well represented. Among the provincial-level delegates, the number of military representatives remained about the same, but there was an increase in the number of civil representatives.

The Tenth Central Committee held its first plenum on August 30. It elected a Politburo of the same size as the previous body, with 21 members and four alternates. Mao was reelected chairman for what would be the last time. The plenum returned to the former multiple-vice-chairman concept by electing Zhou Enlai, Wang Hongwen, Kang Sheng, Ye Jianying, and Li Desheng to this position. The Standing Committee of the Politburo now comprised Mao, Zhou, Wang, Kang, Ye, Li, Zhu De, Zhang Chunqiao, and Dong Biwu, having been enlarged from six to nine members.[24]

Sixteen of the Politburo members had survived from the Ninth Politburo. Five new full members were added, as well as the four alternates. The new Politburo also reflected the reduction of military influence. Only 9 of the 25 had had a primarily military background. Fourteen were civilian cadres and only two were representatives of mass organizations, and both of these were alternates. The average age of the Politburo had advanced from 64 at the end of 1969 to 66.3.[25] There appeared to be a rough balance between those who would support the New Course policies and the Left who opposed them, reflecting what was probably a similar composition in the new Central Committee as a whole.

But throughout the bureaucracy the rehabilitation of previously disgraced cadres would continue in the months ahead, continuously strengthening the moderates under Zhou. Among the restored leading cadres reelected to the Central Committee was Deng Xiaoping, who only six years earlier had been no less than "the second person in authority taking the capitalist road."

The initiative, however, was still with the radical Left at the outset of this final phase of the Cultural Revolution period. This slowed for a time, but did not entirely halt Zhou's protégés. A campaign to criticize Lin Biao began with the Tenth Congress, and the "Criticize Confucius" campaign was resumed. As these campaigns developed, a revised interpretation of the first emperor, Qin Shihuang, in history was debated. He was now depicted in a more positive light, not incidentally responding to the charge made in the "571" outline plan of the Lin conspiracy that Mao was a tyrant like Qin Shihuang. Also, perhaps not incidentally, it was pointed out that Qin Shihuang had ended feudalism in his day.

Likewise in the winter of 1973–1974, Mao, like Qin Shihuang, rent asunder the suspected military regional commands by secretly and swiftly shifting eight of the eleven regional military commanders. The transfers were actually a series of swaps. For example, Guangzhou Regional Military Commander Ding Sheng changed places with Xu Shiyu in Nanjing. Significantly, the transferred military commanders generally relinquished their important concurrent top regional party posts in the shift, and did not assume such positions in their new locations; only one of them did not have the concurrent party position to begin with. The three military commanders who were not transferred were all relatively new at their posts and none concurrently held a top party position. Along with these moves, three civilian Politburo members were assigned as PLA political commissars.[26] It was apparent that the party regained further preeminence by means of this development. The party was also again establishing firmer horizontal links with the center.[27]

But if the military, even though still relatively visible, was becoming less a threat to the party, the latter was increasingly beset by the heightening struggle between the radicals and the moderates or pragmatists who were generally rehabilitated party and government officials.

The campaign against Lin Biao soon turned from criticism of his personal misdeeds, which were seen to have gone back for decades, to his ideology. Thus, it was revealed that Lin was actually a Confucianist. Various arguments were made to prove this, but ultimately, of course, Lin's alleged intention to restore capitalism was the clincher, since Confucius too had been a restorationist. This reasoning, and since otherwise what could be said regarding Lin was nearing exhaustion, led at the beginning of 1974 to the merger of the campaign to criticize Lin with the one criticizing Confucius. The *pi-Lin, pi-Gong* campaign became a fascinating phenomenon that lasted nominally until Mao's death in 1976, but in effect had reached its substantive conclusion by November 1974.

Tien-wei Wu holds that the study and criticism of Confucius generated by the campaign actually developed into an intellectual debate of proportions that were unprecedented in Chinese history. But behind the facade of the intellectual debate was a bitter power struggle between the radical leadership and the party old guard around Zhou Enlai and Deng Xiaoping.[28] In the course of the debates, the Chinese public was treated to a comprehensive review and reconstruction of Chinese ancient society, feudalism, and the historic struggle between Confucianism and legalism. An enormous number of publications relating to these subjects were produced in China, particularly during 1974.

The *pi-Lin, pi-Gong* campaign became in 1974 a "revolutionary great debate" over the direction China was traveling, similar to, but less disruptive than, the Cultural Revolution. Beginning in February, criticism groups were established and wall posters mushroomed. Targets other than Lin and Confucius (and the unnamed Zhou) surfaced, including once again the late educator-diplomat Hu Shi. The campaign atmosphere prompted a transient coolness toward foreigners and criticism of certain foreign cultural expressions. For example, even though during the past year Jiang Qing herself had requested that Beethoven's Sixth Symphony be performed by the visiting Philadelphia Orchestra, Beethoven, along with Schubert, was now under attack by zealous radicals.

However, by mid-year the period of mass criticisms was basically ended. An important editorial in the *People's Daily* indicated that while criticism and supervision by the masses were welcomed, the debate was to be conducted under the leadership of the party committees. The Central Committee simultaneously issued a notice revealing that the revolutionary great debate was causing some serious economic problems.[29] For the rest of the year, the media emphasized the need for unity and order.

In anticipation of the convening of the much-delayed Fourth National People's Congress (NPC), whose impending convocation had been announced at the Tenth Party Congress, three young men placed a hundred-metre-long *dazibao* in Guangzhou in November 1974. Written under the pseudonym Li Yizhe, the wall poster, entitled "Concerning Socialist Democracy and the Legal System," argued for establishing a rule of law based on democracy. Ostensibly, the authors sought to eliminate the continuation of a "social fascist autocracy." The only way this could be accomplished, it was suggested, was by making the leadership more accountable to the people. Hence, the proposal constituted a direct challenge to the party and its vanguard role in China. The famous wall poster was dedicated to Mao, but could hardly be endorsed by him. It was quickly removed, and Vice Premier Li Xiannian termed it "reactionary through and through, vicious and malicious in the extreme."[30]

Toward the end of 1974, Mao announced three directives that summarized the year and the situation.[31] Two of these, the enjoining of "Internal Stability and Unity" and "Pushing the National Economy Forward," were congenial to the moderates. The third, however, "Studying the Theory of the Dictatorship of the Proletariat," provided grounds for further ideological disputation.

The Second Plenary Session of the Tenth Central Committee was held from January 8 to 10, 1975.[32] The plenum elected Deng Xiaoping as a vice chairman of the party and a member of the Standing Committee, replacing Li Desheng. This was an important move for the pragmatic veteran cadres, inasmuch as Zhou Enlai's health was rapidly declining.

Following the party plenum, the long-overdue Fourth NPC was held from January 13 to 17. Like the Tenth Party Congress, this NPC was also unannounced and met secretly for only a relatively short period of time. It was the first NPC meeting in ten years, even though this body was supposed to meet annually. The Fourth NPC heard an important report by Zhou Enlai, approved a much-needed new state constitution, and confirmed needed appointments to the government. The meeting cleared the air in certain important respects and restored a sense of legitimacy to the government.

Zhou reported to the NPC that the Third Five-Year Plan had been overfulfilled, as would be, it was expected, the Fourth Five-Year Plan in 1975.[33] Zhou recalled Mao's instructions to the Third NPC in 1964, envisaging the development of the national economy in two stages, beginning from the Third Five-Year Plan:

> The first stage is to build an independent and relatively comprehensive industrial and economic system in 15 years, that is, before 1980; the second stage is to accomplish the comprehensive modernization of agriculture, industry, national defense and science and technology before the end of the century, so that our national economy will be advancing in the front ranks of the world.

The new state constitution contained only 30 articles, against the 106 of the 1954 document.[34] Zhang Chunqiao reported on the revision of the constitution.[35] The new charter eliminated the posts of PRC chairman and vice chairman. It made the party chairman the commander in chief of the armed forces, reflecting the continued strengthening of the party's renewed control of the military. Similarly, with regard to the government, the new constitution explicitly stated that the exercise of its powers are "on the proposal of the Central Committee of the Communist Party." However, the new constitution endorsed the Four Bigs (sida), that is, "speaking out freely, airing views fully, holding great debates and writing big-character posters." It guaranteed the right of persons to lodge complaints against anyone working in an organ of state, and warned against the obstruction of or retaliation against such complaints. For the first time, the state constitution made labor strikes lawful.

The State Council, with its 26 ministries and three commissions, reflected the streamlining that had taken place in recent years. Of the 29 ministers, sixteen were new at their posts, and only half had previously served in the same capacity.

Deng Xiaoping was named first vice premier, and within days also became chief of staff of the PLA, greatly strengthening his hand. Zhang Chunqiao, also on the Politburo's Standing Committee, ranked just behind Deng among the vice premiers, and shortly became head of the PLA's General Political Department. Zhu De continued to serve as chairman of the NPC's Standing Committee, as he had since 1959.

The radicals were not pleased with the results of these two important party and state meetings in January, for after the intense campaigning of the past year they had hoped for more and better posts in the Politburo and the State Council. Mao himself attended neither meeting, although he was healthy enough to continue to receive foreign visitors during the period of the meetings.

The radicals responded with a new campaign, launched in February, this time to study the theory of the dictatorship of the proletariat and to criticize and restrict "bourgeois right," that is, capitalist-like practices that continued to exist in China. Attention soon focused on Mao's observation that China, even though a socialist country, "practices an eight-grade wage system, distribution to each according to his work and exchange by means of money, which are scarcely different from those in the old society. What is different is that the system of ownership has changed." Mao also quoted Lenin's warning that "Small production engenders capitalism and the bourgeoisie continuously, daily, hourly, spontaneously, and on a mass scale." Mao affirmed that among both the workers and state personnel "there are people who follow the bourgeois style of life."[36] What continued to trouble Mao, as many of his comrades once again sought to regularize politics and to emphasize economic development, is that too many of them remained apparently oblivious of inequalities or deliberately perpetuated them. The fact that property was no longer the basis of social class was beside the point, since office and its privileges could be seen to serve just as well as the basis for class distinction. Other Marxists have been aware of this "new class" phenomenon, but, as Richard Kraus has noted, Mao was the first Marxist in power to actually seek to address the issue.[37]

Mao's warning was echoed in two articles that received wide publicity. Yao Wenyuan's essay "On the Social Basis of the Lin Biao Anti-Party Clique" attacked bourgeois tendencies and their practitioners.[38] Zhang Chunqiao's "On Exercising All-Round Dictatorship over the Bourgeoisie" struck at Soviet leadership, holding that while post-Stalin leaders had a good class background, their subsequent betrayal of their own class "accomplished what Hitler tried but failed to accomplish."[39] His main point was that the importance of technocratic competence in modernization should not be overestimated. Both Yao and Zhang discussed the need to change the system of collective ownership gradually and to eradicate corruption and backsliding among cadres and young people. These proved to be the principal pronouncements of the campaign, although many more articles ensued for several months. Zhang and Yao seem to have carried out the spirit of Mao's intentions in their articles, yet it appears that Mao remained indecisive in his support of the activities of the radicals. In May, for example, he reportedly warned them not to form a "Gang of Four."

In the meanwhile, the Central Committee and the State Council, now increasingly under Deng's leadership as Zhou's health deteriorated, held a series of meetings during 1975 to deal with specific measures to hasten economic development. The discussions eschewed ideological debate. Instead, practical measures to enhance performance, particularly in the fields of industrial management, education, and science, were stressed. More and better education and professionalism were advocated. Also a general rectification campaign against the noisome radical Left was promoted, to be conducted within the ranks of the party, for the purpose of strengthening the party committees. Deng asked, pointedly, how there could be stability and unity when a small group continues to make trouble.[40]

Three very important reports emerged from these meetings. Two of these, "On the General Program for All Work of the Whole Party and the Whole Country" (also known as the General Program) and "Some Problems in Accelerating Industrial Development" (the Twenty Points), were drafted under the supervision of Deng. The third (the only one publicized in 1975) was a report given by Hua Guofeng at a national conference on agricultural mechanization, called the Dazhai conference, held during September and October. The drafters of the comprehensive General Program took pains to refer to Mao's three directives collectively as "the key link" in proceeding with the work to be done.[41] However, Mao himself would later object to this juxtapositioning of the three directives in this way, asking "What 'taking the three directives as the key link'! Stability and unity does not mean writing off class struggle: class struggle is the key link and everything else hinges on it."[42]

There were serious industrial work stoppages during 1975. The sources of this labor unrest were unclear. They may have stemmed in part from the leftist campaign against wage incentives, but may also have been prompted by the diminishing of participatory practices in the factories. But, although strikes were now legal, they were discouraged. An effort by Wang Hongwen during the summer to settle a strike in Hangzhou failed. Deng Xiaoping, on the other hand, settled matters during July and August, although he had to use the military and shake up the factory administrations to do so.[43]

In September, Mao instigated another ideological counterattack, this time selecting the famous popular novel *The Water Margin* for intensive public criticism.[44] The object of this exercise was to show that the novel's hero, Song Jiang, despite a heroic career, had been guilty in the end of capitulation to the class enemy (similar to the alleged behavior of the Taiping loyal prince, Li Xiucheng). This historical negative example was being criticized now with Zhou Enlai and Deng Xiaoping obviously in mind. By November a more explicit campaign was launched to defend the "newborn things" of the Cultural Revolution against the efforts underway "to reverse the verdicts" of that cataclysmic struggle. This campaign provided the radicals with ample opportunity to address specific policy initiatives being undertaken by Deng, since they had been denied a part in their formulation. Much of this criticism of the "right deviationist wind" was spearheaded by the radical's new journal *Xuexi yu Pipan* (Study and Criticism).

The capable and popular Premier Zhou Enlai finally died of cancer on January 8, 1976, after having been bedridden for months. Deng gave the funeral oration on January 11 and promptly disappeared for the next year and a half. It was not until February that the revelation was made that little-known Hua Guofeng had been appointed acting premier on the day of Zhou's passing. Hua had long been a favorite of Mao, having come to the chairman's attention while serving as a party leader in Hunan, where Hua had been instrumental in establishing the Mao museum. Hua subsequently served as Minister of Public Security, a useful position from which to climb yet further.

An intense indirect campaign was conducted against the absent Deng Xiaoping. Oblique critical references appeared on wall posters and in the media about the "unrepentant capitalist roader," and more explicitly about the person who talked about the irrelevance of the color of cats as long as they caught mice! On March 21, the *People's Daily* quoted Mao to the effect that Deng was symbolic of everything wrong in the party, although it also gave assurances that this campaign would concentrate on Deng only, despite the clamor regarding the "reversal of verdicts." Deng was to be the lightening rod to absorb the ire of the radicals. Thus, the Four Modernizations (agriculture, industry, national defense, and science and technology) program of Zhou and Deng, basically supported by Hua, continued unabated.

A massive riot erupted on Tiananmen Square on April 5 as crowds reacted to the premature clearance of wreaths that had been placed there during the Xing Ming Festival in memory of the late Zhou Enlai. Tens of thousands of militiamen, police, and soldiers finally dispersed the crowd. The incident was interpreted as a "counterrevolutionary movement" and the blame for it was conveniently fixed on Deng Xiaoping. Only two days later Deng was removed from all of his positions both inside and outside the party, and the campaign against him intensified. Hua Guofeng immediately benefited from this turn of events. Having been a compromise acting premier primarily because he was the least threatening among the available able leaders in January, Hua was now named premier and first vice chairman of the party. This strengthening of Hua's personal position and his reluctance to encourage the anti-Deng campaign incurred the resentment of the radicals. But their growing opposition to him in turn awakened support for Hua among the moderates.[45]

In mid-June, the Central Committee announced that Mao would no longer meet with foreign visitors. That Mao himself did not announce such a decision seemed to suggest that he was indeed weakening, and this awareness inevitably eroded the position of the radicals. On July 6, Zhu De, the co-founder of the Red Army, passed away at the age of 90.

Dramatically underscoring the momentous power struggle and the passing of the old guard in 1976, China experienced a series of natural catastrophes. A large meteor struck Manchuria in March, and several earthquakes in May preceded the disastrous quakes of July 28 and 29, registering 8.2 and 7.9 on the Richter scale, near the city of Tangshan in north China. The casualties numbered in the hundreds of thousands, with enormous deleterious consequences for the economy. Less than a month later, another severe earthquake struck Gansu Province. Premier Hua won the sympathies of many Chinese by working hard to provide relief to the Tangshan victims. In contrast, the radicals appeared insensitively shrill, especially in these circumstances, with their incessant demands to intensify the already unpopular campaign against Deng Xiaoping.

Finally, just after midnight on September 9, 1976, Mao Zedong died at the age of 82. That same day, a lengthy "Message to the Whole Party, the Whole Army and the People of All Nationalities Throughout the Country" from the Central Committee, the Standing Committee of the NPC, the State Council, and the Military Commission of the Central Committee was released. The statement acknowledged Mao's revolutionary accomplishments with the rhetoric of the Cultural Revolution.[46] More than 300,000 persons filed by the late chairman's body as it lay in state for eight days in the Great Hall of the People. On September 18, Hua Guofeng gave the only speech during a half-hour ceremony on Tiananmen Square with a million Chinese, but no foreigners, in attendance. Hua's comments went beyond the "Message" of September 9 in references to class struggle and he reiterated Mao's "scientific conclusion" that the bourgeoisie were "right in the Communist Party," and that "the capitalist roaders are still on the capitalist road."[47] Hua also repeated the "Message's" specific reference to Deng Xiaoping, both as a target during the Cultural Revolution and in the current campaign. A distinctive epoch of the CCP had come to a close, but it appeared that through Hua Guofeng some of the essentials of its Maoist legacy would be preserved.

PART FIVE

The "Second Revolution"

· 13 ·

Changing Directions

Hua Guofeng was in an advantageous position after Mao's passing. An adroit, opportunistic politician, he sensed that his support from the conservative old guard was intact for the moment, especially in the absence of Deng Xiaoping, whose continued absence he fervently wished. This enabled Hua to co-opt some of the policies and rhetoric of the radicals in order to split their ranks and to strengthen the legitimacy of his own succession to the mantle of Mao. In the meanwhile, the radicals, as part of their own plans either to make a bid for power, as hopeless as this would be, or to help their own prospects as best they could without Mao, began to publicize on September 16 and 17 Mao's alleged dictum: "Act according to the principles laid down."[1] Significantly, Hua did not use this quotation in his memorial service speech on September 18. An intensive media war of slogans ensued. Perhaps the radicals believed, as Parris Chang asserts, that they had an ace in their possession in the form of Mao's will (whether real or forged) which anointed his widow as his successor.[2] The "will" may have been the two documents Jiang Qing was subsequently accused of having altered. One of these involved the instructions Mao gave Hua on April 30, 1976, according to Hua, to "Act according to past principles" but which Jiang is said to have changed to "Act according to the principles laid down," and which had already been widely publicized. The other was a record of Mao's meeting with Hua, Ye, Wang, and Zhang on June 3, 1976, at which time Mao allegedly asked them to help Jiang Qing "carry the Red Banner."[3]

In any case, however, on October 6, Hua and Ye Jianying struck preemptively. With the cooperation of Mao's long-time bodyguard, Wang Dongxing, and his 8341 Guard Unit, they had Jiang Qing, Zhang Chunqiao, Wang Hongwen, Yao Wenyuan, and several of their principal supporters taken into custody. Thus, the intensified struggle between the radicals and the moderates that everyone had expected in the weeks and months ahead, perhaps eventuating in a final bloody test of arms, was suddenly very neatly precluded.[4] The cultivation of the rebuilt mass organizations and the construction of new urban militias (a poor substitute for the loss of the military support once enjoyed under Lin Biao) had all been of no avail to the radicals.

On October 8, the Central Committee adopted two decisions. First, a memorial hall would be built for Mao in which his body would be permanently displayed, even though this was against his own and his widow's wishes. The memorial hall was subsequently built in only a single year, but the embalmers were able to do less than a perfect job with rather unfortunate consequences. Second, a new edition of Mao's *Selected Works* was to be published under Hua's editorship, and work would begin on Mao's *Collected Works*.[5] Both decisions were designed to appropriate Mao's remains and his writings so that they might serve the political objectives of Hua and his supporters.

The news of the arrest of the radicals gradually surfaced over the next several days. A campaign vilifying the Gang of Four was initiated, employing the same kind of personal attacks that the radicals had frequently used against others. As the shock wore off, it became quite clear that the vast majority of the Chinese people felt a great sense of relief as well. Thus, festive parades were staged throughout China from October 21 to 23 in which many millions participated.

On October 24 a similar demonstration was held on Tiananmen Square to celebrate the announcement that on October 7 Hua had become party chairman and chairman of the Military Affairs Commission, in addition to being premier of the State Council and minister of Public Security. Hua now held more titles simultaneously than Mao ever did in his long career. Also on the rostrum with Hua was Wu De, the first secretary of the Beijing Municipal Party Committee and a Politburo member, who explained to the throng that Mao himself had selected Hua as his successor. According to Wu, on April 30, Mao had written to Hua in his own handwriting, "With you in charge, I'm at ease." Wu also catalogued many of the alleged crimes of the radicals. Perhaps the most ironic of the many charges was that they were "typical representatives of the bourgeoisie inside the Party, unrepentent capitalist-roaders still travelling on the capitalist road and a gang of bourgeois conspirators and careerists."[6]

The campaign condemning the Gang of Four would continue for many months, and was joined by many who were anxious to express their pent-up rage. The combined November–December issue of *China Reconstructs* displayed copies of photographs originally published in *Peking Review* on September 24, but in this version pictures of the fallen radicals were blotted out, a particularly graphic expression of rejection. On December 10, the Central Committee issued a lengthy document, *Zhongfa 24*, on the crimes of the Gang of Four. This document was divided into four parts: The first part dealt with the attempt by the Four to seize power, beginning with a secret visit by Wang Hongwen to Mao in October 1974, during which he accused Zhou of conspiring with Deng and others. The second part concerned their adulteration of Mao's political line, and their defiance of Mao's admonitions. The third part dealt with their opposition to Hua, while the fourth covered their activities during Mao's illness and following his death.[7]

While there may have been considerable truth in some of these accusations, there was a monumental problem of differentiating between what the Gang may have done on their own and what they had done that was in compliance with Mao's own intentions. Yet few of the surviving Chinese leaders wished to take on the task of accusing Mao of anything at this point, particularly Hua, whose legitimacy was so closely tied to the late chairman.

In late December, the Second National Dazhai Conference was held, at which the first authorized public version of Mao's speech of April 25, 1956, "On the Ten Great Relationships," was circulated to the 5,000 delegates. Of significance was the revelation for the first time that Mao had been very critical of the Soviet Union in that speech, something that had been edited from previous versions. The timing of the release of this version was also significant, for ever since the death of Mao the Soviets had refrained from anti-Chinese polemics. For their part, however, the Chinese did not take advantage of this Soviet signal to explore a new relationship now that Mao was gone. On the contrary, on April 15, 1977, the Chinese published volume five of Mao's *Selected Works*, which made the full version of Mao's 1956 speech permanently available and part of the CCP's canon. Furthermore, Hua introduced the volume with a review article entitled "Continue the Revolution under the Dictatorship of the Proletariat to the End." Hua called upon the Chinese people to "carry to its conclusion the struggle against Soviet social-imperialism."

This ended the Soviet moratorium on polemics. An article in *Pravda* on May 14 by V. Alexandrov (a pseudonym) revealed interesting comments attributed to Mao. For example, Mao allegedly said to the Central

Committee in September 1959 that "We must rule the world." The Chinese responded to this *Pravda* disclosure with a lengthy article in *Hongqi* on July 4 entitled "Soviet Social-Imperialism is the Most Dangerous Source of World War." This point became a central thesis of the major foreign policy statement made by the CCP later in the year—a 35,000-word editorial department article in the *People's Daily* on November 1, 1977, entitled "Chairman Mao's Theory of the Differentiation of the Three Worlds is a Major Contribution to Marxism-Leninism."

In March 1977, a compromise was finally agreed on at a central work conference whereby Deng Xiaoping would be returned to leadership positions. Thus, in April, Deng wrote a letter to the party leadership pledging support for Hua and acknowledging that he had made mistakes in 1975.[8] Deng's popularity was apparent at the first anniversary in April of the Tiananmen Incident during which many posters called for Deng's reinstatement. At the Third Plenum of the Tenth Central Committee, between July 16 and 21, 1977, Deng was restored to all his previous posts. For his part, Hua was confirmed as party chairman—his original posting had been on a hasty, expedient decision of a truncated Politburo only. But Hua was undoubtedly unnerved by the spectacle of millions of people going "on a joyful rampage . . . in one of the most deafening and chaotic street parties ever seen," triggered by the news of Deng's reemergence.[9] Deng made his first official public appearance on the 50th anniversary of the PLA on August 1.

The Eleventh Party Congress was held in Beijing from August 12 to 18, 1977, attended by 1,510 delegates, who now represented more than 35 million party members.[10] The transitional character of this congress is nowhere better expressed than in its resolution to unanimously approve the "strategic decision" to "grasp the key link of class struggle and bring about great order across the land."[11]

Hua's four-hour political report to the congress summarized the "eleventh struggle between the two lines," the now official designation of the contest with the radicals.[12] The latter, Hua said, had equated veteran cadres with "democrats," and "democrats" with "capitalist-roaders," and slanderously alleged that there was a "bourgeois class" inside the party and the army. Defensively, Hua argued that "as long as supreme party and state power rests with a leading core that adheres to the Marxist-Leninist line, the capitalist-roaders cannot grow into a bourgeois class inside the party because they are only a handful and are constantly being exposed and weeded out."

In his report on the revision to the party constitution, Ye Jianying emphasized that Mao had chosen Hua as his successor, and that Hua could "certainly" lead the party triumphantly into the 21st century![13]

Reflecting the considerable confusion in the party as a result of the events of recent years, coupled with the fact that the party had recruited 7 million new members since the Tenth Congress in 1973, Ye also explained the need to establish commissions for the inspection of discipline at the county level and upwards.

Deng Xiaoping gave only a brief closing address, noting that the party "must revive and carry forward the practice of seeking truth from facts" and that "theory and practice must be closely integrated." "There must be less empty talk," Deng exclaimed, "and more hard work."[14]

The congress elected a new Central Committee of 201 members and 132 alternates. The Eleventh Central Committee differed greatly from its predecessor. It was dominated by older, experienced cadres, at least 76 of whom had been purged in the Cultural Revolution and many others who had been criticized. Seventy-one new members were added to the 110 who continued, displacing 59 who were removed and 16 who had died. Among the alternates, only 52 were carried over, while 80 persons were added to this category, including 5 who had been demoted. Provincial leaders were especially prominent. Even with the considerable changeover in military representation, the military presence remained notable.

The Eleventh Central Committee elected the new Politburo and leadership at its First Plenary Session on August 19, 1977. Hua was chairman, while Ye Jianying, Deng Xiaoping, Li Xiannian, and Wang Dongxing were the four vice chairmen. This "top five" leadership group also constituted the new Standing Committee. There were 22 members of the Politburo and three alternates. Within the Politburo, Hua and Deng each seemed to have nine supporters, while Ye, who had five supporters, held the balance.[15]

The Second Session of the Eleventh Central Committee met from February 18 to 23, 1978, primarily to complete arrangements for the convocation of both the Fifth NPC and the Fifth National Committee of the CPPCC, which would meet concurrently with the NPC. The latter organization was meeting for the first time since 1964.

The 3,460 deputies of the Fifth NPC met in Beijing from February 26 to March 5. Hua gave the principal government report, a new state constitution was adopted, and important official appointments were made at the Fifth NPC.[16]

Hua's report was another lengthy one of three and a half hours. He announced that the once ubiquitous revolutionary committees were being abolished everywhere except to serve as the unit of local government. Hua claimed that $60 billion had been lost in industrial output during 1974–1976 because of the sabotage and interference of the radicals. He announced an exceedingly ambitious ten-year plan, from 1976 to 1985, incorporating the Fifth Five-Year Plan, which sought to raise farm output from 4 to 5 percent and industrial output at the rate of 10 percent.[17]

Ye Jianying reported on the revision of the state constitution, as he had on the 1977 party charter.[18] The new state constitution was about double the size of the 1975 document it supplanted, restoring a number of provisions from the 1954 version. It now provided that material rewards could be combined with moral encouragement (Article 10). However, it incongruously noted that the production brigade could become the basic accounting unit when its "conditions are ripe" (Article 7). "Letting a hundred flowers blossom and a hundred schools of thought contend" became applicable to state policy (Article 14). Deputies of the NPC were given the right to address inquiries to government organs (Article 28). The people's procuratorates were restored "to ensure compliance with the constitution." The right of an accused person to a defense was restored (Article 41).[19]

Hua was renamed premier. Ye was named chairman of the NPC. Soong Ching Ling became chairman of the NPC's Standing Committee. Deng Xiaoping became first vice premier, basically in charge of the Four Modernizations. Deng also became chairman of the Fifth National Committee of the CPPCC, the leading united front organization.

In the weeks and months that followed these important meetings, a series of unprecedented large gatherings were held as the party and government once again sought to institutionalize political and administrative processes, and to stimulate serious economic development. In late March 1978, heralded by the detonation of a nuclear device, the first National Science Conference was held with almost 6,000 participants. In his opening address, Deng announced that science and technology specialists should also be considered workers. This blurring of the distinction between manual and mental work immediately afforded some relief to other intellectuals as well. In April, at a similar national educational conference, Deng called for strict standards and discipline in schools, and for raising the political and social status of teachers.

At an important All-Army Political Work Conference held from April 27 to June 6 in Beijing, Deng again expounded "Mao's concept of seeking truth from the facts" and enjoined his listeners "to proceed from reality and integrate theory with practice."[20] In the meanwhile, societal tensions were relieved somewhat more when in May it was announced that the many thousands of persons who twenty years earlier had been labeled rightists were now considered to be rehabilitated, and the term "rightist" itself was banned.[21]

Deng continued to score victories as the year wore on. Wu De was replaced as "mayor" of Beijing in October. The Beijing Municipal Committee now decided to reverse the verdict on the April 1976 Tiananmen Incident, calling it a completely revolutionary action. This enlivened a growing wall poster campaign in November, which was deftly utilized by Deng's supporters. The posters included further denunciations of the Cultural Revolution, suggestive comments about Mao's role in it, and outspoken charges against party vice chairman Wang Dongxing. However, also included were intriguing questions about electoral processes and human rights, for which it is unlikely Deng was responsible. By late November, large groups of Chinese held impromptu street discussions and Chinese became increasingly bold in asking foreigners for information on a range of fascinating topics. This lively activity came to a sudden halt on December 1, following the circulation of a central document warning that a state of confusion could adversely affect China's economic development. Chinese were specifically cautioned not to discuss the wall posters with foreigners.

Following an important central work conference that lasted from November 11 to December 15, the Eleventh Central Committee held its historic Third Plenum from December 18 to 22, 1978, attended by 169 members and 112 alternates. The plenum was subsequently hailed officially as "a crucial turning point of far-reaching significance in the history of our party,"[22] which has indeed proved to be the case. It represented a major victory for Deng and a crushing defeat for Hua. The plenum condemned the "erroneous" "two-whatevers" policy, that is, the contention of Hua Guofeng's that the party "firmly uphold whatever policy decisions Chairman Mao made, and . . . unswervingly adhere to whatever instructions Chairman Mao gave." Instead, it "decided on the guiding principle of emancipating the mind, using our brains," and "seeking truth from facts." Most significantly it "firmly discarded the slogan 'Take class struggle as the key link,' " which, it affirmed, "had become unsuitable in a socialist society," and it "made the strategic decision to shift the focus of work to socialist modernization."[23]

The plenum elected four additional members to the Politburo: Chen Yun, the 73-year-old former economic administrator, who became a party vice chairman and member of the Standing Committee, and the first secretary of the newly established Central Commission for Discipline Inspection; Deng Yingzhao, Zhou Enlai's widow; Hu Yaobang, a former youth leader who now headed the party's Organization Department; and General Wang Zhen, a vice premier. Deng's supporters now outnumbered the "whatever faction," although Ye Jianying's neutral contingent continued to maintain a balance for the time being. Hua was not yet displaced, nor were Wu De and Wang Dongxing. But the sudden change of direction was immediately evident.

The plenum "solved a number of important questions left over from history," including the reversal of the charge that Deng's line of 1975 was a "Right-deviationist wind to reverse correct verdicts." The Tiananmen Incident, which Hua and Wu had suppressed, was now adjudged to have been entirely revolutionary. Peng Dehuai and Tao Zhu were posthumously rehabilitated. Local authorities throughout the country were left to make similar verdict reversals. In Guangzhou, for example, this led to the rehabilitation of the famous Li Yizhe wall poster authors.[24]

The Third Plenum made very important economic policy decisions. It directed attention "to solving the problem of serious imbalances between the major branches of the economy."[25] Most important was the basic change in agricultural policy. It recognized that "private plots, family sideline occupations, and the trade in rural collective markets are necessary supplements of the socialist economy." The production team was clearly regarded as the basic unit. "This system needs to be stabilized, it must not be changed," declared the plenum communiqué.[26] Furthermore, the possibility of subdividing the production teams into small working groups of three to five families was introduced. These small groups could contract for land, seeds, and tools on a one-to-three-year basis, in return for which they guaranteed an agreed-on amount of production (baochan).[27] These reforms were immediately pioneered with considerable success in Sichuan and Anhwei provinces by provincial party leaders Zhao Ziyang and Wan Li respectively. Within months, small work groups were to be found throughout the country as peasants enthusiastically responded to the new opportunities.

Deng Xiaoping visited the United States for nine days in January–February 1979, symbolizing both his enhanced stature in the party and the improved relationship between Beijing and Washington, which had finally established formal diplomatic relations on January 1. During this visit to the United States, Deng spoke of the possibility of "punishing" Vietnam for its invasion of Cambodia the previous December. On February 17, soon after Deng's return to Beijing, the Chinese invaded Vietnam with some 330,000 men deployed against about 150,000 better armed defenders.[28] This action terminated on March 16, when the Chinese withdrew their troops after having lost 26,000 soldiers, with another 37,000 wounded.[29] The results were inconclusive, but the Soviet Union had refrained from responding militarily on behalf of the Vietnamese, with whom they had signed a treaty in November 1978. The Chinese subsequently decided not to renew their own lapsing treaty with the Soviet Union, but did offer to begin talks to improve relations, to which the Soviets responded favorably. The first round of these talks was held in October and November 1979 in Moscow.

The questionable success of the invasion of Vietnam made Deng somewhat vulnerable to his critics within the party. So did the wall-poster campaign and other demonstrations that continued into 1979. These included poor peasants protesting living conditions in the countryside and rusticated youth who had returned to the cities demanding jobs and housing. There were also representations on behalf of the many thousands who had been persecuted during the Cultural Revolution and who had not yet been rehabilitated or recompensed. But most threatening were continued demands for the Fifth Modernization, that is, genuine democracy. Having already used the wall-poster phenomenon to his advantage, Deng was now in the forefront of the crackdown on these activities, preempting thereby the charges of some of his critics. On March 30, 1979, Deng, addressing a party conference on theoretical work, conveyed the Central Committee's admonition to adhere to the Four Cardinal Principles.[30] These are the path of socialism, the dictatorship of the proletariat, the leadership of the party, and Marxism-Leninism and Mao Zedong Thought. Several dissident leaders were arrested in April, including Wei Jingsheng, the outspoken editor of the underground magazine *Explorations*. After a televised trial in October, Wei was sentenced to 15 years of imprisonment. The so-called democracy wall near Tiananmen was moved to a less congested area, and by the following year such wall posters were outlawed entirely.

The Second Session of the Fifth NPC was held from June 18 to July 1, 1979. This session reflected the decisions of the Central Committee's Third Plenum, and followed a candid admission made in April by Li Xiannian that China faced an economic crisis, with a deficit of $6.5 billion, 20 million people unemployed, and 100 million undernourished.[31] Accordingly, Hua announced to the NPC that the economy would undergo a three-year adjustment in which the ambitious targets he had set only a year earlier were to be scaled down. Recently rehabilitated Peng Zhen became a vice chairman of the NPC's Standing Committee. Peng, who favored the enactment of a law code, but with party controls, also became chairman of a newly established NPC Commission on Legal Affairs.[32]

In the latter capacity Peng Zhen saw to the approval of seven laws that represented a major effort to reestablish a legal system for the PRC and to facilitate economic relations with the outside world. Six of the laws went into effect on January 1, 1980. These were the Organic Law of the People's Courts, the Organic Law of the People's Procuratorates, the Criminal Law, the Law of Criminal Procedure, the Organic Law of the Local People's Congresses and the Local People's Governments, and the Electoral Law for the NPC and the Local People's Congresses. The seventh law, on Joint Ventures with Chinese and Foreign Investment, had become effective earlier, in July 1979.[33]

The Fourth Plenary Session of the Eleventh Central Committee met from September 25 to 28, 1979, attended by 189 members and 118 alternates. This plenum confirmed the decisions of the Third Plenum regarding the acceleration of agricultural development. Twelve additional persons were elected to the Central Committee. Zhao Ziyang, an alternate member of the Politburo, and Peng Zhen were both made full members of the Politburo. Deng Xiaoping's hand was further strengthened. The plenum also approved a speech that Ye Jianying would give on the occasion of the 30th anniversary of the PRC.[34]

Ye's lengthy speech made a "preliminary basic assessment" of the history of the last 30 years. Ye made the first official qualification of Maoist ideology, indicating that the Thought of Mao Zedong is not the product of Mao's wisdom alone, but is the "crystallization of the collective wisdom of the CCP." Ye acknowledged that serious mistakes were made in the first 17 years of the PRC. However, while these were generally rectifiable mistakes, since correct principles were not always applied "we had to pay a very bitter price and, instead of avoiding errors which could have been avoided, we committed even more serious ones." He said that, while it was necessary to be vigilant against revisionism, "at the time when the Cultural Revolution was launched, the estimate made of the situation within the Party and the country ran counter to reality, no accurate definition was given of revisionism, and an erroneous policy and method of struggle were adopted, deviating from the principle of democratic centralism." Ye made the first official public criticism of the Cultural Revolution, noting that it had "brought to the country a whole decade of suppression, tyranny, and bloodshed."[35]

The Fifth Plenary Session of the Eleventh Central Committee was held from February 23 to 29, 1980, attended by 201 members, 118 alternates, and 37 "leading comrade" observers.[36] It constituted yet one more significant victory for Deng Xiaoping. Hu Yaobang and Zhao Ziyang were elevated to the Politburo's Standing Committee, while four supporters of Hua Guofeng were removed from the Politburo: Wang Dongxing, Chen Xilian, Wu De, and Ji Dengkui. This gave Deng Xiaoping a majority both on the Standing Committee and in the Politburo as a whole. Deng took advantage of this majority to reestablish the Secretariat of the Central Committee, which had been abolished in 1967. Hu Yaobang was named general secretary of this body, now responsible for handling the day-to-day business of the party leadership. A clear majority of the ten members of the Secretariat were Deng supporters, while none represented Hua. The plenum also proposed that the NPC delete Article 45 of the state constitution, which gave citizens the cultural revolutionary *sida*, that is, the right to "speak out freely, air their views fully, hold great debates and write big-character posters."

The Fifth Plenum discussed the draft of the revised party constitution and approved the document "Guiding Principles for Inner-Party Political Life."[37] This document was drafted a year earlier and underwent several revisions during 1979. It was published in the media for the first time on March 15, 1980. The document consists of twelve points which generally prescribe Dengist party ideals. The plenum also decided that the Twelfth Party Congress was to be convened before its due date in 1982.

Symbolizing the quickening pace of the party's departure from the Maoist era, the Fifth Plenum also took the major step of rehabilitating Liu Shaoqi, the foremost target of the Cultural Revolution. Three months later, on May 17, 1980, most of the CCP leadership gathered in the Great Hall of the People to listen to Deng Xiaoping deliver the memorial speech at a service for Liu. Conspicuously absent from this service, however, was Ye Jianying. This signaled concern on the part of some over Deng Xiaoping's policies, and fear that he was gaining power too completely and extending the range of criticism of the Left, and of Mao, too rapidly.

Even so, Deng continued to reinforce his position by eliminating opponents and elevating his supporters. Thus, at the fourteenth session of the NPC Standing Committee in April, Ji Dengkui and Chen Xilian were replaced as vice premiers of the State Council by Deng supporters Zhao Ziyang and Wan Li, while Wu De resigned as a vice chairman of the NPC Standing Committee.[38]

Deng was able to capitalize upon the 1979 capsizing of an offshore oil rig that resulted in the death of 72 workers to place pressure on several officials in the so-called petroleum faction, resulting in key dismissals and reprimands. This faction consisted basically of those who represented the interests of the central planning bureaucracy and who favored more Soviet-style economic policies. They enjoyed encouragement from Li Xiannian, and opposed Deng's economic readjustment policy.

Deng gave an important speech on the reform of party and state leadership systems at an enlarged Politburo meeting on August 18.[39] The participants discussed his ideas from August 18 to 23, and again on August 31, when they approved it. Deng explained the shifting of personnel that had taken place at the Fifth Plenum and that would occur at the impending NPC Third Session in terms of the need to prevent overcentralization of power, the practice of holding too many concurrent posts, and the confusing of the party with the government and of substituting the party for the government. He said the problem of transferring power to successors still needed to be resolved. He also spoke out against bureaucratism, paternalism, the lifelong tenure system for leading cadres, and "privileges of every description."

Deng's speech was highly significant, too, for its explicit criticism of the Soviet and Comintern inheritance.[40] Deng spoke of the concentration of power in the hands of individual party leaders during the days of the Comintern, which led to a bad system. Deng noted that Mao had once said when Stalin gravely disrupted the socialist legal system that this kind of thing could not have happened in Western countries. But, Deng had to add, "there none the less came about the ten years of calamity of the 'cultural revolution.' "[41] Such outspoken commentary by Deng was subsequently extended even further by Liao Gailong, a leading reformer and party historian, in October 1980. Liao unprecedentedly traced such party errors back to Lenin himself, asserting that Lenin had not placed the Soviet Communist party on a democratic basis after it had become the ruling party.[42]

Hua Guofeng was replaced as premier by Zhao Ziyang at the Third Session of the Fifth NPC, which was held from August 30 to September 10, 1980. Hua still retained his positions as chairman of the party and of the Military Affairs Commission, but he was, in fact, increasingly isolated among the top decisionmakers. Hua delivered the major address in which he had to explain that his own ambitious ten-year plan had been abandoned in favor of a new one for 1981–1990 and the Sixth Five-Year Plan for 1981–1985.[43]

This NPC session also furthered the drive to provide a new legal system—to strengthen socialist democracy—by adopting a revised Marriage Law, a Nationality Law, and income tax laws both for individuals and for joint ventures.[44] The NPC complied with the party's resolution from the Fifth Plenum and deleted the *sida* Article 45 from the state constitution, arguing that adequate guarantees for and means of expression were already provided for constitutionally.

Zhao Ziyang, the new premier, was a leading protégé of Deng Xiaoping. Born in Henan in 1919, Zhao had been the hard-line leader of the land reform program in Guangdong in 1951, eventually becoming first secretary of the Guangdong Provincial Party Committee. After the Cultural Revolution, he became secretary of the Inner Mongolian Regional Party Committee, then returned to Guangdong, where he again became first secretary. After 1975 he served as first secretary of the

Sichuan Provincial Party Committee, and concurrently as first political commissar of the Chengdu units of the PLA, vice chairman of the National Committee of the CPPCC, and vice premier of the State Council. He was a member of the Tenth and Eleventh Central Committees and, as noted above, became first an alternate member and then a full member of the Politburo, including a member of its Standing Committee. He had recommended himself to Deng particularly because of his post–Third Plenum economic successes in Sichuan.[45]

The long-awaited trial of the Gang of Four took place from November 20, 1980, to January 23, 1981. There was little sympathy for the defendants by this juncture. The tide was running strongly against the political Left. Deng Xiaoping's position and policies were widely supported. And more and more, since Ye Jianying's speech a year earlier, criticism had mounted against the Cultural Revolution and those institutions or individuals who had been identified with it. Hence, the credibility of the model Dazhai Production Brigade was dealt a severe blow in July when it was revealed that its leaders had falsely reported grain output during the years between 1973 and 1977.[46] In late October, Kang Sheng and Xie Fuzhi, who had died in 1975 and in 1972 respectively, were both posthumously expelled from the party, and the speeches delivered at their memorial ceremonies were rescinded. The Central Committee charged that both had participated in the plots of Lin Biao and Jiang Qing and had committed grave crimes.[47]

The trial was actually of the so-called Lin-Jiang cliques, with sixteen principals named in the indictment, although six of these, Lin Biao, Kang Sheng, Xie Fuzhi, Ye Qun, Lin Liquo, and Zhou Yuqi, had already died. The remaining ten stood trial. These included the Gang of Four, Jiang Qing, Zhang Chunqiao, Yao Wenyuan, and Wang Hongwen, and the Clique of Six comprising Chen Boda, Huang Yongsheng, Wu Faxian, Li Zuopeng, Qiu Huiquo, and Jiang Tengjiao. The trial received great publicity and, although foreigners were not allowed to attend the proceedings, edited television coverage was made available for foreign consumption. The indictment cited 48 specific offenses, including "four major crimes."[48] Among the generally haggard defendants, only Jiang Qing and Zhang Chunqiao remained defiant throughout. Jiang refused to admit any guilt, while Zhang would neither sign the indictment nor reply to questions. Jiang charged that Mao was being vilified by her arrest and trial, and that she had only implemented and defended Mao's line.

This presented a ticklish issue for the court and for the political leadership, which had avoided indicting Mao himself.[49] The defense was virtually nonexistent and dwelt on the admissions of guilt and behavior in court where this was appropriate.[50] Thus, despite the unpopularity of the defendants, there was an air of unfairness about the trial that seemed to contradict concurrent efforts to establish, ostensibly, the rule of law in China. Sentences ranged from death for Jiang Qing and Zhang Chunqiao (later commuted to life imprisonment, although neither recanted) to varying terms of imprisonment for the others.

The trial put Hua Guofeng on the spot, for even though he had played a key role in the arrest of the Gang, he was generally identified with some of the policies of the Left and had been involved in some of the actions attributed to them. Ever since stepping down as premier, Hua had been under increasing pressure. At several meetings of the Politburo between November 20 and December 5, 1980 (during the early weeks of the trial of the Gang), Hua was severely criticized. These criticisms included Hua's resistance to the reinstatement of Deng and others, the fostering of a new personality cult for himself, the promotion of the "two-whatevers" policy, the seeking of too quick economic results, the promotion of certain leftist policies, and the suppression of the discussion on the criterion of truth.[51]

On December 5, the Politburo passed a resolution that held that Hua lacked the political and organizational ability to be party chairman. It also snidely asserted that "That he should never have been appointed chairman of the Military Commission, everybody knows." The resolution recommended that the Sixth Plenum formally remove Hua from both chairmanships. In the meanwhile, Hu Yaobang would immediately take up the duties of the party chairmanship and Deng those of the Military Affairs Commission. Hua was left only with the responsibility of receiving foreign guests.[52] Hu Yaobang, 65 at the time, was a longtime associate and bridge partner of Deng and shared the latter's pragmatism. Hu had long been the leader of the Communist Youth League in the 1950s and 1960s but had had only limited military experience. He was an early forthright critic of the Cultural Revolution and of Mao's role in it.

The Central Committee now held an important central work conference from December 15 to 25, 1980, to discuss the state of the economy. Chen Yun, Zhao Ziyang, and Deng Xiaoping spoke, with the latter giving the concluding address on the 25th. At this point, it was clear that a new approach to development was being formulated. Chen Yun's retrenchment and austerity programs were endorsed. In 1981, agriculture and light industry, including consumer goods, were to take priority over heavy industry, and investment in the latter was to be reduced drastically. Deng also expressed the need for greater political stability and called for resolute efforts to "trounce and break up" various threatening influences. Deng had in mind radical remnants, those who were talking about a second cultural revolution, those who were engaged in antiparty publications and activities, and outright criminal elements.[53]

In emphasizing the need for greater discipline and order, Deng was again adroitly anticipating and outmaneuvering his opposition, which asserted itself in early 1981, although he certainly basically meant what he said. Disgruntled military interests, concerned about their budgetary cutbacks and diminishing influence, were apparent in the stiffening opposition. The effort in February 1981 to revitalize a Lei Feng model soldier campaign was not without significance, inasmuch as a Lei Feng campaign in 1963 had been part of the buildup to the Cultural Revolution. Similarly, conservative elements in the PLA attacked Bai Hua and his drama entitled *Bitter Love*. By mid-year the party itself took up this effort to enjoin a return to socialist realism in cultural expression. At the same time, more positive assessments of Mao were again appearing in the media.

The Sixth Plenum of the Eleventh Central Committee met from June 27 to 29, 1981, attended by 195 members, 114 alternates, and 53 others. Hu Yaobang and Deng Xiaoping were formally elected chairmen of the Central Committee and of its Military Affairs Commission respectively. Zhao Ziyang and Hua Guofeng were elected vice chairmen of the party. The Standing Committee of the Politburo now consisted of these four, plus Ye Jianying, Li Xiannian, and Chen Yun.[54] Contrary to expectations, Mao's token peasant, Chen Yonggui of the now criticized Dazhai model, remained on the Politburo. No mention was made of a senior advisory group, which Deng had been advocating, nor was anything said about plans for the Twelfth Party Congress, nor even about the draft constitutional revisions, which had already been discussed at the earlier Fifth Plenum. Thus, even though Deng continued to make headway in consolidating power and promoting his policies, it was not without notable disappointments.

The Sixth Plenum also adopted the important "Resolution on Certain Issues in the History of the Party Since the Founding of the People's Republic of China," which was the result of the call made by Ye Jianying in September 1979 for a formal summing up of recent party history. The resolution's chief significance lies in its unprecedented official public assessment of Mao, which contains some criticism. Thus, Mao was acknowledged to have made "gross mistakes" during the Cultural Revolution, which in itself was a "comprehensive, long-drawn out and grave blunder." However, when all of his activities are considered, Mao's contributions "far outweigh his mistakes."[55] Mao Zedong Thought, a "valuable spiritual asset" and "guide to action for a long time to come," was not just Mao's ideas but, as Ye Jianying had previously disclosed, a "crystallization of the collective wisdom" of the party.[56] Nevertheless, it was made clear that a dogmatic attitude toward Mao's sayings was "entirely wrong."[57] Deng had had the greatest influence in the composition of this historic document, but it is evident that he had to make some concessions, specifically in the softening and limiting of the criticism of Mao.

Thus, while Deng continued to advance, it was not without stiff opposition. The crackdown on dissidents continued through 1981. And, despite China's opening door to the outside world, efforts were again made on the part of some authorities to limit contacts between Chinese and foreigners, a problem which continued well into 1982. A Dutch journalist was expelled in June 1981, and a *Washington Post* correspondent was warned for reporting the account of an imprisoned political dissident that had become available.[58] Some of the adverse atmosphere was linked to the U.S.-PRC relationship, which had not continued to develop according to Chinese expectations. There was some notable progress in this regard as registered in a visit to Beijing by Secretary of State Alexander Haig in June, which revealed that American arms sales to China were in the offing. But continued American arms sales to Taiwan, and particularly the prospect that advanced FX military aircraft would soon be sold to the latter, met with strong Chinese objections. It was in this atmosphere that Ye Jianying, on October 1, 1981, with considerable media fanfare, elaborated on a policy of reunification with Taiwan.[59] This was followed on October 10 by Hu Yaobang's speech commemorating the anniversary of the 1911 revolution by inviting Nationalist President Chiang Ching-kuo and others "to visit the mainland and their natal places."[60]

Despite the adverse current and the distraction of the Taiwan issue and temporary disappointments in the American relationship, the reformers continued with their program. Premier Zhao made it clear in his speech to the Fourth Session of the Fifth NPC, which was held between November 30 and December 13, 1981, that the economic retrenchment would continue for the next five years. He said that government organs would be reduced in size in order to overcome bureaucracy and to raise efficiency. Zhao also said that China should discard the notion of total self-sufficiency and, instead, advance into the world market, increase exports, including some surplus labor, and increase other ties with foreign nations. Foreign companies were welcome to invest in certain joint ventures. Special economic zones in Guangdong and Fujian were told to take bold measures to introduce advanced technology and systems of management, and to employ foreign capital.[61]

The Chinese government had created concern among foreign businessmen by suspending and canceling a number of major contracts in 1980 and 1981 as part of the retrenchment and shifting of development priorities. This included the celebrated Baoshan steel complex near Shanghai, being built by the Nippon Steel Corporation. Deng Xiaoping later decided to honor such contracts to allay the apprehensions of foreign business interests and perhaps because he himself was interested in such contracts in order to hasten economic development. But the experience would also strengthen arguments for tightening administrative procedures and controls over such contract-making in the future.[62]

Premier Zhao's plan for overhauling the State Council was approved by the NPC Standing Committee at its 22d session from February 22 to March 8, 1982. Thus, the number of vice premiers was reduced from thirteen to two, and the 98 ministries, commissions, and agencies of the State Council were merged into 52. The staff of the central bureaucracy was reduced from 49,000 to 32,000. Some of the former vice premiers would be redesignated state councillors, a new position that was considered equal to the vice premiership. Progress was quickly made in streamlining the bureaucracy. By the time of the next meeting of the NPC Standing Committee, between April 22 and May 4, 1982, Zhao could say that the number of ministers and vice ministers, aside from those of the latter rank who concurrently held the post of minister, had been cut by 67 percent. He also announced that the 52 ministries and commissions would be further reduced to 41.

Some of the negative atmospherics regarding unofficial associations with foreigners and concern for undue foreign influences continued well into 1982. In April, Hu Qiaomu, then president of the Academy of Social Sciences, elaborated on comments he had made the previous year saying that the tendency toward bourgeois liberalization was characterized by "calling for the adoption of the bourgeois parliamentarism, including the two-party system, campaigning for office, bourgeois freedoms of speech, press, assembly and association, bourgeois individualism and even anarchism." "The essence of this," he said, "lies in consciously or unconsciously demanding China forsake the socialist road and install the so-called capitalist liberal system."[63] An anticorruption campaign was related to the renewed vigilance against the unwanted outside influences. In May, a Chinese trade magazine editor was given a prison term for "betraying state secrets."[64] An American teacher was expelled from China in June for allegedly "stealing China's secret information."[65]

Despite these negative and contrary manifestations, the undaunted Deng moved ahead. A central work conference met from July 30 to August 5, 1982, and worked out the necessary compromises to clear the way for the Twelfth Party Congress, which was supposed to have been convened early. The Seventh Plenary Session of the Eleventh Central Committee was then held on August 6, 1982, attended by 185 members, 112 alternates, and 21 observers, which formally decided to convene the Twelfth Party Congress on September 1. The plenum approved the report to be given to the congress and the draft of the again-revised party constitution.[66]

· 14 ·

Quickening the Pace of Reform

The Twelfth Party Congress, which was held from September 1 to 11, 1982, represented another decisive, although not complete, victory for Deng Xiaoping. The congress was attended by 1,545 delegates and 145 alternate delegates, representing more than 39 million members. In his opening address to the congress, Deng reiterated the three major tasks of the party for the 1980s: "To intensify socialist modernization, to strive for reunification and particularly for the return of Taiwan to the motherland, and to combat hegemonism and safeguard world peace." At the core of these tasks, Deng stressed, was economic construction.[1]

Hu Yaobang, as party chairman, gave the principal report of the Central Committee. Hu, too, made it clear that the development of the economy was the most important of the tasks ahead. But economic readjustment would have to be extended through 1985, and the introduction of reforms in economic administration delayed until the following five-year period. He affirmed, however, that the general objective was to quadruple the gross annual value of industrial and agricultural production in the twenty years from 1981 to the end of the century.

Hu also made an authoritative statement regarding the concept of a "socialist spiritual civilization," which had first been mentioned in Ye Jianying's speech on September 29, 1979, and was elaborated upon somewhat by Deng Xiaoping in his speech of December 25, 1980.[2] The discussion of the concept was clearly in response to the growing need perceived by the party leadership to fill what was becoming an ideological void. Hu said, "Socialist spiritual civilization not only gives a tremendous impetus to the building of material civilization, but also guarantees that it will develop according to a correct orientation."[3] Of course, this partly reflects the Maoist view that the superstructure can influence historical development, as well as suggests limits to what can be tolerated in the realm of "spiritual civilization."

In foreign relations, Hu used the congress to announce that China would adhere to an "independent foreign policy." This new tack reflected a revised perception of the Soviet threat. It also reflected continued disappointment with the progress being made in relations with the United States. Another Sino-American communiqué, of August 17, 1982, had only partially arrested the temporarily deteriorating relationship with the United States, occasioned by President Ronald Reagan's sentiments regarding Taiwan, American plans to sell FX fighter aircraft to Taiwan, by Chinese impatience over technology transfers, and several other issues.[4] In the meanwhile, Chinese leaders were seeking to normalize their relationship with the Soviet Union, although not much headway was made for a time. A series of semiannual roundtable discussions that began in late 1979 saw only one round of meetings before these were reluctantly suspended by Beijing because of the Soviet invasion of Afghanistan in December of that year. These roundtable "consultations" (as the Chinese called them) were not resumed until October 1982, following the Twelfth Party Congress, when more notable progress would quickly be registered in Sino-Soviet relations.[5]

With regard to party policy, Hu declared that improvement of the system of democratic-centralism and further normalization of inner-party political life was to be sought, as was reform of the leading organs and the cadre system so as to introduce more revolutionary, younger, better-educated, and more professionally competent cadres. Work was to be strengthened among workers, peasants, and intellectuals and close ties established between the party and the masses. Finally, party organizations were to be consolidated systematically, so as to bring about a fundamental turn for the better in the party's work style. To ensure that these "problems" would be addressed seriously, Hu announced that a comprehensive rectification of the party would begin in the latter half of 1983. Chen Yun's report on the work of the greatly expanding Central Commission for Discipline Inspection[6] also spoke to the need of purifying the ranks and improving the party's standing with the public.

The congress adopted a new constitution that eschewed the radical rhetoric of the previous version and defined the party's tasks in terms of economic modernization. Presumably to promote this single-minded objective, the new charter even asserted that "the Party must conduct its activities within the limits permitted by the Constitution of the laws of the state." Stricter requirements for party members, especially for officials, were set, although nothing was said about age restrictions and limitations on tenure in office. The Central Advisory and the Discipline Inspection Commissions were included, although these bodies were not accorded the stature the reformists desired. To safeguard against future domination by a single leader, the posts of party chairman and vice chairmen were abolished. Hu Yaobang, now no longer party chairman, but still general secretary, would henceforth continue to preside over the Secretariat and would also convene meetings of the Politburo as well. Thus, for the first time, the CCP began to follow the Soviet practice of having the general secretary (*zongshuji*) of the Central Committee perform the function of party leader.

The new constitutional provisions were only partially satisfying to Deng and his reformists, who particularly had wished to eliminate the Politburo's Standing Committee, which they wanted to replace with the Secretariat, for the latter organ did not include any opponents of Deng's reforms. They also had hoped for the retirement of Ye Jianying and Li Xiannian, which did not come about.[7]

The Twelfth Central Committee of 210 members and 138 alternates was elected on September 10 and 11. Almost half (98) of the regular members of the new Central Committee were newly elected to the body, and 15 alternates from the previous body were promoted to full membership. As many as 83 percent of the alternates were elected to the Central Committee for the first time. Of the 98 new members as many as 33 had positions in the State Council. In fact, as many as 25 percent of all the full members of the Central Committee now represented the state government. Only three of the newcomers represented the central military leadership, so that, significantly, for the first time since the Cultural Revolution the government cadres outnumbered the military on the Central Committee.[8] Only three newcomers represented the mass organizations. The latter organizations were the biggest losers in the new Central Committee, which now had a total of only fourteen such representatives (eight full members and six alternates).[9] Nineteen party officials from the provinces were also among the new members. The number of provincial representatives had declined considerably, from 44 percent on the Eleventh Central Committee to 35 percent on the new body.[10] Altogether, the new members comprised 42 civil administration cadres, 33 party officials, twelve PLA leaders, four scientists, and three mass organization officials.[11]

Even with this large infusion of new members, the Twelfth Central Committee retained many members who had served on the body for decades. Nevertheless, the radically changed composition of the new Central Committee was similar to the basic overhauling that had taken place on the Seventh and Ninth Central Committees in 1945 and 1969 respectively. Each of these three Central Committees represented the beginning of a significant new period in the history of the party.

The Twelfth Central Committee held its First Plenary Session from September 11 to 13, 1982. The session elected a Politburo of 25 members and three alternates. Seven new members and two alternates were elected. These were Hu Qiaomu, Liao Chengzhi, Song Renqiong, Wan Li, Xi Zhongxun, Yang Dezhi, and Yang Shangkun as members, and Qin Jiwei and Yao Yilin as alternates. All of these cadres, with the exception of Yang Dezhi, had been persecuted during the Cultural Revolution. Interestingly, Yang, who may not have enjoyed Deng's approval in being elected to the Politburo, became the first active-duty chief of the general staff of the PLA to serve on this body. Seven cadres were removed from the Politburo: Liu Bocheng, Geng Biao, Hua Guofeng, Peng Chong, Xu Shiyou, Seypidin, and the Dazhai peasant, Chen Yonggui, who had already been absent for more than two years. Except for Liu Bocheng, all the other former members had gained during the Cultural Revolution.[12] The new composition of the Central Committee gave Deng the support of thirteen members who had been victims of the Cultural Revolution and perhaps eight others on the Politburo. But it did not entirely reflect his personal preferences. For one thing, the average age of the Politburo was now 73 at least, and this did not symbolize the new leadership image Deng desired.[13] And Deng would be constrained somewhat by the remaining five senior military leaders, particularly the aged Ye Jianying.

The Politburo's Standing Committee now consisted of Hu Yaobang, Ye Jianying, Deng Xiaoping, Zhao Ziyang, Li Xiannian, and Chen Yun.

Less than two weeks after the congress, the *Liberation Army Daily* acknowledged that an article it had published just before the congress had "serious theoretical and political mistakes," and had propagated a leftist viewpoint to oppose bourgeois liberalization. The newspaper reaffirmed its need to "obey the party's absolute leadership."[14] Efforts to harness the military more closely, as well as to curtail such leftist sentiment in the PLA, continued to be evident into the following year. General Li Desheng, for example, who was known to be sympathetic to leftists in the past, acknowledged that in carrying out leftist policies "we often also said it was the mass line," but "in reality" it was "canvassing the masses based on our subjective will." He admitted that policies "were not created by the masses or based on the consciousness of the masses" but "exactly the reverse."[15] Yu Qiuli, director of the PLA's General Political Department called for a shake-up in the PLA in

July, and put forth guidelines for the military based on Deng Xiaoping's ideas.[16] Military academies that had been closed during the Cultural Revolution were reopened with the expectation that most officers would pass through them, and no one in the future would be promoted without having done so.[17]

The Fifth Session of the Fifth NPC was held between November 26 and December 10, 1982, attended by 3,155 delegates. Here, Premier Zhao presented the Sixth Five-Year Plan, the first such plan to be made public since the first plan in 1953 and the only one ever to be approved by the NPC.[18] Zhao optimistically promised an average 6 percent rise in income per year. Urban housing construction was to be accelerated, and increased expenditures made on education, science, and culture. The Chinese public soon came to appreciate this change from the earlier plans, which had emphasized heavy industry at the expense of consumer needs. But Zhao warned that among the many obstacles to progress was the continued population growth. The Chinese census of June 1982, the largest ever undertaken in human history, had revealed a population of over 1 billion. Zhao stressed that the population growth rate would have to be reduced to under thirteen births per thousand. Agricultural production, he said, would have to increase by an average of 4 to 5 percent per year, compared to the average of 3.4 percent per year during the 28 years from 1953 to 1980. As for industry, Zhao conceded that the results of the previous 28 years had been very poor.[19] He revealed that China would develop two major economic zones, one in the Chang Jiang delta centered on Shanghai, the other in north China centered on Shanxi province and including part of Inner Mongolia, Shaanxi, Ningxia, and Henan provinces.

The NPC adopted a newly revised state constitution, the fourth since the founding of the PRC.[20] This version consisted of a preamble and 138 articles in four chapters, making it the most comprehensive charter thus far. While the distinction between what was on paper and what was practiced still needs to be recognized, the new document did appear to be a serious attempt to provide a legal framework for the country.[21] The constitution proclaimed that "all state organs, the armed forces, all political parties and public organizations and all enterprises and undertakings must abide by the constitution and the law." The document restored an earlier provision that "all citizens are equal before the law," which had been deleted from the 1975 and 1978 versions. Other articles provided for the inviolability of the personal dignity of citizens, freedom of religious belief, the inviolability of the home, and freedom and privacy of correspondence. The role of intellectuals in building socialism was underscored for the first time. However, the right of workers to strike, a prominent feature of the previous constitution, was now deleted.

The new state constitution also made some significant changes in the structure of the state. Members of the NPC's Standing Committee were prohibited from holding posts in any of the administrative, judicial, or procuratorial organs of the state. The position of president (previously translated as chairman) of state was restored. The system of lifetime tenure in office was ended, with several principal posts limited to two consecutive five-year terms. A State Central Military Commission was established to lead the armed forces. The relationship of this new body to the similar organ of the party's Central Committee was not made clear, although this would remain a moot point as long as Deng Xiaoping (who would be elected chairman of this new commission at the Sixth NPC in June 1983) chaired both commissions. The system of people's congresses and local organs of state power was strengthened, albeit "under the unified leadership of the central authorities." The constitution also significantly divested the rural people's communes of governmental responsibilities by establishing new township governments.

The Communist Youth League held its Eleventh National Congress from December 19 to 30, 1982. It adopted a new constitution and elected the league's eleventh central committee. At the latter's first plenum on December 31, Wang Zhaoguo was elected the league's first secretary,[22] but would be succeeded by Hu Jingtao at the third plenum in December 1984.[23]

The reformist momentum was registered again only six months later at the Sixth NPC, which held its First Session from June 6 to 21, 1983. A total of 2,978 deputies were elected to the Sixth NPC, 76 percent of whom were new. The number of intellectuals in the NPC had now increased, it was said, to 41.5 percent of the deputies, while the percentage of party members had decreased, so that non-CCP deputies now comprised 37.5 percent of the total, 10 percent more than the previous NPC.[24] The NPC elected its own 133-member Standing Committee, with Peng Zhen as its chairman. Li Xiannian was elected president of the PRC.[25]

Premier Zhao's report on the work of the government reviewed the previous five years, from 1978 through 1982, and gave an outline of the main tasks for the next five years, through 1987.[26] Zhao also announced the establishment of a new Ministry of State Security, which seemed to underscore a nagging concern even as the open door policy continued apace. But this may have represented basically a transfer of such responsibilities and personnel from the party apparatus to the state rather than constituting another instance of the expansion of the bureaucracy in absolute terms.

In any case, concern for security and order was seen in a campaign against crime that had been initiated in 1982 and continued throughout 1983. Economic crimes had reportedly reached a record high since 1949. By April 1983 more than 30,000 criminals had been sentenced and 8,500 of these were expelled from the party.[27] Serious abuses by party cadres in the construction and distribution of housing was reported.[28] On September 2, Peng Zhen in an important speech addressed the need to punish criminals severely.[29] In fact, during 1983, tens of thousands of accused persons, many of them young people, were arrested, and more than a thousand of these were executed.[30] A number of executions were carried out in public settings. One *Hongqi* commentator candidly noted that the current "hard blows" against criminal offenders constituted "a serious struggle against the enemies in the political realm."[31]

In the meanwhile, at a meeting on national organization work sponsored by the Central Committee's Organization Department in mid-1983, it was reported that by the end of 1982 "unjust and erroneous cases involving some 3 million cadres were redressed, more than 470,000 party members were reinstated with their party membership, erroneous judgments and actions against some 120,000 party members were revoked, and the problems of millions of innocent cadres and masses who were linked to those cases were solved."[32]

Late 1983 saw important meetings of two of the principal mass organizations. The Fifth National Women's Congress was held in Beijing from September 2 to 12. Kang Keqing was reelected chairwoman.[33] The Tenth National Trade Union Congress was held in Beijing from October 18 to 29. Ni Zhifu was reelected first secretary.[34] Both organizations adopted new constitutions.

The Second Plenary Session of the Twelfth Central Committee was held October 11 and 12, 1983, following a two-day preparatory session. In attendance were 201 members, 136 alternates, 150 members of the Central Advisory Commission, 124 members of the Central Commission for Discipline Inspection, and 11 leading members of central organs and local party committees as observers. The plenum issued a 13,000-word decision to undertake a party consolidation.[35] Hu Yaobang was made the chairman of a central commission to conduct the important campaign.

The new rectification campaign was aimed at two categories of problems. The first was ideological and included those party members who were reluctant to comprehend the current line whether because of influences from the left or the right, with the result that many had adopted a passive attitude. The second category comprised the "three types of persons": those who became prominent by following the Gang of Four and practicing the "right to rebel"; those who held serious factional views; and those who had indulged in "beating, smashing, and looting." It also included those guilty of serious economic and other kinds of crimes. These members were to be dealt with more severely. The campaign was scheduled to be completed in two stages (subsequently changed to three stages) stretching over a period of three years, beginning with the impending winter season. The first stage would concentrate on leading party organs at the central, provincial, municipal, and autonomous regional levels and the leading party organs in the PLA.

The material for study during the campaign was the *Selected Works of Deng Xiaoping*, which was published on July 1, the 62d anniversary of the CCP. The volume included 47 of Deng's speeches and talks, 39 of them published for the first time, given between January 1975 and September 1982. The Central Committee had already in July issued a circular enjoining the entire party to study the volume earnestly as an important preparation for the impending consolidation campaign. Also to be studied were three pieces: *A Must Book for Party Members*, *A Concise Edition of Important Documents Since the Third Plenary Session of the 11th Party Central Committee*, and *Comrade Mao Zedong on the Party's Style of Work and Party Organization*.

The decision made it clear that "On no account should the past erroneous practice of 'letting the masses consolidate the party' or letting nonparty members decide the issues in the party be repeated." The late Chairman Mao's propensity to invite criticism from the outside, which had always discomfited most of the party leadership, was thus explicitly rejected. Instead, in late October the Central Committee invited more than 200 nonparty public personalities to a meeting to discuss the party consolidation campaign. At this meeting Peng Zhen emphasized the problem of "spiritual contamination."[36] Deng Liqun, head of the Propaganda Department, explained that it was necessary to clear away cultural contamination in order to achieve the unity of thinking that was the first task of party consolidation.[37]

This gave rise to a secondary campaign against "spiritual contamination" or "spiritual pollution" that received much media attention for several months. It actually distracted from the party consolidation or rectification campaign. A temporary victim of the new campaign was Zhou Yang, chairman of the China Federation of Literary and Art Circles, who had ventured relatively accommodating views on the subjects of humanism and "alienation" during the celebration of the centennial of the death of Marx earlier in the year. Two other prominent early victims were Hu Jiwei and Wang Ruoshui, respectively the director and deputy editor in chief of the *People's Daily*.

As the new campaigns began, the Central Committee's History Research Center together with the National Party History Society sponsored a national symposium on Mao Zedong Thought in early November 1983 in Nanning at which 300 papers were presented. The participants agreed with the new interpretation that Mao's Thought was indeed the "crystallization of the collective wisdom of the Chinese Communists."[38]

The ancillary spiritual pollution campaign did succeed in raising apprehensions among Chinese and foreigners alike for several months, but especially during the first two months or so into 1984. Novelist Zhang Xiaotian, among others, made self-criticisms publicly in January. The spiritual pollution campaign was clearly a leftist trend and was obviously manipulated to slow or reverse Deng Xiaoping's reform and rectification programs. But Deng and his supporters, principally Hu Yaobang, quickly diffused it. They circulated a confidential directive in January that attached many restrictions to the leftist effort.[39] In March, the *People's Daily* still conceded that the rectification campaign was being impeded by "an obstruction in the middle." However, more and more articles appeared stressing the party's policy on raising the status of intellectuals, including their induction into the party in greater numbers. Attacks on leftists became bolder. By mid-year, there were demands again to negate the Cultural Revolution, and with it the radical slogan "Politics in Command," a hallmark of the Cultural Revolution.[40]

Another indication of the Deng leadership's determination to underscore its growing commitment to the reformation of the party despite recurrent leftist outbursts was the publication for the first time on an unclassified basis of a new updated edition of its organizational handbook, entitled *Questions and Answers on Party Organizational Work*, edited by the Research Office and Organization Bureau of the Central Organization Department. The detailed handbook revealed that the party's cadre management system was beset with contradictions, with evidence of both centralization and fragmentation, and of both institutionalization and personal intervention.[41]

The Sixth NPC held its Second Session from May 15 to 31, 1984, with over 2,700 deputies in attendance. The session underscored the basic trend being pursued by the Deng Xiaoping leadership, contrary to the leftist sentiments of the spiritual pollution campaigners, by resolving that the government at all levels implement the economic reforms. Premier Zhao was able to report economic progress since the previous year, but he stressed that various economic relations were yet to be straightened out and that the price system, in particular, was irrational. He said that two major issues were to receive special attention: the restructuring of the economic system and the opening to the outside world. Zhao emphasized five points: (1) overcoming, step by step, the defect of everyone eating from the same big pot in the urban economy; (2) restructuring the managerial system of the building industry, which was notoriously beset by inefficiency and by a high rate of consumption, wastefulness, and technical stagnation; (3) reform of the circulation system (that is, circulation of supplies, commodities, and money); (4) striving to make the special economic zones a success, opening more coastal cities, and expanding economic and technological exchanges with other countries; and (5) giving full play to the role of intellectuals in socialist construction.[42]

This strong reaffirmation of the determination to continue with the economic reforms actually followed by several months the publication of the Central Committee's highly important Document No. 1 for 1984, the Circular on Rural Work during 1984. This document added significantly to a similarly numbered Central Committee circular of the previous year, which had also extended the rural reforms already underway. The 1984 document extended the contract period to "at least" 15 years. It encouraged the concentration of land in the hands of the most productive households, allowing for the actual subleasing of contracts. It encouraged investment in other regions. And it changed the rules whereby collectives had been obtaining funds from peasants so that such exactions were likely to be reduced.[43] K. K. Kueh has referred to this latest step in the reparcelization of collective farmland as having been "not less spectacular than the land reform of 1949–52."[44] The extension of the rural reform represented a furthering of the decollectivization process, which appeared to have been undertaken mainly on the basis of spontaneous local economic pressures.[45] However, there is also evidence that the new transformation was, in fact, accomplished by fiat, with few villages being given any choice in the matter. Thus, once again, the countryside was channeled from above into a new unitary organizational structure, regardless of the types of crops grown or the level of economic development of the locality.[46] In any case, as popular as these moves were with many peasants, concern was soon expressed regarding the possible loss of certain of the benefits of rural collectivization, for example, water conservation works and agricultural extension services.[47]

With regard to the role of the party itself, the new rural liberalization was fraught with implications. Franz Schurmann thought it was the party that had provided the cohesion for the decentralization program of the late 1950s. But now, as Joyce Kallgren has noted, the responsibility for this rested with technicians and experts who possessed special skills.[48] In any case, government administration continued to separate from commune management as well, following the state constitution's new provision. Thus, townships continued to take over these local governmental responsibilities throughout the country. By October 1984, 60,000 township cadres had already been selected and employed on the basis of a contract system that was now being used to recruit better-educated and more professional cadres.[49]

Providing additional ideological justification for the economic reforms was the prospect of a new 60-volume Chinese-language edition of the *Collected Works of Lenin*. The new corpus was based on the fifth Russian edition (with some pieces added from the Russian edition of the *Works of Lenin*). When completed, it would replace the current 39-volume collection. The latter, based on the fourth Russian edition and published two decades previously, was said to have "some faults and can no longer meet today's needs." A large proportion of the newly collected works "were written after the October Revolution" and therefore were seen to be "more realistic and significant to China's present situation." The entire collection was to be made available by 1990.[50]

On the 63d anniversary of the party, on July 1, 1984, the party's Organization Department announced that the party now had more than 40 million members. More than 4.8 million of these had been admitted over the past five years. Only 10 percent of the 800,000 who had joined in 1983 were peasants. Almost 10,000 college students were being admitted each year.[51] Even so, dissatisfaction was expressed with the slow pace of this reform of party ranks, since only 4 percent of the overall membership had a college education. Furthermore, some intellectuals were being blocked from admission into the party for fear that they would threaten the "iron seats" (the positions) of party functionaries.[52]

Later in July, it was announced that the Central Committee's Secretariat had decided to decentralize personnel and a relevant Organization Department circular indicated that the change was to take effect on August 1, 1984. This meant that cadres under the direct management of the Central Committee would mainly be senior officials of the level of vice minister of ministries and provincial vice governor and above and leading cadres of big and influential enterprises, institutions of scientific research, and major institutions of higher education. The next lower level of cadres would henceforth be managed by the ministries, provinces, regions, municipalities, and other institutions of the same level. The change cut the number of cadres managed directly by the Central Committee by two-thirds.[53]

The party also conducted an especially interesting, unprecedented experiment in Shaanxi province, where the provincial party secretary, Bai Jinian, was elected by secret ballot from among thirteen nominees, later reduced by ballot to eleven, then to six. This was done at a meeting of more than 300 cadres at the level of county party secretary and above. Reportedly, neither the central nor the provincial leadership intervened in the election, nor had the higher authorities had a hand in the nominations. The successful Bai had met the three conditions of eligibility; he was under 60, highly educated, and he had not compromised himself during the Cultural Revolution.[54] But there did not seem to be any other such experiments, and by September 1987 Bai, despite the good performance record of Shaanxi, was removed in what was "regarded as part of the rejuvenation program."[55] In actual fact, Bai was an associate of Hu Yaobang, whose career was affected by Hu's reversal in January 1987.

Nevertheless, by September 5, 1984, considerable further progress was reported in the streamlining of the government structure. This program was now considered completed at the central, provincial, prefectural, and city levels. Leading cadres at the provincial level were reduced by 34 percent, their average age was lowered by seven years, and those with college education had increased from 20 to 43 percent. Similar figures were cited for the changes at the prefectural and city levels.[56] This unprecedented amount of shifting of personnel continued into 1985.

Deng Xiaoping was honored and given enormous publicity at the celebration of the 35th anniversary of the PRC on October 1, 1984. He gave the only speech—twelve minutes long—and reviewed the pre-parade formations of the PLA, and then the parade itself. This was a high point in Deng's career. He had easily weathered the machinations of the spiritual pollution campaigners earlier in the year. And only a few days earlier, on September 16, he had overseen, after two years of secret, intensive negotiations, the conclusion of a historic draft agreement between Beijing and London that returns Hong Kong to China in 1997. China agreed in this arrangement to maintain Hong Kong's capitalist system and life style for at least 50 years after 1997. It also affirmed that Hong Kong would remain an international financial center (it was the world's third largest in 1984) and free port; hold on to its convertible currency, its gold, its securities and futures markets, and its free flow of capital. China, however, would assume responsibility for foreign affairs and defense. The latter responsibility would entail the stationing of PLA units in Hong Kong. The agreement was subsequently signed by Prime Minister Margaret Thatcher and Premier Zhao Ziyang in Beijing, in front of Deng and more than a hundred other dignitaries, on December 19, 1984.[57]

Following six days of preparatory meetings, the Third Plenary Session of the Twelfth Central Committee was held on October 20, 1984, attended by the 321 members and alternate members of the Central Committee. Another 297 persons also attended as members of the Central Advisory Commission and of the Central Commission for Discipline Inspection, and principal leading cadres from relevant local and central departments. It was another landmark meeting. The plenum adopted a 39-page document on the reform of the economic structure. It also decided on the convocation in September 1985 of a national conference of party delegates, which would discuss the Seventh Five-Year Plan and the election of additional members of the Central Committee, along with other organization matters.[58]

The important decision on reforming the economic structure basically extended the rural economic reforms that had been initiated at the 1978 Third Plenum to the rest of the country's economy. Greater autonomy was now to be given to state-owned enterprises, making it necessary for them to compete in order to survive. Government functions were to be separated from purely economic ones, which were to be left to enterprise managers to operate within guidelines. Central planning would be limited. Many consumer subsidies were to be phased out. Prices of many products were to be determined by supply and demand. Urban wage increases were to be based on increases in productivity.

The reformists had capitalized on the momentum that the popularity of the reforms had so far afforded them. Yet these new reforms were generally stated and were not intended to change the socialist system, other than, as Robert Dernberger has said, to make it uniquely Chinese, based on trial and error, not some theoretical model, nor borrowed from another socialist country.[59] Even so, they were ambitious measures, with fascinating implications for China's socialist system.

· I5 ·

Socialism with Chinese Characteristics

With the Central Committee's decision at the October 1984 Third Plenum to extend the economic reforms to the entire economy, Deng Xiaoping's reformers were in buoyant spirits by late 1984. Adding to the euphoria, the grain crop for the year provided the first surplus in the history of the PRC, giving yet further credibility to the rural reforms. Therefore, by the end of December another major concession was made in agriculture. Peasants would no longer have to sell part of their grain to the state. Instead, grain would now be purchased through contracts with the state or sold on the open market.[1] Only two months earlier, the designations of landlords, rich peasants, counterrevolutionaries, and bad elements had been removed from a final group of 79,000 people out of a total of 20 million, who, in the 1950s, had been convicted in these four categories.[2]

In this atmosphere, the party reformist leadership was in an expansive mood. It sought to capitalize on the reform momentum by moving into the ideological field, the domain of the party conservatives. This was begun with three articles published in the *People's Daily* on November 30 and December 5 and 7.[3] The first hinted that resistance to reforms came from some leaders who had not been liberated from old ideas, while the second openly accused propaganda departments and departments of politics and law of being seriously tainted by leftist ideology. The third piece, a lead article, generated considerable comment throughout the world. The article said: "We cannot expect the works of Marx and Lenin in their day to solve the problems of today." Subsequently, the daily printed a correction saying that the word "all" (following the word "solve") had been inadvertently omitted. But even the corrected version had to be regarded as a bold assertion. Less than a month later, the same newspaper reminded critics that "Marxism is not a dogma but a guide to action." An accompanying commentary remarked that at present "there are many new things that do not appear in books at all." It added, eloquently: "More than ever before, we cannot cut our feet to fit our shoes."

The conservatives countered on the pages of the *Liberation Army Daily*, emphasizing party discipline and proper work style and referring to the many serious problems caused by economic reforms.[4] But within days, a new compilation of Deng's speeches was made available with the provocative title *Building Socialism with Chinese Characteristics*. The publication assured readers that China would remain socialist despite the experiments with capitalism that were designed to advance modernization. But it also suggested that the parameters of such a national socialism were yet to be determined.

The reformist ideological offensive continued at the Fourth National Writers' Congress, held in Beijing from December 29, 1984, to January 5, 1985, at which leading conservatives Hu Qiaomu, perhaps the premier party theoretician, and Deng Liqun, director of the Propaganda Department, were conspicuously absent. The assembled intellectuals greeted the speech given by Hu Qili, who was reputed at the time to be the likely successor to Hu Yaobang as party general secretary, with 33 bursts of spontaneous applause, the lengthiest of which lasted more than a minute.[5] Hu Qili acknowledged that "literary freedom is a vital part of socialist literature" and he admitted that " 'leftist' tendencies are still an obstacle to progress."[6] This was heartening talk, but many Chinese intellectuals had long learned the need to remain cautious. Their caution seemed somewhat justified when only three months later Hu Yaobang himself was constrained to make it clear that the party's journalism "is the party's mouthpiece and . . . the mouthpiece of the people's government, which is led by the party."[7]

At the same time, the Central Commission for Discipline Inspection cracked down on a number of "unhealthy" tendencies. These included engaging in commerce, running enterprises, and abuse of power by buying and reselling products for profit by party and government cadres; raising prices indiscriminately in violation of policy; increasing wages at will; dispensing bonuses indiscriminately; and fraudulent practices, among other violations.[8] Ensuing investigations resulted in almost 9,000 businesses that had been formed by party and government departments being closed down, and more than 90 percent of the 67,041 party and government officials connected with businesses being enjoined to sever such ties.[9] But such practices would remain a continuing problem. In May, when Beijing residents along nine major city thoroughfares were told to convert or rent their premises for commercial purposes, it had to be made clear that party members were not eligible for such capitalist pursuits. Only one day earlier, it was reported that hundreds of party cadres and other bureaucrats in the city were punished for engaging in commercial activities.

In the meanwhile, the first stage of the rectification campaign was completed by early 1985. Some 960,000 party members in central, provincial, and municipal organs had participated. The second stage would now involve as many as a third of the party membership—about 13.5 million members, located in prefectural and city organs, universities, colleges, and large enterprises. Officials revealed that relatively few would be expelled from the party, perhaps only about 0.1 percent of the total membership.[10] It was evident that the party had relaxed its determination to root out the "three types of persons" who had gained from the Cultural Revolution. Instead, as Hu Qili now explained, the most fundamental guideline for party rectification during this stage was "to ensure and expedite reform, and this guideline will never vacillate."[11]

This continued concentration on the all-important economic reforms, referred to by Deng Xiaoping as a "second revolution,"[12] was evident at the Third Session of the Sixth NPC, which was held from March 27 to April 10, 1985. Here, Premier Zhao's report on the work of the government departed from previous such reports, which usually reviewed comprehensively both domestic and external developments, by concentrating on the economy exclusively.[13] He did have good news. The total value of industrial and agricultural output, which had averaged 7.9 percent annually between 1979 and 1983, increased by 14.2 percent over the previous year. The national income and state revenue both rose by 12 percent, so that national finances were also steadily improving. Bumper harvests also continued. There were increases in the number of Chinese-foreign joint ventures, more in 1984 than in all of the previous five years combined.

Zhao also addressed the continued economic reforms, indicating how unhealthy tendencies would be dealt with and what new measures would be undertaken. The practice of "eating from the same big pot" was to be gradually abolished. Wage earners could expect to pay taxes on personal income above a certain level. With regard to the price system, a policy of combining relaxed control with readjustments would be adopted.

On August 1, 1985, the PLA was compelled to celebrate its 58th birthday "on the operating table," to use the expression Deng Xiaoping had uttered ten years earlier regarding the need to reduce the size of the army. Deng had repeated this need only two months earlier, saying that the PLA would be reduced by 1 million men, or one-fourth of its personnel over a period of two years.[14] Also, in June, eight of the eleven regional commanders were either retired or transferred, and the number of military regions was reduced from eleven to seven. By September, it was reported that the average age of the officers in the leading bodies of all major units had been lowered from 64.9 to 56.7 years.[15]

The party and the government, too, continued to register similar dramatic personnel changes, as had been occurring since 1983. During the spring and summer, more than half of the party secretaries of the 29 provinces and autonomous regions were changed. During the same period some fifteen of the government's 45 ministers were replaced, while nine governors were removed and new mayors were appointed in many major cities including Shanghai. From January through September 1985, more than 200,000 younger, better-educated cadres were given leadership responsibilities at and above the county level. Below the county level, it was reported that by June the five-year drive to dismantle the 56,000 rural communes as the basic unit of state power had been completed. They were now replaced by more than 92,000 new local township governments.[16]

The amount of personnel shifting that took place between 1983 and 1985 should not be underestimated. For example, the restructuring of party and state provincial positions that took place during only six weeks in the spring of 1983 involved 650 of 1,082 provincial leaders who were replaced by 362 new appointments. But even more interesting, among these same categories of leaders, David Goodman found that only 75 of the 656 cadres in provincial leadership in September 1983 were still provincial leaders two years later.[17]

The reformers also launched a major effort to replace China's Soviet-style educational system with one closer to Western models and to counter certain stubbornly persistent traditional pedagogical practices. Deng Xiaoping initiated this effort during a national conference on education on May 19.[18] The Central Committee subsequently issued a "Decision on the Reform of the Educational System." The momentum was continued with the elevation of the former Ministry of Education to a higher status as the State Education Commission, whose first director was Vice Premier Li Peng.[19]

Following four days of preliminary meetings, the Fourth Plenary Session of the Twelfth Central Committee was held on September 18. The plenum came on the heels of a dramatic announcement that 131 elderly party leaders had asked to be allowed to resign from the Central

Committee, the Central Advisory Commission, and the Central Commission for Discipline Inspection. These retirees included Ye Jianying and Deng Yingchao.[20] Only a few days later, it was announced that 1.1 million elderly party leaders had suddenly retired.[21]

From September 18 to 23, 1985, the extraordinary National CCP Conference of Party Delegates was held, with 992 delegates in attendance. The conference was called primarily to facilitate the orderly transfer of power to a new generation of officials, and to discuss the draft of the next five-year plan. The only other such conference, held in 1955, had similarly dealt with a personnel situation, that is, the Gao Gang-Rao Shushi case and the five-year plan of that period. Deng Xiaoping had been prominently involved in the 1955 conference as well. The delegates conference is a useful device for implementing personnel shifts when the outcome might otherwise be in doubt if left to the regularly elected party congress. The delegates to the conference are appointed from above, not elected. Nor, constitutionally, does such a conference have the power to elect a new central committee, this being the responsibility of the party congress.[22]

Nevertheless, the conference elected 64 new leaders to the Central Committee—29 full members and 35 alternates. It also placed 56 officials on the Central Advisory Commission and 31 on the Central Commission for Discipline Inspection. The conference also discussed the draft of the Seventh Five-Year Plan, which would be presented in final form to the NPC in 1986.

The Fifth Plenary Session of the Twelfth Central Committee met on September 24, 1985, immediately after the conclusion of the party conference. The plenum dramatically changed the composition of the Politburo. Ten of the 27 members of the Politburo resigned and were replaced by six, for the most part, younger men, some considerably younger. Resigning were: Deng Yingchao, Li Desheng, Nie Rongzhen, Song Renqiong, Ulanfu, Wang Zhen, Wei Guoqing, Xu Xiangqian, Ye Jianying, and Zhang Tingfa. The six new members were Hu Qili, Li Peng, Qiao Shi, Tian Jiyun, Wu Xueqian, and Yao Yilin (formerly an alternate member). Except for Ye Jianying, now resigned, the Standing Committee remained the same. Almost all of those who retired had had military backgrounds, which is natural considering their ages and experience in the revolution, but the relative absence of military background among the replacements certainly indicated the further strengthening of party civilian control of political decisionmaking once again. Five new members joined the Secretariat, including two former alternate members, replacing three who had resigned.[23] Significantly, however, Deng Xiaoping was unable to find a suitable and acceptable successor to his position as chair of the Military Affairs Commissions. It was apparent that Hu Yaobang was not acceptable to the military.

The reform atmosphere was highlighted in 1985 by the reevaluation and partial rehabilitation of Chen Duxiu, the principal original founder of the CCP. Chen had been expelled from the party in 1929, but this more balanced consideration in the mid-1980s of his role was consonant with the party's effort to elevate the status of intellectuals. Chen had been a prominent and highly respected intellectual throughout much of his career.[24] Similarly, for the same reasons, Hu Yaobang positively reevaluated Hu Feng, the prominent party literary figure who had been imprisoned in 1955 for alleged counterrevolutionary statements. Hu Feng had been exonerated in 1980 and died in 1985.[25]

By the end of 1985, Deng Xiaoping could view with some satisfaction what he and his fellow reformers had wrought thus far. He told the Conference of Party Delegates in September that the seven years since the Third Plenum of the Eleventh Central Committee in December 1978 had been one of the best periods the country had had since 1949. He said: "We have set wrong things right." Indeed, measured by the number of persons who had been rehabilitated or who had gained restitution since the Cultural Revolution or who had been released from harmful designations dating from the 1950s, this was clearly the case. The economic reforms also were showing evidence of success. Some did create serious dilemmas. But the reform movement was popular nonetheless.

Vice Premier Li Peng could say in November 1985 that the economy had shown sustained, balanced, and steady development over the preceding seven years. He announced that the total product of society, the total industrial and agricultural output value, and the total national income had increased an average of 10 percent a year during the Sixth Five-Year Plan period. The three-year decline in state revenues had been halted in 1982. The readjustment of the structure of industry in recent years had rectified the long-standing, serious imbalances in the national economy. And the structural reform, Li added, had ushered in a period of economic prosperity unprecedented in the PRC. With genuine satisfaction he could say that although China's arable land accounted for only 7 percent of the world's total farmland, China had satisfied the basic needs of 22 percent of the world's population in food and clothing. He stated that the open door policy had turned a closed economy into an open one, enabling the country to make "fairly good achievements" in developing economic and technological cooperation with foreign countries. The total volume of the import-export trade during the period of the Sixth Five-Year plan was double that of the previous five years, and exports increased more than imports. Finally, Li pointed out that urban and rural living standards had improved to varying degrees, against the record of no such remarkable changes for many years in the past.[26] And whatever the methods employed at times, and whatever the ultimate social consequences, it seemed that by 1985 the population control program was meeting with considerable success. But the population growth rate could and would rise again.

Also at the Conference of Party Delegates, significant changes had taken place among the top leadership, but these were not as sweeping as the personnel changes that had taken place at the provincial level over the previous two years. There were still an appreciable number of aged cadres at the very top, but in the provinces it could now be said that the "revolutionary generation" had been almost entirely displaced by much younger leaders. The average age of the provincial party secretaries after August 1985 was about 53 years.[27] Thus, the success of Deng's cadre personnel changes had been overwhelming, and were much more profound than was discernible in the Central Committee or in the Politburo itself. In discussing the need for reducing leading organs and making needed personnel changes, Deng Xiaoping had declared in December 1983 that such "streamlining is a revolution and selecting those with virtue and specialized knowledge is also a revolution."[28] In actual fact, it is likely that the official bureaucracy at that time continued to grow despite the efforts to streamline it. But, to a significant extent, Deng was able to realize the "revolution" of making key personnel changes by mid-1985.

With such a thoroughgoing changeover of personnel from the central level down through the provinces to the counties, the party was better prepared to launch the third stage of the party rectification campaign, which it did by the end of 1985. This final stage extended the campaign to the more than 1.1 million rural party branches throughout the country, whose combined numbers totaled more than 22 million party members, or more than half of the entire party membership. The plan was to complete the campaign by the spring of 1987.

It would not be easy to accomplish. Resistance to change by some local cadres had been noted for some time.[29] It was acknowledged that, because of the rapid and profound changes that had occurred in recent years, "many rural Party members have found themselves lacking mental preparations for and an understanding of all that has happened."[30] It was also acknowledged that a number of "undisciplined" party branches had slackened their ideological and political work, and this had compounded the problem. According to an authoritative *Beijing Review* article, the problems were essentially ideological. Thus, education work was to "focus first on reiterating the sole purpose of the Chinese Communist Party, which is to serve the people wholeheartedly." However, the ambiguity of the situation created by the reforms was nowhere better seen than in the same author's assertion that many party members "have not only worked hard to better their own lives, but have also done their best to help other peasants improve their income." This statement undoubtedly reflected the reality that many party cadres were indeed looking after their own interests first.[31] In fact, even before the full brunt of the rectification campaign hit the local level, most cadres had probably accommodated themselves to the changed circumstances one way or another. John P. Burns suggests that they adopted various strategies, depending on the leadership style each cadre employed. The options were either acceptance of the changes or resignation.[32] Jean C. Oi pointed out, however, that while government policies did seek to serve the peasants' interests, inasmuch as centralized control was not abandoned, cadres were able to appropriate the new administrative opportunities to bolster their own power.[33]

Despite his many successes, Deng Xiaoping continued to court opposition. This was apparent even at the Conference of Party Delegates when Chen Yun provocatively suggested that Deng had had too free a hand in setting policy. Chen also warned of the possibility of social disorder if the flight by peasants from the farms was not arrested. Also, Chen argued that the economy should continue to be based on central planning and not on market forces. This criticism did not necessarily signal a serious breach between the two old comrades. Deng and Chen had long agreed on many aspects of the reform programs, and Deng had certainly long shown respect for Chen's contributions and views. There had been differences between the two all along, but these were mostly on how certain policies should be promoted, as David Bachman has pointed out.[34] It was perhaps another measure of the success Deng was achieving that such differences between himself and Chen Yun began to surface. Deng was simply more willing to take risks than Chen, but he was no less a committed Marxist.

Deng continued to employ tactics that would help cover points of vulnerability from the left, which were always there because of his risk-taking. For example, a national forum on theoretical work was sponsored by the Central Committee's Propaganda Department in Chengdu from November 18 to 24, 1985, in response to a demand from Deng Xiaoping himself that both new and old cadres study Marxist theory.[35]

After the massive changes of 1985, the following year began on an entirely different basis. Premier Zhao announced in January 1986 that the major goals for the new year would be to "consolidate, digest, supplement and improve on" the reforms of 1985, which he revealed had "turned out to be bigger than we expected, and so were the effects." Zhao made it clear that there would be no major steps to implement price and wage reforms in 1986.[36]

The party held, without prior public notice, two large meetings on January 6 and 9, 1986, attended by 8,000 senior party, army, and government officials. The meetings were dominated by the reformers, who announced a yet new campaign against corruption in the senior ranks. But instead of the campaign being entrusted to the Central Commission for Discipline Inspection, a new anticorruption team was established, headed by Qiao Shi, who in August 1985 had become secretary of the important Commission of Political Science and Law, and the following month was promoted to the Politburo. Curiously, Deng Xiaoping, Li Xiannian, and Chen Yun did not attend.[37]

In the months that followed there were a number of arrests, sentencings, and imprisonments of the offspring of prominent cadres, including the son of the leading conservative, Hu Qiaomu.[38] This was another indication of the intense struggle that was transpiring between reformers and conservatives. But it also highlighted a very profound problem in the regime, the rise to influence and power of the progeny of leading cadres and their all-too-frequent abuse of such positions. In February, three children of senior Shanghai party officials were executed for rape and "hooliganism." The general crackdown on crime continued as well, with 31 criminals executed in Beijing in June, in what was the largest single mass execution since the inception of the campaign in 1983.[39]

The Seventh Five-Year Plan, for 1986–1990, was launched in an atmosphere of consolidation and contention. Nevertheless, it was approved at the Fourth Session of the Sixth NPC on April 12, 1986.[40] Significantly, this was the first time that such a plan had been discussed and endorsed by the NPC before being promulgated or, as was sometimes the case previously, simply being implemented without having been promulgated.

The new plan gave priority to continued reform—in order to lay the foundation, it was said, for the establishment of a socialist economic structure with Chinese characteristics. To accomplish this, reforms were to be carried out in three fields: (1) enterprises were to be invigorated, especially large and medium-sized state-owned ones, "so that they will truly become relatively independent economic entities"; (2) the socialist commodity market was to be further developed, "gradually perfecting the market system"; and (3) state management of enterprises would change gradually from direct to indirect control, and a new socialist macroeconomic management system was to be established. The growth rate (total industrial and agricultural output value) was projected to be at the average annual rate of 6.7 percent; the GNP was set for an average annual rate of 7.5 percent. An average accumulation rate of 30 percent was projected, as was a 5 percent annual increase of consumption. Science, technology, and education continued to receive important attention.[41]

The reformers secured further evolution of the nation's legal structure and two important promotions at the Fourth Session of the Sixth NPC. Endorsed were the General Principles of the Civil Code scheduled to come into force in 1987; the Law Governing Enterprises with Foreign Capital, which became effective upon publication; and the Law Governing Compulsory Education, which went into effect on July 1, 1986. Qiao Shi was made the fifth vice premier of the State Council and Song Jian, the minister in charge of the State Scientific and Technological Commission, was appointed state councillor.[42]

Political reform was prominently discussed throughout 1986. From July 10 to 12, 1986, more than 130 researchers and others from the Central Committee and the State Council participated in a symposium to discuss the theory of political structural reform. The discussion focused on the basic objective of decentralizing power, and included pointed comments on the functions of the party itself. Most of the participants held that the "overconcentration of power finds expression in Party organizations so that generally speaking, the Party functions in place of the state."[43]

On July 31, Vice Premier Wan Li, speaking to a national symposium on "soft science," or policy research, acknowledged that to develop a scientific approach "it is necessary first to create a political environment in which democracy, equality, and the free exchange of views and information are the norms of life." He continued: "Leaders must respect other people's democratic right to air their opinions without fear, including, of course, those that contradict their own." He added that this was all the more important for soft science research "because it comprises mental work involving political as well as academic questions."[44]

In the meanwhile, other developments were at work that would have their effect on the economy. Urban dwellers were feeling the effects of an inflation rate of about 6 percent. On July 5, 1986, the *Renminbi* was devalued by 15.8 percent, the biggest such devaluation in the history of the PRC.[45] And, in August, the news of an explosion-prevention equipment factory in Shenyang actually having gone bankrupt—a heretofore unprecedented phenomenon in the PRC—sent shock waves throughout the country.[46] The complaints and apprehensions generated by such developments strengthened the hand of the conservatives and made the reformers more cautious. Even so, on September 9, the State Council promulgated four sets of regulations on reforming the country's labor system. The aim of the reform, according to Minister of Labor and Personnel He Guang, was to eliminate the defects of the "iron rice bowl" practice, and establish the relationship between workers and enterprises on a rational basis in order to meet the needs of a planned commodity economy.[47]

The Sixth Plenary Session of the Twelfth Central Committee was held on September 28, 1986, following a five-day preparatory meeting. There were 199 members and 126 alternate members in attendance, along with members of the Central Advisory Committee and the Central Commission for Discipline Inspection. The economy was discussed at the lengthier preparatory meeting, but the plenum made only one minor personnel change (Yin Changmin, a former alternate member was promoted to full membership) and passed two resolutions. One of these announced that the Thirteenth Party Congress would be held the following October. The other was a 10,000-character statement of "guiding principles for building a socialist society with an advanced culture and ideology."

The resolution declared: "As a basic, unalterable state policy, opening to the outside world applies to our efforts to achieve cultural and ideological progress as well as to our work for material progress." It said:

> Taking economic development as the key link, China is to continue to reform its economic and political structure and at the same time speed up the country's cultural and ideological progress, making sure that these aspects of work are co-ordinated and promote each other. The cultural and ideological progress provides a powerful guarantee for the correct orientation of the material progress.[48]

Even though the resolution conceded that opening to the outside world is an unalterable state policy and that economic development is the key link, the plenum was basically a victory for the conservatives. This is because the issue of political reforms, which had been so intensively discussed for months, and which many reformers believed was essential to further economic reform, was not on the agenda. Later, a commentary in the *People's Daily* revealed that the government would be putting forward a "practical" plan for political reform in a year's time, presumably in time for the Thirteenth Party Congress.[49]

In light of the stiffening opposition, and because of the inherent contradictions in reforming the political system, especially under the overwhelming strictures of the Four Cardinal Principles, promoting greater democratization was proving to be more difficult than the reformers had expected. Even so, the Central Committee's Organization Department issued a circular late in the year urging all regions and departments to have their rank and file make public assessments of the abilities, moral character, conscientiousness, and achievements of leading officials at the county level and above during the winter and spring of 1987. This came on the heels of initiatives by the Guangdong Provincial and the Beijing Municipal party committees that suggested the use of public opinion polls to evaluate the performance of officials.[50]

With reformist domination of key party organs, conservative opposition to some of Deng Xiaoping's policies began manifesting itself in the NPC. Veteran China analyst Louis Ladany, S.J., concluded that Peng Zhen, the chairman of the NPC's Standing Committee, was building an institutional base from which to challenge Deng and Zhao Ziyang. In January 1986, Peng Zhen had objected to a person being considered conservative and an opponent of reform if he stressed Marxism-Leninism. He said: "It is the theories of the capitalist class and its apologists that are conservative and ossified. Bourgeois thoughts may look very fresh and jaunty today, but they serve only to defend capitalism's status quo."[51] Later, Peng rebuked those who denigrated the communist ideal. He defended the superiority of socialist democracy and urged the strengthening of socialist legal and democratic systems, so that they "are not subject to change with the change of leadership, or changes in the views and attention of the leaders."[52] Some observers interpreted such warnings of the danger of personal rule as being directed against Deng Xiaoping and Zhao Ziyang. Various reform measures, and most particularly a bankruptcy law, were extensively debated, and sometimes delayed, in Peng Zhen's NPC Standing Committee.[53]

The conservative position may have been enhanced with the publication of the first Chinese edition of the *Complete Works of Karl Marx and Frederick Engels* in late 1986. The 50-volume collection was translated from the Russian edition, with only minor differences.[54] Serving the same purpose, the third volume of the *Selected Works of Chen Yun (1956–1985)* appeared in print in 1986. Moreover, the tenth anniversary of Mao Zedong's death was commemorated by the publication of an edition of 68 of his articles written between 1921 and 1965.

However, the conservative dampener on political reforms contributed to the frustrations of many increasingly restive Chinese students, who finally mounted major demonstrations beginning in December 1986. The demonstrations began at the prestigious Chinese University of Science and Technology in Hefei, Anhui, where ideas freely circulated under the leadership of its outspoken vice president, astrophysicist Fang Lizhi.[55] From Hefei, where the primary issue had to do with a local election, the activity soon spread to Shanghai and then to Beijing. A march of about 30,000 students in Shanghai on December 20 was the largest student demonstration in China since the Cultural Revolution. The students demonstrated for various reasons, including for better living and study conditions at their universities. But they also clearly called for more democracy in their locales and for the country. The authorities handled the massive demonstrations with surprising restraint, and remarkably few students were arrested. Nevertheless, it was evident that conservative officials were disturbed by such representations. The occasion provided them with a convenient pretext for attacking the reformists.

Their pressure led Deng Xiaoping himself to criticize the handling of the students and the behavior of some leading cadres, including Hu Yaobang, perhaps to forestall further attacks. Deng's ploy was insufficient. A top-level conference on party life was held from January 10 to 15, 1987, that began with a self-criticism by Hu Yaobang, who admitted violating the party principle of collective leadership and of making other serious errors. On January 16, the Politburo held an extraordinary enlarged meeting, which accepted Hu Yaobang's resignation as general secretary. Premier Zhao Ziyang was named acting general secretary.[56] It bears noting that this major personnel action took place under extraordinary circumstances and was not strictly legal, according to the party constitution, inasmuch as the general secretary is elected by and removed by the Central Committee.

The January 16 Politburo meeting was attended by eighteen members of the Politburo itself, along with the two alternate members, four representatives from the Secretariat, seventeen leading cadres from the Central Advisory Commission, two members from the Central Commission for Discipline Inspection, "and others." Bo Yibo, the deputy director of the Central Advisory Commission, reported to the meeting on the details of the preceding party life conference. This action was a stinging rebuke to Deng Xiaoping and the reformers. However, Hu was replaced by another leading reformer, and did retain, for the time being, his position on the Standing Committee of the Politburo.

A Central Committee document was circulated on January 17 that listed six mistakes Hu Yaobang had made. He had not taken a clear-cut stand against bourgeois liberalization; had transformed the central authorities' proposal to unify thinking into the "straightening-out of vocation thinking"; had erroneously put forward the slogan of "high consumption" and set excessively high targets; had advocated the rule of man; had "said something which should not have been said" regarding the effort to crack down on economic crimes; and had violated discipline by making speeches everywhere, often without authorization.[57]

There were further immediate setbacks for the reformers. Three prominent party intellectuals lost their positions and were expelled from the party: Wang Ruowang, a writer; Fang Lizhi, referred to above; and Liu Binyan, a writer and reporter for the *People's Daily.* The three were charged with advocating "bourgeois liberalization." The *People's Daily* had already editorialized on "resolutely combating bourgeois liberalization,"[58] indicating that momentum was building for a new campaign that would target intellectuals. Intellectuals throughout China became apprehensive.

On February 4, Wang Renzhi, the former deputy editor-in-chief of *Hong Qi,* was made head of the party's propaganda department, replacing Zhu Houze, a former associate of Hu Yaobang.[59] Bo Yibo and Peng Zhen were appointed to a triumvirate to head a preparatory committee for the upcoming party congress. Bo Yibo, among others, revived the "three-in-one combination" concept, which this time suggested providing a place for party elders at the congress (in contrast to the slogan's implication at the Tenth Party Congress, which was to make room for younger cadres—in the young, middle-aged, and older cadre formulation).

Meanwhile, however, the reform leaders attempted to assure the public that the campaign against bourgeois liberalization would not get out of hand. Assurances were given that the major reform policies would remain unchanged. The open door was to open even more widely. Experiments in economic reforms were to go forward, including the shareholding system and the renting out of smaller state enterprises to colectives and individuals, which should "not be misconstrued as 'bourgeois liberalization.' "[60] Acting General Secretary and Premier Zhao, speaking at a Spring Festival gathering in Beijing on January 29, indicated that the work of opposing bourgeois liberalization "is strictly an inner-Party issue, to be handled mainly in the political and ideological fields." Zhao said the "nothing of the sort will be conducted in rural areas, while in enterprises and institutions the task will be handled in the form of study and self-education."[61]

Zhao's injunction was largely ignored initially, as the conservatives mounted their drive. There was even talk of extending the antibourgeois liberalization campaign to the PLA. The leftist *Beijing Daily,* which had been sharply criticized during the demonstrations, suggested that students should serve time in the fields, factories, or armed forces, revealing that several thousand students in Beijing had already spent their month-long winter vacation doing so.[62]

Wang Zhen, vice-chairman of the Central Advisory Commission and president of the Central Party School, ominously warned that the party was plagued by weakness and confusion in the political and ideological fields and was more divided than it had ever been in the previous eight years.[63]

Nevertheless, Zhao Ziyang remained undaunted, and by mid-March it was apparent that a reform resurgence was underway. A new edition of Deng Xiaoping's *To Build Socialism with Chinese Characteristics* was published containing an additional 22 speeches since the initial edition of December 1984, including some given as recently as January 1987. The publication symbolized Deng's main concern for reform, although it included abundant evidence of his concern for order and stability. With regard to the latter, documents had been released in January that again revealed Deng's toughness. These documents contained speeches in which Deng told Chinese officials to use "dictatorial" methods, such as Poland used against the Solidarity trade union, to quell the student protests. Deng's tactical reaffirmation of such a hard line against disorder (and Western democracy) served to blunt the criticism of his detractors.[64] In the weeks that followed, Deng's unqualified support for Zhao Ziyang became absolutely clear.

However, the Fifth Session of the Sixth NPC, held from March 25 to April 11, 1987, again showed the propensity of this body under the leadership of Peng Zhen to criticize the work of the State Council. It approved Premier Zhao's report on the work of the government but took the government to task for not having taken more prompt and effective measures to solve certain problems in agriculture production, especially in grain production, and for neglecting the "fine tradition" of building up China through thrift and hard work—well-chosen leftist expressions. Concern was expressed regarding the large deficit in 1986 and the "longstanding" problem of overextended capital construction. The NPC urged the government to eliminate or reduce the deficit, to limit the price hikes, to end the import of large numbers of autos, and to make efficient use of foreign currency. In several respects, the premier's work report was revised accordingly. Even so, the main thrust of Zhao's message was the reformist determination to "deepen the reform of the economic structure and open wider to the outside world."[65]

In April, authorities of three publications—*Red Flag, Theory and Critics of Literature,* and *Guangming Daily*—held a conference in Zhuozhou to solicit articles nationwide for the antibourgeois liberalization campaign. With 120 participants, this was regarded as the largest meeting of conservatives (again, read 'leftists') since Deng Xiaoping had assumed power in late 1978. The conference advocated the initiation of a new movement "to right all wrongs in the areas of economy, philosophy, literature and arts since the Third Plenary Session." This was clearly construed as a challenge to Deng Xiaoping and the reformers.[66]

But Zhao Ziyang decisively outmaneuvered the conservatives at a meeting of propaganda, media, and party school cadres at Huairen Hall in Zhongnanhai, Beijing on May 13. Actually, the conservatives had sought to circumvent Zhao by not inviting him to speak at the session. But Zhao exercised his prerogative as party leader and took the occasion to give one of the most important speeches of the year, in which he systematically criticized various views that had been voiced by conservatives in recent months. That same evening an enlarged meeting of the Politburo was held. Here, Zhao accused three of the most prominent critics—Bo Yibo, Hu Qiaomu, and Deng Liqun—of leftist deviations.[67] Zhao's speech was then circulated as a Central Committee document and was discussed in two *People's Daily* editorials, although it was not openly published until July 9, indicative of the continuing obstructive tactics of Deng Liqun and others.[68]

Nevertheless, on May 21–22, the Central Committee's Propaganda Department held a forum in which the call was made "to integrate firmly and in an organic way the two basic points, namely, upholding the Four Cardinal Principles, and reform and opening up, in propaganda and theoretical research work." This was an important turning point. Henceforth, the idea was given prominence that in building socialism with Chinese characteristics, "the main obstacle came from 'leftism,' and from force of habit and ossification in people's ideological understanding."[69] On May 25 at a meeting of "responsible cadres," Hu Qili explained the background to Zhao's May 13 speech in a lengthy talk. He noted that Deng Xiaoping had commented that the party had no option other than making the report to the Thirteenth Congress a report about reform. Therefore, it was necessary to coordinate propaganda work in order to maintain an atmosphere strongly supportive of reform.[70]

On the following day, May 26, the three-and-a-half-year party rectification campaign finally came to an end. The Central Commission for Guiding Party Rectification met to summarize and evaluate the campaign. Bo Yibo, the vice-chairman of the commission, delivered the main report. He said the consolidation had been successful, although the outcome was unbalanced inasmuch as some party organs had not completed their work and "some even did it superficially." Bo reported that 33,896 persons were expelled from the party, including some high-ranking cadres. This was far fewer than had been expected. Bo's report itself was regarded by many as not having been much more satisfactory than the campaign itself.[71] For his part, Zhao Ziyang took the occasion once more to emphasize the need to adhere simultaneously to the Four Cardinal Principles *and* to the general policies of reform, thus opening to the outside world and invigorating the economy.[72]

However, Propaganda Department director Wang Renzhi described the ongoing campaign against bourgeois liberalization as the party's "second drive to bring order out of chaos." This, in effect, reiterated the sentiment that Deng Liqun had expressed to trade union leaders in Tianjin earlier in May regarding the need to "quell chaos and return to the right path." But Wang Renzhi's comments brought immediate criticism, including an unprecedented rebuke from a lower-level propaganda department (of the Shanghai Municipal Party Committee).[73] As for Deng Liqun, Deng Xiaoping was furious when he heard that the former used a phrase that Deng Xiaoping himself had earlier employed in the struggle against the Gang of Four and Hua Guofeng.[74] Deng Xiaoping later told Deng Liqun that his comments and actions in extending the campaign against bourgeois liberalization were "not conducive to reform and openness." Deng Liqun was replaced by Qiao Shi on the preparatory group for the impending party congress.[75]

It became more fully apparent that the reformers were again dominant when Premier Zhao made a visit to Eastern Europe in June. On the eve of his departure from Beijing, Zhao announced that Hu Qili would act in his stead in presiding over the Secretariat, although Hu would not use the title of acting general secretary. Wan Li performed the duties of acting premier in Zhao's absence. On June 12, Deng Xiaoping publicly supported this bold assertion of reformist confidence by calling for a speedup in reform and declaring that reform of the political structure would be one of the main topics at the party congress. He also noted, pointedly, that the average age of members of the CCP Central Committee "is higher than it is in the central committee of any other Communist Party in the world."[76]

During Zhao's absence from the country, a resentful Deng Liqun arranged for criticism of State Council work habits through *Xinhua*.[77] Also, a Central Committee document was circulated revealing that Hu Yaobang's self-criticism had included comments about Liu Binyan (calling him a "rightist") that seriously detracted from the popularity Hu Yaobang had come to enjoy since his resignation as general secretary. Subsequently, however, it was charged that Deng Liqun had actually tampered with Hu's self-criticism, adding the offending phrases, specifically for the purpose of eroding Hu's popularity.[78]

Conservatives also took advantage of the serious forest fire that had raged during the summer in the Greater Hinggan Mountains of Heilongjiang province to criticize officials close to Zhao at the 21st Session of the Sixth NPC Standing Committee in June. The NPC Standing Committee also appointed Vice-Premier Yao Yilin to head the State Planning Commission. This important commission's former minister, Song Ping, had earlier taken over the Central Committee's Organization Department, and the former head of the latter department, Wei Jianxing, was now appointed minister of the newly established Ministry of Supervision. This ministry would monitor the performance of government departments, government officials, and government-appointed factory managers.[79]

The anniversary of the CCP was marked on July 1 by the republication in all major Chinese newspapers of Deng Xiaoping's speech on "Reform of the Leadership Systems of the Party and State" that he originally gave on August 18, 1980. This rendition of the speech contained an additional paragraph that dealt with changes in the responsibility systems of plant directors and managers, school principals, academy presidents, and institute directors.[80] Yet another compilation of 44 speeches by Deng Xiaoping given since December 1984, entitled *Fundamental Issues in Present-Day China*, was made available for wide distribution in the weeks just before the party congress. The two main themes stressed were opposition to bourgeois liberalization and adherence to the policies of reform and opening to the world.[81] In addition, on July 1 *Xinhua* announced that some 50 reference books on political structural reform were to be made available shortly.[82]

Some of the cost of such progress by the reformers was borne by the students of China whose demonstrations six months earlier had provided the pretext for the demotion of Hu Yaobang and the launching of the antibourgeois liberalization campaign. Students were frequently accused by authorities of indiscipline and extravagances. During the summer recess more than one million college students were sent to work in factories and rural villages as part of a program to remold their views. This constituted the first mass migration of students since the Cultural Revolution. On July 1 it was reported that most of the nearly 400,000 college graduates and postgraduates of the current class were to be sent to work at the grass roots for two years instead of being assigned to government positions. Also, the number of graduates assigned to ten remote provinces and autonomous regions was to be increased by 30 percent over 1986,[83] and tighter restrictions were announced on Chinese students going abroad for further study. Finally, the Chinese government began to replace the system whereby almost two million college students had been provided grants to cover the expense of their education with a new loan system.[84] As a result of such measures, many students became increasingly cynical and apathetic.[85]

Meanwhile, across the Taiwan Strait the government in Taiwan undertook two decisive actions on July 15, 1987, that reformers and conservatives alike in Beijing had to ponder. The government abolished the 38-year-old Emergency Decree, which had been referred to over the years as "martial law," and it removed restrictions on the possession and use of foreign currency by Taiwan citizens. Moreover, on the following day it also lifted the ban on direct travel to Hong Kong and Macao by Taiwan citizens, a restriction imposed in April 1979 to prevent capital flight. The relaxation of foreign currency controls had immediate beneficial effect. Within a week, Taiwan's foreign exchange holdings dropped from the record high of almost $62 billion to $60.7 billion.[86] It also encouraged speculation that Taiwan could become an international banking, insurance, and marine industry center in the future.

Party leaders had other concerns, too, which generally strengthened the hand of the conservatives. There were manifestations of societal tension and instability, seen in the recurrent bomb plots and actual detonations in Beijing during 1987. There was evidence of assassination plans, and in late July slogans critical of the "new gang of four" appeared, as did appeals for "democracy and freedom, not autocratic rule."[87] The economy required close attention. All major economic indicators for several months prior to June 1987 rose at a speed comparable to the previous such boom in late 1984, implying that inflation was much higher than the official rate of 8.8 percent at the end of June. This was something that had an impact on everyone, and complaints abounded. Similarly, the budget deficit was expected to be much larger than what had been forecast.[88] In foreign relations, tension had increased considerably during the preceding several months along the Sino-Indian border, with military deployment on either side far exceeding that used during the 1962 border war. (In September and October, demonstrations, rioting, and killing would take place in Lhasa. This outbreak was apparently provoked by comments and actions by the Dalai Lhama abroad, but it drew attention to the sensitive issue of Chinese rule there.)

Such was the atmosphere as party leaders gathered at the seaside resort of Beidaihe for important working vacation meetings preparatory to the imminent party congress. Discussions concentrated on three topics: the reaffirmation of reform and the opening-up policy; political structural reform; and the important personnel decisions that had to be made.

It was clear by now that the congress would reaffirm reform and that political structural reform would be spotlighted. The group formed in 1986 to design a plan for structural reform had suspended work for a couple of months after the unexpected turn of events in January 1987.

However, that group too had been given heart by Deng Xiaoping's renewed support for this agenda, and after resuming work it was able to complete its initial draft in May. With regard to personnel decisions, a key role in implementing this responsibility had been given initially to Bo Yibo, but during the year Deng Xiaoping himself became much more actively involved.[89]

Perhaps the key move on Deng's part was his decision, announced repeatedly during the summer, that he would retire from the Central Committee. This would have the effect of compelling his more conservative elderly comrades to do the same, which would facilitate the work of the reformers in the years immediately ahead. It was apparent that the personnel negotiations proved to be difficult at Beidaihe and afterward.

Zhao Ziyang tried to set a positive tone for the discussions by meeting with a group of middle-aged scientists and their families at Beidaihe on July 20. This was the first time the Central Committee had invited intellectuals to spend a holiday at the summer resort.[90] But on August 1, the conservatives countered by arranging for the threatened expulsion of eight prominent intellectuals from the party. One of these intellectuals, the playwright Wu Zuguang, revealed that Hu Qiaomu visited his apartment and told him to quit the party of his own accord or be expelled. Hu read to him a document accusing him of opposing the party leadership in the 1950s and of publicly criticizing the more recent campaign against spiritual pollution. Wu, 70 years old, who had only joined the party in 1981, agreed to resign.

The others who were told to resign were: Wang Ruoshui, the well-known theorist who had been attacked during the anti-Spiritual Pollution campaign; Su Shaozhi, director of the Research Institute of Marxism-Leninism–Mao Zedong Thought; Zhang Xianyang, a member of the same institute; Sun Changjia, deputy editor of *Science News*; Ge Yang, editor of *New Observer* magazine and co-author of a controversial ten-year history of the Cultural Revolution; Yu Haocheng, an editor at the Masses Publishing House; and Li Honglin, a literary critic.[91] However, these seven intellectuals refused to leave the party, and although some of them were further criticized and demoted, they were not expelled. In the meanwhile, tit for tat, Xiong Fu, a conservative hardliner who had been outspoken at the so-called Zhuozhou Conference in April, was removed from his post as editor in chief of *Hong Qi* magazine. His superior, Deng Liqun, was also criticized and relieved of his responsibility for supervising ideological matters.[92]

Thus, Deng Xiaoping and Zhao Ziyang remained steadfast. They were greatly bolstered in this by the results of unprecedented polls taken during the year that underscored support for the reform programs. Accordingly, by the beginning of September the Politburo proposed to the Central Committee that the party congress be convened on October 25.[93]

The Seventh Plenary Session of the Twelfth Central Committee met on October 20, 1967. The plenum approved the key documents to be presented to the congress. It approved in principle "general ideas on the reform of the political structure," the major points of which would be in the Central Committee's work report to the congress. It also accepted Hu Yaobang's resignation of January 16 from the general secretaryship and approved Zhao Ziyang's appointment as acting general secretary. Hu Yaobang was present at the plenum.[94]

Hu Qili, as secretary general of the congress, presided over the first meeting of the 187-member Presidium of the Thirteenth Congress on October 24, 1987. Zhao Ziyang spoke to the presidium, which elected 30 members of its standing committee and three deputy secretaries general of the congress: Qiao Shi, Song Ping, and Wen Jiabao. Qiao Shi, as chairman of the eighteen-member credentials committee, gave a report on the delegates to the congress.

Qiao Shi reported that the election of the delegates, from the preliminary discussions and nomination of candidates to deciding the short lists of candidates and formal elections, was conducted "in a democratic way following the principle of democratic centralism and respecting the will and democratic rights of the electors." All delegates were said to have been elected by secret ballot from among multiple candidates. The resulting 1,936 delegates were broadly representative. They included 1,465 cadres from various levels, accounting for 75.7 percent of the total; 366 persons from the professions, accounting for 18.9 percent; and 105 delegates were combat heroes and model workers, accounting for 5.4 percent. As many as 59.5 percent of the delegates had some college or higher educational background. Women delegates accounted for 14.9 percent of the total. Minority nationalities were represented by 10.8 percent of the delegates. In terms of age, 58.8 percent of the total were below the age of 55. (It was not officially mentioned, nor was it a part of Qiao Shi's report, but former party chairman Hua Guofeng reportedly received the largest number of votes among the delegates. The significance of this surprising development, if it is true, is not clear.) Also invited to the congress were 61 veteran cadres who had joined the party before 1927 and who have served in important leadership positions in the party. A number of observers and guests were similarly invited to attend.

On the day before the congress, the first of several press conferences was given by Zhu Muzhi, the spokesman of the Thirteenth Party Congress. The conference was chaired by Gao Liang, director of the well-equipped press center established for the congress. Utilizing the services of this press center were more than 400 journalists, including at least 300 foreign reporters who would be permitted to cover the opening and closing sessions of the congress. Except for the Soviet and East European reporters who had covered the Eighth Party Congress in 1956, this was another unprecedented example of *kaifang* or opening up by the CCP—signifying, perhaps, China's reform-era unwillingness to be upstaged by the Soviet policy of *glasnost'* that had been getting so much attention under Soviet general secretary Mikhail Gorbachev in recent months.

The Thirteenth Party Congress, which had been awaited with such suspense and apprehension and which was now suddenly attended by such well-orchestrated publicity, was declared open by Deng Xiaoping at 9 A.M. on October 25, 1987. The band played the "Internationale." The 1,953 actual delegates stood in silence to mourn deceased veteran leaders. They represented a membership of 46,011,951, including 2,410,831 probationary members, at the end of 1986. Acting General Secretary Zhao Ziyang then took two and a half hours to deliver the 34,000-character work report entitled "Advance Along the Road of Socialism with Chinese Characteristics." A draft of this report had been circulated to more than 5,000 party leaders in August and had seen successive drafts. Its main points had come to be pretty well known within the party by this time. The report comprised seven parts with these respective headings: historic achievements and the tasks of the present congress; the primary stage of socialism and the basic line of the party; the strategy of economic development; restructuring the economy; reform of the political structure; strengthening party building while carrying out reform and the open policy; and striving to win victories for Marxism in China.[95]

Zhao announced that the central task of the congress was to accelerate and deepen China's reform, holding that "Reform is the only process through which China can be revitalized. It is a process which is irreversible and which accords with the will of the people and the general trend of events."

Zhao noted the great changes that had taken place in China in the nine years since the Third Plenum of the Eleventh Central Committee, whose line was upheld and would be further developed. During the nine years, there had been sustained, stable growth in the national economy. China's gross national product, state revenue, and the average income of both urban and rural residents had roughly doubled. He said that the overwhelming majority of the country's one billion people had secured a life with sufficient food and clothing and that people in some areas were beginning to become well-off. Job opportunities for 70 million urban residents had been created. In the countryside, 80 million peasants had now shifted wholly or part time from farming to industry. Market supplies had improved greatly. China had basically put an end to the situation in which there were acute and long-lasting shortages of consumer goods. There had been a marked improvement with regard to the serious imbalance among major sectors of the national economy, which had gradually been set on a course of more or less coordinated development.

Zhao praised Deng Xiaoping, saying: "With his courage in developing Marxist theory, his realistic approach, his rich experience, and his foresight and sagacity, Comrade Deng Xiaoping has made significant contributions to the formulation and development of this line and to decisionmaking on a series of key issues, as well as to the creation of a new situation in construction, reform, and opening to the outside world."

Zhao expounded on an important ideological finding that had been under discussion for some time—that China "is now in the primary stage of socialism, and it will be for at least 100 years from the 1950s, when the socialist transformation of private ownership of the means of production was basically completed, to the time when socialist modernization will have been in the main accomplished, and all these years belong to this stage." Zhao pointed out that "a correct understanding of this present historical stage" was "of prime importance as the essential basis on which to formulate and implement a correct line and correct policies." He explained that this primary stage "is not the initial phase in a general sense, a phase that every country will go through in the process of building socialism. Rather, in a particular sense, [it is] the specific stage China must necessarily go through while building socialism under conditions of backward productive forces and an underdeveloped commodity economy." Put this way, the Chinese sought to avoid unnecessary ideological polemics with other communist parties on a reading of current history that was particularly important for giving China latitude to conduct its reforms.

According to Zhao, the basic line of the party in this stage is as follows: "To lead the Chinese people of all nationalities in a united, self-reliant, intensive, and pioneering effort to turn China into a prosperous, strong, democratic, culturally advanced, and modern socialist country by making economic development the central task while adhering to the four cardinal principles and persevering in reform and the open policy."

Zhao said that China's development strategy involved three steps, the first of which—doubling the GNP of 1980 and the solution of the problem of food and clothing—has already been largely fulfilled. The second step is to double it again by the end of the twentieth century in order to enable the Chinese people to lead a more comfortable life. The third step is to reach the per capita GNP level of medium-developed countries by the middle of the next century. This will enable the Chinese people to enjoy a relatively affluent life and will provide the basis for further economic advance. For the present, it was important to succeed with the second step. In this regard, he outlined three major tasks: give priority to expanding scientific, technological, and educational undertakings; maintain a rough balance between total demand and total supply and rationally adjust and reform the structure of production; and open wider to the outside world, constantly expanding economic and technological exchange and cooperation with other countries.

As for restructuring the economy, Zhao asserted that the socialist economy in China is a planned commodity economy based on pubic ownership, and this, he said, "is the theoretical basis for the reform of the economic structure." But the reforms, which are conducive to the development of the socialist economy, include the development of different types of ownership, even allowing the private sector to exist and develop, with public ownership remaining predominant. Zhao said that the main task is to change the managerial mechanism of enterprises and, with that end in view, to institute supporting reforms in the systems of planning, investment, allocation of materials, finance, monetary affairs, and foreign trade. In this way, China will gradually establish a basic framework for a planned commodity economy. The socialist planned economy should be a system that integrates planning with the market.

It is noteworthy that political structural reform was included as one of the seven topics of the work report, rather than placed on the agenda of the congress as a separate, more prominent topic. Even so, Zhao seemed to make the most of this opportunity. He reaffirmed that China is a socialist country under the people's democratic dictatorship and that its "basic political system is good." He conceded, however, that "there are major defects in our system of leadership, in the organizational structure and style of work, which mainly find expression in overconcentration of power, a serious degree of bureaucratism, and feudal influences that are far from being eliminated."

Zhao held that the purpose of reforming the political structure is "to promote what is beneficial and eliminate what is harmful and to build a socialist democracy with Chinese characteristics." He said that the long-range goal of the reform is to build a socialist political system with a high degree of democracy and a complete set of laws, a system that is effective and full of vitality. He added that the immediate objective is to institute a system of leadership that will help to raise the efficiency, increase the vitality, and stimulate the initiative of sectors of society.

Zhao explained that by the immediate objective he meant separation of the functions of the party and the government, delegating powers to lower levels, reforming government organs, reforming the personnel system concerning cadres, establishing a system of consultation and dialogue, improving a number of systems regarding socialist democracy, and strengthening the socialist legal system. He also made it clear that China would never introduce a Western system of separation of legislative, executive, and judicial powers and of different parties ruling the country in turn.

With regard to party building, Zhao indicated that party members are to be dealt with strictly. During the years of the revolutionary wars, he said, party members had to go through the test of sacrificing their lives. "Today they must stand the test of holding office and working for reform and the open policy." Strengthening the party's collective leadership and democratic centralism, he said, should start with the Central Committee and include: establishing a system of regular reporting by the Politburo Standing Committee to the Politburo and by the latter to the Central Committee; increasing the number of Central Committee plenary sessions each year; and formulating work rules and a system for holding democratic meetings of the Politburo, its Standing Committee, and the Secretariat, so as to institutionalize collective leadership and place party leaders under stricter supervision and control.

Zhao called for adhering to the policy of making the ranks of the party's cadres more revolutionary, younger, better educated, and more professionally competent. "In our efforts to promote younger cadres to leading posts, we should now focus on members of the central leading bodies. We propose that this congress take a big step in this respect."

Zhao said that in more than 60 years of integrating Marxism with practice in China there have been two major historic leaps. The first leap took place during the new democratic revolution, when the CCP, by trial and error, found a road of revolution based on China's particular conditions and led the revolution to victory. The second took place after the Third Plenum of December 1978. Having analyzed both the positive and negative experiences of more than 30 years since the founding of the PRC and studied the experience of other countries and the world situation, the CCP found a way to build socialism with Chinese characteristics, thus ushering in a new period of socialist development in China.

From October 26 to 31, the delegates divided into 33 groups to discuss the report and the candidates for the Central Committee, the Central Advisory Commission, and the Central Commission for Discipline Inspection. The name lists of these candidates were presented by the presidium, which held its second meeting on October 27 to decide on the name lists and the electoral procedures. Both Zhao Ziyang and Bo Yibo spoke at the meeting. The presidium decided that the elections would be conducted by secret ballot. The candidates for the members and alternate members of the Central Committee and the members of the Central Commission for Discipline Inspection were to be decided by the results of preliminary elections, with more people proposed than the number to be selected. There were to be at least five percent more people standing for the preliminary elections than the number selected for the full members of the Central Committee and for the members of the Central Commission for Discipline Inspection. There were to be at least twelve percent more people standing for the preliminary election of alternate members of the Central Committee. As for the Central Advisory Commission, the election would be conducted with an equal number of candidates and actual places. The meeting also endorsed the "lists of scrutineers [vote counters], selected by the various delegations, for the preliminary elections and of the general scrutineers selected from among the scrutineers."[96]

The resulting elections appeared to respond, at least in part, to the calls of Deng Xiaoping and Zhao Ziyang for younger party leaders and for organizational streamlining. The Thirteenth Central Committee was smaller than its predecessor, having only 175 full members as compared with 210 in the former, and only 110 alternate members as compared with 133 in the Twelfth Central Committee. The new Central Advisory Commission had 200 members, which was an increase from the former body's 162 members. This increase reflected the departure of many of the older cadres from the Central Committee. The new Central Commission for Discipline Inspection had 69 members.

The chief characteristic of the new Central Committee was the absence of the older cadres, a feat that was facilitated by Deng Xiaoping's decision to leave the Central Committee. It was a surprise to find that Deng Liqun was not elected to the Central Committee inasmuch as many expected him to appear on the Politburo as a result of the bargaining for posts. He was elected to the Central Advisory Commission, but his antics had so infuriated Deng Xiaoping, and many others, as to preclude a larger continuing role for him.

Closer inspection, however, suggests that the Thirteenth Central Committee was not so revolutionary after all. The average age of the 175 members was 58.5 years as compared to 59.6 years for the 210 members of the Twelfth Central Committee at the time of their election.[97] The age difference is only one year younger. The election was soon characterized as one of "de-ossification" rather than "rejuvenation." The new Central Committee is heavily male dominated; there are only 10 female members. Provincial leaders form the largest number of members (69), central party and government next (48), and the military is third (32). With regard to the military, there are four fewer members than on the 210-member former Central Committee, but this amounts to a slightly higher proportion on the new body. There is a correspondingly smaller central party and government representation. There is an increase in representation of minority nationalities: 16 on the new body as compared to 14 on the larger former Central Committee. This is the net result of having retired 95 members from the Twelfth Central Committee (at an average age of 67.8), re-electing 114 members from the former body (with an average age of 60.4), and electing 61 others, 22 of whom were alternate members of the Twelfth Central Committee (with an average age of 55.9 years).[98]

The following proportional differences between the two Central Committees are based on a preliminary computerized analysis conducted by the *South China Morning Post*[99] in Hong Kong:

	12th CC	13th CC
Average age at election	59.6	58.8
Women	5.7%	5.7%
Minorities	6.1%	6.7%
Provincial	36.8%	39.4%
Government	29.2%	27.4%
Military	17.2%	18.3%
Central Party	9.1%	8.0%
Technology	2.4%	2.3%
Others	5.3%	4.6%

The congress also approved the reports of the Central Advisory Commission and the Central Commission on Discipline Inspection, and it approved the revision of several articles of the party constitution.

Among the party constitution revisions were: the number of members and alternate members of the Central Committee to be replaced or newly elected is limited so that they do not exceed one-fifth of the respective totals of members and alternate members of the Central Committee; the Secretariat is specified as the working body of the Politburo and its Standing Committee, whose members are nominated by the latter body, subject to the endorsement of the Central Committee in plenary session; the chairmen of the Military Affairs and Central Advisory Commissions and the first secretary of the Central Commission for Discipline Inspection no longer must be members of the Politburo Standing Committee; the people's communes are no longer listed as a venue of the ubiquitous primary party organizations; in enterprises and organizations where the responsibility management system is practiced, the primary party organization is supportive of the administrative leaders and concentrates on party ideological, political, and mass work; the formation of leading party members' groups in leading bodies is not strictly obligatory and such leading bodies are now to be elected; and similarly, it is left to the Central Committee to determine whether party committees should even be formed in government departments that need to exercise highly centralized and unified leadership, rather than simply to determine the powers, functions, and tasks of such committees.[100]

The new Thirteenth Central Committee held its First Plenary Session on November 2. Zhao presided over the 173 members and 106 alternate members who attended along with members of the Central Advisory Commission and the Central Commission for Discipline Inspection.

The First Plenary Session elected the members and alternate member of the Politburo (listed in the order of the number of strokes in their surname characters): Wan Li, Tian Jiyun, Qiao Shi, Jiang Zemin, Li Peng, Li Tieying, Li Ruihuan, Li Ximing, Yang Rudai, Yang Shangkun, Wu Xueqian, Song Ping, Zhao Ziyang, Hu Qili, Hu Yaobang, Yao Yilin, and Qin Jiwei. Ding Guangen was the only alternate member. The new Politburo was thus reduced in size to 17 members and 1 alternate, as compared with the displaced Politburo's 20 members and 2 alternate members. Except for Yang Shangkun, who was 80, the other octogenarians were gone. It was clearly a reform-oriented Politburo. Hu Yaobang's re-election to the Politburo further symbolized the reformist thrust.

The session elected Zhao Ziyang, Li Peng, Qiao Shi, Hu Qili, and Yao Yilin to the Politburo's Standing Committee. This all-important body also appeared to be basically reformist, although Li Peng and Yao

Yilin, while reformers themselves, had shown conservative instincts as well, particularly favoring the predominance of central planning.

Zhao Ziyang was elected general secretary of the Central Committee. In the preceding several months, Zhao had repeatedly expressed his desire to remain premier of the State Council instead. Indeed, his forte does seem to be in the realm of government, particularly economic work. With his technocratic leanings, he had not built a patronage network in the party organization that in any way could be said to rival that of Hu Yaobang or of some of his conservative competitors. Yet Zhao finally acceded because of Deng Xiaoping's insistence.

The session approved the nominations by the new Politburo Standing Committee of Hu Qili, Qiao Shi, Rui Xingwen, and Yang Mingfu as members of the Secretariat and Wen Jiabao as the alternate member. Thus, this body was much reduced in size from eleven members to only four members and one alternate member.

The First Plenum decided on the appointment of Deng Xiaoping as chairman of the Military Affairs Commission. This was the only post Deng retained, enabling him to keep the military in line. Significantly, Zhao Ziyang was elected first vice-chairman, a strategically important position that Deng Xiaoping had not been able to secure for Hu Yaobang. Yang Shangkun remained as permanent vice-chairman of the Military Affairs Commission.

Chen Yun was approved as chairman of the Central Advisory Commission (replacing Deng Xiaoping), and Bo Yibo and Song Renqiong were approved as vice-chairmen. Twenty-seven members were elected as the commission's standing committee. It appeared for the time being that this commission, as a repository of aged conservatives, could constitute a serious challenge to the reformers.

The plenum also approved the election of the officers of the Central Commission for Discipline Inspection: Qiao Shi as first secretary; Chen Zuolin, Li Zhengting, and Xiao Hongda as deputy secretaries; and Wang Deying, Qiao Shi, Liu Liying, Li Zhengting, Xiao Hongda, Chen Zuolin, Guo Linxiang, and Fu Jie as standing committee members.[101] The rapidly rising Qiao Shi's election to this important secretaryship, which many had expected to go to Peng Zhen or Bo Yibo, was significant. Given Qiao Shi's other assignments (Politburo Standing Committee, membership on the Central Committee's Secretariat, secretary of the Political Science and Law Committee, and experience since 1982 as director of the General Office, head of the Organization Department, and head of the Central Leading Group for Improving the Party's Style of Work—all of the Central Committee—and as a vice premier of the State Council), his strategic position in the party was exceeded only by Zhao Ziyang's, whose responsibilities were now manifold.

At its first work conference, the new Central Committee decided on the division of work among the five Politburo Standing Committee members and on the functions and operations of the central departments, and it made general arrangements regarding the work of the following year. It decided that Zhao Ziyang would deal with matters generally; Li Peng would focus on State Council matters; Qiao Shi on party affairs; Hu Qili on propaganda, the work of the Secretariat, and routine matters; and Yao Yilin on the economy.[102]

On November 24, 1987, the NPC Standing Committee accepted Zhao Ziyang's resignation as premier and appointed Li Peng as acting premier. It was expected that Li would be elected premier at the next meeting of the NPC in March 1988. Li Peng had a reputation as a technocrat. His father had been an early martyr of the party and a friend of Zhou Enlai. Subsequently, Li Peng was adopted by Zhou and his wife Deng Yingchao. Li was educated as a hydraulic engineer in the Soviet Union in the 1950s but was not considered particularly oriented toward the Soviet Union, despite a personal preference for aspects of the Soviet political and economic system. There was talk, however, that in the past Li's promotion had been opposed by Hu Yaobang and Zhao Ziyang.

By the end of 1987, it is evident that Deng Xiaoping has continued to secure marked successes with his reform agenda. There continue to be disappointments, but Deng has himself cautioned against undue optimism. During the summer of 1987 he said that the reform of the political structure could not be completed within three or five years; it certainly could not be completed at the Thirteenth Party Congress. "We tentatively plan to make further progress" at the Fourteenth Party Congress, he said, "and complete the task" at the Fifteenth Party Congress, at least a decade hence.[103]

Of course, it remains to be seen just how far political structural reform can go. It is still unclear exactly what is meant by such reform or how it might be achieved. The party is hardly united on the subject. Separation of functions raises the spectre of diminished importance for many party positions and of diminished or lost perquisites. The aim is greater political authority, more effectively exercised. This implies appropriate power distribution and more accountability, yet democracy, except as a well-used term in socialist countries, is still regarded only with the greatest caution. For a party that earlier lost so much credibility, there is still a well-justified concern as to how much support it really enjoys among the people. Hence, there is a desire to achieve accountability by means of consultation and opinion polls—the "mass line" in new guise—in lieu of truly meeting the real democratic challenge of allowing genuine political choices.

But if meaningful political structural change is slow in coming, what then are the prospects for continued serious economic reform, which, it is increasingly being realized, is predicated on successful political reform? Already some of the economic reforms, particularly the more difficult ones such as price reform, are encountering great resistance. Furthermore, after years of significant advances, it appears that agricultural output is beginning to stagnate. Some consumer goods are again being rationed. Attempts to decentralize economic decisions often result in price hikes and in the spectre of an inflation that might get out of hand. The population is again growing faster than had been planned or expected.[104] The rarely discussed phenomenon of unemployment constitutes a severe obstacle to economic growth and performance.[105] Fortunately for China, the economy does continue to register respectable growth.

The party conveys an unmistakable impression of commitment to reform as it faces the difficult months and years ahead. Indeed, a broad consensus for reform among the party leadership mirrors a similar disposition throughout society. Even most of the leftist-conservatives are in favor of some reform, and there are genuine reformers dedicated to making the reforms succeed. The reformers have an agenda. But the task before them is immense.

The reformers can take some heart from favorable responses abroad, where many nations applaud their efforts. Market-economy nations welcome China's participation in the global economy, and socialist nations observe with real interest China's experiments with economic and political reforms that compete with or inspire their own uncertain efforts. Even Soviet general secretary Gorbachev's well-publicized policies of glasnost' and perestroika can be said to be in part inspired or incited by China's bold programs. But just as Gorbachev's reforms face considerable domestic opposition, so do various particulars of the Chinese reforms. If the reforms falter, there are those who await the opportunity to redirect China once again to a more orthodox orientation, either modified Stalinist or, less likely (ironically), modified Maoist. In either case, the regime would be more authoritarian. After so much reform and effort to institutionalize China's political processes, ominously, a great deal continues to depend on the longevity of Deng Xiaoping, who is now in his 84th year.

What will happen when Deng passes from the scene is uncertain. China is, however, a predominantly youthful country, and younger

Chinese, who are now in the process of inheriting its leadership, will undoubtedly bring to this responsibility new ideas and fresh vision. These younger men and women will decide the shape and the role of the party in the future as they pursue the tasks of modernization and of making China an influential global power.

Notes

Introduction

1. China had "used" $10.3 billion of foreign loans from a larger amount of foreign loan commitments available by the end of 1986, according to official statements. Some estimate that China may borrow more than $20 billion during the current Seventh Five-Year Plan. See A. Doak Barnett, "Ten Years After Mao," *Foreign Affairs* (Fall 1986): 54–55.

2. See, for example, Richard Baum, "Modernization and Legal Reform in Post-Mao China: The Rebirth of Socialist Legality," *Studies in Comparative Communism* 19, no. 2 (Summer 1986): 69–104.

3. Lucian W. Pye, "On Chinese Pragmatism in the 1980s," *China Quarterly* 106 (June 1986): 232.

4. This appears to be the case, even though there is some serious Marxist scholarship in China today. For views on the latter, see, for example, Gordon H. Chang, "Perspectives on Marxism in China Today: An Interview with Su Shao-zhi, Director of the Marxism-Leninism-Mao Zedong Thought Institute, Academy of Social Sciences, Beijing, China," *Monthly Review* 38, no. 4 (September 1986): 14–28; and Maurice Meisner, "The Chinese Rediscovery of Karl Marx," *Bulletin of Concerned Asian Scholars*, no. 3 (1985): 2–16.

Chapter 1

1. See Mark Elvin, *The Pattern of the Chinese Past* (Stanford, Calif.: Stanford University Press, 1973).

2. Excellent accounts of events leading to the war are Maurice Collis, *Foreign Mud* (New York: Knopf, 1947), and Hsin-pao Chang, *Commissioner Lin and the Opium War* (Cambridge, Mass.: Harvard University Press, 1964).

3. Standard accounts of the Opium War, of the treaties and of events of the next few years are to be found in John K. Fairbank, *Trade and Diplomacy on the China Coast* (Cambridge, Mass.: Harvard University Press, 1953), and H. B. Morse, *The International Relations of the Chinese Empire*, vol. 1, *The Period of Conflict, 1834–1860* (Shanghai, 1910). A very readable more recent account is Peter Ward Fay, *The Opium War 1840–1842* (Chapel Hill: University of North Carolina Press, 1975).

4. See Stephen Uhalley, Jr., "The Taiping Movement: A Proposal for a Proper Designation," in Laurence G. Thompson, ed., *Studia Asiatica: Essays in Asian Studies in Felicitation of the Seventy-Fifth Anniversary of Professor Ch'en Shou-yi* (Taibei: Association for Asian Studies, 1975).

5. See Stephen Uhalley, Jr., *The Foreign Relations of the Taiping Revolution* (Ann Arbor, Mich.: University Microfilms International, 1967).

6. See Jen Yu-wen, *The Taiping Revolutionary Movement* (New Haven, Conn.: Yale University Press, 1973), and Franz Michael, *The Taiping Rebellion* (Seattle: University of Washington Press, 1966).

7. See Franz Michael's introduction to Stanley Spector, *Li Hung-chang and the Huai Army* (Seattle: University of Washington Press, 1964).

8. See Mary C. Wright, *The Last Stand of Chinese Conservatism: The T'ung-chih Restoration* (Stanford, Calif.: Stanford University Press, 1957).

9. For example, see the statement of Grand Secretary Wo-jen in Ssu-yu Teng and John K. Fairbank, eds., *China's Response to the West: A Documentary Survey 1839–1923* (Cambridge, Mass.: Harvard University Press, 1954), pp. 75–77.

10. See Joseph R. Levenson, *Confucian China and Its Modern Fate: A Trilogy*, vol. 1 (Berkeley: University of California Press, 1968), pp. 59–78.

11. Many useful ideas and relevant information on this general topic may be found in Paul A. Cohen and John E. Schrecker, eds., *Reform in Nineteenth Century China* (Cambridge, Mass.: Harvard University Press, 1976).

12. See Richard O'Connor, *The Spirit Soldiers: A Historical Narrative of the Boxer Rebellion* (New York: G. P. Putnam's Sons, 1973), and Victor Purcell, *The Boxer Uprising: A Background Study* (Cambridge, Eng., Cambridge University Press, 1963). The foreign relations of the incident is well covered in Chester C. Tan, *The Boxer Catastrophe* (New York: Columbia University Press, 1955).

13. A very early study of this decade remains the best on the reforms undertaken. See Meribeth E. Cameron. *The Reform Movement in China, 1898–1912* (Stanford, Calif.: Stanford University Press, 1931). See also the important relevant essays in Mary C. Wright, ed., *China in Revolution: The First Phase, 1900–1913* (New Haven, Conn.: Yale University Press, 1968).

14. See Wolfgang Franke, *The Reform and Abolition of the Traditional Chinese Examination System*, Harvard East Asian Monographs, no. 10 (Cambridge, Mass.: Harvard University Press, 1960).

15. Good biographies of Sun are by Lyon Sharman, *Sun Yat-sen: His Life and Its Meaning* (Stanford, Calif.: Stanford University Press, 1968), a new

printing of the original 1934 edition by John Way in New York; Harold Schiffrin, *Sun Yat-sen and the Origins of the Chinese Revolution* (Berkeley: University of California Press, 1968); and C. Martin Wilbur, *Sun Yat-sen: Frustrated Patriot* (New York: Columbia University Press, 1976).

16. Wright, *China in Revolution*, p. 50.

17. See Charlton M. Lewis, *Prologue to the Chinese Revolution: The Transformation of Ideas and Institutions in Hunan Province, 1891–1907* (Cambridge, Mass.: Harvard University Press, 1976), and Joseph W. Esherick, *Reform and Revolution in China: The 1911 Revolution in Hunan and Hubei* (Berkeley: University of California Press, 1976).

18. See Ernest P. Young, *The Presidency of Yuan Shih-k'ai: Liberalism and Dictatorship in Early Republican China* (Ann Arbor: University of Michigan Press, 1977).

19. Prominent examples of this literature are: James Peck, "The Roots of Rhetoric: The Professional Ideology of America's China Watchers," *Bulletin of Concerned Asian Scholars (BCAS)* 2, no. 1 (October 1969): 59–69, and John K. Fairbank and James Peck, "An Exchange," *BCAS* 2, no. 3 (April–July 1970): 51–70. Andrew J. Nathan, "Imperialism's Effects on China," *BCAS* 4, no. 4 (December 1972): 3–8; Joseph Esherick, "Harvard on China: The Apologetics of Imperialism," ibid., pp. 9–16; "Imperialism in China: An Exchange" (letters from John K. Fairbank, Joseph Esherick, and Marilyn B. Young), *BCAS* 5, no. 2 (September 1973); Cheryl Payer, "Harvard on China II: Logic, Evidence, and Ideology," *BCAS* 6, no. 2 (April–August 1974): 62–68; and Robert F. Dernberger, "The Role of the Foreigner in China's Economic Development, 1840–1949," in Dwight H. Perkins, ed., *China's Modern Economy in Historical Perspective* (Stanford, Calif.: Stanford University Press, 1975), pp. 19–47.

20. Albert Feuerwerker, *The Chinese Economy, ca. 1870–1911* (Ann Arbor: University of Michigan Center for Chinese Studies, 1969), p. 72.

21. Stephen C. Thomas, *Foreign Intervention and China's Industrial Development, 1870–1911* (Boulder, Colo.: Westview Press, 1984), p. 5.

22. Albert Feuerwerker, *The Chinese Economy, 1912–1949* (Ann Arbor: University of Michigan Center for Chinese Studies, 1968), p. 17–19.

23. Hou Chi-ming, *Foreign Investment and Economic Development in China, 1840–1937* (Cambridge, Mass.: Harvard University Press, 1965), p. 130.

24. See Stanley F. Wright, *Hart and the Chinese Customs* (Belfast: Mullan, 1950).

25. See S. A. M. Adshead, *The Modernization of the Chinese Salt Administration* (Cambridge, Mass.: Harvard University Press, 1970).

26. See, for example, Knight Biggerstaff, *The Earliest Modern Government Schools in China* (Ithaca, N.Y.: Cornell University Press, 1961).

27. Ramon Myers, *The Chinese Peasant Economy: Agricultural Development in Hopei and Shantung, 1890–1949* (Cambridge, Mass.: Harvard University Press, 1970).

28. See Jerome Ch'en, *Yuan Shih-k'ai, 1859–1916* (Stanford, Calif.: Stanford University Press, 1961).

29. Among good accounts of the warlord period are James Sheridan, *Chinese Warlord* (Stanford, Calif.: Stanford University Press, 1966); Donald Gillin, *Warlord: Yen Hsi-shan in Shansi Province, 1911–1949* (Princeton, N.J.: Princeton University Press, 1967); Lucian W. Pye, *Warlord Politics: Conflict and Coalition in the Modernization of Republican China* (New York: Praeger, 1971); Ch'i Hsi-sheng, *Warlord Politics in China 1916–1928* (Stanford, Calif.: Stanford University Press, 1976); Jerome Ch'en, *The Military-Gentry Coalition: China under the Warlords* (Toronto: University of Toronto-York University, Joint Centre on Modern East Asia, 1979); and Donald S. Sutton, *Provincial Militarism and the Chinese Republic: The Yunnan Army, 1905–25* (Ann Arbor: University of Michigan Press, 1980).

30. Levenson, *Confucian China and Its Modern Fate*, vol. 1, pp. 103–108.

31. See Chow Tse-tsung's still excellent study, *The May Fourth Movement: Intellectual Revolution in Modern China* (Cambridge, Mass.: Harvard University Press, 1960).

Chapter 2

1. Leong Sow-Theng, *Sino-Soviet Diplomatic Relations, 1917–1926* (Honolulu: University Press of Hawaii, 1976), p. 131.

2. Don C. Price, *Russia and the Roots of the Chinese Revolution, 1896–1911* (Cambridge, Mass.: Harvard University Press, 1974), p. 220.

3. Maurice Meisner, *Li Ta-chao and the Origins of Chinese Marxism* (Cambridge, Mass.: Harvard University Press, 1967), p. xii.

4. Chang Kuo-t'ao, *The Autobiography of Chang Kuo-t'ao*, vol. 1, *The Rise of the Chinese Communist Party 1921–1927* (Lawrence: University Press of Kansas, 1971), p. 101.

5. Ibid., p. 88.

6. Lee Feigon, *Chen Duxiu, Founder of the Chinese Communist Party* (Princeton, N.J.: Princeton University Press, 1983), p. 11.

7. Chang, *Autobiography*, vol. 1, p. 99.

8. Ibid., p. 124.

9. Other foreigners were similarly impressed by Wu Peifu. See Robert A. Scalapino and George T. Yu, *Modern China and Its Revolutionary Process: Recurrent Challenges to the Traditional Order 1850–1920* (Berkeley: University of California Press, 1985), p. 603.

10. See the excellent firsthand account of this important institution in Moscow between 1925 and 1930 by Sheng Yueh, *Sun Yat-sen University in Moscow and the Chinese Revolution: A Personal Account* (Lawrence: University of Kansas Center for East Asian Studies, 1971).

11. Ibid., p. 128.

12. Robert A. Scalapino, "The Evolution of a Young Revolutionary—Mao Zedong in 1919–1921," *Journal of Asian Studies* 42, no. 1 (November 1982): 59.

13. See the interesting account of a participant who later wrote about his experiences while a student in the United States: Ch'en Kung-po, *The Communist Movement in China*, edited with an introduction by C. Martin Wilbur (New York: Columbia University East Asian Institute, 1960).

14. James Pinckney Harrison, *The Long March to Power: A History of the Chinese Communist Party, 1921–72* (New York: Praeger, 1972), p. 32.

15. Chang, *Autobiography*, vol. 1, p. 137.

16. Tony Saich, "Hank Sneevliet and the Origins of the First United Front (1921–1923)," *Issues & Studies* 22, no. 8 (August 1986): 126.

17. Chang, *Autobiography*, vol. 1, p. 143.

18. Ibid., pp. 144–45.

19. Allen S. Whiting, *Soviet Policies in China, 1917–1924* (New York: Columbia University Press, 1954), p. 56.

20. X. J. Eudin and Robert C. North, *Soviet Russia and the East, 1920–1927: A Documentary Survey* (Stanford, Calif.: Stanford University Press, 1957), p. 144.

21. Harrison, *The Long March*, p. 39.

22. Ibid., p. 38; Warren Kuo, *Analytical History of the Chinese Communist Party* (Taibei: Institute of International Relations, 1966), p. 96.

23. Chang, *Autobiography*, vol. 1, p. 222.

24. However, quoting Pavel Mif, the much lower figure of 2,365 by 1925, although still larger than the party, is used by C. Martin Wilbur and Julie Lien-ying How, *Documents on Communism, Nationalism, and Soviet Advisers in China, 1918–1927: Papers Seized in the 1927 Peking Raid* (New York: Columbia University Press, 1956), p. 90.

25. Harrison, *The Long March*, p. 38.

26. Chang, *Autobiography*, vol. 1, pp. 114–20.

27. Stuart R. Schram, *Mao Tse-tung* (Middlesex, Eng.: Penguin, 1966), p. 69.

28. Harrison, *The Long March*, p. 36.

29. Ibid., p. 37.

30. Ibid., pp. 38–39.

31. Chang, *Autobiography*, vol. 1, p. 207.

32. Ibid., p. 241.

33. Harrison, *The Long March*, p. 41.

34. Chang, *Autobiography*, vol. 1, p. 250.

35. Dov Bing refers to Maring's concept as the "Sneevletian strategy" in his article "Sneevliet and the Early Years of the CCP," *China Quarterly (CQ)* 48 (October–December 1971): 678. Of some interest, too, is the subsequent dispute over certain points made by Bing and his responses: Mrs. Muntjewerf's comment

in *CQ* 53 (1973): 159–68; Bing's response in *CQ* 54 (1973): 160–62; Adrian Chan's comment in *CQ* 56 (1973): 749–51; and Bing's response in ibid., pp. 751–61.

36. Lyman P. Van Slyke, *Enemies and Friends: The United Front in Chinese Communist History* (Stanford, Calif.: Stanford University Press, 1967), p. 13, fn. b.

37. Chang, *Autobiography*, vol. 1, p. 294.

38. Ibid., p. 268.

39. Leng Shao-chuan and Norman Palmer, *Sun Yat-sen and Communism* (New York: Praeger, 1961), p. 174.

40. Chang, *Autobiography*, vol. 1, pp. 264–68.

41. Harrison, *The Long March*, p. 53.

42. Chang, *Autobiography*, vol. 1, p. 295.

43. Conrad Brandt, Benjamin Schwartz, and John K. Fairbank, *A Documentary History of Chinese Communism* (London: Allen & Unwin, 1952), pp. 71–73.

44. Harrison, *The Long March*, pp. 58–59.

45. Ibid., p. 61.

46. Kuo, *Analytical History*, p. 103.

47. Ibid., p. 148.

48. Harrison, *The Long March*, p. 62.

49. See Richard W. Rigby, *The May 30 Movement, Events and Themes* (Canberra: Australian National University Press, 1980), pp. 9–16.

50. Ibid., p. 169.

51. Ibid., p. 170.

52. Conrad Brandt, *Stalin's Failure in China* (Cambridge, Mass.: Harvard University Press, 1958), p. 50.

53. Van Slyke, *Enemies and Friends*, p. 22.

54. Harrison, *The Long March*, p. 65.

55. Gregor Benton's introduction to Wang Fan-hsi, *Chinese Revolutionary: Memoirs 1919–1949* (New York: Oxford University Press, 1980), p. xiii.

56. Harrison, *The Long March*, p. 73.

57. Mao Zedong, "Report on an Investigation of the Peasant Movement in Hunan," in *Selected Works*, vol. 1 (Beijing: Foreign Language Press, 1950), pp. 23–59.

58. Robert B. Marks, *Rural Revolution in South China: Peasants and the Making of History in Haifeng County, 1850–1930* (Madison: University of Wisconsin Press, 1984).

59. Fernando Galbiati, *P'eng P'ai and the Hai-Lu-feng Soviet* (Stanford, Calif.: Stanford University Press, 1985), p. 4.

60. Eto Shinkichi, "Hai-lu-feng—The First Chinese Soviet Government, part 2," *China Quarterly* 9 (January–March 1962): 157.

61. David P. Barrett, "The Role of Hu Hanmin in the 'First United Front': 1922–1927," *China Quarterly* 89 (March 1982): 50–51.

62. Daniel Norman Jacobs, *Borodin, Stalin's Man in China* (Cambridge, Mass.: Harvard University Press, 1981), pp. 199–200.

63. Chang, *Autobiography*, vol. 1, p. 517.

64. Ibid., p. 519.

65. Donald A. Jordan, *The Northern Expedition: China's National Revolution of 1926–1928* (Honolulu: University Press of Hawaii, 1976), pp. 293–94.

66. Jacques Guillermaz, *A History of the Chinese Communist Party 1921–1949* (New York: Random House, 1972), pp. 119–20.

67. Harold R. Isaacs's account remains one of the most eloquent: *The Tragedy of the Chinese Revolution*, 2d rev. ed. (New York: Atheneum, 1966), pp. 175–85.

68. Kuo, *Analytical History*, pp. 229–33.

69. Mao, *Selected Works*, vol. 1, pp. 23–28.

70. Isaacs, *Tragedy*, pp. 234–36.

71. Eudin and North, *Soviet Russia and the East*, Doc. no. 109.

72. Isaacs, *Tragedy*, p. 247.

73. Wu Tien-wei, "A Review of the Wuhan Debacle: The Kuomintang-Communist Split of 1927," *Journal of Asian Studies* 29, no. 1 (November 1969): 143.

74. Zhang Guotao gives the differing view that the two were to have resigned in protest, but they did not in fact give such an impression in their resignation letters. Chang, *Autobiography*, vol. 1, p. 650.

75. Kuo, *Analytical History*, p. 260–61.

76. Chang, *Autobiography*, vol. 1, p. 676.

77. See Benjamin Schwartz, *Chinese Communism and the Rise of Mao* (Cambridge, Mass.: Harvard University Press, 1958), p. 92.

78. Ibid., p. 93; and the review of the newly published *Selected Works of Qu Qiubai* in Chinese, in *Beijing Review* 33 (August 19, 1985): 33–34.

79. Chang, *Autobiography*, vol. 1, p. 94.

80. Ibid., p. 95.

81. Roy Hofheinz, Jr., "The Autumn Harvest Insurrection," *China Quarterly* 32 (October–December 1967): 37–87.

82. Roy Hofheinz, Jr., *The Broken Wave: The Chinese Communist Peasant Movement, 1922–1928* (Cambridge, Mass.: Harvard University Press, 1977), p. 283.

83. Schwartz, *Chinese Communism*, p. 106.

84. S. Bernard Thomas, *"Proletarian Hegemony" in the Chinese Revolution and the Canton Commune of 1927* (Ann Arbor: University of Michigan Center for Chinese Studies, 1975), p. 3.

Chapter 3

1. Richard C. Thornton, *The Comintern and the Chinese Communists, 1928–1931* (Seattle: University of Washington Press, 1969), pp. 32–38.

2. Chang Kuo-t'ao, *The Autobiography of Chang Kuo-t'ao*, Vol. 2, *The Rise of the Chinese Communist Party 1928–1938* (Lawrence: University Press of Kansas, 1972), p. 74.

3. C. Martin Wilbur, "The Influence of the Past: How the Early Years Helped to Shape the Future of the Chinese Communist Party," *China Quarterly* 36 (October–December 1968): 23–44.

4. See Peng Dehuai, *Memoirs of a Chinese Marshal* (Beijing: Foreign Languages Press, 1985), pp. 193–215.

5. Ibid., pp. 232–49; 252–61.

6. Mao Zedong, "The Struggle in the Chingkang Mountains," November 25, 1928, *Selected Works*, vol. 1 (Beijing: Foreign Languages Press, 1950), p. 73.

7. Jacques Guillermaz, *A History of the Chinese Communist Party 1921–1949* (New York: Random House, 1972), p. 183.

8. Mao, *Selected Works*, vol. 1, pp. 105–16.

9. Edgar Snow, *Red Star Over China* (New York: Random House, 1938), p. 176.

10. Thornton, *The Comintern and the Chinese Communists*, p. 225.

11. Guillermaz, *History of the CCP*, p. 195.

12. James Pinckney Harrison, *The Long March to Power: A History of the Chinese Communist Party, 1921–72* (New York: Praeger, 1972), p. 167.

13. Ibid., p. 169.

14. Ibid., p. 171.

15. Translation by Hsiao Tso-liang, in Guillermaz, *History of the CCP*, p. 197; fn. on p. 198.

16. Agnes Smedley, *The Great Road* (New York: Monthly Review Press, 1956), p. 27.

17. See comparisons of these documents in Hsiao Tso-liang, *Power Relations within the Chinese Communist Movement, 1930–1934: A Study of Documents* (Seattle: University of Washington Press, 1961), pp. 25–26.

18. Thornton, *The Comintern and the Chinese Communists*, p. 175.

19. Peng, *Memoirs*, pp. 295–97.

20. Thornton, *The Comintern and the Chinese Communists*, pp. 187–200.

21. Ibid., pp. 203–4.

22. Ibid., pp. 213–17.

23. Benjamin Schwartz, *Chinese Communism and the Rise of Mao* (Cambridge, Mass.: Harvard University Press, 1958), p. 166.

24. Lynda Schaefer Bell, "Agricultural Laborers and Rural Revolution," in Philip C. C. Huang et al., *Chinese Communists and Rural Society, 1927–1934* (Berkeley: University of California Center for Chinese Studies, 1978), pp. 41–44.

25. Ronald Suleski, "The Fu-t'ien Incident, December 1930," in *Early Communist China: Two Studies* (Ann Arbor: University of Michigan Center for Chinese Studies, 1969), pp. 3–4; see also Suleski's later article "The Futian Incident Reconsidered," *China Quarterly* 89 (March 1982): 97–104, in which he compares his own interpretation with the book he is reviewing, i.e., Xuejia Zheng's *Zhonggong Futian shibian zhenxiang* (The truth about the Futian Incident) (Taibei: Guoji gongdang wenti yanchiushe, 1976).

26. Suleski, *Early Communist China*, p. 7.

27. Based on an account by Agnes Smedley, ibid., p. 12.

28. Ibid., p. 13.

29. Derek J. Waller, *The Kiangsi Soviet Republic: Mao and the National Congresses of 1931 and 1934* (Berkeley: University of California Center for Chinese Studies, 1973), p. 25.

30. Ibid., p. 26.

31. Ibid., p. 31.

32. Ibid., pp. 42–43.

33. Ibid., pp. 50–51.

34. Lawrence R. Sullivan, "Reconstruction and Rectification of the Communist Party in the Shanghai Underground: 1931–34," *China Quarterly* 101 (March 1985): 78–97.

35. See Ilpyong J. Kim, *The Politics of Chinese Communism: Kiangsi under the Soviets* (Berkeley: University of California Press, 1973), p. 116.

36. John E. Rue, *Mao Tse-tung in Opposition, 1927–1935* (Stanford, Calif.: Stanford University Press, 1966), pp. 251–53. William Dorrill, however, argues that Mao did not lose military power but was later said to have done so in order that he be disassociated from the subsequent defeat and hence appear to be infallible. See William F. Dorrill, "Rewriting History to Further Maoism: The Ningtu Conference of 1932," in J. C. Hsiung, ed., *The Logic of "Maoism": Critiques and Explication* (New York: Praeger, 1974), pp. 62–85.

37. Waller, *The Kiangsi Soviet Republic*, pp. 55–56.

38. Ibid., pp. 84–85.

39. Trygve Lotveit, *Chinese Communism 1931–1934: Experience in Civil Government*, Scandinavian Institute of Asian Studies Monograph Series, no. 16 (Lund, Sweden: Studentlitteratur, 1973), p. 139.

40. Bell, "Agricultural Laborers and Rural Revolution," pp. 29–56.

41. Otto Braun subsequently published his memoirs of this and other experiences—*A Comintern Agent in China, 1932–1939* (London: C. Hurst & Co., 1982).

42. William F. Dorrill, "The Fukien Rebellion and the CCP: A Case of Maoist Revisionism," *China Quarterly* 37 (January–March 1969): 31–53.

43. Hu Chi-hsi, "Mao, Lin Biao, and the Fifth Encirclement Campaign," *China Quarterly* 82 (June 1980): 250–80.

44. Benjamin Yang, "The Zunyi Conference as One Step in Mao's Rise to Power: A Survey of Historical Studies of the Chinese Communist Party," *China Quarterly* 106 (June 1986): 256.

45. Zhou Enlai reportedly conceded many years later that he had failed to vote for Mao, even at the more important Zunyi Conference that soon followed. Nor is Zhou's name listed among the leaders who, among the majority, supported Mao at Zunyi, according to the authoritative *Guanyu jianguo yilai dangde rogan lishi wenti de jueyi: zhushiben, xiu ding* (Annotated Edition of the Resolution on Certain Issues in the History of the Party Since the Founding of the People's Republic of China), compiled by the Party Literature Research Center of the Central Committee (Beijing: People's Publishing House, 1985), p. 125.

46. Ibid.

47. See Jerome Ch'en, "Resolutions of the Tsunyi Conference," *China Quarterly* 40 (October–December 1969): 1–38; also Benjamin Yang, "Historical Studies," *China Quarterly* 106 (June 1986): 235–71; Ch'en's response, *China Quarterly* 111 (September 1987): 450–65; and Yang's reply, pp. 466–68.

48. Dick Wilson, *The Long March 1935: The Epic of Chinese Communism's Survival* (New York: Avon Books, 1971), pp. 132–33.

49. Yang, "Historical Studies," 257.

50. The original classic account in English was Edgar Snow, *Red Star Over China* (New York: Random House, 1938). See also Harrison E. Salisbury, *The Long March: The Untold Story* (New York: Harper & Row, 1985), and Wilson, *Long March*.

51. Chang, *Autobiography,* vol. 2, pp. 379–82.

52. Ibid., p. 387.

53. This was made clear in Zhang's own account of the meeting, ibid., p. 416; and in Gregor Benton's article, "The 'Second Wang Ming Line' (1935–38)," *China Quarterly* 61 (March 1975): 64.

54. Chang, *Autobiography,* vol. 2, pp. 416–17.

55. Wilson, *Long March,* p. 279.

Chapter 4

1. Mao Zedong, "Problems of War and Strategy," November 6, 1938, *Selected Works,* vol. 2 (Beijing: Foreign Languages Press, 1950–1977), p. 224.

2. See John Israel and Donald W. Klein, *Rebels and Bureaucrats: China's December 9ers* (Berkeley: University of California Press, 1976).

3. Lyman P. Van Slyke, *Enemies and Friends: The United Front in Chinese Communist History* (Stanford, Calif.: Stanford University Press, 1967), pp. 58–59.

4. Ibid., p. 60.

5. The best and most comprehensive account is Wu Tien-wei, *The Sian Incident: A Pivotal Point in Modern Chinese History* (Ann Arbor: University of Michigan Papers in Chinese Studies, 1976). See also Van Slyke, *Enemies and Friends*, pp. 75–91; James Pinckney Harrison, *The Long March to Power: A History of the Chinese Communist Party, 1921–72* (New York: Praeger, 1972), pp. 268–70.

6. See Party Literature Research Center, Central Committee, CCP, *Guanyu jianguo yilai dangde rogan lishi wenti de jueyi: zhushiben, xiu ding* (Annotated Edition of the Resolution on Certain Issues in the History of the Party since the Founding of the People's Republic of China) (Beijing: People's Publishing House, 1985), p. 127.

7. Van Slyke, *Enemies and Friends*, pp. 90–93.

8. Gregor Benton, "The 'Second Wang Ming Line' (1935–38)," *China Quarterly* 61 (March 1975): 80.

9. Carl Dorris, "Peasant Mobilization in North China and the Origins of Yenan Communism," *China Quarterly* 68 (December 1976): 702.

10. Mark Selden, *The Yenan Way in Revolutionary China* (Cambridge, Mass.: Harvard University Press, 1971), pp. 175–76.

11. Dorris, "Peasant Mobilization," 698.

12. Ibid., 704.

13. Extracts from Stuart R. Schram, "On the New Stage," in *The Political Thought of Mao Tse-tung*, rev. enl. ed. (New York: Praeger, 1969), pp. 172–73.

14. Dorris, "Peasant Mobilization," 707.

15. Ibid., 707–8.

16. See, for example, Jane Price, *Cadres, Commanders, and Commissars: The Training of the Chinese Communist Leadership, 1920–45* (Boulder, Colo.: Westview Press, 1976), pp. 135–72.

17. Boyd Compton, "Reform in Learning, the Party and Literature," in *Mao's China: Party Reform Documents, 1942–1944* (Seattle: University of Washington Press, 1966), pp. 21–22.

18. Ibid., p. 21.

19. Ibid., pp. 31–32.

20. Ibid.

21. Harrison, *The Long March*, pp. 323–45; Selden, *The Yenan Way*, pp. 188–207.

22. Mao, *Selected Works*, vol. 3, p. 94.

23. Selden, *The Yenan Way*, pp. 212–16.

24. Ibid., pp. 224–29.

25. Ibid., pp. 229–37.

26. Ibid., 237–49.

27. Elizabeth J. Perry, *Rebels and Revolutionaries in North China 1845–1945* (Stanford, Calif.: Stanford University Press, 1980), p. 245.

28. Selden, *The Yenan Way*, pp. 249–67.

29. Peter Schran, *Guerrilla Economy: The Development of the Shensi-Kansu-Ninghsia Border Region, 1937–1945* (Albany: State University of New York Press, 1976), pp. 249–52.

30. Lloyd E. Eastman, *The Abortive Revolution: China under Nationalist Rule 1927–1937* (Cambridge, Mass.: Harvard University Press, 1974), p. 226.

31. Ibid., pp. 271–72.

32. Ibid., p. 236; David Buck, *Urban Change in China: Politics and Development in Tsinan, Shantung, 1890–1949* (Madison: University of Wisconsin Press, 1978).

33. See Richard C. Bush, *The Politics of Cotton Textiles in Kuomintang China 1927–1937* (New York: Garland Publishing Co., 1982), pp. 18–21.

34. See Peng Zhen's speech of September 3, 1985, marking the 40th anniversary of the victory in the War of Resistance against Japanese Aggression in *Beijing Review* (September 9, 1985): i–vii (document insert).

35. Otto Braun, *A Comintern Agent in China, 1932–1939* (London: C. Hurst & Co., 1982), p. 215.

36. See Chalmers Johnson, ed., *Ideology and Politics in Contemporary China* (Seattle: University of Washington Press, 1973).

37. See, e.g., Y. L. Ting, "Nanjing Massacre: A Dark Page in History," *Beijing Review* (September 2, 1985): 15–21.

38. Peng Dehuai, who engineered this campaign of 104 regiments, said that Mao congratulated him for it. Peng Dehuai, *Memoirs of a Chinese Marshal* (Beijing: Foreign Languages Press, 1985), p. 441. Peter Vladimirov claims that the campaign was initiated by Mao, who even informed the Comintern about the plan. Peter Vladimirov, *The Vladimirov Diaries: Yenan, China: 1942–1945* (Garden City, N.Y.: Doubleday, 1975), p. 418. But the campaign seems to have been highly uncharacteristic of Mao's military style.

39. See, e.g., David D. Barrett, *Dixie Mission: The United States Army Observer Group in Yenan, 1944* (Berkeley: University of California Center for Chinese Studies, 1970), and Joseph W. Esherick, ed., *Lost Chance in China: The World War II Despatches of John S. Service* (New York: Vintage Books, 1975).

40. Joseph W. Stilwell, *The Stilwell Papers*, ed. Theodore H. White (New York: Sloane, 1948), and Barbara W. Tuchman, *Stilwell and the American Experience in China, 1911–1945* (New York: Bantam, 1972).

41. Harrison, *The Long March*, p. 358.

42. Vladimirov, *Diaries*, p. 479.

43. Mao, *Selected Works*, vol. 3, pp. 205–70.

44. Ibid., pp. 231 and 233.

45. Ibid., p. 232.
46. Ibid., p. 255.
47. Ibid., pp. 271–74.
48. Harrison, *The Long March*, p. 359.

Chapter 5

1. Colin Mackerras, *Modern China: A Chronology from 1842 to the Present* (San Francisco: W. H. Freeman & Co, 1982), p. 412.

2. Tang Tsou, *America's Failure in China*, vol. 1 (Chicago: University of Chicago Press, 1963), p. 325.

3. See O. Borisov (Borisov-Rakhmanin), *The Soviet Union and the Manchurian Revolutionary Base, 1945–1949* (Moscow: Progress Publishers, 1977), p. 46.

4. Lee Chong-sik, *Revolutionary Struggle in Manchuria: Chinese Communism and Soviet Interest, 1922–1945* (Berkeley: University of California Press, 1983), p. 320.

5. Steven I. Levine, *Anvil of Victory: The Communist Revolution in Manchuria, 1945–1948* (New York: Columbia University Press, 1987), p. 245.

6. Tang Tsou, *America's Failure*, vol. 1, p. 308.

7. O. Borisov quotes American sources in confirming this point, *Soviet Union and the Manchurian Revolutionary Base*, p. 46.

8. James Pinckney Harrison, *The Long March to Power: A History of the Chinese Communist Party, 1921–72* (New York: Praeger, 1972), p. 375.

9. Mao Zedong, "The Situation and Our Policy after the Victory in the War of Resistance against Japan," *Selected Works*, vol. 4 (Beijing: Foreign Languages Press, 1950–1977), p. 21.

10. See Ch'i Hsi-sheng, *Nationalist China at War: Military Defeats and Political Collapse, 1937–45* (Ann Arbor: University of Michigan Press, 1982), pp. 128–31.

11. Harrison, *The Long March*, p. 377.

12. See Joseph W. Esherick, ed., *Lost Chance in China: The World War II Despatches of John S. Service* (New York: Vintage Books, 1975).

13. See George C. Marshall, with introduction by Lyman Van Slyke, *Marshall's Mission to China: The Report and Appended Documents*, 2 vols. (Washington, D.C.: University Publications of America, 1976).

14. James Reardon-Anderson, *Yenan and the Great Powers: The Origins of Chinese Communist Foreign Policy, 1944–1946* (New York: Columbia University Press, 1980), p. 166.

15. Ibid., pp. 170–71.

16. Mao, "The Present Situation and Our Tasks," Selected Works, vol. 4, pp. 157–71.

17. J. Leighton Stuart to George C. Marshall, January 9, 1948, U.S. Department of State, United States Relations with China: With Special Reference to the Period 1944–1949 (Washington, D.C.: U.S. Government Printing Office, 1949), p. 841.

18. Chang Kia-ngau, The Inflationary Spiral: The Experience of China 1939–1950 (New York: John Wiley & Sons, 1958), p. 367.

19. Harrison, The Long March, pp. 406–7.

20. See, e.g., Ramon Myers, The Chinese Peasant Economy: Agricultural Development in Hopei and Shantung, 1890–1949 (Cambridge, Mass.: Harvard University Press, 1970), and Dwight Perkins, Agricultural Development in China, 1368–1968 (Cambridge, Mass.: Harvard University Press, 1970).

21. Suzanne Pepper, Civil War in China: The Political Struggle 1945–1949 (Berkeley: University of California Press, 1978), p. 244.

22. Harrison, The Long March, p. 413.

23. See, e.g., Tanaka Kyoko, "Mao and Liu in the 1947 Land Reform: Allies or Disputants?" China Quarterly 75 (September 1978): 593. This author seeks to demonstrate that Liu Shaoqi may initially have erred on the side of equal distribution, but that in 1947 the choice was not deliberately made since probably neither Mao nor Liu realized the incompatibility of the two objectives at the time.

24. Mao, "On Some Important Problems of the Party's Present Policy," Selected Works, vol. 4, p. 183.

25. Mao, "Different Tactics for Carrying Out the Land Law in Different Areas," Selected Works, vol. 4, pp. 193–94.

26. Mao, "On the People's Democratic Dictatorship," Selected Works, vol. 4, p. 415.

27. Peng Dehuai saw the victory at Wazijie, where the Nationalists lost five brigades in early March 1948, as the beginning of the offensive. Peng Dehuai, Memoirs of a Chinese Marshal (Beijing: Foreign Languages Press, 1985), p. 469.

28. Stuart, United States Relations with China 1944–1949, pp. 330–31.

29. Testimony of the U.S. consul-general at Cingdao, ibid., p. 319.

30. Lionel Max Chassin, The Communist Conquest of China: A History of the Civil War 1945–1949 (Cambridge, Mass.: Harvard University Press, 1965), p. 188.

31. Ibid., pp. 189–91.

32. See O. Edmund Clubb, "Chiang Kai-shek's Waterloo: The Battle of the Hwai-Hai," Pacific Historical Review 25 (November 1956): 389–99.

33. Chassin, Communist Conquest, pp. 209–11.

34. Kenneth G. Lieberthal, A Research Guide to Central Party and Governmental Meetings in China 1949–1975 (White Plains, N.Y.: International Arts and Sciences Press, 1976), p. 50.

35. Mao, "Report to the Second Plenary Session of the Seventh Central Committee of the Communist Party of China," *Selected Works*, vol. 4, p. 363.

36. Pepper, *Civil War*, p. 332.

37. See Levine, *Anvil of Victory*, p. 239.

38. See Seymour Topping, *Journey Between Two Chinas* (New York: Harper & Row, 1972), p. 86; Nancy Bernkopf Tucker, *Patterns in the Dust: Chinese-American Relations and the Recognition Controversy, 1949–1950* (New York: Columbia University Press, 1983), and Yu-ming Shaw, "John Leighton Stuart and U.S.-Chinese Communist Rapprochement in 1949: Was There Another 'Lost Chance in China'?" *China Quarterly* 89 (March 1982): 74–96.

Chapter 6

1. James Pinckney Harrison, *The Long March to Power: A History of the Chinese Communist Party, 1921–72* (New York: Praeger, 1972), pp. 427–28.

2. Mao Zedong, *Selected Works*, vol. 4 (Beijing: Foreign Languages Press, 1950–1977), pp. 411–24.

3. W. W. Rostow et al., *The Prospects for Communist China* (Cambridge, Mass.: MIT Press, 1954), p. 238.

4. Ibid., citing Chen Yun, "The Financial and Food Situation," in *New China's Economic Achievements, 1949–1952* (Beijing: Foreign Languages Press, 1952), pp. 53–54.

5. John Gardner, quoting Chen Yi in "The Wu-fan Campaign in Shanghai," in A. Doak Barnett, ed., *Chinese Communist Politics in Action* (Seattle: University of Washington Press, 1969), p. 493.

6. Alexander Eckstein, *China's Economic Development: The Interplay of Scarcity and Ideology* (Ann Arbor: University of Michigan Press, 1975), p. 174.

7. Ibid.

8. Mao Zedong, "Long Live the Great Unity of the Chinese People!" September 30, 1949, *Selected Works*, vol. 5 (Beijing: Foreign Languages Press, 1977), pp. 20–21.

9. *Handbook on People's China* (Beijing: Foreign Languages Press, 1957), p. 95.

10. Mao, *Selected Works*, vol. 5, p. 20.

11. Mao, *Selected Works*, vol. 5, p. 40n1.

12. Dorothy J. Solinger, *Regional Government and Political Integration in Southwest China, 1949–1954: A Case Study* (Berkeley: University of California Press, 1977).

13. Tianjin initially was designated a special municipality, too, but lost this distinction with the 1954 reorganization.

14. Franz Schurmann, *Ideology and Organization in Communist China*, 2d enl. ed. (Berkeley: University of California Press, 1968), p. 372.

15. Ibid., p. 373.

16. Ibid., pp. 374–76.

17. See A. Doak Barnett, *Communist China: The Early Years, 1949–1955* (New York: Praeger, 1964), pp. 29–44. This account, written in September 1951, has been one of the most informative on mass organizations.

18. Richard L. Walker, *China under Communism: The First Five Years* (New Haven, Conn.: Yale University Press, 1955), p. 37.

19. Ibid.

20. Ibid., p. 39.

21. Ibid., p. 40.

22. Ibid., p. 42.

23. See James R. Townsend's important treatise, *Political Participation in Communist China*, new ed. (Berkeley: University of California Press, 1969).

24. See Gordon Bennett, *Yundong: Mass Campaigns in Chinese Communist Leadership* (Berkeley: University of California Center for Chinese Studies, 1976).

25. Martin King Whyte, *Small Groups and Political Rituals in China* (Berkeley: University of California Press, 1974), pp. 230–35; based on interviews with emigrés in Hong Kong in 1971.

26. Among the best studies on mass media in the PRC are Frederick T. C. Yu, *Mass Persuasion in Communist China* (New York: Praeger, 1964); Franklin W. Houn, *To Change a Nation: Propaganda and Indoctrination in Communist China* (Glencoe, Ill.: Free Press, 1961); Alan P. Liu, *The Press and Journals in Communist China* (Cambridge, Mass.: MIT Press, 1966); Alan P. Liu, *Communications and National Integration in Communist China* (Berkeley: University of California Press, 1971); and Godwin C. Chu, *Radical Change Through Communication in Mao's China* (Honolulu: University Press of Hawaii, 1977).

27. Schurmann, *Ideology and Organization*, p. 110.

28. See John W. Lewis, *Leadership in Communist China* (Ithaca, N.Y.: Cornell University Press, 1963), for a full study of the party's role.

Chapter 7

1. Mao Zedong, "Don't Hit Out in All Directions," *Selected Works*, vol. 5 (Beijing: Foreign Languages Press, 1977), p. 35.

2. Ibid., pp. 33–34.

3. Mao, "Be a True Revolutionary," *Selected Works*, vol. 5, p. 39.

4. E.g., Mao, "On the People's Democratic Dictatorship," *Selected Works*, vol. 5, p. 421.

5. Kenneth G. Lieberthal, *Revolution and Tradition in Tientsin, 1949–1952* (Stanford, Calif.: Stanford University Press, 1980), p. 48.

6. W. W. Rostow et al., *The Prospects for Communist China* (Cambridge, Mass.: MIT Press, 1954), p. 241.

7. Ibid., p. 237, citing Edwin W. Pauley, *Report on Japanese Assets in Manchuria to the President of the United States*, July 1946, p. 37.

8. Rostow, *Prospects*, pp. 239–40.

9. Ibid., pp. 238–39.

10. Ibid., pp. 241–42.

11. Ibid., p. 243.

12. Ibid., p. 243.

13. Deng Yingchao, "Breaking the Yoke of the Feudal Marriage System," in *The Marriage Law of the People's Republic of China* (Beijing: Foreign Languages Press, 1959), p. 35.

14. M. J. Meijer, *Marriage Law and Policy in the Chinese People's Republic* (Hong Kong: Hong Kong University Press, 1971), pp. 134–53.

15. Deng Yingchao, *The Marriage Law*, p. 42.

16. Lin Ching-fan's "Report on the Movement for Implementation of the Marriage Law, November 11, 1953," Appendix X, in Meijer, *Marriage Law and Policy*, pp. 307–14.

17. See Kay Ann Johnson, *Women, the Family and Peasant Revolution in China* (Chicago: University of Chicago Press, 1983).

18. John Wong, *Land Reform in the People's Republic of China* (New York: Praeger, 1973), p. 77.

19. Ibid., p. 78.

20. Ibid., pp. 92–95.

21. Ibid., pp. 108–9; see also the detailed account of this phenomenon in William Hinton, *Fanshen: A Documentary of Revolution in a Chinese Village* (New York: Random House, 1966).

22. *Beijing Review* (February 9, 1979).

23. Wong, *Land Reform*, p. 138.

24. See Ezra F. Vogel, *Canton under Communism: Programs and Politics in a Provincial Capital, 1949–1968* (Cambridge, Mass.: Harvard University Press, 1969), pp. 106–24.

25. Wong, *Land Reform*, p. 153.

26. John Gittings, *The Role of the Chinese Army* (London: Oxford University Press, 1967), pp. 79–83.

27. Ibid., pp. 83–85.

28. Excellent accounts of these campaigns include Sherwin Montell, "The San-Fan Wu-Fan Movement in Communist China," *Papers on China*, vol. 8 (Cambridge, Mass.: Harvard University Regional Studies Seminar, February 1954); John Gardner, "The Wu-fan Campaign in Shanghai," in *Chinese Communist Politics in Action*, ed. A. Doak Barnett (Seattle: University of Washington Press, 1969), pp. 477–539; A. Doak Barnett, *Communist China: The Early*

Years, 1949–1955 (New York: Praeger, 1964); and Lieberthal, *Revolution and Tradition in Tientsin.*

29. Roxane Witke, *Comrade Chiang Ch'ing* (Boston: Little, Brown & Co., 1977), p. 238.

30. Guy S. Alitto, *The Last Confucian: Liang Shu-ming and the Chinese Dilemma of Modernity* (Berkeley: University of California Press, 1979), p. 330.

31. Theodore H. E. Chen, *Thought Reform of the Chinese Intellectuals* (Hong Kong: Hong Kong University Press, 1960), pp. 43–46.

32. A particularly penetrating study is Robert Jay Lifton, *Thought Reform and the Psychology of Totalism: A Study of "Brainwashing" in China* (Middlesex, Eng.: Penguin Books, 1961).

33. Stuart R. Schram, *Mao Tse-tung* (Middlesex, Eng.: Penguin, 1966), p. 256.

34. Alekseyev, "Important Document in the History of Soviet-Chinese Relations," *Izvestia*, February 14, 1985; *Foreign Broadcast Information Service*, February 14, 1985, p. B1.

35. Franz Schurmann, *The Logic of World Power: An Inquiry into the Origins, Currents, and Contradictions of World Politics* (New York: Pantheon, 1974), p. 241.

36. Barry M. Richman, *Industrial Society in Communist China* (New York: Random House, 1969), pp. 405–6.

37. Ibid., p. 406.

38. A. Doak Barnett, quoting Hans Heymann, in *China and the Major Powers in East Asia* (Washington, D.C.: Brookings Institute, 1977), p. 28.

39. Richman, *Industrial Society,* p. 407.

40. Liao Gailong (Liao Kai-lung), "Historical Experiences and Our Road of Development, part 1," a report on the history of the party delivered on October 25, 1980, at the National Party-School Forum, translated in *Issues & Studies* 17 (October 1981): 79.

41. Kenneth G. Lieberthal, *A Research Guide to Central Party and Governmental Meetings in China 1949–1975* (White Plains, N.Y.: International Arts and Sciences Press, 1976), p. 59.

42. Edward E. Rice, *Mao's Way* (Berkeley: University of California Press, 1972), pp. 129–31.

43. *People's Daily,* April 5, 1955.

44. Mao, "On the Draft Constitution of the People's Republic of China," June 14, 1954, *Selected Works,* vol. 5, p. 146.

45. Mao, "On the Co-operative Transformation of Agriculture," July 31, 1955, *Selected Works,* vol. 5, p. 184.

46. Ibid.

47. Jurgen Domes, *Socialism in the Chinese Countryside: Rural Societal Policies in the People's Republic of China 1949–1979* (London: C. Hurst & Co., 1980), p. 15.

48. Lieberthal, *Research Guide*, p. 74.

49. General Office of the Central Committee of the CCP, ed., "Preface," *Socialist Upsurge in China's Countryside* (Beijing: Foreign Languages Press, 1978), p. 3.

50. Roderick MacFarquhar, *The Origins of the Cultural Revolution*, vol. 1, *Contradictions among the People, 1956–1957* (New York: Columbia University Press, 1974), pp. 22–24.

51. Richman, *Industrial Society*, pp. 894–912.

52. Lieberthal, *Research Guide*, pp. 78–79.

53. Huang Daqiang, "The Theoretical Basis for Building Socialism with Chinese Characteristics—In Commemoration of the 90th Anniversary of Comrade Mao Zedong's Birthday," *Guangming Ribao*, Beijing, December 26, 1983, p. 3; in *Foreign Broadcast Information Service*, January 11, 1984, p. K3.

54. The speech was subsequently included in Mao, *Selected Works*, vol. 5, pp. 284–307.

55. MacFarquhar, *Origins*, vol. 1, p. 53.

56. Lieberthal, *Research Guide*, p. 83.

57. Jacques Guillermaz, *The Chinese Communist Party in Power 1949–1976* (Boulder, Colo.: Westview Press, 1976), p. 131.

58. Roberta Martin, *Party Recruitment in China: Patterns and Prospects: A Study of the Recruitment Campaign of 1954–56 and Its Impact on Party Expansion through 1980* (New York: Columbia University East Asian Institute, 1981), pp. 14–17.

59. Ibid., p. 133.

60. MacFarquhar, *Origins*, vol. 1, p. 119.

61. Ibid., pp. 173–74.

62. Ibid., pp. 177–78.

63. Mao, *Selected Works*, vol. 5, pp. 384–421.

64. Lieberthal, *Research Guide*, p. 94.

65. MacFarquhar, *Origins*, vol. 1, pp. 175–76 and 181.

66. Ibid., p. 210.

67. Ibid., p. 288.

68. Alexander Eckstein, *China's Economic Revolution* (Cambridge, Eng.: Cambridge University Press, 1977), p. 54.

Chapter 8

1. Roderick MacFarquhar, *The Origins of the Cultural Revolution*, vol. 2, *The Great Leap Forward, 1958–1960* (New York: Columbia University Press, 1983), p. 330, citing estimates made by John Aird.

2. See in particular William A. Joseph, "A Tragedy of Good Intentions: Post-

Mao Views of the Great Leap Forward," *Modern China* 12, no. 4 (October 1986): 419–57.

3. See Ramon H. Myers' review of Jean-Luc Domenach, *Aux Origines du Grand Bond en Avant: Le cas d'une province Chinoise, 1956–1958* [The origins of the Great Leap Forward: A conjunction in a Chinese province, 1956–1958] (Paris: Editions de l'Ecole des Hautes Etudes en Sciences Sociales, Presses de la Fondation Nationale des Sciences Politiques, 1982), in *Journal of Asian Studies* 45, 2 (February 1986): 373–75.

4. A good effort to explain sympathetically the rationale of the Great Leap is Victor D. Lippit, "The Great Leap Forward Reconsidered," *Modern China* 1, no. 1 (January 1975): 92–115.

5. MacFarquhar, *Origins*, vol. 2, p. 17.

6. Mao Zedong, *Miscellany of Mao Tse-tung Thought (1949–1968)*, part 1 (Arlington, Va.: Joint Publications Research Service, 1974), pp. 77–84.

7. MacFarquhar, *Origins*, vol. 2, p. 55.

8. Mao, *Miscellany*, part 1, p. 109.

9. Roberta Martin, *Party Recruitment in China: Patterns and Prospects: A Study of the Recruitment Campaign of 1954–56 and Its Impact on Party Expansion through 1980* (New York: Columbia University East Asian Institute, 1981), p. 17.

10. Ibid., p. 67.

11. Ibid.

12. Kenneth G. Lieberthal, *A Research Guide to Central Party and Governmental Meetings in China 1949–1975* (White Plains, N.Y.: International Arts and Sciences Press, 1976), p. 114.

13. Franz Schurmann, *Ideology and Organization in Communist China*, 2d enl. ed. (Berkeley: University of California Press, 1968), pp. 465–77.

14. Ibid., p. 85.

15. MacFarquhar, *Origins*, vol. 2, p. 98.

16. Ibid., p. 102.

17. Ibid., pp. 89–90.

18. Lieberthal, *Research Guide*, pp. 123–24.

19. *Sixth Plenary Session of the Eighth Central Committee of the Communist Party of China* (Beijing: Foreign Languages Press, 1958).

20. Mao Zedong, *Mao Zedong ssu-xiang wan sui* [Long live the thought of Mao Zedong] (Red Guard publication, 1969), p. 41.

21. Lieberthal, *Research Guide*, p. 134, referring to ibid., p. 35.

22. Ibid., pp. 136–37.

23. Ibid., p. 138; MacFarquhar, *Origins*, vol. 2, p. 154, also citing *Mao Zedong ssu-xiang wan-sui* (1967), p. 22, noted that Mao called for the brigade as the basic accounting unit.

24. Parris Chang, *Power and Policy in China*, 2d enl. ed. (University Park: Pennsylvania State University Press, 1978), p. 108.

25. Ibid., p. 140.

26. Peng Dehuai, *Memoirs of a Chinese Marshal* (Beijing: Foreign Languages Press, 1985), pp. 510–20.

27. *The Selected Works of Zhang Wentian*, published in Chinese by the People's Publishing House in Beijing in August 1985, contains the speech that Zhang delivered at Lushan, now published for the first time. *Beijing Review* (November 4, 1985): 34.

28. Chang, *Power and Policy*, p. 115.

29. MacFarquhar, *Origins*, vol. 2, p. 206.

30. Stuart R. Schram, ed., *Chairman Mao Talks to the People: Talks and Letters: 1956–1971* (New York: Pantheon Books, 1974), pp. 131–46.

31. Ibid., p. 145.

32. Ibid., p. 146.

33. Ibid., p. 139.

34. MacFarquhar, *Origins*, vol. 2, p. 228.

35. Ibid., p. 233.

36. Central Committee, Communist Party of China, *Resolution on CPC History (1949–81)* (Beijing: Foreign Languages Press, 1981), p. 29.

37. Ibid., p. 234.

38. Peng, *Memoirs*, p. 522.

39. MacFarquhar, *Origins*, vol. 2, p. 237.

40. Ibid., pp. 236–37.

41. Ibid., p. 229.

42. Ibid., p. 247.

43. Ibid., p. 249–51.

44. A. M. Halpern, "Communist China and Peaceful Coexistence," *China Quarterly* (July–September 1960): 18–21.

45. Donald S. Zagoria, *The Sino-Soviet Conflict 1956–1961* (Princeton, N.J.: Princeton University Press, 1962), pp. 320–25.

46. MacFarquhar, *Origins*, vol. 2, p. 277.

47. John Gittings, *Survey of the Sino-Soviet Dispute: A Commentary and Extracts from the Recent Polemics, 1963–1967* (London: Oxford University Press, 1968), p. 139.

48. Central Committee, *Resolution on CPC History (1949–81)*, p. 29.

49. Ellis Joffe, *Between Two Plenums: China's Intraleadership Conflict, 1959–1962* (Ann Arbor: University of Michigan Center for Chinese Studies, 1975), pp. 22–23.

50. Ahn Byung-joon, *Chinese Politics and the Cultural Revolution: Dynam-

ics of Policy Processes (Seattle: University of Washington Press, 1976), pp. 45–47.

51. MacFarquhar, *Origins*, vol. 2, p. 293.

Chapter 9

1. William A. Joseph, *The Critique of Ultra-Leftism in China, 1958–1981* (Stanford, Calif.: Stanford University Press, 1984), p. 119.

2. Mao Zedong, *Miscellany of Mao Tse-tung Thought (1949–1968)*, part 2 (Arlington, Va.: Joint Publications Research Service, 1974), p. 242.

3. Ahn Byung-joon, *Chinese Politics and the Cultural Revolution: Dynamics of Policy Processes* (Seattle: University of Washington Press, 1976), p. 54.

4. Roderick MacFarquhar, *The Origins of the Cultural Revolution*, vol. 2, *The Great Leap Forward, 1958–1960* (New York: Columbia University Press, 1983), pp. 209–12.

5. Stephen Uhalley, Jr., "The Cultural Revolution and the Attack on the 'Three Family Village,'" *China Quarterly*, no. 26 (July–September 1966): 149–61.

6. Stephen Uhalley, Jr. "The Wu Han Discussion: Act One in a New Rectification Campaign," *China Mainland Review* 1, no. 4 (March 1966): 24–38.

7. Ahn, *Chinese Politics*, pp. 65–66.

8. Ibid., pp. 66–67.

9. Mao Zedong, "Talk at an Enlarged Central Work Conference," January 30, 1962, in Stuart R. Schram, ed., *Chairman Mao Talks to the People: Talks and Letters: 1956–1971* (New York: Pantheon Books, 1974), pp. 183–84.

10. Ahn, *Chinese Politics*, p. 76.

11. Ibid., p. 77.

12. Ibid., p. 65.

13. Stated at the Seventh Plenum of the Third CYL Central Committee, ibid., p. 76.

14. Mao, "Speech at the Tenth Plenum," September 24, 1962, in Schram, ed., *Chairman Mao Talks*, pp. 188–96.

15. Central Committee, Communist Party of China, *Resolution on CPC History (1949–81)* (Beijing: Foreign Languages Press, 1981), p. 30.

16. Mao Zedong, *Quotations from Chairman Mao Tse-tung* (Beijing: Foreign Languages Press, 1966), p. 279.

17. Ahn, *Chinese Politics*, pp. 79–80.

18. Ibid., p. 79–80.

19. See Jurgen Domes, *Socialism in the Chinese Countryside: Rural Societal Policies in the People's Republic of China 1949–1979* (London: C. Hurst & Co., 1980), pp. 55–116.

20. Ellis Joffe, *Between Two Plenums: China's Intraleadership Conflict, 1959–1962* (Ann Arbor: University of Michigan Center for Chinese Studies, 1975), p. 57.

21. See Zhou Enlai, *Premier Chou En-lai's Letter to the Leaders of Asian and African Countries on the Sino-Indian Boundary Question*, November 15, 1962 (Beijing: Foreign Languages Press, 1973); Neville Maxwell, *India's China War* (New York: Pantheon Books, 1970); and Allen S. Whiting, *The Chinese Calculus of Deterrence: India and Indochina* (Ann Arbor: University of Michigan Press, 1975).

22. Central Committee, CPC, *Resolution on CPC History (1949–81)*, p. 30.

23. See Harry Harding, ed., *Organizing China: The Problem of Bureaucracy, 1949–1976* (Stanford, Calif.: Stanford University Press, 1982), pp. 201–34; Richard Baum, *Prelude to Revolution: Mao, the Party, and the Peasant Question 1962–66* (New York: Columbia University Press, 1975); and Richard Baum and Frederick C. Teiwes, *Ssu-Ch'ing: The Socialist Education Movement of 1962–1966* (Berkeley: University of California Center for Chinese Studies, 1968).

24. Baum, *Prelude to Revolution*, pp. 21–28.

25. Ibid., pp. 43–59. Baum believed that Deng Xiaoping did not consciously seek to obfuscate matters, although the document "may have had the effect of tacitly undermining the spirit, if not the letter, of Mao's thesis on class struggle." However, from what has transpired in the years since, it would appear that Deng may well have been obfuscating. See ibid., p. 59.

26. Baum and Teiwes, *Ssu-Ch'ing*, pp. 72–94.

27. Ibid., pp. 102–17.

28. Baum, *Prelude to Revolution*, pp. 103–4.

29. Ibid., pp. 118–26.

30. Ibid., pp. 215–16.

31. Merle Goldman, *China's Intellectuals: Advise and Dissent* (Cambridge, Mass.: Harvard University Press, 1981), pp. 90–91.

32. See, for example, Merle Goldman, "The Chinese Communist Party's 'Cultural Revolution' of 1962–64," in Chalmers Johnson, ed., *Ideology and Politics in Contemporary China* (Seattle: University of Washington Press, 1973), pp. 219–54.

33. See Stephen Uhalley, Jr., "The Controversy over Li Hsiu-ch'eng: An Ill-timed Centenary," *Journal of Asian Studies* 25, no. 2 (February 1966): 305–17.

34. Goldman, *China's Intellectuals*, pp. 95–101.

35. John Gittings, *Survey of the Sino-Soviet Dispute: A Commentary and Extracts from the Recent Polemics, 1963–1967* (London: Oxford University Press, 1968), p. 184.

36. *Beijing Review* 29 (July 17, 1964): 7–28.

37. Gittings, *Sino-Soviet Dispute*, p. 229.

38. See Peter Van Ness, *Revolution and Chinese Foreign Policy* (Berkeley: University of California Press, 1971).

39. K. Fan, ed., *Mao Tse-tung and Lin Piao* (New York: Anchor Books, 1972), pp. 357–412.

Chapter 10

1. See Harry Harding, *Organizing China: The Problem of Bureaucracy, 1949–1976* (Stanford, Calif.: Stanford University Press, 1982), pp. 219–23.

2. Kenneth G. Lieberthal, *A Research Guide to Central Party and Governmental Meetings in China 1949–1975* (White Plains, N.Y.: International Arts and Sciences Press, 1976), p. 229.

3. Ibid., p. 231.

4. Edward Rice, *Mao's Way* (Berkeley: University of California Press, 1972), p. 230.

5. See, e.g., Stephen Uhalley, Jr., "The Wu Han Discussion: Act One in a New Rectification Campaign," *China Mainland Review* 1, no. 4 (March 1966): 24–38.

6. *Hongqi*, no. 9 (1966): 27; *Summary of the Forum on Work in Literature and Art in the Armed Forces Which Comrade Lin Piao Entrusted to Comrade Chiang Ching* (Beijing: Foreign Languages Press, 1968).

7. Stephen Uhalley, Jr., "The Cultural Revolution and the Attack on the 'Three Family Village,'" *China Quarterly* 26 (July–September, 1966): 149–61.

8. *Important Documents on the Great Proletarian Cultural Revolution in China* (Beijing: Foreign Languages Press, 1970), pp. 107–28.

9. Central Committee, Communist Party of China, *Resolution on CPC History (1949–81)* (Beijing: Foreign Languages Press, 1981), p. 33.

10. Ahn Byung-joon, *Chinese Politics and the Cultural Revolution: Dynamics of Policy Processes* (Seattle: University of Washington Press, 1976), p. 216.

11. Harding, *Organizing China*, p. 239.

12. Edgar Snow, *The Long Revolution* (New York: Random House, 1972), p. 70.

13. Lee Hong Yung, *The Politics of the Chinese Cultural Revolution: A Case Study* (Berkeley: University of California Press, 1978), p. 65.

14. "Decision of the Central Committee of the Chinese Communist Party Concerning the Great Proletarian Cultural Revolution," August 8, 1966, *Important Documents*, pp. 129–56.

15. Initiated on August 18, 1966, when Mao accepted an armband from an organized group of middle school students. The armband was inscribed with the words *hong wei bing*, or red guard. See Gordon A. Bennett and Ronald N. Montaperto, *Red Guard: The Political Biography of Dia Hsiao-ai* (Garden City, N.Y.: Anchor Books, 1972), p. 66.

16. Ibid., p. 138.

17. See Parris H. Chang, "Provincial Party Leaders' Strategies for Survival during the Cultural Revolution," in Robert A. Scalapino, ed., *Elites in the People's Republic of China* (Seattle: University of Washington Press, 1972), pp. 501–39.

18. Special Procuratorate of the People's Republic of China, *The Indictment against Lin Biao–Jiang Qing Cliques,* English supplement (Hong Kong: Ta Kung Pao, 1980), p. 23.

19. Bennett and Montaperto, *Red Guard,* pp. 119–21.

20. See, e.g., Lee, *Politics of the Chinese Cultural Revolution,* pp. 59–63.

21. Peter Moody, "Policy and Power: The Career of T'ao Chu, 1956–66," *China Quarterly* 54 (April–June 1973): 291.

22. See, e.g., Jean Daubier, *A History of the Chinese Cultural Revolution* (New York: Vintage Books, 1974), pp. 124–29.

23. Andrew G. Walder, *Chang Ch'un-ch'iao and Shanghai's January Revolution* (Ann Arbor: University of Michigan Center for Chinese Studies, 1977), pp. 47–48.

24. Harding, *Organizing China,* p. 247.

25. See John Bryan Starr, "Revolution in Retrospect: The Paris Commune through Chinese Eyes," *China Quarterly* 49 (January–March 1972): 106–25.

26. Harding, *Organizing China,* pp. 252–53.

27. Walder, *Chang Ch'un-ch'iao,* pp. 62–63.

28. Lee, *Politics of the Chinese Cultural Revolution,* pp. 168–82.

29. Ibid., p. 188.

30. Ibid., p. 195.

31. Ibid., pp. 202–3; see also Barry Burton, "The Cultural Revolution's Ultraleft Conspiracy: The May 16 Groups," *Asian Survey,* no. 11 (November 1971): 1029–53.

32. See Thomas W. Robinson, "The Wuhan Incident: Local Strife and Provincial Rebellion during the Cultural Revolution," *China Quarterly* 47 (July–September 1971): 413–18.

33. Lee, *Politics of the Chinese Cultural Revolution,* p. 247.

34. See Melvin Gurtov, "The Foreign Ministry and Foreign Affairs during the Cultural Revolution," *China Quarterly* 40 (October–December 1969): 65–102.

35. Lee, *Politics of the Chinese Cultural Revolution,* pp. 251–52.

36. Bennett and Montaperto, *Red Guard,* p. 197.

37. Ibid., pp. 252–54.

38. Such as Dai Hsiao-ai, the subject of Bennett's and Montaperto's *Red Guard,* p. 205.

39. Harding, *Organizing China,* pp. 257–60; the documents are included in Klaus Mehnert, *Peking and the New Left: At Home and Abroad* (Berkeley: University of California Center for Chinese Studies, 1969).

40. Lee, *Politics of the Chinese Revolution*, p. 271.

41. William L. Parish, "Factions in Chinese Military Politics," *China Quarterly* 56 (October–December 1973): 680.

42. Jurgen Domes, *China after the Cultural Revolution: Politics between Two Party Congresses* (Berkeley: University of California Press, 1977), p. 12.

43. Canton Area Workers' Revolutionary Committee, *Thirty-Three Leading Counterrevolutionary Revisionists*, translated in *Current Background*, no. 874 (Hong Kong: American Consulate General, March 17, 1969).

44. See William Hinton, *Hundred Day War: The Cultural Revolution at Tsinghua University* (New York: Monthly Review Press, 1972).

45. Ibid., pp. 226–27.

46. Quoted in David Milton and Nancy Dall Milton, *The Wind Will Not Subside: Years in Revolutionary China—1964–1969* (New York: Pantheon Books, 1976), p. 275.

47. Lee, *Politics of the Chinese Cultural Revolution*, p. 298.

48. Lowell Dittmer, *Liu Shao-ch'i and the Chinese Cultural Revolution: The Politics of Mass Criticism* (Berkeley: University of California Press, 1974), pp. 108–9.

49. See Thomas W. Robinson, *The Sino-Soviet Border Dispute: Background Development and the March 1969 Clash* (Santa Monica, Calif.: Rand Corp., 1970).

50. See Neville Maxwell, "The Chinese Account of the 1969 Fighting at Chenpao," *China Quarterly* 56 (October–December 1973): 730–39.

51. Among others, including Thomas Robinson, who conclude that the Chinese provoked the incident is Harold Hinton. See his *Bear at the Gate: Chinese Policymaking under Soviet Pressure* (Stanford, Calif.: Hoover Institution Press, 1971).

52. Delivered on April 1 and adopted on April 14, 1969, in *The Ninth National Congress of the Communist Party of China (Documents)* (Beijing: Foreign Languages Press, 1969), pp. 1–108.

53. Ibid., pp. 109–28.

54. Names of members listed ibid., pp. 165–70.

55. Communiqué with list of officers, members, and alternates of the Politburo, ibid., pp. 173–76.

Chapter 11

1. Jurgen Domes, *China after the Cultural Revolution: Politics between Two Party Congresses* (Berkeley: University of California Press, 1977), p. 54.

2. This is quoted from an editorial in *Hongqi* of October 14, 1968, subtitled "An Important Question in Party Consolidation." The editorial was reprinted as a pamphlet under that title by Foreign Languages Press, 1968. See p. 9.

3. This sequence of stages for the rebuilding of the party coincides with that of John W. Garver in his *China's Decision for Rapprochement with the United States, 1968–1971* (Boulder, Colo.: Westview Press, 1982), pp. 118–24.

4. Philip Bridgham, "The Fall of Lin Piao," *China Quarterly* 55 (July–September 1973): 444.

5. Domes, *China after the Cultural Revolution*, p. 50.

6. Gordon Bennett, "Military Regions and Provincial Party Secretaries: One Outcome of China's Cultural Revolution," *China Quarterly* 54 (April–June 1973): 294.

7. Kenneth G. Lieberthal, *A Research Guide to Central Party and Governmental Meetings in China 1949–1975* (White Plains, N.Y.: International Arts and Sciences Press, 1976), pp. 275–76.

8. Harry Harding, *Organizing China: The Problem of Bureaucracy, 1949–1976* (Stanford, Calif.: Stanford University Press, 1982), pp. 302–3.

9. Mao Zedong, "Summary of Chairman Mao's Talks with Responsible Comrades at Various Places during his Provincial Tour from the Middle of August to 12 September 1971" in Stuart R. Schram, ed., *Chairman Mao Talks to the People: Talks and Letters: 1956–1971* (New York: Pantheon Books, 1974), p. 296.

10. Harold Hinton, "Critical Factors in Chinese Policy Making since the Cultural Revolution," *First Sino-American Conference on Mainland China, Proceedings* (Taibei: Institute for International Relations, 1970), cited in Garver, *China's Decision for Rapprochement*, p. 122.

11. Bridgham, "Fall of Lin Biao," 433.

12. *Communiqué of the Second Plenary Session of the Ninth Central Committee of the Communist Party of China*, September 6, 1970 (Hong Kong: Joint Publishing Co., 1970), p. 1.

13. Schram, *Chairman Mao Talks*, pp. 293–94.

14. Bridgham, "Fall of Lin Piao," 435; also Schram, *Chairman Mao Talks*, p. 295; and Michael Y. M. Kau, *The Lin Piao Affair: Power Politics and Military Coup* (White Plains, N.Y.: International Arts and Sciences Press, 1975), p. xxiii.

15. Domes, *China after the Cultural Revolution*, pp. 62–66.

16. This figure is used by Domes, *China after the Cultural Revolution*, p. 66. The most comprehensive study of the *xia-fang* movement, however, holds that the figure is probably less than 12 million. See Thomas P. Bernstein, *"Up to the Mountains and Down to the Villages": The Transfer of Youth from Urban to Rural China* (New Haven, Conn.: Yale University Press, 1977), p. 31.

17. Domes, *China after the Cultural Revolution*, pp. 108–12.

18. See Ellis Joffe, "The Chinese Army after the Cultural Revolution: The Effects of Intervention," *China Quarterly* 55 (July–September 1973): 450–77.

19. See both Harold C. Hinton, *Bear at the Gate: Chinese Policymaking under Soviet Pressure* (Stanford, Calif.: Hoover Institution Press, 1971), and

Garver, *China's Decision for Rapprochement*, pp. 64–67, for differing assessments of this encounter.

20. Garver, *China's Decision for Rapprochement*, pp. 84–107.

21. Ibid., p. 102.

22. See, for example, Robert G. Sutter, *China-Watch: Toward Sino-American Reconciliation* (Baltimore, Md.: Johns Hopkins University Press, 1978), p. 118.

23. Special Procuratorate of the People's Republic of China, *The Indictment against Lin Biao–Jiang Qing Cliques*, English supplement (Hong Kong: Ta Kung Pao, 1980), p. 28.

24. From the confession of Li Weixin of the Fourth Air Force Group's Political Department, in Kau, *The Lin Piao Affair*, pp. 90–95.

25. "Outline of 'Project 571,' " in Kau, *The Lin Piao Affair*, pp. 81–90.

26. Yao Ming-le, *The Conspiracy and Murder of Mao's Heir* (New York: Knopf, 1983). This book reads like a thriller novel, and the validity of many of its claimed sources are debatable. See, e.g., the review by Stephen Uhalley, Jr., in *Asian Wall Street Journal* (June 13, 1983).

27. Central Committee Document, *Zhongfa*, September 18, 1971, no. 60, in Kau, *The Lin Piao Affair*, pp. 69–70.

28. Early Soviet sources indicated that none of the bodies in the crashed Trident plane was above the age of 50. However, Xu Wenyi, the Chinese ambassador to Mongolia at the time, had pictures taken of the remains, which, he said, later specified the identities. *Wen Wei Po*, Hong Kong, January 14, 1988, p. 2; in *Foreign Broadcast Information Service*, January 15, 1988, p. 11.

29. Central Committee, Communist Party of China, *Resolution on CPC History (1949–81)* (Beijing: Foreign Languages Press, 1981), p. 38.

Chapter 12

1. Central Committee, Communist Party of China, *Resolution on CPC History (1949–81)* (Beijing: Foreign Languages Press, 1981), pp. 38–39.

2. Jurgen Domes, *China after the Cultural Revolution: Politics between Two Party Congresses* (Berkeley: University of California Press, 1977), pp. 140–43.

3. Parris Chang, "Political Rehabilitation of Cadres in China: A Traveller's View," *China Quarterly* 54 (April–June 1973): 337.

4. Jim Townsend, "Political Institutions," in Joyce Kallgren, ed., *The People's Republic of China after Thirty Years: An Overview* (Berkeley: University of California Institute of East Asian Studies, Center for Chinese Studies, 1979), p. 16.

5. Domes, *China after the Cultural Revolution*, p. 148.

6. Ibid., p. 149.

7. See Ahn Byung-joon, "The Cultural Revolution and China's Search for Political Order," *China Quarterly* 58 (April–May, 1974): 277.

8. Domes, *China after the Cultural Revolution*, pp. 153–56.

9. Ibid., pp. 156–63.

10. Mao Zedong, *Selected Works*, vol. 4 (Beijing: Foreign Languages Press, 1950–1977), pp. 47–51 and 53–63.

11. See A. Doak Barnett, *China and the Major Powers in East Asia* (Washington, D.C.: Brookings Institute, 1977), pp. 113–37.

12. William A. Joseph, *The Critique of Ultra-Leftism in China, 1958–1981* (Stanford, Calif.: Stanford University Press, 1984), pp. 124–29.

13. Harry Harding, *Organizing China: The Problem of Bureaucracy, 1949–1976* (Stanford, Calif.: Stanford University Press, 1982), pp. 308–9.

14. Domes, *China after the Cultural Revolution*, p. 179.

15. See Richard Wich, "The Tenth Party Congress: The Power Structure and the Succession Question," *China Quarterly* 58 (April–June 1974): 231–48.

16. Ibid., 232.

17. Report delivered August 24 and adopted August 28, 1973, in *The Tenth National Congress of the Communist Party of China (Documents)* (Beijing: Foreign Languages Press, 1973), pp. 12–13.

18. Ibid., p. 34.

19. Ibid., pp. 21–22.

20. Ibid., p. 29.

21. See Pierre M. Perrolle, ed., *Fundamentals of the Chinese Communist Party* (White Plains, N.Y.: International Arts and Sciences Press, 1976), for comparisons between the 1969 and 1973 documents.

22. Wich, "The Tenth Party Congress," 235.

23. The names are included in *The Tenth National Congress (Documents)*, pp. 89–93.

24. Ibid., pp. 97–98.

25. Domes, *China after the Cultural Revolution*, p. 198.

26. *Current Scene* 21, no. 2, February 1974, pp. 19–23.

27. See Robert A. Scalapino, "The CCP's Provincial Secretaries," *Problems of Communism* (July–August 1976): 18–35.

28. See Wu Tien-wei's excellent study of this fascinating campaign, *Lin Biao and the Gang of Four, Contra-Confucianism in Historical and Intellectual Perspective* (Carbondale: Southern Illinois University Press, 1983).

29. Harding, *Organizing China*, p. 314.

30. Bill Brugger, *China: Radicalism to Revisionism 1962–1979* (London: Croom Helm, 1981), pp. 179–80.

31. Wu, *Lin Biao and the Gang of Four*, p. 202.

32. Communiqué in *Beijing Review* (January 24, 1975): 6.

33. "Report on the Work of the Government," ibid., 21–25.

34. Full text, ibid., 12–17.

35. Zhang's report, ibid., 18–20.

36. *Beijing Review* (February 14, 1975): 4.

37. Richard C. Kraus, *Class Conflict in Chinese Socialism* (New York: Columbia University Press, 1981), p. 17.

38. In *Hongqi*, no. 3 (1975), translated as a booklet, *On the Social Basis of the Lin Piao Anti-Party Clique* (Beijing: Foreign Languages Press, 1975).

39. In *Hongqi*, no. 4 (1975), translated as a booklet, *On Exercising All-Round Dictatorship Over the Bourgeoisie* (Beijing: Foreign Languages Press, 1975).

40. Speaking on July 4, 1975, to students of the fourth study class arranged by the Central Committee, in *Selected Works of Deng Xiaoping (1975–1982)*, Beijing: Foreign Languages Press, 1984, p. 25.

41. Translated in Chi Hsin, *The Case of the Gang of Four—With First Translation of Teng Hsiao-ping's "Three Poisonous Weeds"* (Hong Kong: Cosmos Books, 1977), p. 232.

42. Parris Chang, *Power and Policy in China* (University Park: Pennsylvania State University Press, 1967 and 1975), p. 212.

43. Leo Goodstadt, " 'Hangchow' and the Crises Still to Come," *Far Eastern Economic Review* (August 29, 1975): 27–28.

44. Once translated into English as *All Men Are Brothers* by Pearl Buck.

45. See Chang, *Power and Policy in China*, pp. 218–19.

46. Full text in *Beijing Review* (September 13, 1976): 6–13.

47. *Beijing Review* (September 24, 1976): 12–16.

Chapter 13

1. This was said to be a falsification of Mao's comment on April 30 "to act according to past principles."

2. Parris Chang, *Power and Policy in China* (University Park: Pennsylvania State University Press, 1967 and 1975). This "deathbed adjuration" was regarded as one of the two documents Jiang Qing had tampered with.

3. Immanuel C. Y. Hsu, *China Without Mao: The Search for a New Order* (New York: Oxford University Press, 1982), p. 15.

4. The distribution of 6 million rounds of ammunition to the Shanghai urban militia on the day after Mao's death certainly aroused apprehensions. Andres D. Onate, "Hua Kuo-feng and the Arrest of the 'Gang of Four,' " *China Quarterly* 75 (September 1978): 555–56.

5. *Beijing Review* (October 15, 1976): 3–4.

6. *Beijing Review* (October 29, 1976): 13.

7. Hsu, *China Without Mao,* p. 21; complete text in *Issues & Studies* (September–October, 1977).

8. Chang, *Power and Policy in China,* p. 231.

9. *Washington Post,* July 23, 1977.

10. "Press Communiqué," August 18, 1977, in *The Eleventh National Congress of the Communist Party of China (Documents)* (Beijing: Foreign Languages Press, 1977), p. 200.

11. "Resolution," August 18, 1977, ibid., p. 116.

12. "Political Report," ibid., pp. 1–112.

13. "Report on the Revision of the Constitution," ibid., pp. 146–49.

14. "Closing Address," ibid., pp. 192–93.

15. Hsu, *China Without Mao,* p. 32.

16. See *Documents of the First Session of the Fifth National People's Congress of the People's Republic of China* (Beijing: Foreign Languages Press, 1978).

17. Ibid., pp. 1–118.

18. Ibid., pp. 173–220.

19. Ibid., pp. 125–72.

20. *Beijing Review* (June 23, 1978).

21. *Foreign Broadcast Information Service,* May 19, 1978.

22. Central Committee, Communist Party of China, *Resolution on CPC History (1949–81)* (Beijing: Foreign Languages Press, 1981), p. 49.

23. Ibid., pp. 49–50.

24. See Stanley Rosen, "Guangzhou's Democracy Movement in Cultural Revolution Perspective," *China Quarterly* 101 (March 1985): 7–12.

25. *Resolution on CPC History (1949–81),* p. 50.

26. In Jurgen Domes, *The Government and Politics of the PRC* (Boulder, Colo.: Westview Press, 1985), p. 164.

27. Ibid., pp. 164–65.

28. See King C. Chen, *China's War Against Vietnam, 1979: A Military Analysis,* Occasional Papers/Reprints Series in Contemporary Asian Studies, no. 5 (University of Maryland School of Law, 1983).

29. Ibid., p. 25.

30. *Selected Works of Deng Xiaoping* (Beijing: Foreign Languages Press, 1984), pp. 166–91.

31. *Manchester Guardian,* June 24, 1979.

32. See Pitman B. Potter, "Peng Zhen," in Carol Lee Hamrin and Timothy Cheek, eds., *China's Establishment Intellectuals* (New York: M. E. Sharpe, 1986), pp. 40–50.

33. *Beijing Review* (July 13 and 20, 1979).

34. Delivered at a celebration in the Great Hall of the People on September 29, 1979, rather than on October 1.

35. *Beijing Review* (October 5, 1979): 7–32.

36. Text of the communiqué of the Fifth Plenum, *Beijing Review* (March 10, 1980): 7–10.

37. Text in *Beijing Review* (April 7, 1980): 11–19.

38. *Beijing Review* (April 28, 1980): 3.

39. *Selected Works of Deng Xiaoping*, pp. 302–25.

40. Stuart R. Schram, " 'Economics in Command?' Ideology and Policy since the Third Plenum, 1978–84," *China Quarterly* 99 (September 1984): 425–26.

41. *Beijing Review,* no. 40 (October 6, 1980): p. 21.

42. Liao Gailong (Liao Kai-lung), "Historical Experiences and Our Road of Development," part 2, a report on the history of the party delivered on October 25, 1980, at the National Party-School Forum, translated in *Issues & Studies* (November 1981): 93.

43. *Main Documents of the Third Session of the Fifth National People's Congress of the People's Republic of China* (Beijing: Foreign Languages Press, 1980), pp. 143–201.

44. "Appendices," ibid., pp. 209–45.

45. See David L. Shambaugh, *The Making of a Premier: Zhao Ziyang's Provincial Career* (Boulder, Colo.: Westview Press, 1984).

46. *Beijing Review* (July 21, 1980): 6.

47. *Beijing Review* (November 10, 1980): 3.

48. Special Procuratorate of the People's Republic of China, *The Indictment against Lin Biao–Jiang Qing Cliques*, English supplement (Hong Kong: Ta Kung Pao, 1980).

49. See James C. Hsiung, ed., with contributions by H. Lyman Miller, Hung-dah Chiu, and Lillian Craig Harris, *Symposium: The Trial of the "Gang of Four" and its Implication in China*, Occasional Papers/Reprints Series in Contemporary Asian Studies, no. 3 (University of Maryland School of Law, 1980).

50. See also David Bonavia, *Verdict in Peking: The Trial of the Gang of Four* (New York: G. P. Putnam's Sons, 1984).

51. Parris Chang, *Elite Conflict in Post-Mao China*, rev. ed., Occasional Papers/Reprints Series in Contemporary Asian Studies, no. 2 (University of Maryland School of Law, 1983), p. 24.

52. Domes, *Government and Politics of the PRC*, p. 176.

53. *Selected Works of Deng Xiaoping, China Report*, pp. 335–55.

54. Communiqué of the Sixth Plenary Session, adopted on June 29, 1981, in Central Committee, CPC, *Resolution on CPC History (1949–81)*, pp. 124–25.

55. Central Committee, CPC, *Resolution on CPC History (1949–81)*, p. 56.

56. Ibid., p. 57.

57. Ibid., p. 73.

58. Michael Weisskopf of the *Washington Post* had given an account of Liu

Qing's 196-page handwritten document. See James P. Sterba, Beijing, *New York Times*, September 22, 1981.

59. Xinhua (Beijing), September 30, 1981; text in *Beijing Review* (October 5, 1981): 10–11.

60. *Beijing Review* (October 19, 1981): 6.

61. *Beijing Review* (December 21, 1981): 6–36.

62. Ryosei Kokubun, "The Politics of Foreign Economic Policy-making in China: The Case of Plant Cancellations with Japan," *China Quarterly* 105 (March 1986): 19–44.

63. *Beijing Review* (June 7, 1982): 20–21.

64. *Beijing Review* (May 17, 1982): 3.

65. *Beijing Review* (June 14, 1982): 7.

66. *Beijing Review* (August 16, 1982): 4–5.

Chapter 14

1. *Beijing Review* (September 6, 1982): 5.

2. Deng still referred to the concept as the "so-called spiritual civilization" at that time. *Selected Works of Deng Xiaoping, China Report* (Arlington, Va.: Foreign Broadcast Information Service/Joint Publications Research Service, 1983), p. 262. Interestingly, the later official version of this talk does not use the term at all. See *Selected Works of Deng Xiaoping (1975–1982)* (Beijing: Foreign Languages Press, 1984), e.g., pp. 344–50.

3. Stuart R. Schram, "Economics in Command," *China Quarterly* 99 (September 1984): 433.

4. See, e.g., Stephen Uhalley, Jr., "The Reagan Administration Turnaround on China," in James C. Hsiung, ed., *Beyond China's Independent Foreign Policy: Challenge for the U.S. and Its Asian Allies* (New York: Praeger, 1985), pp. 55–70.

5. See Peter Berton, "A Turn in Sino-Soviet Relations?" ibid., pp. 32–35.

6. Membership on that commission had increased from 76 in December 1978 to about 132 by the time of the Twelfth Party Congress.

7. See Jurgen Domes, *The Government and Politics of the PRC* (Boulder, Colo.: Westview Press, 1985), pp. 184–85, and Wolfgang Bartke and Peter Schier, *China's New Party Leadership: Biographies and Analysis of the Twelfth Central Committee of the Chinese Communist Party* (Armonk, N.Y.: M. E. Sharpe, 1985), p. 11.

8. Ibid., p. 65.

9. Ibid., p. 71.

10. Ibid., p. 68.

11. Ibid., pp. 55–57.

12. Ibid., pp. 45–50.

13. Ibid., p. 49.

14. The article was entitled "Communist Ideology Is the Core of Socialist Spiritual Civilization," in *Foreign Broadcast Information Service*, September 29, 1982, p. K3.

15. *People's Daily* (Beijing), April 13, 1983, p. 5; *Foreign Broadcast Information Service*, April 14, 1983, pp. K1–K5.

16. Xinhua (Beijing), July 26, 1983; *Foreign Broadcast Information Service*, July 26, 1983, p. K1.

17. David Bonavia, "Back to School," *Far Eastern Economic Review* (September 22, 1983): 50.

18. "Report on the Sixth Five-Year Plan," November 30, 1982, *Beijing Review* (December 20, 1982): 10–35.

19. Zhao's public admission of the poor performance of the Chinese economy in the past was refreshing and affords interesting comparisons with other evaluations of the same performance. See Ramon H. Myers, "How Well Did American Economists Understand Communist China's Economy?" *Issues & Studies* (November 1984): 33–49.

20. *Issues & Studies* (December 27, 1982): 10–18.

21. See Byron Weng, "Some Key Aspects of the 1982 Draft Constitution of the PRC," *China Quarterly* 91 (September 1982): 492–506, for a good analysis of this version of the constitution. A sobering study that puts the latest changes into fuller perspective is John F. Copper, Franz Michael, and Wu Yuan-li, *Human Rights in Post-Mao China* (Boulder, Colo.: Westview Press, 1985).

22. *Beijing Review* (January 10, 1983): 5.

23. *Asiaweek* (January 4, 1985): 68.

24. *Asiaweek* (May 30, 1983): 5.

25. A complete listing of the new officers is in *Asiaweek* (June 27, 1983): 9, 12.

26. Report delivered June 6, 1983, *Asiaweek* (July 4, 1983): ii–xxiv.

27. *Beijing Review* (August 15, 1983): 7.

28. Xinhua (Beijing), July 13, 1983; *Foreign Broadcast Information Service*, July 14, 1983, pp. K9–K10.

29. Xinhua (Beijing), September 2, 1983; *Foreign Broadcast Information Service*, September 6, 1983, pp. K1–K2.

30. Agence France-Presse (Hong Kong), October 21, 1983; *Foreign Broadcast Information Service*, October 25, 1983, p. K6.

31. *Hongqi*, no. 18 (September 16, 1983): 2–8; *Foreign Broadcast Information Service*, October 21, 1983, pp. K14–K23.

32. Xinhua (Beijing), July 21, 1983; *Foreign Broadcast Information Service*, July 22, 1983, pp. K1–K4.

33. *Beijing Review* (September 19, 1983): 5.

34. *Beijing Review* (November 7, 1983): 5–6.

35. Text of the decision on party consolidation in *Beijing Review* (October 17, 1983): i–xii.

36. Xinhua (Beijing), October 23, 1983; *Foreign Broadcast Information Service*, October 24, 1984, pp. K2–K6.

37. Xinhua (Beijing), November 1, 1983; *Foreign Broadcast Information Service*, November 2, 1983, pp. K1–K2.

38. *Beijing Review* (November 28, 1983): 5.

39. *New York Times*, January 24, 1984, p. A1.

40. Xinhua (Beijing), July 15, 1984; *Foreign Broadcast Information Service*, July 16, 1984, pp. K1–K2.

41. See Melanie Manion, "The Cadre Management System, Post-Mao: The Appointment, Promotion, Transfer and Removal of Party and State Leaders," *China Quarterly* 102 (June 1985): 203–4.

42. Full text in *Beijing Review* (June 11, 1984): i–xiv.

43. See the translation of Document No. 1 for 1984 and the commentaries on the document by Joyce Kallgren, Kenneth Lieberthal, Bruce Stone, and Y. Y. Kueh in *China Quarterly* 101 (March 1985): 104–42.

44. Ibid., p. 122.

45. Ibid., p. 124.

46. Jonathan Unger, "The Decollectivization of the Chinese Countryside: A Survey of Twenty-eight Villages," *Pacific Affairs* 58 (Winter 1985–1986): 588.

47. Y. Y. Kueh, "The Economics of the 'Second Land Reform' in China," *China Quarterly* 101 (March 1985): 127.

48. Ibid., p. 106.

49. *People's Daily* (Beijing), October 15, 1984, p. 1; *Foreign Broadcast Information Service*, October 19, 1984, pp. K6–K7.

50. *Beijing Review* (May 28, 1984): 34.

51. Xinhua (Beijing), July 1, 1984; *Foreign Broadcast Information Service*, July 2, 1984, p. K4.

52. Mary Lee, *Far Eastern Economic Review* (December 20, 1984): 38–39.

53. *China Daily* (Beijing), July 21, 1984, p. 1.

54. *People's Daily* (Beijing), November 13, 1984, p. 1; *Foreign Broadcast Information Service*, November 14, 1984, pp. K7–K9.

55. Quoting David Chen, *South China Morning Post* (Hong Kong), September 11, 1987, pp. 1–2; *Foreign Broadcast Information Service*, September 11, 1987, pp. 9–10.

56. *China Daily*, September 5, 1984, p. 4; *Foreign Broadcast Information Service*, September 5, 1984, pp. K2–K3.

57. Full text of this joint declaration is in the *Beijing Review* (October 1, 1984), centerfold.

58. Xinhua (Beijing), October 20, 1984; *Foreign Broadcast Information Service*, October 22, 1984, p. K1.

59. See Robert F. Dernberger, "Economic Policy and Performance," in *China's Economy Looks Toward the Year 2000*, vol. 1, *The Four Modernizations*, Selected Papers Submitted to the Joint Economic Committee, Congress of the United States (Washington, D.C.: U.S. Government Printing Office, 1986): 41.

Chapter 15

1. See "Second Stage Rural Structural Reform," *Beijing Review* (June 24, 1985): 15–17.

2. Announced by the Ministry of Public Security on November 2, 1984. Another 195 persons reportedly still remained in jail or were undergoing forced labor for actual offenses committed. Xinhua (Beijing), November 2, 1984; *Foreign Broadcast Information Service*, November 5, 1984.

3. See Yu Yu-lin, "Mainland China's Political Structure since the Third Plenary Session of the CCP's 12th Central Committee," *Issues & Studies* 22 (July 1986): 48–49.

4. Ibid., referring specifically to an article of December 12, p. 49.

5. *Asiaweek* (January 18, 1985): 18.

6. *Beijing Review* (February 14, 1985): 6.

7. *People's Daily* (Beijing), April 14, 1985; *Foreign Broadcast Information Service*, April 15, 1985, p. K1.

8. Xinhua (Beijing), February 8, 1985; *Foreign Broadcast Information Service*, February 11, 1985, p. K20.

9. Nie Lisheng, "State Closes 9,000 Firms Run by Cadres," *China Daily* (Beijing), October 28, 1985, p. 3.

10. See comments by Bo Yibo, *Far Eastern Economic Review* (February 14, 1985): 8.

11. Xinhua (Beijing), July 14, 1985; *Foreign Broadcast Information Service*, July 15, 1985, p. K1.

12. The expression was first used in Deng's talk with visiting Japanese Liberal Democratic Party vice president Susumu Nikaido on March 28, 1985. *Beijing Review* (April 8, 1985): 6.

13. Full text of Zhao's report is in *Beijing Review* (April 22, 1985): i–xv.

14. *Beijing Review* (June 17, 1985): 6. This confirmed the disclosure made by Hu Yaobang on April 19, 1985, during his visit to New Zealand. Hu had made his own announcement even before the decision was formally adopted by the Military Affairs Commission during its enlarged meeting from May 23 to June 6, 1985. See David Bonavia, *Far Eastern Economic Review* (August 22, 1985): 45.

15. *Zhongguo Xinwen She* (Beijing), September 18, 1985; *Foreign Broadcast Information Service*, September 19, 1985, p. K18.

16. *Beijing Review* (June 17, 1985): 8.

17. See William de B. Mill, "Leadership Change in China's Provinces," *Problems of Communism* 34, no. 3 (1985): 24; and David S. G. Goodman, "The National CCP Conference of September 1985 and China's Leadership Changes," *China Quarterly* 105 (March 1986): 128.

18. *Beijing Review* (June 10, 1985): 15.

19. Wendy Lin, *Chronicle of Higher Education* (June 26, 1985): 1, 28; and (September 11, 1985): 85, 87.

20. *Beijing Review* (September 23, 1985): 6–7.

21. *Wall Street Journal*, September 20, 1985, p. 22.

22. See Louis Ladany, *Wall Street Journal*, September 30, 1985, p. 15.

23. *Beijing Review* (September 30, 1985): 7.

24. *Guangming Daily*, October 30, 1985, publishing excerpts from an article in *China Social Science*, no. 5; *Foreign Broadcast Information Service*, November 4, 1985, p. K1.

25. David Bonavia, *Far Eastern Economic Review* (June 27, 1985): 44.

26. Xinhua (Beijing), November 18, 1985; *Foreign Broadcast Information Service*, November 19, 1985, p. K1.

27. Goodman, "National CCP Conference of September 1985," 128–29.

28. "Streamlining Government Institutions is a Revolution," January 13, 1983, in *Selected Works by Deng Xiaoping* (Beijing: Foreign Languages Press, 1984), p. 304.

29. See, for example, David Zweig, "Opposition to Change in Rural China: The System of Responsibility and People's Communes," *Asian Survey* (July 1983): 879–900.

30. An Zhiguo, "Party Shifts Consolidation to Countryside," *Beijing Review* (December 30, 1985): 4.

31. Ibid.

32. John P. Burns, "Local Cadre Accommodation to the 'Responsibility System' in Rural China," *Pacific Affairs* 58 (Winter 1985–1986): 607–25.

33. Jean C. Oi, "Commercializing China's Rural Cadres," *Problems of Communism* (September–October 1986): 15.

34. David M. Bachman, *Chen Yun and the Chinese Political System* (Berkeley: University of California Institute of East Asian Studies, Center for Chinese Studies, 1985), pp. 161–64. Bachman usefully includes Zhao Ziyang in the comparisons between Deng and Chen.

35. Xinhua, November 25, 1985; *Foreign Broadcast Information Service*, November 27, 1985, p. K5.

36. *Beijing Review* (February 3, 1986): 6–7.

37. Mary Lee, *Far Eastern Economic Review* (January 23, 1986): 28; and (January 30, 1986): 22–24.

38. His son, Hu Shiying, was imprisoned for embezzling education funds on

March 7, 1986. See *Pai Hsing* (Hong Kong), May 1, 1986, pp. 6–7; in *Foreign Broadcast Information Service*, May 12, 1986, p. W1.

39. Agence France-Presse (Beijing), June 25, 1986; in *Foreign Broadcast Information Service*, June 26, 1986, p. K1; and *Zhongguo Xinwen She* (Beijing), February 19, 1986; in *Foreign Broadcast Information Service*, February 21, p. K1.

40. Zhao Ziyang's report on the plan, delivered on March 25, 1986, is in *Foreign Broadcast Information Service*, April 21, 1986, pp. i–xx; major excerpts from the plan are in *Foreign Broadcast Information Service*, April 28, 1986, pp. i–xxiii.

41. *Beijing Review* (April 28, 1986): i–xxiii.

42. *Beijing Review* (April 21, 1986): 5.

43. See *Liaowang Overseas Edition* (Hong Kong), July 21, 1986, pp. 3–4; in *Foreign Broadcast Information Service*, July 23, 1986, p. K1; and Chi Fulin, "Symposium on Theory of Political Structural Reform," *Beijing Review* (November 17, 1986): 14–15.

44. *Beijing Review* (September 29, 1986): 28–29.

45. See Stephen Morgan et al., "Special Report," *Standard* (Hong Kong), July 13, 1986, p. 5; in *Foreign Broadcast Information Service*, July 16, 1986, p. W1.

46. *Beijing Review* (September 8, 1986): 25–27.

47. Interview in *Beijing Review* (September 15, 1986): 16–17.

48. *Beijing Review* (October 6, 1986): i–viii.

49. See *Beijing Review* (December 22, 1986): 5.

50. *Beijing Review* (December 22, 1986): 5.

51. In *Beijing Review* (May 19, 1986): 14, 23.

52. Full text of speech in *Beijing Review* (November 17, 1986): 21–24.

53. See Robert Delfs, *Far Eastern Economic Review* (December 11, 1986): 51–52.

54. *Far Eastern Economic Review* (December 1, 1986): 34.

55. See, for example, Lo Ping, "The Huangpu Jiang Roars On," *Cheng Ming* (Hong Kong), January 1, 1987; in *Foreign Broadcast Information Service*, January 8, 1987, pp. K1–K9.

56. *Beijing Review* (January 26, 1987): 5.

57. See Chang Chieh-feng, "Documents Nos. 2 to 6 Reveal Current Situation . . . ," *Pai Hsing* (Hong Kong), February 16, 1987; in *Foreign Broadcast Information Service*, February 17, 1987, pp. K1–K18.

58. On January 6, 1987; translated and reprinted in *Beijing Review* (January 19, 1987): 15.

59. *Beijing Review* (February 16, 1987): 9.

60. See An Zhiguo, *Beijing Review* (February 9, 1987): 4.

61. Text of Zhao's speech in *Beijing Review* (February 9, 1987): 26–29.

62. *Agence France-Presse* (Beijing) February 13, 1987; in *Foreign Broadcast Information Service*, February 17, 1987, p. K26.

63. *Hong Kong Standard*, February 18, 1987, p. 8; in *Foreign Broadcast Information Service*, February 18, 1987, p. K1.

64. See *Agence France-Presse* (Beijing), February 26, 1987; in *Foreign Broadcast Information Service*, February 26, 1987, pp. K1–K2.

65. Full text in *Beijing Review* (April 20, 1987): i–xx (centerfold).

66. See Yau Shing Mu in *Hong Kong Standard*, September 9, 1987, p. 1; in *Foreign Broadcast Information Service*, September 9, 1987, p. 16.

67. See *Ching Pao* (Hong Kong), June 10, 1987, pp. 34–38; in *Foreign Broadcast Information Service*, June 18, 1987, p. K8; also Lo Ping, "Notes on the Northern Journey," *Cheng Ming* (Hong Kong), August 1, 1987, pp. 6–10; in *Foreign Broadcast Information Service*, August 7, 1987, pp. K1–K3.

68. *Xinhua* (Beijing), July 9, 1987; in *Foreign Broadcast Information Service*, July 10, 1987, pp. K1–K8; see also Lo Ping, "Notes on the Northern Journey."

69. See Kung Shuang-yin, "Oppose 'Leftism,' Oppose 'Ossification'—Current Main Themes in the Chinese Press," *Wen Wei Pao* (Hong Kong), June 15, 1987, p. 1; in *Foreign Broadcast Information Service*, June 16, 1987, pp. K20–K21.

70. Fu Chung, "Hu Yaobang Comes to Political Impasse, Bo Yibo Escalates His Activities—No. 8 Storm Signal on the Eve of the 13th Party Congress," *Ching Pao* (Hong Kong), July 10, 1987, pp. 28–32; in *Foreign Broadcast Information Service*, July 15, 1987, p. K1.

71. For example, on May 22–23, 1987, the Economic Structural Reform Research Institute invited 200 workers from fourteen trades to give their opinions. The workers candidly said that party style did not change much after the campaign. See ibid., p. K2. For the full text of Bo Yibo's report of May 26, 1987, see *Xinhua* (Beijing), May 31, 1987; in *Foreign Broadcast Information Service*, June 2, 1987, pp. K3–K18.

72. *Xinhua* (Beijing), May 31, 1987; in *Foreign Broadcast Information Service*, June 2, 1987, pp. K3–K18; see also *Beijing Review* (June 8, 1987): 6–7.

73. See Chen Ming, "Wang Renzhi Criticized by Lower Levels," *Cheng Ming* (Hong Kong), June 3, 1987; in *Foreign Broadcast Information Service*, June 5, 1987, pp. K7–K8.

74. Terry Cheng, *South China Morning Post* (Hong Kong), June 12, 1987, pp. 1–2; in *Foreign Broadcast Information Service*, June 12, 1987, p. K1.

75. *Cheng Ming* (Hong Kong), July 1, 1987, p. 3; in *Foreign Broadcast Information Service*, July 2, 1987, pp. K11–K12.

76. Deng made his comments during his meeting with Stefan Korosec, member of the Presidium of the Central Committee of the League of Communists of Yugoslavia. *Beijing Review* (August 24, 1987): 15–16.

77. *Foreign Broadcast Information Service*, July 2, 1987, pp. K12–K13.

78. *Kyodo* (Hong Kong), November 8, 1987, referring to Hong Kong's Chinese-

language *Asia Weekly* as its source; in *Foreign Broadcast Information Service*, November 9, 1987, p. 16.

79. *Beijing Review* (July 6, 1987): 6.

80. This is based on a comparison of the versions published in *Foreign Broadcast Information Service*, July 6, 1983, p. K1, and July 7, 1987, p. K22.

81. *Beijing Review* (June 29, 1987): 14–17, and (July 13, 1987): 6–7.

82. Published by Chunqiu Publishing House. See Chen Xiangan, in *Xinhua* (Beijing); in *Foreign Broadcast Information Service*, July 8, 1987, p. K22.

83. Juan Chi-hung, "Graduates Current Class Will First Be Assigned to Grass Roots," *Wen Wei Po* (Hong Kong), July 1, 1987, p. 2; in *Foreign Broadcast Information Service*, July 1, 1987, p. K5.

84. The new restrictions on studying abroad were decided on in December 1986, but their publication awaited the return of a delegation to the United States which sought to persuade the U.S. government to compel Chinese students to return to China. See Wu Xue, in *China Daily* (Beijing), June 29, 1987, p. 3; in *Foreign Broadcast Information Service*, July 2, 1987, p. K14.

85. See, for example, Edward A. Gargan, *New York Times* (Beijing), July 5, 1987, p. E3.

86. *The Free China Journal* (Taipei), July 27, 1987, p. 4.

87. The slogans appeared simultaneously in Chongwenmen, Xidan, and Dongsi in Beijing. See *Cheng Ming* (Hong Kong), August 1, 1987, pp. 12–13; in *Foreign Broadcast Information Service*, August 5, 1987, p. K12.

88. See, for example, Louise do Rosario, *Far Eastern Economic Review* (October 29, 1987): 76.

89. See Chiang Wei-wen, "Major Decision at a Crucial Moment in Beijing," *Kung Chiao Ching* (Hong Kong), July 16, 1987, pp. 6–9; in *Foreign Broadcast Information Service*, July 23, 1987, p. 7.

90. *Beijing Review* (August 3, 1987): 7.

91. See, for example, Jen Chien-pai's analysis in *Cheng Ming* (Hong Kong), September 1, 1987, pp. 12–14; in *Foreign Broadcast Information Service*, September 8, 1987, pp. 22–25.

92. See Yau Shing Mu, *Hong Kong Standard*, September 9, 1987, p. 1.

93. *Xinhua* (Beijing), September 2, 1987; in *Foreign Broadcast Information Service*, September 2, 1987, p. 9.

94. *Xinhua* (Beijing), October 20, 1987; in *Foreign Broadcast Information Service*, October 20, 1987, p. 6.

95. For translations of the full text see *Foreign Broadcast Information Service, China: Supplement*, October 26, 1987, pp. 10–34; and *Beijing Review* (November 9–15, 1987): 23–49 (centerfold).

96. *Xinhua* (Beijing), in English, October 27, 1987.

97. Comparing the entire Central Committees—that is, both members and alternate members—the average age of the new 285-person committee is said

to be 55, or about four years younger. See *Beijing Review* (November 16–22, 1987): 6.

98. *South China Morning Post* (Hong Kong), November 7, 1987, p. 1; in *Foreign Broadcast Information Service*, November 9, 1987, pp. 18–19.

99. Ibid.

100. *Beijing Review* (November 16–22, 1987): 33–34.

101. *Beijing Review* (November 9–15, 1987): 11.

102. Liu Jui-shao, "CPC Central Committee Holds Work Conference," *Wen Wei Pao* (Hong Kong), November 18, 1987, p. 1; in *Foreign Broadcast Information Service*, November 18, 1987, p. 10.

103. *Ta Kung Pao* (Hong Kong), June 28, 1987, p. 1; in *Foreign Broadcast Information Service*, June 29, 1987, p. K2.

104. In November 1987 China Central Television reported that the natural population growth rate in 1987 was 14.8 per thousand, up from 14.03 per thousand in 1986 and a substantial increase over the rate of 11.23 per thousand in 1985. The population had been increasing by an average of almost 13 million annually for the previous five years. On July 1, 1987, the population of China, excluding Taiwan, was 1,072,330,000, an increase of 64.15 million since the 1982 census (*United Press International* [Beijing], November 11, 1987).

105. See Peter F. Drucker, *The Wall Street Journal*, November 19, 1987, p. 30.

Selected Bibliography

This bibliography includes only books, monographs, and certain documents selected from an extensive and burgeoning literature on Chinese communism. The publications are listed in the two separate categories *Pre-1949 China* and *Post-1949 China*. An even vaster periodical literature exists, some of which is exceedingly important for gaining insight into particular aspects of this often elusive subject. Some of those sources have been cited in the text or in the endnotes. Regretfully, they cannot be repeated here, nor supplemented by the many more useful studies that have become available. However, I have listed here the more important periodicals.

Chinese language:

Ban Yue Tan (Fortnightly Talks)
Guowuyuan Gongbao (Bulletin of the State Council)
Hongqi (Red Flag)
Liaowang (Outlook)
Renmin Ribao (People's Daily)
Xiandaihua (Modernization)
Xuexi yu Pipan (Study & Criticism)
Zhongguo Zhishi Fenzi (The Chinese Intellectual)(New York)

English and other languages:

Asian Survey (Berkeley, Calif.)
Asiaweek (Hong Kong)

Australian Journal of Chinese Studies (Canberra)
Beijing Review (China)
Bulletin of Concerned Asian Scholars (Boulder, Colo.)
China Aktuell: PRC Official Activities
China Business Review (Washington, D.C.)
China Daily (China and elsewhere)
China News Analysis (Hong Kong)
China Quarterly (London)
China Reconstructs (China)
China Spring (New York)
China Spring Digest (New York)
Chinese Law and Government (White Plains, N.Y.)
Communist China Problem Research Series (Hong Kong)
Contemporary China (Columbia University, N.Y.)
Current Background (Hong Kong)
Current Scene (Hong Kong)
Far Eastern Economic Review (Hong Kong)
Far Eastern Quarterly
Foreign Broadcast Information Service (FBIS), Daily Report: People's Republic of China (Washington, D.C.)
Issues & Studies (Taibei)
Journal of Asian Studies
Journal of Chinese Studies (American Association for Chinese Studies)
Journal of Northeast Asian Affairs (George Washington University, Washington, D.C.)
Mainland China Review (Hong Kong)
Modern China (UCLA, Calif.)
Newsletter (Center for Chinese Research Materials, Washington, D.C.)
Pacific Affairs (University of British Columbia, Vancouver)
Papers on China (Harvard)
Problems of Communism (Washington, D.C.)
Republican China (University of Illinois)
Social Sciences in China (China)
Summary of World Broadcasts, Part 3: The Far East (London)
Survey of China Mainland Magazines (SCMM) (Hong Kong)
Survey of the China Mainland Press (SCMP) Hong Kong

Pre-1949 China

Adelman, Jonathan R. *The Revolutionary Armies: The Historical Development of the Soviet and Chinese People's Liberation Armies.* Westport, Conn.: Greenwood Press, 1980.

Alitto, Guy S. *The Last Confucian: Liang Shu-ming and the Chinese Dilemma of Modernity.* Berkeley: University of California Press, 1979.

Bertram, James. *First Act in China.* New York: Viking Press, 1938.

———. *Unconquered: Journal of a Year's Adventures among the Fighting Peasants of North China.* New York: John Day, 1939.

Bianco, Lucien. *Origins of the Chinese Revolution 1915–1949.* Stanford, Calif.: Stanford University Press, 1971.

Borg, Dorothy. *American Policy and the Chinese Revolution 1925–1928.* New York: American Institute of Pacific Relations, 1947.

Borisov, O. (Borisov-Rachmanin). *The Soviet Union and the Manchurian Revolutionary Base, 1945–1949.* Moscow: Progress Publishers, 1977.

Brandt, Conrad. *Stalin's Failure in China.* Cambridge, Mass.: Harvard University Press, 1958.

Brandt, Conrad, Benjamin Schwartz, and John K. Fairbank. *A Documentary History of Chinese Communism.* London: Allen & Unwin, 1952.

Braun, Otto. *A Comintern Agent in China, 1932–1939* (London: C. Hurst & Co., 1982).

Brown, David G. *Partnership with China: Sino-Foreign Joint Ventures in Historical Perspective.* Boulder, Colo.: Westview Press, 1985.

Bullard, Monte. *China's Political/Military Evolution.* Boulder, Colo.: Westview Press, 1985.

Chan, F. Gilbert, ed. *China at the Crossroads: Nationalists and Communists 1927–1949.* Boulder, Colo.: Westview Press, 1980.

Chan, F. Gilbert, and Thomas H. Etzold, eds. *China in the 1920s: Nationalism and Revolution.* New York: New Viewpoints, 1976.

Chang Kou-t'ao. *The Autobiography of Chang Kuo-t'ao.* Vol. 1, *The Rise of the Chinese Communist Party 1921–1927.* Lawrence: University Press of Kansas, 1971.

———. *The Autobiography of Chang Kuo-t'ao.* Vol. 2, *The Rise of the Chinese Communist Party 1928–1938.* Lawrence: University Press of Kansas, 1972.

Chen Chang-feng. *On the Long March with Chairman Mao.* Beijing: Foreign Languages Press, 1972.

Chen Po-ta. *Mao Tse-tung on the Chinese Revolution: Written in Commemoration of the 30th Anniversary of the Communist Party of China.* Beijing: Foreign Languages Press, 1953.

———. *Notes on Ten Years of Civil War (1927–1936).* Beijing: Foreign Languages Press, 1954.

Chen Yung-fa. *Making Revolution: The Communist Movement in Eastern and Central China, 1937–1945.* Berkeley: University of California Press, 1986.

Ch'en Jerome. *The Military-Gentry Coalition: China under the Warlords.* Toronto: University of Toronto-York University, Joint Centre on Modern East Asia, 1979.

Ch'en Kung-po. *The Communist Movement in China.* New York: Columbia University East Asian Institute, 1960.

Chesneaux, Jean. *Secret Societies in China in the 19th and 20th Centuries.* Hong Kong: Heinemann Educational Books (Asia) Ltd., 1971.

Chesneaux, Jean, Francoise Le Barbier, and Marie-Claire Bergere. *China from the 1911 Revolution to Liberation.* New York: Pantheon Books, 1977.

Ch'i Hsi-sheng. *Warlord Politics in China 1916–1928.* Stanford, Calif.: Stanford University Press, 1976.

———. *Nationalist China at War: Military Defeats and Political Collapse, 1937–1945.* Ann Arbor, Mich.: University of Michigan Press, 1982.

Chiang Kai-shek. *The Collected Wartime Messages of Generalissimo Chiang Kai-shek 1937–1945.* 2 vols. New York: John Day, 1946.

———. *Soviet Russia in China: A Summing-up at Seventy.* New York: Farrar, Straus & Cudahy, 1957; rev. abr. ed., 1965.

Davis, Russell. "Moscow and the Chinese Communist Party: The Comintern and Sovietniki in China, 1919–1943." M. A. thesis, University of Hawaii Asian Studies Program, Honolulu, 1985.

Eastman, Lloyd E. *The Abortive Revolution: China under Nationalist Rule 1927–1937.* Cambridge, Mass.: Harvard University Press, 1974.

———. *Seeds of Destruction: Nationalist China in War and Revolution, 1937–1949.* Stanford, Calif.: Stanford University Press, 1984.

Elegant, Robert S. *China's Red Leaders: Political Biographies of the Chinese Communist Leaders.* London: Bodley Head Ltd., 1952.

Ellison, Herbert J., ed. *The Sino-Soviet Conflict: A Global Perspective.* Seattle: University of Washington Press, 1982.

Elvin, Mark. *The Pattern of the Chinese Past.* Stanford, Calif.: Stanford University Press, 1973.

Esherick, Joseph W. *Reform and Revolution in China: The 1911 Revolution in Hunan and Hubei.* Berkeley: University of California Press, 1976.

———, ed. *Lost Chance in China: The World War II Despatches of John S. Service.* New York: Vintage Books, 1975.

Eudin, Xenia Joukoff, and Robert C. North. *Soviet Russia and the East, 1920–1927: A Documentary Survey.* Stanford, Calif.: Stanford University Press, 1957.

Feigon, Lee. *Chen Duxiu, Founder of the Chinese Communist Party.* Princeton, N.J.: Princeton University Press, 1983.

Feuerwerker, Albert. *China's Early Industrialization.* Cambridge, Mass.: Harvard University Press, 1958.

———. *The Chinese Economy, ca. 1870–1911.* Ann Arbor: University of Michigan Center for Chinese Studies, 1969.

———. *The Chinese Economy, 1912–1949.* Ann Arbor: University of Michigan Center for Chinese Studies, 1968.

Feuerwerker, Albert, and S. Cheng. *Chinese Communist Studies of Modern Chinese History.* Cambridge, Mass.: Harvard University Press, 1961.

Fitzgerald, C. P. *The Birth of Communist China.* Baltimore, Md.: Penguin Books, 1964.

Furth, Charlotte, ed. *The Limits of Change.* Cambridge, Mass.: Harvard University Press, 1976.

Galbiati, Fernando. *P'eng P'ai and the Hai-Lu-feng Soviet.* Stanford, Calif.: Stanford University Press, 1985.

Gasster, Michael. *China's Struggle to Modernize.* New York: Knopf, 1972.

———. *Chinese Intellectuals and the Revolution of 1911: The Birth of Modern Chinese Radicalism.* Seattle: University of Washington Press, 1969.

Gelder, George Stuart, ed. *The Chinese Communists.* London: V. Gollancz Ltd., 1946.

Gillin, Donald. *Warlord: Yen Hsi-shan in Shansi Province, 1911–1949.* Princeton, N.J. Princeton University Press, 1967.

Griffin, Patricia E. *The Chinese Communist Treatment of Counterrevolutionaries 1924–1949.* Princeton, N.J.: Princeton University Press, 1976.

Guillermaz, Jacques. *A History of the Chinese Communist Party 1921–1949.* New York: Random House, 1972.

Harrison, James Pinckney. *The Communists and Chinese Peasant Rebellions: A Study in the Rewriting of Chinese History.* New York: Atheneum, 1969.

———. *The Long March to Power: A History of the Chinese Communist Party, 1921–72.* New York: Praeger, 1972.

Hinton, William. *Fanshen: A Documentary of Revolution in a Chinese Village.* New York: Vintage Books, 1968.

Hofheinz, Roy, Jr. *The Broken Wave: The Chinese Communist Peasant Movement, 1922–1928.* Cambridge, Mass.: Harvard University Press, 1977.

Holubnychy, Lydia. *Michael Borodin and the Chinese Revolution, 1923–1925.* Ann Arbor, Mich. University Microfilms International, 1979.

Hou Chi-ming. *Foreign Investment and Economic Development in China, 1840–1937.* Cambridge, Mass.: Harvard University Press, 1965.

Hsueh Chun-tu. *The Chinese Communist Movement 1921–1937: An Annotated Bibliography of Selected Materials in the Chinese Collection of the Hoover Institution on War, Revolution, and Peace.* Stanford, Calif.: Hoover Institution Press, 1960.

———. *The Chinese Communist Movement 1937–1949: An Annotated Bib-*

liography of Selected Materials in the Chinese Collection of the Hoover Institution on War, Revolution, and Peace. Stanford, Calif.: Hoover Institution Press, 1962.

Hu Ch'iao-mu. *Thirty Years of the Communist Party of China.* Beijing: Foreign Languages Press, 1959.

Huang, Philip. *Peasant Economy and Social Change in North China.* Stanford, Calif.: Stanford University Press, 1985.

Huang, Philip C. C., Lynda Schaefer Bell, and Kathy Lemons Walker. *Chinese Communists and Rural Society, 1927–1934.* Berkeley: University of California Center for Chinese Studies, 1978.

Isaacs, Harold Robert. *The Tragedy of the Chinese Revolution.* 2d rev. New York: Atheneum, 1966.

Israel, John. *The Chinese Student Movement, 1927–1937: A Bibliographical Essay Based on the Resources of the Hoover Institution.* Stanford, Calif.: Hoover Institution Press, 1959.

Israel, John, and Donald W. Klein. *Rebels and Bureaucrats: China's December 9ers.* Berkeley: University of California Press, 1976.

Jacobs, Daniel Norman. *Borodin, Stalin's Man in China.* Cambridge, Mass.: Harvard University Press, 1981.

Jordan, Donald A. *The Northern Expedition: China's National Revolution of 1926–1928.* Honolulu: University Press of Hawaii, 1976.

Kataoka, Tetsuya. *Resistance and Revolution in China: The Communists and the Second United Front.* Berkeley: University of California Press, 1974.

Kim, Ilpyong J. *The Politics of Chinese Communism: Kiangsi under the Soviets.* Berkeley: University of California Press, 1973.

Kun, Bela, ed. *Fundamental Laws of the Chinese Soviet Republic.* New York: International Publishers, 1934.

Kuo, Warren. *Analytical History of the Chinese Communist Party.* Taibei: Institute of International Relations, 1966.

Lary, Diana. *Region and Nation: The Kwangsi Clique in Chinese Politics 1925–1937.* London: Cambridge University Press, 1974.

Lawrence, Anthony. *China: The Long March.* Hong Kong: International Publishing Corporation, 1986.

Lee Chong-Sik. *Revolutionary Struggle in Manchuria: Chinese Communism and Soviet Interest, 1922–1945.* Berkeley: University of California Press, 1983.

Leng Shao-chuan and Norman D. Palmer. *Sun Yat-sen and Communism.* New York: Praeger, 1961.

Leong Sow-Teng. *Sino-Soviet Diplomatic Relations, 1917–1926.* Honolulu: University Press of Hawaii, 1976.

Levenson, Joseph Richmond. *Confucian China and Its Modern Fate: A Trilogy.* Berkeley: University of California Press, 1968.

Levine, Steven I. *Anvil of Victory: The Communist Revolution in Manchuria, 1945–1948.* New York: Columbia University Press, 1987.

Lewis, Charlton M. *Prologue to the Chinese Revolution: The Transformation of Ideas and Institutions in Hunan Province, 1891–1907.* Cambridge, Mass.: Harvard University Press, 1976.

Li Chien-nung. *The Political History of China 1840–1928.* New York: Van Nostrand, 1956.

Liao Kai-lung (Liao Gailong). *From Yenan to Peking: The Chinese People's War of Liberation from Reconstruction to the First Five-Year Plan.* Beijing: Foreign Languages Press, 1954.

Liao Kuang Sheng. *Antiforeignism and Modernization in China, 1860–1980.* New York: St. Martin's Press, 1984.

Lin Yu-sheng. *The Crisis of Chinese Consciousness: Radical Antitraditionalism in the May Fourth Era.* Madison: University of Wisconsin Press, 1979.

Liu Chun-jo. *Controversies in Modern Chinese Intellectual History: An Analytic Bibliography of Periodical Articles Mainly of the May Fourth and Post–May Fourth Era.* Cambridge, Mass.: Harvard University Press, 1964.

Liu, F. F. *A Military History of Modern China 1924–1949.* Princeton, N.J.: Princeton University Press, 1956.

Loh Pichon Pei Yung, ed. *The Kuomintang Debacle of 1949: Collapse or Conquest?* Boston: D. C. Heath, 1965.

Lotveit, Trygve. *Chinese Communism 1931–1934: Experience in Civil Government.* Scandinavian Institute of Asian Studies Monograph Series, no. 16. Lund, Sweden: Studentliteratur, 1973.

Lowe, Donald M. *The Function of "China" in Marx, Lenin, and Mao.* Berkeley: University of California Press, 1966.

Marks, Robert B. *Rural Revolution in South China: Peasants and the Making of History in Haifeng County, 1850–1930.* Madison: University of Wisconsin Press, 1984.

McDonald, Angus W., Jr. *The Urban Origins of Rural Revolution: Elite and the Masses in Hunan Province, China, 1911–1927.* Berkeley: University of California Press, 1978.

McLane, Charles B. *Soviet Policy and the Chinese Communists, 1931–1946.* New York: Columbia University Press, 1958.

Melby, John Fremont. *The Mandate of Heaven: Record of a Civil War: China 1945–49.* Toronto: University of Toronto Press, 1968.

Metzger, Thomas A. *Escape from Predicament: Neo-Confucianism and China's Evolving Political Culture.* New York: Columbia University Press, 1977.

Mif, P. *Heroic China: Fifteen Years of the Communist Party of China.* New York: Workers' Library Publishers, 1937.

Myers, Ramon H. *The Chinese Economy: Past and Present.* Belmont, Calif.: Wadsworth, 1980.

——. *The Chinese Peasant Economy: Agricultural Development in Hopei and Shantung, 1890–1949.* Cambridge, Mass.: Harvard University Press, 1970.

Nathan, Andrew J. *Peking Politics, 1918–1923: Factionalism and the Failure of Constitutionalism.* Berkeley: University of California Press, 1976.

North, Robert C. *Kuomintang and Chinese Communist Elites.* Stanford, Calif.: Stanford University Press, 1952.

——. *Moscow and the Chinese Communists.* Stanford, Calif.: Stanford University Press, 1953.

Pepper, Suzanne. *Civil War in China: The Political Struggle 1945–1949.* Berkeley: University of California Press, 1978.

Perry, Elizabeth J. *Rebels and Revolutionaries in North China 1845–1945.* Stanford, Calif.: Stanford University Press, 1980.

Political School Communist Party History Instructional Research Office, eds. *Zhonggong dangshi jianghua* [Lectures on Chinese Communist history]. Beijing: People's Liberation Army Political School Publisher, 1986.

Price, Don C. *Russia and the Roots of the Chinese Revolution, 1896–1911.* Cambridge, Mass.: Harvard University Press, 1974.

Pye, Lucian W. *Warlord Politics: Conflict and Coalition in the Modernization of Republican China.* New York: Praeger, 1971.

Qian Wen-yuan. *The Great Inertia: Scientific Stagnation in Traditional China.* Beckenham, Eng.: Croom Helm, 1984.

Rankin, Mary Backus. *Early Chinese Revolutionaries: Radical Intellectuals in Shanghai and Chekiang, 1902–1911.* Cambridge, Mass.: Harvard University Press, 1971.

Rawski, Thomas G. *Economic Growth and Employment in China.* New York: Oxford University Press, 1979.

Reardon-Anderson, James. *Yenan and the Great Powers: The Origins of Chinese Communist Foreign Policy, 1944–1946.* New York: Columbia University Press, 1980.

Rigby, Richard W. *The May 30 Movement, Events and Themes.* Canberra: Australian National University Press, 1980.

Ronning, Chester. *A Memoir of China in Revolution: From the Boxer Rebellion to the People's Republic.* New York: Pantheon Books, 1974.

Rosenberg, William G., and Marilyn B. Young. *Transforming Russia and China: Revolutionary Struggle in the Twentieth Century.* New York: Oxford University Press, 1982.

Roy, Manabendra Nath. *My Experience in China.* Calcutta: Renaissance, 1945.

——. *Revolution and Counter-revolution in China.* Calcutta: Renaissance, 1946. (Translation of the 1930 German edition with two chapters added in 1939 and an epilogue in 1946.)

Rue, John E. *Mao Tse-tung in Opposition, 1927–1935.* Stanford, Calif.: Stanford University Press, 1966.

Salisbury, Harrison E. *The Long March: The Untold Story.* New York: Harper & Row, 1985.

Scalapino, Robert A., and George Yu. *Modern China and Its Revolutionary Process: Recurrent Challenges to the Traditional Order, 1850–1920.* Berkeley: University of California Press, 1985.

Schaller, Michael. *The United States and China in the Twentieth Century.* New York: Oxford University Press, 1979.

Schran, Peter. *Guerrilla Economy: The Development of the Shensi-Kansu-Ninghsia Border Region, 1937–1945.* Albany: State University of New York Press, 1976.

Schwartz, Benjamin. *Chinese Communism and the Rise of Mao.* Cambridge, Mass.: Harvard University Press, 1958.

———. *In Search of Wealth and Power.* Cambridge, Mass.: Harvard University Press, 1964.

Selden, Mark. *The Yenan Way in Revolutionary China.* Cambridge, Mass.: Harvard University Press, 1971.

Sheng Yueh. *Sun Yat-sen University in Moscow and the Chinese Revolution: A Personal Account.* Lawrence: University of Kansas Center for East Asian Studies, 1971.

Sheridan, James E. *China in Disintegration: The Republican Era in Chinese History, 1912–1949.* New York: Free Press, 1975.

———. *Chinese Warlord.* Stanford, Calif.: Stanford University Press, 1966.

Siao Emi. *Mao Tse-tung: His Childhood and Youth.* Bombay: People's Publishing House, 1953.

Siao-yu. *Mao tse-tung and I Were Beggars.* New York: Collier Books, 1973.

Sladkovskii, M. I., ed. *Noveishaia istoriia kitaia, 1928–1949* [Newest history of China, 1928–1949]. Institute of Far Eastern Studies, Soviet Academy of Sciences, Moscow: Nauka, 1984.

Smedley, Agnes. *Battle Hymn of China.* New York: DeCapo Press, 1975.

Snow, Edgar. *Red Star Over China.* New York: Modern Library, 1944.

———. *Random Notes on Red China (1936–1945).* Cambridge, Mass.: Harvard University Press, 1957.

Snow, Helen. *Inside Red China.* New York: Doubleday & Co., 1939.

Spence, Jonathan. *The Gate of Heavenly Peace.* New York: Viking Press, 1982.

Strong, Anna Louise. *China's Millions: The Revolutionary Struggles from 1927–1935.* New York: Knight Publishing Co., 1935.

Sutton, Donald S. *Provincial Militarism and the Chinese Republic: The Yunan Army, 1905–25.* Ann Arbor: University of Michigan Press, 1980.

Swarup, Shanti. *A Study of the Chinese Communist Movement.* London: Oxford University Press, 1966.

Tang, Peter S. H. *Russian and Soviet Policy in Manchuria and Outer Mongolia, 1911–1931.* Durham, N.C.: Duke University Press, 1959.

Thaxton, Ralph. *China Turned Rightside Up: Revolutionary Legitimacy in the Peasant World.* New Haven, Conn.: Yale University Press, 1983.

Thomas, S. Bernard. *Labor and the Chinese Revolution: Class Strategies and Contradictions of Chinese Communism, 1928–48.* Ann Arbor: University of Michigan Center for Chinese Studies, 1983.

———. *"Proletarian Hegemony" in the Chinese Revolution and the Canton Commune of 1927.* Ann Arbor: University of Michigan Center for Chinese Studies, 1975.

Thomas, Stephen C. *Foreign Intervention and China's Economic Development, 1870–1911.* Boulder, Colo.: Westview Press, 1983.

Thornton, Richard C. *China, A Political History 1917–1980.* Boulder, Colo.: Westview Press, 1982.

———. *The Comintern and the Chinese Communists, 1928–1931.* Seattle: University of Washington Press, 1969.

Tien Hung-mao. *Government and Politics in Kuomintang China 1927–1937.* Stanford, Calif.: Stanford University Press, 1972.

Topping, Seymour. *Journey Between Two Chinas.* New York: Harper & Row, 1972.

Trotskii, Lev. *Leon Trotsky on China.* New York: Monad Press, 1976.

Trotsky, Leon. *Problems of the Chinese Revolution.* New York: Paragon Book Reprint Corp., 1966.

Tucker, Nancy Bernkopf. *Patterns in the Dust: Chinese-American Relations and the Recognition Controversy, 1949–1950.* New York: Columbia University Press, 1983.

U.S. Department of State. *United States Relations with China: With Special Reference to the Period 1944–1949.* Washington, D.C.: U.S. Government Printing Office, 1949.

Van Slyke, Lyman P. *Enemies and Friends: The United Front in Chinese Communist History.* Stanford, Calif.: Stanford University Press, 1967.

Vincent, John Carter. *The Extraterritorial System in China: Final Phase.* Cambridge, Mass.: Harvard University Press, 1969.

Vladimirov, Petr Parfenovich. *China's Special Area 1942–1945.* Bombay: Allied Publishers, 1974.

Wakeman, Frederic, Jr. *History and Will: Philosophical Perspectives of Mao Tsetung's Thought.* Berkeley: University of California Press, 1973.

Wales, Nym. *Red Dust: Autobiographies of Chinese Communists as Told to Nym Wales.* Stanford, Calif.: Stanford University Press, 1952.

Waller, Derek J. *The Kiangsi Soviet Republic: Mao and the National Congresses of 1931 and 1934.* Berkeley: University of California Center for Chinese Studies, 1973.

Wang Fan-hsi. *Chinese Revolutionary: Memoirs 1919–1949.* New York: Oxford University Press, 1980.

Wang, Y. C. *Chinese Intellectuals and the West.* Chapel Hill: University of North Carolina Press, 1966.

Wei, William. *Counterrevolution in China: The Nationalists in Jiangxi during the Soviet Period.* Ann Arbor: University of Michigan Press, 1985.

White, Theodore, and Annalee Jacoby. *Thunder Out of China.* New York: Sloane Associates, 1946.

White, Theodore H. *China: The Roots of Madness.* New York: Bantam Books, 1969.

Whiting, Allen S. *Soviet Policies in China, 1917–1924.* New York: Columbia University Press, 1954.

Wilbur, Clarence Martin. *Chinese Sources on the History of the Chinese Communist Movement.* New York: Columbia University East Asian Institute, 1950.

——. *Sun Yat-sen: Frustrated Patriot.* New York: Columbia University Press, 1976.

Wilbur, Clarence Martin, ed., and Ichiro Shirato, compiler. *Japanese Sources on the History of the Chinese Communist Movement.* New York: Columbia University East Asian Institute, 1953.

Wilbur, Clarence Martin and Julie Lien-ying How, eds. *Documents on Communism, Nationalism, and Soviet Advisers in China, 1918–1927: Papers Seized in the 1927 Peking Raid.* New York: Columbia University Press, 1956.

Wilson, Dick. *The Long March 1935: The Epic of Chinese Communism's Survival.* New York: Avon Books, 1971.

Womack, Brantly. *The Foundations of Mao Zedong's Political Thought 1917–1935.* Honolulu: University Press of Hawaii, 1982.

Wu, Eugene. *Leaders of Twentieth-Century China: An Annotated Bibliography of Selected Chinese Biographical Works in the Hoover Library.* Stanford, Calif.: Stanford University Press, 1956.

Yakhontoff, Victor A. *The Chinese Soviets.* New York: Conrad McCann, 1934.

Post-1949 China

Ahn Byung-joon. *Chinese Politics and the Cultural Revolution: Dynamics of Policy Processes.* Seattle: University of Washington Press, 1976.

An Tai-sung. *Mao Tse-tung's Cultural Revolution.* Indianapolis, Ind.: Pegasus, 1972.

Armstrong, J. D. *Revolutionary Diplomacy: Chinese Foreign Policy and the United Front Doctrine.* Berkeley: University of California Press, 1977.

Avakian, Bob. *Mao Tse-tung's Immortal Contributions.* Chicago: RCP Publications, 1979.

Bachman, David. *Chen Yun and the Chinese Political System.* Berkeley: University of California Institute of East Asian Studies, 1985.

Barker, Randolph, and Radha Sinha, eds. *The Chinese Agricultural Economy.* Boulder, Colo.: Westview Press, 1982.

Barnett, A. Doak. *Cadres, Bureaucracy, and Political Power in Communist China.* New York: Columbia University Press, 1967.

———. *China's Economy in Global Perspective.* Washington, D.C.: Brookings Institute, 1981.

———. *Communist China: The Early Years, 1949–1955.* New York: Praeger, 1964.

———. *The Making of Foreign Policy in China.* Boulder, Colo.: Westview Press, 1985.

———. *Uncertain Passage.* Washington, D.C.: Brookings Institute, 1984.

———, ed. *Chinese Communist Politics in Action.* Seattle: University of Washington Press, 1969.

Barnett, A. Doak, and Ralph N. Clough, eds. *Modernizing China: Post-Mao Reform and Development.* Boulder, Colo.: Westview Press, 1986.

Bartke, Wolfgang. *Who's Who in the People's Republic of China.* Armonk, N.Y.: M. E. Sharpe, 1981.

Bartke, Wolfgang, and Peter Schier. *China's New Party Leadership: Biographies and Analysis of the Twelfth Central Committee of the Chinese Communist Party.* Armonk, N.Y.: M. E. Sharpe, 1985.

Baum, Richard. *Prelude to Revolution: Mao, the Party, and the Peasant Question 1962–1966.* New York: Columbia University Press, 1975.

Baum, Richard, ed. *China's Four Modernizations: The New Technological Revolution.* Boulder, Colo.: Westview Press, 1980.

Baum, Richard, and Frederick C. Teiwes. *Ssu-Ch'ing: The Socialist Education Movement of 1962–1966.* Berkeley: University of California Center for Chinese Studies, 1968.

Bernstein, Richard. *From the Center of the Earth: The Search for the Truth about China.* Boston: Little, Brown & Co., 1982.

Bernstein, Thomas. *"Up to the Mountains and Down to the Villages": The Transfer of Youth from Urban to Rural China.* New Haven, Conn.: Yale University Press, 1977.

Bettleheim, Charles, *Cultural Revolution and Industrial Organization in China.* New York: Monthly Review Press, 1974.

Bettleheim, Charles et al. *China Shakes the World Again.* New York: Monthly Review Press, 1959.

Bonavia, David. *Verdict in Peking: The Trial of the Gang of Four.* New York: G. P. Putnam's Sons, 1984.

Borisov, O. B., and B. T. Koloskov. *Sino-Soviet Relations, 1945–1973: A Brief History.* Moscow: Progress Publishers, 1975.

Brugger, Bill. *China, Liberation and Transformation 1942–1962.* London: Croom Helm, 1981.

————. *Democracy and Organisation in the Chinese Industrial Enterprise (1948–1953)*. Cambridge, Eng.: Cambridge University Press, 1976.

Brugger, Bill ed. *Chinese Marxism in Flux*. Beckenham, Eng.: Croom Helm, 1985.

Buck, John Lossing, Owen L. Dawson, and Yuan-li Wu. *Food and Agriculture in Communist China*. New York: Praeger, 1966.

Burns, John P., and Stanley Rosen, eds. *Policy Conflicts in Post-Mao China: A Documentary Survey with Analysis*. Armonk, N.Y.: M. E. Sharpe, 1986.

Camilleri, Joseph. *Chinese Foreign Policy: The Maoist Era and Its Aftermath*. Seattle: University of Washington Press, 1981.

Campbell, Nigel. *China Strategies: The Inside Story*. Hong Kong: University of Hong Kong Press, 1986.

Cell, Charles. *Revolution at Work: Mobilization Campaigns in China*. New York: Academic Press, 1977.

Central Committee, Communist Party of China. *Resolution on CPC History (1949–81)*. Beijing: Foreign Languages Press, 1981.

Chan, Anita. *Children of Mao: Personality Development and Political Activism in the Red Guard Generation*. Seattle: University of Washington Press, 1985.

Chan, Anita, Richard Madsen, and Jonathan Unger. *Chen Village: The Recent History of a Peasant Community in Mao's China*. Berkeley: University of California Press, 1984.

Chan, Anita, Jonathan Unger, and Stanley Rosen, eds. *On Socialist Democracy and the Chinese Legal System: The Li Yizhe Debates*. Armonk, N.Y.: M. E. Sharpe, 1985.

Chang, David W. *Zhou Enlai and Deng Xiaoping in the Chinese Leadership Succession Crisis*. Boston: University Press of America, 1984.

Chang King-yuh, ed. *Perspectives on Development in Mainland China*. Boulder, Colo.: Westview Press, 1985.

Chang, Parris. *Power and Policy in China*. University Park: Pennsylvania State University Press, 1967, 1975, and 1978.

Chen, Erjin, and Robin Munro. *China: Crossroads Socialism*. New York: Schocken, 1984.

Chen, Jack. *Inside the Cultural Revolution*. New York: Macmillan, 1975.

Chen, Theodore H. E. *The Chinese Communist Regime: Documents and Commentary*. New York: Praeger, 1967.

Chen Yung Ping. *Chinese Political Thought: Mao Tse-tung and Liu Shao-chi*. 2d rev. ed. The Hague: Nijhoff, 1971.

Cheng, Chester J. *Documents of Dissent: Chinese Political Thought since Mao*. Stanford, Calif.: Hoover Institution Press, 1980.

Cheng, Peter. *A Chronology of the People's Republic of China*. Totawa, N.J.: Littlefield, Adams, 1972.

Chesneaux, Jean. *China: The People's Republic, 1949–1976*. New York: Pantheon Books, 1979.

Chi Wen-shun. *Ideological Conflicts in Modern China: Democracy and Authoritarianism*. New Brunswick, N.J.: Transaction Books, 1985.

Chi Hsin. *The Case of the Gang of Four—With First Translation of Teng Hsiao-Ping's "Three Poisonous Weeds."* Hong Kong: Cosmos Books, 1977.

Chiu Hungdah, and Jaw-ling Joanne Chang, eds. *Survey of Recent Developments in China (Mainland and Taiwan), 1985–1986*. Occasional Papers/Reprint Series in Contemporary Asian Studies, no. 2. Baltimore: University of Maryland School of Law, 1987.

Cohen, Paul A. *Discovering History in China: American Historical Writing on the Recent Chinese Past*. New York: Columbia University Press, 1984.

Copper, John Franklin. *China's Global Role*. Stanford, Calif.: Hoover Institution Press, 1980.

Copper, John Franklin, Franz Michael, and Wu Yuan-li. *Human Rights in Post-Mao China*. Boulder, Colo.: Westview Press, 1985.

Croizier, Ralph C., ed. *China's Cultural Legacy and Communism*. New York: Praeger, 1970.

Daubier, Jean. *A History of the Chinese Cultural Revolution*. New York: Vintage Books, 1974.

Deng Xiaoping. *Selected Works (1975–1982)*. Beijing: Foreign Languages Press, 1984.

Dernberger, Robert F., ed. *China's Development Experience in Comparative Perspective*. Cambridge, Mass.: Harvard University Press, 1980.

Devillers, Philippe. *What Mao Really Said*. New York: Schocken, 1969.

Dirlik, Arif. *Culture, Society and Revolution: A Critical Discussion of American Studies of Modern Chinese Thought*. Durham, N.C.: Duke University Asian/Pacific Studies Institute, 1985.

Dittmer, Lowell. *Liu Shao-ch'i and the Chinese Cultural Revolution: The Politics of Mass Criticism*. Berkeley: University of California Press, 1974.

Domes, Jurgen. *China after the Cultural Revolution: Politics between Two Party Congresses*. Berkeley: University of California Press, 1977.

———. *The Government and Politics of the PRC*. Boulder, Colo.: Westview Press, 1985.

———. *The Internal Politics of China, 1949–1972*. New York: Praeger, 1973.

———. *Peng Te-huai: The Man and the Image*. London: C. Hurst & Co., 1985.

———. *Socialism in the Chinese Countryside: Rural Societal Policies in the People's Republic of China 1949–1979*. London: C. Hurst & Co., 1980.

Ebon, Martin. *Lin Piao: The Life and Writings of China's New Ruler*. New York: Stein & Day, 1970.

Eckstein, Alexander, Walter Galenson, and Liu Ta-chung, eds. *Economic Trends in Communist China*. Chicago: Aldine Publishing Co., 1968.

Ellison, Herbert J., ed. *The Sino-Soviet Conflict: A Global Perspective.* Seattle: University of Washington Press, 1982.

Fairbank, John King. *China's Revolution from 1800 to the Present.* New York: Harper & Row, 1986.

Feuerwerker, Albert, ed. *History in Communist China.* Cambridge, Mass.: MIT Press, 1968.

Friedman, Edward. *Backward Toward Revolution: The Chinese Revolutionary Party.* Berkeley: University of California Press, 1974.

Frolic, B. Michael. *Mao's People: Sixteen Portraits of Life in Revolutionary China.* Cambridge, Mass.: Harvard University Press, 1980.

Gao Nie and Yan Jiaqi. *'Wenhua dageming' shi nian shi 1966—1976* [A ten-year history of the 'Great Cultural Revolution']. Tianjin: Tianjin People's Publishing House, 1986.

Gao Shangchuan, chief ed. Compiled by the China Economic Structural Reform Research Institute. *Zhungguo: Fazhan vu geming 1984–1985* [China: Development and Reform]. Beijing: Chinese Communist Party Historical Research Materials Publisher, 1987.

Gardner, John. *Chinese Politics and the Succession to Mao.* New York: Holmes & Meier, 1982.

Garside, Roger. *Coming Alive: China after Mao.* New York: McGraw-Hill, 1981.

Gass, Henry B. *Sino-American Security Relations.* Washington, D.C.: National Defense University Press, 1984.

Gelman, Harry. *The Soviet Far East Buildup and Soviet Risk-Taking against China.* Santa Monica, Calif.: Rand Corp., 1982.

Ginneken, Jaap van. *The Rise and Fall of Lin Piao.* New York: Avon Books, 1974.

Ginsburg, Norton, and Bernard A. Lalor, eds. *China: The '80s Era.* Boulder, Colo.: Westview Press, 1984.

Gittings, John. *The Role of the Chinese Army.* London: Oxford University Press, 1967.

———. *Survey of the Sino-Soviet Dispute: A Commentary and Extracts from the Recent Polemics, 1963–1967.* London: Oxford University Press, 1968.

———. *The World and China, 1922–72.* New York: Harper & Row, 1974.

Godwin, Paul H. B., ed. *The Chinese Defense Establishment: Continuity and Change in the 1980s.* Boulder, Colo.: Westview Press, 1983.

Goldman, Merle. *China's Intellectuals: Advise and Dissent.* Cambridge, Mass.: Harvard University Press, 1981.

———. *Literary Dissent in Communist China.* Cambridge, Mass.: Harvard University Press, 1967.

Gourlay, Walter E. *The Chinese Communist Cadre: Key to Political Control.* Cambridge, Mass.: Harvard University Russian Research Center, 1952.

Grasso, June. *Truman's Two-China Policy.* Armonk, N.Y.: M. E. Sharpe, 1987.

Gray, Jack, ed. *Modern China's Search for a Political Form.* London: Oxford University Press, 1969.

Griffin, Keith. *Institutional Reform and Economic Development in the Chinese Countryside.* Armonk, N.Y.: M. E. Sharpe, 1985.

Guillermaz, Jacques. *The Chinese Communist Party in Power 1949–1976.* Boulder, Colo.: Westview Press, 1976.

Gurley, John G. *China's Economy and the Maoist Strategy.* New York: Monthly Review Press, 1976.

Gurtov, Melvin, and Hwang Byong-Moo. *China under Threat: The Politics of Strategy and Development.* Baltimore: Johns Hopkins University Press, 1980.

Hamrin, Carol Lee, and Timothy Cheek, eds. *China's Establishment Intellectuals.* Armonk, N.Y.: M. E. Sharpe, 1986.

Harding, Harry. *Organizing China: The Problem of Bureaucracy, 1949–1976.* Stanford, Calif.: Stanford University Press, 1982.

Harding, Harry, ed. *China's Foreign Relations in the 1980s.* New Haven, Conn.: Yale University Press, 1984.

Hayhoe, Ruth. *Contemporary Chinese Education.* Beckenham, Eng.: Croom Helm, 1985.

Hinton, Harold C. *Bear at the Gate: Chinese Policymaking under Soviet Pressure.* Stanford: Hoover Institution Press, 1971.

———. *China's Turbulent Quest: An Analysis of China's Foreign Relations Since 1949.* New York: Macmillan, 1972.

Hinton, Harold C., ed. *The People's Republic of China, 1949–1979: A Documentary Survey.* 5 vols. Wilmington, Del.: Scholarly Resources, 1980.

———. *The People's Republic of China, 1979–1984. A Documentary Survey.* 2 vols. Wilmington, Del. Scholarly Resources, 1986.

Hinton, William. *Hundred Day War: The Cultural Revolution at Tsinghua University.* New York: Monthly Review Press, 1972.

———. *Shenfan: The Continuing Revolution in a Chinese Village.* New York: Random House, 1983.

Ho Ping-ti and Tang Tsou, eds. *China in Crisis.* 2 vols. in 3 books. Chicago: University of Chicago Press, 1968.

Ho, Samuel P. S., and Ralph W. Huenemann. *China's Open Door Policy: The Quest for Foreign Technology and Capital.* Vancouver: University of British Columbia Press, 1984.

Houn, Franklin W. *A Short History of Chinese Communism.* Englewood Cliffs, N.J.: Prentice-Hall, 1967; completely updated, 1973.

Hsia, T. A. *The Gate of Darkness.* Seattle: University of Washington Press, 1968.

Hsiung, James C., ed. *Beyond China's Independent Foreign Policy.* New York: Praeger, 1985.

Huang, Philip C. C., ed. *The Development of Underdevelopment in China: A Symposium.* Armonk, N.Y.: M. E. Sharpe, 1980.

Hunter, Edward. *Brain Washing in Red China, The Calculated Destruction of Men's Minds.* Rev. ed. New York: Vanguard Press, 1953.

Hsu, Immanuel C. Y. *China Without Mao: The Search for a New Order.* New York: Oxford University Press, 1982.

Hsueh Chun-tu. *Revolutionary Leaders of Modern China.* New York: Oxford University Press, 1971.

Joffe, Ellis. *Between Two Plenums: China's Intraleadership Conflict, 1959–1962.* Ann Arbor: University of Michigan Center for Chinese Studies, 1975.

———. *Party and Army: Professionalism and Political Control of the Chinese Officer Corps.* Cambridge, Mass.: Harvard University Press, 1965.

Johnson, Chalmers, ed. *Ideology and Politics in Contemporary China.* Seattle: University of Washington Press, 1973.

Johnson, Kay Ann. *Women, the Family and Peasant Revolution in China.* Chicago: University of Chicago Press, 1983.

Johnson, U. Alexis, et al. *China Policy for the Next Decade: Report of the Atlantic Council's Committee on China Policy.* Boston: Oelgeschlager, Gunn & Hain, 1984.

Joseph, William A. *The Critique of Ultra-Leftism in China, 1958–1981.* Stanford, Calif.: Stanford University Press, 1984.

Kallgren, Joyce K., ed. *The People's Republic of China after Thirty Years: An Overview.* Berkeley: University of California Institute of East Asian Studies, Center for Chinese Studies, 1979.

Kau, Michael Y. M., ed. *The Lin Piao Affair: Power, Politics and Military Coup.* White Plains, N.Y.: International Arts and Sciences Press, 1975.

Kau, Michael Y. M., and John K. Leung, eds. *The Writings of Mao Zedong 1949–1976.* Vol. 1. *September 1949–December 1955.* Armonk, N.Y.: M. E. Sharpe, 1986.

Kirby, Richard. *Urbanization in China.* New York: Columbia University Press, 1985.

Klein, Donald W., and Ann B. Clark, eds. *Biographical Dictionary of Chinese Communism, 1921–1965.* Cambridge, Mass.: Harvard University Press, 1971.

Kraus, Richard C. *Class Conflict in Chinese Socialism.* New York: Columbia University Press, 1981.

Kuo Tai-chun and Ramon H. Myers. *Understanding Communist China: Communist China Studies in the United States and the Republic of China, 1949–1978.* Stanford: Hoover Institution Press, 1986.

Ladany, Laszlo. *The Communist Party of China and Marxism, 1921–1985: A Self-Portrait.* Stanford: Hoover Institution Press, 1987.

Lampton, D. Michael. *Policy Implementation in the People's Republic of China.* Berkeley: University of California Press, 1986.

———. *The Politics of Medicine in China: The Policy Process, 1949–1977.* Boulder, Colo.: Westview Press, 1977.

Lardy, Nicholas R. *Agriculture in China's Modern Economic Development.* New York: Cambridge University Press, 1983.

Lardy, Nicholas R., and Kenneth Lieberthal, eds. *Chen Yun's Strategy for China's Development: A Non-Maoist Alternative.* Armonk, N.Y.: M. E. Sharpe, 1983.

Lawson, Eugene K. *Sino-Vietnamese Conflict.* New York: Praeger, 1984.

Lee Hong Yung. *The Politics of the Chinese Cultural Revolution: A Case Study.* Berkeley: University of California, 1978.

———. *A Research Guide to Red Guard Publications, 1966–1969.* Armonk, N.Y.: M. E. Sharpe, 1986.

Leng Shao-chuan and Hungdah Chiu. *Criminal Justice In Post-Mao China: Analysis and Documents.* Albany: State University of New York Press, 1985.

Lewis, John W. *Leadership in Communist China.* Ithaca, N.Y.: Cornell University Press, 1963.

Lewis, John W., ed. *The City in Communist China.* Stanford, Calif.: Stanford University Press, 1971.

———. *Party Leadership and Revolutionary Power in China.* Cambridge, Eng.: Cambridge University Press, 1970.

Leys, Simon. *Chinese Shadows.* New York: Viking Press, 1977.

Li Choh-ming. *The Economic Development of Communist China.* Berkeley: University of California Press, 1959.

Li, Victor Hao. *Law Without Lawyers: A Comparative View of Law in the United States and China.* Boulder, Colo.: Westview Press, 1978.

Liang Heng and Judith Shapiro. *Son of the Revolution.* New York: Knopf, 1983.

———. *After the Nightmare: A Survivor of the Cultural Revolution Reports on China Today.* New York: Knopf, 1986.

Liao Gailong. "Historical Experiences and Our Road of Development." A report on the history of the CCP delivered on October 25, 1980, at the National Party-School Forum. Translated in three parts in *Issues & Studies* 17 (October 1981): 65–94; (November 1981): 81–110; and (December 1981): 79–104.

Lieberthal, Kenneth G. *Central Documents and Politburo Politics in China.* Ann Arbor: University of Michigan Center for Chinese Studies, 1978.

———. *A Research Guide to Central Party and Governmental Meetings in China 1949–1975.* White Plains, N.Y.: International Arts and Sciences Press, 1976.

———. *Revolution and Tradition in Tientsin, 1949–1952.* Stanford, Calif.: Stanford University Press, 1980.

Lieberthal, Kenneth, and Michael Oksenberg. *Bureaucratic Politics and Chinese Energy Development.* U.S. Department of Commerce. Washington, D.C.: U.S. Government Printing Office, 1986.

Lifton, Robert Jay. *Thought Reform and the Psychology of Totalism: A Study of "Brainwashing" in China.* Middlesex, Eng.: Penguin Books, 1961.

Lindbeck, John M., ed. *China: Management of a Revolutionary Society.* Seattle: University of Washington Press, 1971.

Lippit, Victor D. *The Economic Development of China.* Armonk, N.Y.: M. E. Sharpe, 1986.

Liu Shao-ch'i. *Collected Works, 1945–1957.* Hong Kong: Union Research Institute, 1969.

———. *Collected Works, 1958–1967.* Hong Kong: Union Research Institute, 1968.

Liu Ta-Chung and Yeh Kung-Chia. *The Economy of the Chinese Mainland: National Income and Economic Development, 1933–1959.* Princeton, N.J.: Princeton University Press, 1965.

Lotta, Raymond, ed. *And Mao Makes 5: Mao Tse-tung's Last Great Battle.* Chicago: Banner Press, 1978.

Low, Alfred D. *The Sino-Soviet Dispute: An Analysis of the Polemics.* Cranbury, N.J.: Associated Universities Press, 1976.

Ma Hong. *New Strategy for China's Economy.* Beijing: Foreign Languages Press, 1983.

MacFarquhar, Roderick. *The Origins of the Cultural Revolution. Vol. 1 Contradictions among the People, 1956–1957.* New York: Columbia University Press, 1974.

———. *The Origins of the Cultural Revolution. Vol. 2. The Great Leap Forward, 1958–1960.* New York: Columbia University Press, 1983.

Mackerras, Colin. *Modern China: A Chronology from 1842 to the Present.* San Francisco: W. H. Freeman & Co., 1982.

Madsen, Richard. *Morality and Power in a Chinese Village.* Berkeley: University of California Press, 1984.

Malraux, Andre. *Anti-Memoirs.* New York: Holt, Rinehart & Winston, 1968.

Mancall, Mark. *China at the Center.* New York: Free Press, 1984.

Mao Zedong (Mao Tse-tung). *A Critique of Soviet Economics.* New York: Monthly Review Press, 1977.

———. *Miscellany of Mao Tse-tung Thought (1949–1968).* Parts 1 and 2. Arlington, Va.: Joint Publications Research Service, 1974.

———. *Selected Works.* Vols. 1–4. Beijing: Foreign Languages Press, 1950–1977.

———. *Selected Works.* Vol. 5. Beijing: Foreign Languages Press, 1977.

Martin, Roberta. *Party Recruitment in China: Patterns and Prospects: A Study of the Recruitment Campaign of 1954–56 and Its Impact on Party Expansion through 1980.* New York: Columbia University East Asian Institute, 1981.

Maxwell, Neville. *India's China War.* New York: Pantheon, 1970.

Maxwell, Neville, ed. *China's Road to Development.* 2d enl. ed. New York: Pergamon Press, 1979.

Maxwell, Neville, and Bruce McFarlane, eds. *China's Changed Road to Development.* New York: Pergamon Press, 1984.

Medvedev, Roy. *China and the Superpowers.* Oxford: Blackwell, 1986.

Mehnert, Klaus. *China Returns.* New York: Dutton, 1972.

Meisner, Maurice. *Mao's China and After.* New York: Free Press, 1985.

Milton, David, and Nancy Dall Milton. *The Wind Will Not Subside: Years in Revolutionary China—1964–1969.* New York: Pantheon Books, 1976.

Moody, Peter R. *Chinese Politics after Mao: Development and Liberalization, 1976–1983.* New York: Praeger, 1983.

———. *Opposition and Dissent in Contemporary China.* Stanford: Hoover Institution Press, 1977.

Morse, Ronald A., ed. *The Limits of Reform in China.* Boulder, Colo.: Westview Press, 1983.

Mosher, Steven W. *Broken Earth: The Rural Chinese.* New York: Free Press, 1983.

———. *Journey to the Forbidden China.* New York: Free Press, 1985.

Muller, David G., Jr. *China as a Maritime Power.* Boulder, Colo.: Westview Press, 1983.

Munro, Donald. *The Concept of Man in Contemporary China.* Ann Arbor: University of Michigan Press, 1977.

Murphey, Rhoads. *The Fading of the Maoist Vision: City and Countryside in China's Development.* New York: Methuen, 1980.

Nathan, Andrew J. *Chinese Democracy.* New York: Knopf, 1985.

Nee, Victor. *The Cultural Revolution at Peking University.* New York: Monthly Review Press, 1969.

Nee, Victor, and David Mozingo, eds. *State and Society in Contemporary China.* Ithaca, N.Y.: Cornell University Press, 1983.

Nee, Victor, and James Peck, eds. *China's Uninterrupted Revolution: From 1840 to the Present.* New York: Pantheon, 1973.

Nelson, Harvey W. *The Chinese Military System: An Organizational Study of the People's Liberation Army.* 2d rev. ed. Boulder, Colo.: Westview Press, 1981.

Oldham, John R., ed. *China's Legal Development.* Armonk, N.Y.: M. E. Sharpe, 1986.

Oksenberg, Michael, ed. *China's Developmental Experience.* New York: Praeger, 1973.

Oksenberg, Michael, and Robert Oxnam, eds. *Dragon and Eagle: United States–China Relations, Past and Future.* New York: Basic Books, 1978.

Orleans, Leo A. *Professional Manpower and Education in Communist China.* Washington, D.C.: U.S. Government Printing Office, 1961.

Orleans, Leo A., ed. *Science in Contemporary China.* Stanford, Calif.: Stanford University Press, 1981.

Parish, William L., ed. *Chinese Rural Development: The Great Transformation.* Armonk, N.Y.: M. E. Sharpe, 1985.

Parish, William L., and Martin K. Whyte. *Village and Family in Contemporary China.* Chicago: University of Chicago Press, 1978.

Party Literature Research Center, Central Committee, CCP. *Guanyu jianguo yilai dangde rogan lishi wenti de jueyi: zhushiben, xiu ding* [Annotated Edition of the Resolution on Certain Issues in the History of the Party since the Founding of the People's Republic of China]. Beijing: People's Publishing House, 1985.

Peng Dehuai. *Memoirs of a Chinese Marshal.* Beijing: Foreign Languages Press, 1985.

P'eng Shu-tse. *The Chinese Communist Party in Power.* New York: Monad Press, 1980.

Perkins, Dwight H. *Market Control and Planning in Communist China.* Cambridge, Mass.: Harvard University Press, 1966.

Perkins, Dwight, and Shahid Yusuf. *Rural Development in China.* Baltimore, Md.: Johns Hopkins University Press, 1984.

Perrolle, Pierre M., ed. *Fundamentals of the Chinese Communist Party.* White Plains, N.Y.: International Arts and Sciences Press, 1976.

Pollack, Jonathan. *The Lessons of Coalition Politics: Sino-American Security Relations.* Santa Monica, Calif.: Rand Corp., 1984.

———. *Security, Strategy, and the Logic of Chinese Foreign Policy.* Berkeley: University of California Institute of East Asian Studies, 1981.

———. The Sino-Soviet Rivalry and Chinese Security Debate. Santa Monica, Calif. Rand Corp., 1982.

Prybyla, Jan S. *The Chinese Economy: Problems and Policies.* 2d rev. ed. Columbia: University of South Carolina Press, 1981.

Pye, Lucian W. *Chinese Commercial Negotiating Style.* Cambridge, Mass.: Oelgeschlager, Gunn & Hain, 1982.

———. *The Dynamics of Chinese Politics.* Cambridge, Mass.: Oelgeschlager, Gunn, & Hain, 1981.

———. *The Spirit of Chinese Politics: A Psychocultural Study of the Authority Crisis in Political Development.* Cambridge, Mass.: MIT Press, 1968.

Pye, Lucian W., with Mary W. Pye. *Asian Power and Politics: The Cultural Dimensions of Authority.* Cambridge, Mass.: Harvard University Press, Belknap Press, 1985.

Reynolds, Bruce L., ed. *Reform in China: Challenges & Choices: A Summary and Analysis of the CESRRI Survey.* Prepared by the Chinese Economic System Reform Research Institute. Armonk, N.Y.: M. E. Sharpe, 1987.

Rhee Sang-Woo, ed. *China's Reform Politics: Policies and Their Implications.* Seoul: Sogang University Press, 1986.

Rice, Edward. *Mao's Way.* Berkeley: University of California Press, 1972.

Richman, Barry M. *Industrial Society in Communist China.* New York: Random House, 1969.

Riskin, Carl. *The Political Economy of Chinese Development since 1949.* New York: Oxford University Press, 1986.

Rostow, Walter W., et al. *The Prospects for Communist China.* Cambridge, Mass.: MIT Press, 1954.

Rozman, Gilbert. *A Mirror for Socialism: Soviet Criticisms of China*. Princeton, N.J.: Princeton University Press, 1985.

———. *The Chinese Debate about Soviet Socialism, 1978–1985*. Princeton, N.J.: Princeton University Press, 1987.

Saich, Tony. *China: Politics and Government*. New York: St. Martin's Press, 1981.

Scalapino, Robert A., ed. *The Communist Revolution in Asia: Tactics, Goals, and Achievements*. Englewood Cliffs, N.J.: Prentice-Hall, 1965.

———. *Elites in the People's Republic of China*. Seattle: University of Washington Press, 1972.

Schell, Orville. *To Get Rich is Glorious: China in the Eighties*. New York: Pantheon, 1984.

Schram, Stuart R. *Mao Tse-tung*. Middlesex, Eng.: Penguin, 1966.

———. *The Political Thought of Mao Tse-tung*. New York: Praeger, 1969.

Schram, Stuart R., ed. *Authority Participation and Cultural Change in China*. Cambridge, Eng.: Cambridge University Press, 1973.

———. *Mao Tse-tung Unrehearsed: Talks and Letters, 1956–71*. Middlesex, Eng.: Penguin Books, 1974.

———. *The Scope of State Power in China*. Hong Kong: Chinese University Press, 1985.

Schurmann, Franz. *Ideology and Organization in Communist China*. 2d enl. ed. Berkeley: University of California Press, 1968.

———. *The Logic of World Power: An Inquiry into the Origins, Currents, and Contradictions of World Politics*. New York: Pantheon Books, 1974.

Schwartz, Benjamin. *Communism and China: Ideology in Flux*. Cambridge, Mass.: Harvard University Press, 1968.

Segal, Gerald. *Defending China*. New York: Oxford University Press, 1985.

Selden, Mark, ed. *The People's Republic of China: A Documentary of Revolutionary Change*. New York: Monthly Review Press, 1979.

Selden, Mark, and Victor Lippit, eds. *The Transition to Socialism in China*. Armonk, N.Y.: M. E. Sharpe, 1982.

Seybolt, Peter J., ed. *The Rustification of Urban Youth in China*. Armonk, N.Y.: M. E. Sharpe, 1977.

Seymour, James D. *China's Satellite Parties*. Armonk, N.Y.: M. E. Sharpe, 1987.

Seymour, James D., ed. *The Fifth Modernization: China's Human Rights Movement, 1978–79*. New York: Human Rights Publishing Group, 1980.

Shalom, Stephen R. *Deaths in China Due to Communism*. Tempe: Arizona State University Center for Asian Studies, 1984.

Shambaugh, David L. *The Making of a Premier: Zhao Ziyang's Provincial Career*. Boulder, Colo.: Westview Press, 1984.

Shaw Yu-ming, ed. *Chinese Modernization*. San Francisco: Chinese Materials Center Publications, 1985.

————. *Mainland China: Politics, Economics, and Reform.* Boulder, Colo. Westview Press, 1986.

————. *Power and Policy in the PRC.* Boulder, Colo.: Westview Press, 1985.

Shirk, Susan. *Competitive Comrades.* Berkeley: University of California Press, 1981.

Shue, Vivienne. *Peasant China in Transition: The Dynamics of Development toward Socialism, 1949–1956.* Berkeley: University of California Press, 1980.

Singer, Martin. *Educated Youth and the Cultural Revolution in China.* Ann Arbor: University of Michigan Center for Chinese Studies, 1971.

Siu, Helen F., and Zelda Stern, eds. *Mao's Harvest.* London: Oxford University Press, 1983.

Snow, Edgar. *The Long Revolution.* New York: Random House, 1972.

————. *The Other Side of the River: Red China Today.* London: V. Gollancz Ltd., 1963.

Socialist Upsurge in China's Countryside. Beijing: Foreign Languages Press, 1978.

Solinger, Dorothy J. *Chinese Business under Socialism: The Politics of Domestic Commerce, 1949–1980.* Berkeley: University of California Press, 1984.

————. *Regional Government and Political Integration in Southwest China, 1949–1954: A Case Study.* Berkeley: University of California Press, 1977.

Solomon, Richard. *Mao's Revolution and the Chinese Political Culture.* Berkeley: University of California Press, 1971.

Staar, Richard F., ed. *The Yearbook on International Communist Affairs.* Stanford: Hoover Institution Press, annually.

Stacey, Judith. *Patriarchy and Socialist Revolution in China.* Berkeley: University of California Press, 1983.

Starr, John Bryan. *Continuing the Revolution: The Political Thought of Mao.* Princeton, N.J.: Princeton University Press, 1979.

————. *Ideology and Culture: An Introduction to the Dialectic of Contemporary Chinese Politics.* New York: Harper & Row, 1973.

Stavis, Benedict. *The Politics of Agricultural Mechanization in China.* Ithaca, N.Y.: Cornell University Press, 1978.

Stolper, Thomas E. *China, Taiwan and the Offshore Islands.* Armonk, N.Y.: M. E. Sharpe, 1985.

Stuart, Douglas T., and William T. Tow. *China, the Soviet Union and the West: Strategic and Political Dimensions for the 1980s.* Boulder, Colo.: Westview Press, 1981.

Sutter, Robert G. *The China Quandary: Domestic Determinants of U.S.-China Policy, 1972–1982.* Boulder, Colo.: Westview Press, 1983.

————. *China-Watch: Toward Sino-American Reconciliation.* Baltimore, Md.: Johns Hopkins University Press, 1978.

———. *Chinese Foreign Policy: Developments after Mao.* New York: Praeger, 1986.

———. *Reform in China and Its Implications for the United States.* Congressional Research Service. Washington, D.C.: Library of Congress, 1985.

Tang Tsou. *The Cultural Revolution and Post-Mao Reforms: A Historical Perspective.* Chicago: University of Chicago Press, 1986.

Teiwes, Frederick C. *Leadership, Legitimacy, and Conflict in China: From a Charismatic Mao to the Politics of Succession.* Armonk, N.Y.: M. E. Sharpe, 1984.

———. *Politics and Purges in China.* Armonk, N.Y.: M. E. Sharpe, 1979.

Ten Great Years. Beijing: Foreign Languages Press, 1960.

Terrill, Ross. *The White-Boned Demon: A Biography of Madame Mao Zedong.* New York: Morrow, 1984.

Thurston, Anne F. *Enemies of the People.* New York: Knopf, 1987.

Thurston, Anne F., and Burton Pasternak, eds. *The Social Sciences and Fieldwork in China: Views from the Field.* Boulder, Colo.: Westview Press, 1983.

Tien Hung-Mao, ed. *Mainland China, Taiwan, and U.S. Policy.* Boston: Oelgeschlager, Gunn & Hain, 1985.

Treadgold, Donald W., ed. *Soviet and Chinese Communism: Similarities and Differences.* Seattle: University of Washington Press, 1967.

Tung Chi-ping and Humphrey Evans. *The Thought Revolution.* New York: Coward-McCann, 1966.

Uhalley, Stephen, Jr. *Mao Tse-tung: A Critical Biography.* New York: New Viewpoints, 1975.

Unger, Jonathan. *Education under Mao: Class and Competition in Canton Schools 1960–1980.* New York: Columbia University Press, 1982.

U.S. Congress. Joint Economic Committee. *China's Economy Looks Toward the Year 2000. Volume 1, The Four Modernizations.* Washington, D.C.: GPO, 1986.

———. *China's Economy Looks Toward the Year 2000. Volume 2, Economic Openness in Modernizing China.* Washington, D.C.: GPO, 1986.

———. *An Economic Profile of Mainland China.* New York: Praeger, 1968.

Vogel, Ezra F. *Canton under Communism: Programs and Politics in a Provincial Capital, 1949–1964.* Cambridge, Mass.: Harvard University Press, 1969.

Walder, Andrew G. *Chang Ch'un-ch'iao and Shanghai's January Revolution.* Ann Arbor: University of Michigan Center for Chinese Studies, 1977.

———. *Communist Neo-traditionalism: Work and Authority in Chinese Industry.* Berkeley: University of California Press, 1986.

Walker, Richard L. *China under Communism: The First Five Years.* New Haven, Conn.: Yale University Press, 1955.

Waller, Derek J. *The Government and Politics of the People's Republic of China.* London: Hutchinson, 1981.

Wang Ming. *Mao's Betrayal.* Moscow: Progress Publishers, 1979.

Watson, James L. *Class and Social Stratification in Post-Revolution China*. New York: Cambridge University Press, 1984.

White, Gordon. *Party and Professionals: The Political Role of Teachers in Contemporary China*. Armonk, N.Y.: M. E. Sharpe, 1981.

White, Lynn T., III. *Careers in Shanghai: The Social Guidance of Personal Energies in a Developing Chinese City, 1949–1966*. Berkeley: University of California Press, 1980.

Whiting, Allen S. *The Chinese Calculus of Deterrence: India and Indochina*. Ann Arbor: University of Michigan Press, 1975.

Whyte, Martin King. *Small Groups and Political Rituals in China*. Berkeley: University of California Press, 1974.

Whyte, Martin King, and William L. Parish. *Urban Life in Contemporary China*. Chicago: University of Chicago Press, 1984.

Wich, Richard. *Sino-Soviet Crisis Politics: A Study of Political Change and Communication*. Cambridge, Mass.: Harvard University Press, 1980.

Witke, Roxane. *Comrade Chiang Ch'ing*. Boston: Little, Brown & Co., 1977.

Wolf, Margery. *Revolution Postponed: Women in Contemporary China*. Stanford, Calif.: Stanford University Press, 1984.

Wong, John. *Land Reform in the People's Republic of China*. New York: Praeger, 1973.

Wu Tien-wei. *Lin Biao and the Gang of Four: Contra-Confucianism in Historical and Intellectual Perspective*. Carbondale: Southern Illinois University Press, 1982.

Xue Muqiao. *China's Socialist Economy.* Beijing: Foreign Languages Press, 1981.

Yahuda, Michael. *Towards the End of Isolationism: China's Foreign Policy after Mao*. London: Macmillan, 1983.

Yang Ch'ing-kung. *Chinese Communist Society: The Family and the Village*. Cambridge, Mass.: MIT Press, 1959.

Yao Ming-le [pseud.]. *The Conspiracy and Murder of Mao's Heir*. New York: Knopf, 1983.

Yu Guangyuan, ed. *China's Socialist Modernization*. Beijing: Foreign Languages Press, 1984.

Zagoria, Donald S. *The Sino-Soviet Conflict 1956–1961*. Princeton, N.J.: Princeton University Press, 1962.

Zhou Ming, chief ed. *Lishi zai zheli chensi—1966–1976 nian jishi* [History ponders here—some facts from 1966 to 1976]. 3 vols. Beijing: Hua Xia Publishing House, 1986.

Index